SECOND EDITION

BUSINESS, GOVERNMENT, AND THE PUBLIC

MURRAY L. WEIDENBAUM

Director, Center for the
Study of American Business
Washington University
St. Louis, Missouri

Prentice-Hall, Inc., Englewood Cliffs, New Jersey 07632

Library of Congress Cataloging in Publication Data

WEIDENBAUM, MURRAY L
   Business, government, and the public.

   Bibliography: p.
   Includes index.
   1. Industry and state — United States.
I. Title.
HD3616.U46W44 1980   322'.3'0973   80–12553
ISBN 0–13–099325–5

Editorial/production supervision and
  interior design by Alice Erdman
Cover design by M. Recio
Manufacturing buyer: Gordon Osbourne

Printed in the United States of America

10 9 8 7 6 5 4 3 2

Prentice-Hall International, Inc., *London*
Prentice-Hall of Australia Pty. Limited, *Sydney*
Prentice-Hall of Canada, Ltd., *Toronto*
Prentice-Hall of India Private Limited, *New Delhi*
Prentice-Hall of Japan, Inc., *Tokyo*
Prentice-Hall of Southeast Asia Pte. Ltd., *Singapore*
Whitehall Books Limited, *Wellington, New Zealand*

contents

Part Two
THE ADAPTATION BY BUSINESS

Part Three
SHAPING THE BUSINESS-GOVERNMENT ENVIRONMENT

case studies /appendices

preface

This revised edition is an attempt to provide an updated, more balanced, and thorough view of the impact of government and other external influences on the operations of business firms. Traditional books in this area have emphasized antitrust activities and independent regulatory agencies, such as the Interstate Commerce Commission.

Although it is useful insofar as it covers important aspects of business-government relations, the traditional approach ignores the newer types of public concerns and the resultant government activities that have a daily impact on virtually every enterprise in the nation. Hence, this book tries to break some new ground. Rather than being concerned with the specialized part of the public-private relationship, which is primarily the domain of lawyers (and secondarily of economists), it emphasizes the more far-ranging regulatory activities which impinge on almost every business executive, line or staff, headquarters or divisional, in small companies and large, and in industries that are not ostensibly "regulated," as well as those that are.

This book is not designed to be a comprehensive encyclopedia of the entire gamut of business-government-public activities. Part One deliberately presents a point of view, albeit at times it is an unconventionally critical view of federal intervention. As tested in the author's classroom, it can be effective in stimulating thought and discussion, both pro and con, on the many provocative issues that are raised.

After thus whetting the readers' intellectual appetites, Part Two shifts the focus to a more positive approach. It deals with the varied nature of the business responses — passive and active — to an environment increasingly influenced by government and public-interest groups, indicating how business can survive and even prosper in the new situation. Part Three deals with the interaction of business and the broader social-political environment of which it is a part. Possibilities of reshaping that environment are also considered.

The focus throughout is on improving the understanding of current and future generations of business executives with reference to an increasingly important, but basically neglected, aspect of their job. In the past at least, the failure of many business firms to respond voluntarily to the changing needs of the society has contributed to increased government involvement in internal business decision-making. Also, hopefully, this book will assist government officials and members of various interest groups to appreciate better the various consequences of their actions on the private sector of the economy.

The preparation of this book was supported in part by the Center for the Study of American Business at Washington University. The author is indebted to Ronald Penoyer for helpful research and editorial assistance. Rachel Knipp carefully typed the drafts and final version of the manuscript.

Portions of various chapters have appeared in earlier form in *Business Horizons, Business and Society Review, Journal of Economic Issues, Michigan Business Review, Policy Analysis,* and in the American Enterprise Institute's monograph, *Government-Mandated Price Increases.* In each case, the editors have kindly consented to the use of these materials.

Murray L. Weidenbaum

Part One

REGULATION BY GOVERNMENT

1

an overview of
government regulation

An examination of the emerging business-government relationship from the business executive's viewpoint shows a very considerable public presence in what historically have been private matters. No company, large or small, can operate without obeying a myriad of government restrictions and regulations. Entrepreneurial decisions fundamental to the functioning of enterprise are increasingly becoming subject to governmental influence, review, or control — decisions such as what lines of business to go into, what products and services to produce, which investments to finance, how to produce goods and services, where to make them, how to market them, what prices to charge, and what profit to keep.

Virtually every major department of the typical corporation in the United States has one or more counterparts in a government agency that controls or strongly influences its internal decision making. There is almost a "shadow" organization chart of public officials matching the organizational structure of each private company. For example, much of the work of the scientists in corporate research laboratories is now involved with ensuring that the products they develop are not rejected by lawyers in regulatory agencies. The engineers in manufacturing departments must make sure the equipment they specify meets the standards promulgated by Labor Department authorities. Marketing staffs must follow procedures established by government administrators in product safety agencies. The location of business facilities must conform with a variety of environmental statutes. The activities of personnel staffs are increasingly geared to meeting the standards of the various agencies concerned with employment conditions. Finance departments often bear the brunt of the rising paperwork burden imposed on business by government agencies. In short, there simply are few aspects of business activities that escape some type of government review or influence.

Clearly, a massive expansion of government involvement in private industry is under way in the United States. Impetus for this expanded government participation is being provided by a variety of consumer groups, environmental organizations, civil rights advocates, labor unions, and other citizens' institutions. In many cases, the increasing regulation reflects public and congressional concern that traditional federal and state-local government programs have not been effective. The rise of regulation is also reinforced by the belief that the private sector itself is responsible for many of the problems facing society — pollution, discrimination in employment, unsafe products, unhealthy working environments, misleading financial reporting, and so forth.

The regulatory process is undoubtedly one of the most powerful ways in which government can influence economic activity. As an alternative to taxing and spending to achieve national objectives, federal, state, and local governments have come to rely increasingly on mechanisms that operate through directly controlling the actions of institutions and people in the private sector of the society. Over the course of four different presidential administrations — Johnson, Nixon, Ford, Carter — we have witnessed a rising tide of involvement by government in the internal decision making of individual businesses. Government looms increasingly large between business and its customers, its employees, its shareholders, and the public.

GOVERNMENT'S INFLUENCE OVER BUSINESS

The development and introduction of technology related to automobile exhaust emissions furnishes a cogent and representative example of this involvement. Rather than relying on indirect means of encouragement, such as expenditure, tax, or credit subsidies, or waiting for the market to respond on its own, the federal government has established by law and regulation allowable emissions from motor vehicles. Automobile manufacturers are thus made to innovate to bring their products within the performance standards established by law.

This automotive case, however, is no isolated instance. What the typical business manager sees is that the government is influencing, if not controlling, more and more of the basic management decisions of the firm, ranging from choosing new products and processes to setting prices and determining which production methods to use. The government of the modern state thus has become an active partner in the management of business.

Obviously, the sphere of influence of the government-as-partner is extremely broad. This fact becomes particularly evident for new firms — and what is a more basic entrepreneurial function than starting a new enterprise? In many cases, the requirement to obtain a license before commencing operations is merely an annoying method used by state and local governments to raise revenue. At the federal level, however, for many types of businesses, regulatory activity is far more widespread and almost always more stringent, as in such diverse examples as the operation of airlines (the Civil Aeronautics Board) and railroads (the Interstate Commerce Commission), the management of radio and television stations (the Federal Communications Commission), the distilling of alcohol (the Treasury), the manufacturing of ethical drugs (the Food and Drug Administration), and the production of nuclear materials (the Nuclear Regulatory Commission).

In addition, prior to marketing new products, a company must obtain government approval of its items or at least demonstrate that they will meet federal standards. Many clothes, for example, must meet the requirements of the Wool Labeling Act. Other commodities are subject to a far wider range of regulations. In particular, the Consumer Product Safety Commission has the authority to set safety standards for consumer products and to ban those presenting "undue" risk of injury.

Although government contractors which produce military materiel are accustomed to working under a variety of government directives concerning prices and profits, other segments of the private market likewise are subject to the influence of federal pricing decisions. The extractive industries and their customers, for instance, keenly feel the effects of government control of the prices of agricultural, forestry, and mining output. Additionally, transportation, communications, and utility companies must deal with a host of federal, state, and at times local regulatory agencies in setting price schedules and in making other basic managerial decisions.

Many federal regulations directly affect the internal working procedures of businesses. A firm is obliged to follow the accounting methods of the Internal Revenue Service in at least one set of its books, as well as the increasingly detailed requirements of the Securities and Exchange Commission in its public reporting. More recent innovations in federal regulatory activities include Truth-in-Lending (requiring full disclosure of finance charges), the Wholesome Poultry Products Act, the Poison Prevention Packaging Act, and the Clean Air Act.

In the area of employee compensation, government contractors must adhere to the pay and related standards of the Walsh-Healey and Davis-Bacon Acts. But a far wider array of companies is subject to laws governing minimum wages, equal pay, overtime hours, and the entire area of recognizing, bargaining with, and maintaining day-to-day relations with labor unions.

GOVERNMENT'S SCRUTINY OF BUSINESS

A role of government in business affairs not often in the public eye is that of a virtual intruder. The literature on public administration does not place much emphasis on this role of the government official as *inspector.* Yet this uninvited visitor tends to make appearances in business firms with increasing frequency and often without prior notice. Inspections and audits are made by all levels of government and a host of departments and agencies. Their coverage of business activities varies from sanitation to working conditions to financial records.

Obviously, then, federal inspectors — an increasingly important physical presence in private industry — are concerned with a growing list of responsibilities. In the mid-1970s the Supreme Court ruled that air pollution inspectors do not need search warrants to enter the property of suspected polluters as long as they do not enter areas closed to the public. These unannounced and warrantless inspections were held not to be in violation of the constitutional protections against unreasonable search and seizure.[1]

However, on the restraining side of this regulatory phenomenon, the "no-knock" power of the inspectors of the Labor Department's Occupational Safety and Health Administration (OSHA) has been

---

[1] Air Pollution Variance Board of the State of Colorado v. Western Alfalfa Corporation, 94 S. Ct. 2114 (May 20, 1974).

limited by the courts.[2] If employers insist, OSHA must obtain a search warrant prior to entering the premises. But for various reasons, including perhaps a fear of antagonizing inspectors, most companies have been waiving their right to demand a court-issued warrant.

In the broad picture of government regulation briefly sketched here, it is clear that corporations of all sizes, all types, and all "shapes" must pay close attention to and assiduously comply with rules set down for them by regulatory bureaucracies. This is no small matter for America's private enterprise system, and one way to understand it better is to examine briefly the recent, nearly meteoric rise in the scope and variety of federal regulatory programs.

NEW REGULATORY PROGRAMS

Table 1-1 lists the major expansions in federal regulatory activities enacted by Congress since 1962. They cover four major areas of involvement: consumer products, employment conditions, environment, and energy. The pace of the development of these regulatory activities, we may note, has varied substantially within each area.

One constant theme since 1962, however, has been the increasingly stringent consumer product regulations, which started with the requirement in the Food and Drug Amendments that all drugs be tested for safety and effectiveness prior to marketing. Several federal statutes have required the labeling of cigarettes with official statements concerning their health hazard. Children's toys received special attention in 1966, as did flammable products in 1967. The broad-gauged consumer safety legislation was enacted in 1972, and warranty protection tightened in 1974.

The catalogue of regulatory activity has also grown in other directions. Modern traffic safety regulation commenced in 1966 with the Traffic Safety Act. That law provides for a national safety program, including setting national safety standards for motor vehicles. Consumer finance legislation was later in getting started; its landmark statute, the Consumer Credit Protection Act (usually called Truth-in-Lending), was passed in 1968. This law requires full disclosure of the terms and conditions of finance charges in credit transactions. The 1970 amendments regulate credit bureaus and give consumers access to their files.

A series of equal employment opportunity laws also was enacted

[2] Marshall v. Barlow's, Inc., 29 U.S.S.C., sec. 657(a) (1977).

Table 1-1   Extension of government regulation of business, 1962–78

Year of Enactment	Name of Law	Purpose and Function
1962	Food and Drug Amendments	Requires pretesting of drugs for safety and effectiveness and labeling of drugs by generic names
1962	Air Pollution Control Act	Provides first modern ecology statute
1963	Equal Pay Act	Eliminates wage differentials based on sex
1964	Civil Rights Act	Creates Equal Employment Opportunity Commission (EEOC) to investigate charges of job discrimination
1965	Water Quality Act	Extends environmental concern to water
1965	Cigarette Labeling and Advertising Act	Requires labels on hazards of smoking
1966	Fair Packaging and Labeling Act	Requires producers to state what a package contains, how much it contains, and who made the product
1966	Child Protection Act	Bans sale of hazardous toys and articles
1966	Traffic Safety Act	Provides for a coordinated national safety program, including safety standards for motor vehicles
1966	Coal Mine Safety Amendments	Tightens controls on working conditions
1967	Flammable Fabrics Act	Broadens federal authority to set safety standards for inflammable fabrics, including clothing and household products
1967	Age Discrimination in Employment Act	Prohibits job discrimination against individuals aged 40 to 65
1968	Consumer Credit Protection Act (Truth-in-Lending)	Requires full disclosure of terms and conditions of finance charges in credit transactions
1968	Interstate Land Sales Full Disclosure Act	Provides safeguards against unscrupulous practices in interstate land sales
1969	National Environmental Policy Act	Requires environmental impact statements for federal agencies and projects
1970	Amendments to Federal Deposit Insurance Act	Prohibits issuance of unsolicited credit cards. Limits customer's liability in case of loss or theft to $50. Regulates credit bureaus and provides consumers access to files
1970	Securities Investor Protection Act	Provides greater protection for customers of brokers and dealers and members of national securities ex-

Table 1-1 (contd.)

Year of Enactment	Name of Law	Purpose and Function
		changes. Establishes a Securities Investor Protection Corporation, financed by fees on brokerage houses
1970	Poison Prevention Packaging Act	Authorizes standards for child-resistant packaging of hazardous substances
1970	Clean Air Act Amendments	Provides for setting air quality standards
1970	Occupational Safety and Health Act	Establishes safety and health standards that must be met by employers
1972	Consumer Product Safety Act	Establishes a commission to set safety standards for consumer products and bans products presenting undue risk of injury
1972	Federal Water Pollution Control Act	Declares an end to the discharge of pollutants into navigable waters by 1985 as a national goal
1972	Noise Pollution and Control Act	Regulates noise limits of products and transportation vehicles
1972	Equal Employment Opportunity Act	Gives EEOC the right to sue employers
1973	Vocational Rehabilitation Act	Requires federal contractors to take affirmative action on hiring the handicapped
1973	Highway Speed Limit Reduction	Limits vehicles to speeds of 55 miles an hour
1973	Safe Drinking Water Act	Requires EPA to set national drinking water regulations
1974	Campaign Finance Amendments	Restricts amounts of political contributions
1974	Employee Retirement Income Security Act	Sets new federal standards for employee pension programs
1974	Hazardous Materials Transportation Act	Requires standards for the transportation of hazardous materials
1974	Magnuson-Moss Warranty Improvement Act	Establishes federal standards for written consumer product warranties
1975	Energy Policy and Conservation Act	Authorizes greater controls over domestic energy supplies and demands
1976	Hart-Scott-Rodino Antitrust Amendments	Provides for class action suits by state attorneys general; requires large companies to notify the Department of Justice of planned mergers and acquisitions.

(continued)

Table 1-1 (contd.)

Year of Enactment	Name of Law	Purpose and Function
1976	Toxic Substances Control Act	Requires advance testing and restrictions on use of chemical substances
1977	Department of Energy Organization Act	Establishes a permanent department to regulate energy on a continuing basis
1977	Surface Mining Control and Reclamation Act	Regulates strip mining and the reclamation of abandoned mines
1977	Fair Labor Standards Amendments	Increases the minimum wage in three steps
1977	Export Administration Act	Imposes restrictions on complying with the Arab boycott
1977	Business Payments Abroad Act	Provides for up to $1 million penalties for bribes of foreign officials
1977	Saccharin Study and Labeling Act	Requires warning labels on products containing saccharin
1978	Fair Debt Collection Practices Act	Provides for the first nationwide control of collection agencies
1978	Age Discrimination in Employment Act Amendments	Raises the permissible mandatory retirement age from 65 to 70 for most employees

early in this period. The Equal Pay Act of 1963 eliminated wage differentials based on sex. The Equal Employment Opportunity Commission was established in 1964 and was strengthened in 1972. Job discrimination against individuals aged 40 to 65 was outlawed in 1967, and the permissible mandatory retirement age was raised in 1978 from 65 to 70. Affirmative action on behalf of handicapped workers was included in the Vocational Rehabilitation Act of 1973.

Job safety legislation has a long tradition, going back to federal and state workmen's compensation laws. The Occupational Safety and Health Act of 1970 is the major statute in the recent wave of regulatory legislation in this area. It establishes national employee safety and health standards, which must be met by employers.

But the area of government regulation that has received the most substantial amount of public interest relates to the environment. Beginning with the Air Pollution Control Act of 1962, Congress successively has legislated federal controls over water pollution, required environmental impact statements, and regulated noise of products and transportation vehicles. In more recent years the federal government has also enacted a series of laws emphasizing the development and conservation of energy resources — and, ironically, some of these statutes have tended to create conflicts with ecology objectives. The latter include the Emergency Petroleum Allocation Act of 1973, the Federal Energy Administration Act of 1974, and the creation of the Department of Energy in 1977. As will be shown, the expansion of regulation often results in problems of adjusting to its varying objectives and approaches.

Certainly, perspective is needed after examining such a lengthy and complex catalogue of regulatory activity. Thus we should note that although in general the scope of federal influence is expanding, there are limits to this trend. Some controls do end. For example, in January 1974 the federal government terminated the interest equalization tax on American holdings of foreign stocks and bonds, as well as the five-year-old program of controls over direct investments abroad by United States corporations. Simultaneously, the Federal Reserve System ended its guidelines limiting lending and investments overseas by United States banks and other financial institutions. Under the Airline Deregulation Act of 1978 entry and price regulation of domestic airlines has been reduced and will be phased out by 1982 and 1983, respectively.

Also, the federal government does not adopt every suggestion for increasing government regulation of the private sector. In April 1974 the Food and Drug Administration (FDA) rejected a petition by 37 members of Congress and nine consumer groups calling for warning labels on all packaged foods that do not list each ingredient. The commissioner of FDA stated that the proposed label would confuse and mislead consumers, and expressed doubt whether most buyers read the relatively simple statement of ingredients that is now available.[3]

So, sometimes reasonable limitations and changes are made. But although the precise changes that will occur in the years ahead are basically a matter for conjecture, the overall trend seems to be fairly clear: On balance there is likely to be more and not less government intervention in internal business decision making. Despite differences in philosophy and outlook, changes in control of the executive branch and in the composition of Congress and the judiciary seem to have little effect in altering that trend.[4]

[3] "Stricter Food Labeling Is Rejected," *St. Louis Globe-Democrat*, April 20, 1974, p. 4D.

[4] See Murray L. Weidenbaum, *The Future of Business Regulation* (New York: Amacom Press, 1979).

REASONS FOR REGULATION

Why should governments want to become involved in regulating private industry? The question is not, of course, a simple one to answer. But numerous justifications for public intervention in the private sector have been offered. The basic reason advanced by economists is "market failure," which occurs when, for natural reasons, competitive or market forces fail to function properly in the allocation of goods and services.

These market failures come in many forms. In one set of instances, *inadequate information* may contribute to consumers' making unwise purchases. For example, in regulating the use of certain chemicals in the treatment of baby clothes, the Consumer Product Safety Commission has sought to mitigate any harm which might come to babies exposed to that hazard. The rationale for government action in such a situation is that consumers lack knowledge either of the chemicals with which the clothing is treated or of the hazards that they may give rise to.

Other types of informational failures in the consumer product area have given rise to regulatory mandates such as labeling requirements, grading standards, weight and size information, truth-in-advertising enforcement, and many product safety standards. Likewise, in the area of job safety and working conditions, inadequate information about health hazards has spurred regulators to set down a wide array of rules for on-the-job operations.

In other instances of market failures, *externalities* — also known as "spillover" or neighborhood effects — consist of costs or benefits which accrue not to the person producing them but to other individuals or society as a whole. Externalities result in the wasteful use of resources or in unfair costs being shifted to third parties. Environmental problems are, of course, the major cases in point here. For example, persons living along a river downstream from a polluting factory may have to endure poor water quality when the factory dumps wastes into the river. The Environmental Protection Agency, however, has the regulatory power to enforce the use of less polluting waste disposal systems, thus lessening the involuntary burden placed on the factory's neighbors.

In the absence of governmental intervention, voluntary action to deal with such problems may place a firm under a competitive disadvantage. The specific company attempting to correct a situation such as the one just described would tend to bear the full costs, while the benefits of the improvement would be widely dispersed in the society. "Free riders," or firms which do not make the expensive changes, may nevertheless share in the benefit. An example of this situation is provided by the regulation of pollution standards in the motor vehicle area. The basic justification given by government for setting such standards was clearly stated by a senior executive of a major automotive manufacturer:

> . . . a large part of the public will not voluntarily spend extra money to install emission control systems which will help clean the air. Any manufacturer who installs and charges for such equipment while his competition doesn't soon finds he is losing sales and customers. In cases like this, a government standard requiring everyone to have such equipment is the only way to protect both the public and the manufacturer.[5]

Another important type of market failure is caused by *natural monopolies.* These monopolies occur in industries where certain economies associated with large-scale production make it plausible and reasonable for only one firm to produce the entire industry's output (at least in a given geographic area). An obvious example here is the reliance on only one electric company to run one set of wires to users of electric power in a specific region. Other examples of natural monopolies often occur in the natural gas transmission, telephone, and telegraph industries. Duplication of services such as these by a competing company would be wasteful and would also be likely to raise the cost of the service for users. However, if only one such utility is allowed to operate without any regulation, then we might expect that utility to restrict its output and to charge higher, monopoly prices to its customers. Under the threat of such a circumstance, utility commissions have been established to watch over the operations of utility companies.

Although regulation is often used by the government as a means of correcting market failures, we must be aware that regulatory actions are not necessarily the only means available. For instance, consumers can be educated and provided with information in making purchases. Employees can be made more aware of on-the-job hazards — and presumably bargain for improved working conditions or higher pay as compensation for the risks. Taxes can be levied on polluters and/or subsidies can be paid to those unfairly harmed by pollution, to compensate them for the cleanup burden imposed on them.

Outside the realm of market failures, it is often claimed that

[5] John J. Riccardo, "Regulation: A Threat to Prosperity," *The New York Times,* July 20, 1975, p. F-12.

"distributive justice," or concern with political or social equity, is a reason for governmental intervention. In other words, the government's involvement is seen primarily as a way of bringing about the transfer of wealth to a worthy segment of society. But, in practice, a small group (that is, a "special interest") usually benefits at the expense of the mass of consumers. Regulation has been used in this way to redistribute income among the regions of the nation, to promote new industries, to provide services for small communities, and to give special protection to those deemed especially "worthy" (small businesses, family farms, and so forth). This type of regulation is different in practice from that designed to correct market failures, although the stated rationale may be similar.

Interstate trucking may be a pertinent example here, for regulation of this industry merely serves to insulate existing trucking firms and their employees from competition created by new trucking companies which have not received the approval of a regulatory agency (the Interstate Commerce Commission) to enter the business. The redistribution of income in this case is from consumers in general to the owners, managers, and employees of the regulated industry.[6]

AN OVERVIEW OF REGULATION

Proponents of regulation contend that many of the rules and directives have yielded numerous benefits to the public. The National Highway Traffic Safety Administration claims that seat belts, head restraints, and other mandated safety devices saved 55,000 lives between 1966 and 1978. The Environmental Protection Agency notes that, because of its controls over industrial discharges, fish and marine life are returning to the Naugatuck River in Connecticut and shrimp and crab are back in the Neches River in Texas.

However, the regulatory process may generate its own set of "externalities." Voters in one congressional district may achieve the bulk of the benefits from a federal regulation, but the costs may be borne primarily by citizens in other parts of the nation. For example, regulations making it uneconomical to use low-sulfur (that is, low-polluting) coal have been supported by those areas producing high-sulfur coal. Consumers generally have borne the costs that result from such "self-interested" regulation.

In any event, there are real, albeit vague, limits on the ability

---

[6] Thomas G. Moore, "Beneficiaries of Trucking Regulation," *Journal of Law and Economics*, October 1978.

of government to regulate the private sector while still retaining that sector's private characteristics. This point was clearly enunciated in a landmark decision written by Supreme Court Justice Oliver Wendell Holmes: ". . . while property may be regulated to a certain extent, if regulation goes too far it will be recognized as a 'taking.' "[7]

These are the issues, then, in a general overview of government regulation of business: Regulatory legislation can bring about important benefits for society, but simultaneously it can generate disadvantages for business which are usually passed on to consumers. The balance between the benefit and harm brought about by any given regulation can be, at best, a very delicate one. And, knowing that regulatory activity has a clear tendency to grow rather than to shrink, we might suspect that this balance may rapidly become more precarious.

[7] Pennsylvania Coal v. Mahon, 260 U.S. 393 (1922).

2

the new wave of government regulation

The current wave of government regulation delineated in the previous overview is not merely an intensification of traditional activities. In good measure it is a new departure. The standard theory of government regulation of business, which is still in general use and has dominated thinking on the subject, is based on the model of the Interstate Commerce Commission. Under this approach, a federal commission is established to regulate a specific industry, with the related concern of promoting the well-being of that industry. Often the public or consumer interest is viewed as subordinate, or is even ignored, since the agency focuses on the needs and concerns of the industry that it is regulating.[1]

This specialized focus can acquire curious features. In some cases — because of the unique expertise possessed by the members of the industry or because of job enticements for regulators who leave government employment — the regulatory commission is alleged to

[1] See, for example, George J. Stigler, *The Citizen and the State: Essays on Regulation* (Chicago: University of Chicago Press, 1975).

become a captive of the industry it is supposed to regulate. This is a widely held view of the development of the regulatory process. In addition to the ICC, other examples of this development that have been cited from time to time include the Civil Aeronautics Board, the Federal Communications Commission, the Federal Energy Regulatory Commission, and the Federal Maritime Commission. The head of one of these agencies resigned in 1975 amid charges of excessive zeal in promoting the interests of the industry being regulated.[2] The head of another agency (the Commodity Futures Trading Commission) was put in charge of an investment banking firm's commodity marketing efforts within one month of leaving that regulatory agency in 1979.[3]

Thus, the popular view of regulatory "capture" or "collusion" is not held without some substantiation in fact. A comprehensive study by Professor Victor H. Kramer of the Georgetown University Law School showed that, from 1960 to 1975, 30 percent of the persons appointed to nine regulatory commissions came from the industry they were to regulate. The study's definition of "regulated industry" included employment in companies directly involved in the regulated activity as well as those people working in law firms which consult with companies wishing to further industry interests. Of the 85 commissioners who left the agencies within that period, 32 became employed in the regulated industry within five years.[4]

But regulatory agencies do have rules that restrict the private employment of former employees. Federal law forbids any former federal official from participating in a matter in which he or she was involved while in government service for at least one year after leaving the government. Some agencies have even more stringent rules. The Federal Energy Regulatory Commission will not permit a former employee ever to appear in a case before the Commission if he or she participated in the case while working for the agency. The Federal Trade Commission is even stricter; it bars any previous employee from participating in a proceeding pending while that person was employed by the FTC.

In recent years economists have developed a more general theory of the regulatory process. This theory pictures it as the arena in which various interest groups invest their resources in order to effect an outcome more to their liking. The "capture theory" in this

---

[2] Albert R. Karr, "Helen Bentley Quits Her Position as Head of Maritime Agency," *Wall Street Journal*, June 18, 1975, p. 14.
[3] "Seevers, Ex-Official of Futures Agency, Joins Goldman Sachs," *Wall Street Journal*, May 11, 1979, p. 30.
[4] "Quality of Appointments to 9 U.S. Agencies Scored," *The New York Times*, November 7, 1975, p. 14.

traditional view is seen in terms of the dominance of a small group with a relatively large stake in the affairs of the society as a whole, whose interests are more diffused.[5] For example, the major proponents of job safety regulation are labor unions; these unions have a strong desire to "lock into," or capture, the regulatory activities of job safety agencies. The costs of the standards are borne by consumers generally in the form of higher prices for services and manufactured goods. The benefits accrue almost exclusively to the special interest group itself.

THE NEW MODEL OF GOVERNMENT REGULATION

Although the traditional type of federal regulation of business surely continues, the regulatory efforts established by Congress in recent years — as described in chapter 1 — follow, in the main, a fundamentally different pattern. The new federal regulatory agencies are broader in the scope of their jurisdiction than the ICC-CAB-FCC model. Yet simultaneously in important aspects they are far more restricted. This paradox lies at the heart of the problem of relating their efforts to the national interest.

The changing nature of regulation can be seen with reference to figure 2-1. The vertical lines show the traditional relationship between the old style of governmental commission (ICC, CAB, FCC, etc.) and the specific industry that it regulates. However, the great bulk of the economy — the manufacturing, trade, and services sectors — is virtually exempt from that type of intervention.

In contrast, the horizontal lines show the newer breed of regulation — the EPA, EEOC, OSHA, CPSC, and so on. In the case of each of these relative newcomers to the federal bureaucracy, jurisdiction extends to the great bulk of the private sector, cutting through whole segments of the marketplace. It is this far-ranging characteristic that makes it impractical for any single industry to dominate these regulatory activities in the manner of the traditional model. After all, what specific industry is going to capture the EEOC or OSHA, or would have the incentive to do so?

Yet in comparison with the older agencies, the newer regulators in many important ways operate in a far narrower sphere. That is, they are not usually concerned with the totality of a company or industry, but only or primarily with the one segment of operations

---

[5] Sam Peltzman, "Toward a More General Theory of Regulation," *Journal of Law and Economics,* August 1976.

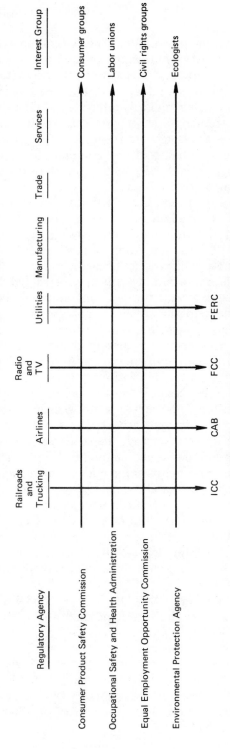

Figure 2-1 VARIATIONS IN FEDERAL REGULATION OF BUSINESS

that falls under their jurisdiction. The ICC, as an example of a traditional regulator, must pay attention to the basic mission of the trucking industry — to provide transportation services to the public — as part of its supervision of rates and entry into the trucking business. The EPA, on the other hand, is interested almost exclusively in the effect of those trucking operations on the environment. This limitation prevents the newer agency from developing too close a concern with the overall well-being of any company or industry. But it can certainly result in a lack of concern for the effects of its specific actions on a company or industry.

If there is any special interest that may come to dominate such an agency, it is not the industry being regulated but rather the group that is preoccupied with its specific task — environmental cleanup, elimination of job discrimination, establishment of safer working conditions, reduction of product hazards, and so forth.

Thus, while important benefits may be gained, little attention is given by the regulators to the *basic* mission of industry, to provide goods and services to the public. Also ignored or downplayed are crosscutting concerns and matters broader than those dealt with in the specific charter of the regulating agency, such as productivity, economic growth, employment, cost to the consumer, effects on overall living standards, and inflationary impacts.

Some important cases, however, may blend the old and the new forms of regulation. The Securities and Exchange Commission (SEC) is a good example. In one aspect of its activities, it regulates a specific branch of the economy, the securities industry. Yet, as will be brought out in subsequent chapters, its rules also influence the way in which a great many companies prepare their financial statements and reports to shareholders. These economywide regulatory agencies (such as the SEC) are not entirely a recent creation; the Federal Trade Commission has existed since 1914. Moreover, a few one-industry agencies continue to be created, notably the Commodity Futures Trading Commission (1974). This commission regulates the financial markets dealing with products of agriculture and other extractive industries.

In short, then, even though the new model has hybrid exceptions, we can see on the one hand that the traditional theory of regulation is geared to a world where the regulators — as well as the various private adversaries in the process — are concerned with prices and entry. But, on the other hand, the new breed of regulators — and the public interest groups supporting their efforts — are usually oblivious to those economic factors. Many of them condemn as callous, or worse, any consideration of cost or other business aspects in deliberations on product, personnel, or environmental safety. In this respect, therefore, the new wave of government regulation is a markedly different phenomenon.

The results of the new approach to government regulation of business may be the reverse of the traditional "capture" situation. Rather than being dominated by a given industry, the newer type of federal regulatory activity is far more likely to utilize the resources of various industries, or to ignore their needs, to further the specific objectives of the regulatory agency. Detailed study of the activities of these newer agencies reveals many negative aspects — for business, the economy, and the public — as well as the intended benefits.

To begin with, we must recognize that it is difficult to criticize the basic mission of these newer regulatory agencies. Only a Scrooge or a misanthrope would quarrel with the intent of the new wave of federal regulation — safer working conditions, better products for the consumer, elimination of discrimination in employment, reduction of environmental pollution, and so forth. And we must recognize that the programs were deliberately established by Congress in response to a surge of rising public expectations about corporate performance. Each of these programs has yielded significant benefits to society as a whole, and at times to business specifically. Some companies have found new outlets for their products in the emerging market for pollution control equipment, and society certainly benefits from the reduction in pollution that results. Opening new employment opportunities for minority groups not only eliminates a basic social inequity but expands the effective labor force that can produce the goods and services desired by the society.

But even though the new wave of regulation may be the reverse of the "capture" situation, we discover that strange and varying alliances may arise in the process of either promoting or attempting to reform a given type of regulatory activity. We find business firms and labor unions becoming supporters of the traditional, industry-oriented commission to which they have adapted. An example of this phenomenon is the opposition in the railroad and trucking industries to efforts on the part of consumer groups and economists to reduce the traditional "protective" regulation. In the area of occupational safety, however, labor unions and consumer groups may form an alliance to encourage the expansion of regulation, while — conversely — business groups and economists may oppose such regulation for the reason of excessive costs.

Hence, compatriots on one issue may find themselves competitors on others: Specific safety regulations for automobiles may be opposed by both unions and companies in the motor vehicle industry, although the two groups may differ strongly on job safety standards. Further, labor, management, and local governments may form a coalition when regulations such as environmental standards threaten the economy of their community, although some of these groups may advocate general ecological advances.

The present trends in federal government regulation in the United States do not represent an abandonment of an idealized and competitive free market economy, but rather they represent a rapid intensification of the long-term expansion of government influence over the private sector. Moreover, the new wave of regulation is reinforced by the widespread belief that many business firms will face the difficult and costly questions of public demands and public actions only if they are forced to by government edict.

THE GROWTH OF GOVERNMENT REGULATION

The process of government intervention in the private sector has become so pervasive that we have, by now, almost come to take its labyrinthine complexity for granted. But merely skimming newspaper headlines will convey to us an understanding of the depth and variety of the trend of government regulation. As an example, let us examine one issue (March 5, 1979) of *The Wall Street Journal*:

> "Airline Deregulation Causes Anger and Joy at Nation's Airports"
> "Energy Department Recommends Carter Call for 3% Voluntary Cut in Energy Use"
> "U.S. Widens Price-Monitoring Program to Cover Small, Medium-Sized Industries"
> "Consent Decree Filed in Bid to Settle Suit Against 9 Steel Firms"
> "Unitex is Cleared to Resume Buying Dan River Common"
> "Dome Petroleum Bid to Sell U.S. Ethane to Get Hearing"
> "Steel Producers Lose Bid for Restrictions on Exports of Scrap"
> "Great Northern Iron Needn't End Trust, State Court Rules"
> "Use of Aluminum Wiring in Homes is Ruled Safe"
> "U.S. Considers Issuing Tougher Safety Rules for Some Wheel Rims"
> "UV Industries to Seek Enforcement of Curb on Sharon's Purchases"
> "Four Are Convicted in Florida Power Case Involving Oil Pricing"
> "U&I Sugar Workers Qualify for Federal Aid Due to Higher Imports"
> "Mercedes-Benz Recalls 3,913 Autos"
> "Hunt Oil, Sedco Inc., to Apply to Chinese for Drilling Rights"
> "Pacific Lighting Unit Asks Rate Rise of $398 Million"
> "Court Clears Much of Tough U.S. Plan on Lead Exposure"

"Revamp of Food-Safety Laws Is Sought"

"Canadian Board Clears Oil Swap"

"SEC Charges Settled by a Senior Partner in Chicago Law Firm"

"Outcome of Foreign Bids for U.S. Banks Put in Doubt by New Interest in Congress"

"Canadian Government Creates a Commission to Monitor Inflation"

"Indiana Lawyers Plot Is Alleged [by Justice Department] on Cornering Title-Search Activity"

"Upkeep Firms Settle Case in New York City about Price-Fixing"

"NLRB Is Told to Review Election of USW as Bargaining Agent at Newport News"

"Bell Canada Appeals a Ruling about Profit from Saudi Contract"

"Carter Names James Duffy to Postal Rate Commission"

"Exxon Corp. Gets $79 Million Contract for Fuel, Gasoline"

"Ex-Im Bank Approves Loan [for purchase of two Lockheed jetliners]"

"Sale of 3 Boeing 747s to Libya Is Approved by State Department"

"Justice Agency Opposes Airline Uniform Fees for Ticketing Duty"

"Bonds for Financing of Home Mortgages [issued by local governments] Seen As Hazardous"

"IRS Examines Charges That an Options Firm Manipulated Records"

"Edward Greene Named Head of SEC Division"

"Morgan Stanley's Rivals Lose Their Smirks Over Olinkraft As Fear of [Government] Crackdown Dawns"

"Robert Maheu Agrees to an Order Settling Charges Filed by SEC"

If this list of headlines shows anything, it demonstrates that both the number and size of the agencies carrying out federal regulation are expanding—and far more rapidly than the industries they are regulating. Since the mid-1960s we have seen the formation of the Consumer Product Safety Commission, the Environmental Protection Agency, the Department of Energy, the Cost Accounting Standards Board, the Mining Health and Safety Administration, the National Highway Traffic Safety Administration, and the Occupational Safety and Health Administration, to cite just the better known ones. This growth is more rapid than that which took place during the New Deal period of the 1930s (see fig. 2-2).

The direct costs of these agencies to the taxpayers are large and growing. As shown in Table 2-1, the operating expenses of the 56 major federal regulatory agencies came to about $2.8 billion in the fiscal year 1974. Their budgets doubled over the following five years, with the total federal costs of these regulatory activities rising to $5.8 billion in fiscal 1979. A further increase to $6.0 billion was budgeted for 1980.

It is apparent, however, that the biggest regulatory budgets are

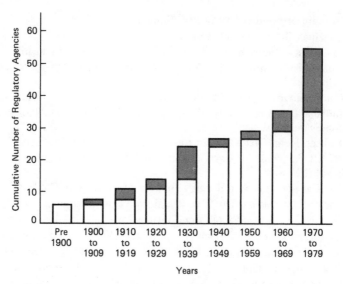

Figure 2-2 GROWTH OF FEDERAL REGULATORY AGENCIES

not those for the traditional independent regulatory commissions, such as the ICC ($80 million) or the CAB ($102 million). Rather, the largest proportion of the funds is devoted to the broader regulatory activities, such as those conducted by EPA ($1.2 billion), Department of Agriculture ($977 million, largely for food inspection), Transportation ($781 million, mainly for vehicle safety), and Labor ($463 million, mainly for employment standards and job safety).

The labor force of inspectors, reviewers, and other regulators maintained by these programs is also growing, from 66,406 in fiscal year 1974 to 80,826 in fiscal 1979 (see table 2-2). Increases are concentrated primarily in the newer agencies, especially in the areas of energy and environmental regulation and occupational safety. But those increases represent only the tip of the iceberg. The costs imposed by these agencies on the private sector are far larger, and these secondary costs are eventually paid by the consumer.

At first glance, government imposition of socially desirable requirements on business appears to be an inexpensive way of achieving national objectives: It seems to cost the government little (aside from the usually overlooked expenses of the regulatory agencies themselves) and therefore is not recognized as much of a burden on the taxpayer. But, on reflection, it can be seen that the public does not escape paying the full cost. For example, every time the Occupational Safety and Health Administration (Department of Labor) imposes on business a more costly, albeit safer, method of produc-

Table 2-1   Expenditures by federal regulatory agencies (fiscal years, $ millions)

Agency	1974	1975	1976	1977	1978	1979	1980
Agriculture	410	447	475	590	915	1,051	977
Commerce	76	75	86	94	99	105	105
Defense	10	16	22	32	38	43	40
Energy	33	6	40	49	79	110	156
Health, Education, and Welfare	165	201	218	245	276	306	317
Interior	5	6	9	13	22	90	168
Justice	22	30	30	35	45	58	61
Labor	208	257	314	332	325	455	463
Transportation	466	460	506	603	679	762	781
Treasury	161	166	185	246	267	297	253
Civil Aeronautics Board	89	81	91	103	101	101	102
Commodity Futures Trading Commission	—	1	11	13	14	16	16
Comptroller of the Currency	50	65	77	83	91	103	190
Consumer Product Safety Commission	19	34	38	40	40	41	41
Environmental Protection Agency	629	850	772	718	885	1,094	1,154
Equal Employment Opportunity Commission	42	56	59	72	74	114	124
Federal Communications Commission	38	48	52	56	64	70	71
Federal Deposit Insurance Corporation	58	66	74	88	105	113	122
Federal Energy Regulatory Commission	27	34	36	41	38	59	70
Federal Maritime Commission	6	7	8	8	9	11	11
Federal Trade Commission	32	39	44	52	59	65	68
International Trade Commission	7	8	10	11	12	14	15
Interstate Commerce Commission	38	44	47	59	65	66	80
National Labor Relations Board	55	61	68	81	90	102	107
National Transportation Safety Board	8	9	11	13	16	16	16
Nuclear Regulatory Commission	80	86	180	231	271	305	345
Securities and Exchange Commission	35	44	51	54	61	68	68
All other	65	71	83	100	122	147	120
Total	2,834	3,268	3,597	4,062	4,862	5,782	6,041

Source: Center for the Study of American Business

Table 2-2   Employment of federal regulatory agencies

Agency	1974	1975	1976	1977	1978	1979
Agriculture	14,854	14,223	14,582	17,193	16,725	17,186
Commerce	2,993	3,014	3,014	2,932	2,937	2,894
Health, Education and Welfare	6,116	6,206	6,362	7,340	7,490	7,583
Justice	629	712	856	907	920	977
Labor	5,643	6,728	7,134	7,709	7,874	8,349
Transportation	1,250	1,479	1,527	1,528	1,550	1,601
Treasury	4,015	4,123	4,401	4,376	4,140	4,068
Civil Aeronautics Board	718	718	758	787	802	830
Commodity Futures Trading Commission	—	496	497	470	470	530
Comptroller of the Currency	2,499	2,546	3,075	2,907	3,069	3,282
Consumer Product Safety Commission	836	890	896	889	900	899
Environmental Protection Agency	5,467	5,365	5,501	6,360	6,420	7,043
Equal Employment Opportunity Commission	2,416	2,384	2,584	2,487	2,487	3,219
Federal Communications Commission	2,021	2,020	2,129	2,159	2,128	2,186
Federal Deposit Insurance Corporation	3,005	3,164	3,600	4,162	4,362	4,500
Federal Energy Regulatory Commission	1,300	1,320	1,398	NA	NA	NA
Federal Maritime Commission	309	319	319	319	348	354
Federal Trade Commission	1,560	1,569	1,638	1,668	1,670	1,716
International Trade Commission	398	408	426	395	395	395
Interstate Commerce Commission	2,035	2,142	2,237	2,205	2,233	2,172
National Labor Relations Board	2,573	2,573	2,670	2,901	3,025	3,123
National Transportation Safety Board	291	310	386	385	385	385
Nuclear Regulatory Commission	1,538	2,006	2,289	2,499	2,662	2,788
Securities and Exchange Commission	1,919	2,144	2,054	2,117	2,092	2,132
All other	2,021	2,270	2,323	2,366	2,559	2,614
Total	66,406	69,129	72,656	77,061	77,643	80,826

Source: Center for the Study of American Business

tion, the cost of the resultant product necessarily will tend to rise. Every time that the Consumer Product Safety Commission imposes a standard which is more costly to attain, some product expenses will tend to rise. The same holds true for the activities of the Environmental Protection Agency, the Food and Drug Administration (Department of Health, Education and Welfare), and so forth.

The point being made in these examples should not be misunderstood. What is at issue is not the worthiness of the objectives of these agencies. Rather, the point is that the public does not get a "free lunch" by imposing public requirements on private industry.[6] Although the costs of government regulation are not borne by the taxpayer directly, in large measure they show up in higher prices of the goods and services that consumers buy. These higher prices represent the "hidden tax," which is shifted from the taxpayer to the consumer. Moreover, to the extent that government-mandated requirements impose similar costs on all price categories of a given product (say, automobiles), this hidden tax will tend to be more regressive than the federal income tax. That is, the costs may place a heavier relative burden on lower income groups than on higher income groups.

THE RANGE OF CONTROLS OVER BUSINESS

Many types of government controls may not be as obvious as some of those just mentioned. They may accompany programs that are promotional or supportive activities for an industry or economic sector. For example, the federal government's efforts to assist in the maintenance of a merchant marine consist primarily of direct subsidies to shipbuilders and ship operators. However, to qualify for the government funds, the ships must incorporate specific national defense and safety features spelled out by the government. These added features raise both acquisition and operating costs.

Other controls contained in government procurement contracts dictate not only what goods and services the contractors must provide but also how they should go about producing them. These requirements range from hiring and training minority groups to adopting federally set wage and hour standards and to favoring depressed areas and small business firms in subcontracting.

[6] See Murray L. Weidenbaum, *Government-Mandated Price Increases* (Washington, D.C.: American Enterprise Institute for Public Policy Research, 1975). See also Murray L. Weidenbaum, *The Future of Business Regulation* (New York: Amacom Press, 1979).

In addition, the tax collector also serves as regulator or at least as a source of strong influence. Using the carrot of tax incentives, the federal government is fostering greater social responsibility on the part of business. Specific Internal Revenue Service provisions that have been adopted in recent years include tax credits for hiring certain categories of people (minority groups), tax deferrals for income from exports, and outright tax reductions for investing in capital goods (the investment tax credit). At times there is a direct linkage between taxes and controls. For example, to qualify for rapid tax amortization of pollution control devices, a company's facility must first be certified by both the state involved and the regional office of the Environmental Protection Agency. For the company contributions to qualify as a tax deduction, a pension program must meet detailed requirements spelled out in the Employee Retirement Income Security Act of 1974. Also, the Internal Revenue Code denies various foreign tax benefits (credits, deferrals, etc.) to taxpayers who participate in or cooperate with an international boycott.

Obviously, however, regulatory activity is so complex that we need to make important distinctions in evaluating the impacts of government controls over business activity. Many controls clearly are going to be present, at least in some form, for the foreseeable future. Others may be of an intermittent or short-term nature.

The tax system just mentioned is the most obvious example of a constant and ongoing control, although even the revenue structure is hardly a static affair. Congress frequently enacts new or modified provisions in the Internal Revenue Code. The Internal Revenue Service, in turn, regularly reviews and often changes its administrative regulations. Nevertheless, business firms can plan their future activities on the assumption that taxes will continue to be an important form of government intervention in internal business decision making.

By contrast, wage and price controls have been an on-again, off-again affair. There are many ways in which government intervenes in private wage and price determination (that is, the so-called incomes policies). At one end of the spectrum are generalized government appeals to business and labor to exercise restraint in increasing wages and prices. This practice is often referred to as moral suasion, or "jawboning." A more specific step is the government effort to set voluntary standards, or "guideposts," for wage and price changes considered to be in the public interest (however that is determined). These nominally voluntary approaches may be supplemented by various forms of government pressure or even coercion, ranging from public chastisement of individual businesses and labor unions to threats to cancel government contracts or other benefits. At the compulsory end of the wage and price control spectrum are formal systems that limit increases and absolute freezes that prohibit them for a fixed period of time.

Between the two types of government intervention represented by the durable tax structure and the relatively unpredictable wage- and price-control actions lies a third area of federal regulation of business. This large and growing intermediate zone consists of evolving programs. The general objective of each of these regulatory programs usually is clear, but the specific means of implementation may be uncertain because changes are made as unexpected problems emerge in the process of applying broad and relatively new policies to operational situations. Environmental and equal employment opportunity programs are perhaps the largest and best-known examples of this middle category of federal regulation.

Although specific regulations may be revised repeatedly, the basic federal presence in these areas of business decision making is likely to prove long lasting. But because government policies are relatively new and volatile, the business response to this sort of government regulation in many cases is not as fully developed as it is for well-established types of government intervention.

The federal government also uses influence in a way that is less direct than controls or regulations. A government agency may monitor a firm's operations, requesting various categories of data and other information; the Treasury Department, for example, monitors financial institutions. Not only are business executives troubled by the paperwork burden that government requests may place on a company, but many are often concerned that the monitoring or disclosure requirements are merely initial steps toward more formal intervention. Although these concerns are occasionally justified, at times use of the information-monitoring approach may be a desirable alternative to more direct federal intervention in business decision making.

Many problems relating to the range of government controls of business result from the fact that these controls all arise out of the political process. Often an extended period of uncertainty predates the congressional mandate for a new regulatory program. In the interim, company decisions on new investments and product lines are often held in limbo. An extra degree of risk is attached to those corporate innovations that do go forward during such periods. In the early 1970s, for example, some petroleum companies were reported to have held off on the construction of new domestic refining facilities partly because of uncertainty about future restrictions on certain types of gasoline resulting from increasingly stringent environmental controls. A more recent example has been the uncertainty over whether the Standard Oil Company of Ohio would continue with its proposed oil pipeline from California to the Midwest. The company attributed its indecision to cumbersome, lengthy, overlappping, and indecisive regulatory procedures.

Other problems may arise when Congress responds to public pressures before the ramifications of the proposed laws — or the possible alternatives to such measures — can be fully considered. Thus, legitimate public concern over the deterioration of the nation's rivers led to a statutory goal of zero discharge of pollutants by 1985, a goal regarded by many economists and industry experts as unattainable. Such quickly enacted legislation also may exacerbate day-to-day business-government relations because executive branch officials find themselves administering policies that are sometimes both unpopular and difficult to carry out. A related problem at times is the lack of knowledge about business operations on the part of many civil servants whose education and experience is in the field of public administration. Consequently, business faces a tremendous challenge in providing pertinent information to these government officials in an open and proper manner.

CONCLUSION

There is little justification for a general attack by business or other groups on all forms of government regulation. Unless we are anarchists, we believe that government should set rules for the society. A society working through government can and should act to protect consumers against rapacious sellers, individual workers against unscrupulous employers, and future generations against those who would waste the nation's resources. But, as in most things in life, the sensible questions are not matters of either-or but rather of more, or less, and how. Thus, we can enthusiastically advocate stringent controls to avoid infant crib deaths without simultaneously supporting a plethora of detailed federal rules and regulations dealing with the color of exit lights and the maintenance of cuspidors. Simply put, there are serious questions as to what rules to set, how detailed they should be, and how they should be administered. That, of course, is the substance of this book.

Because of the very substantial costs and other adverse side effects that government regulation gives rise to, society is beginning to take a new and hard look at the existing array of government controls over business. Efforts are being made to eliminate those controls that generate excessive costs, rather than merely to continue proliferating more and more government controls. In theory, government regulation should be carried to the point where the incremental benefits equal the incremental costs; overregulation (which can be defined as situations where the costs to society exceed the benefits) thus would be avoided.

In the short run, nevertheless, the frontiers of control are expanding. Controls are increasing in a geographic sense as local regulation is followed by state or regional regulation and as federal control is supplemented by that of international regulatory agencies. Thus, the forecast of government intervention by John Maurice Clark in the 1930s has turned out not only to be accurate but also to apply to the future outlook:

> Whether one believes government control to be desirable or undesirable, it appears fairly obvious that the increasing interdependence of all parts of the economic system . . . will force more control in the future than has been attempted in normal times in the past.[7]

We can expect, however, that as corporate managers become more sensitive to evolving social demands, and more aware of the "interdependence" Clark speaks of, they will understand that responses to at least some of the public's expectations are a normal aspect of conducting business. To the extent that this development occurs voluntarily, businesses themselves will be providing an important constraint on the degree of political pressure that social-action interests effectively can exert against them.

[7] John Maurice Clark, "Government Regulation of Industry," *Encyclopedia of the Social Sciences* (New York: Macmillan, 1932), 3, p. 129.

3

government and
automobile production

The most extensive case of the new wave of government regulation of business relates to the production of the passenger automobile, where intervention has taken many forms. In the words of a former chairman of the board of General Motors, "Government today has something to say about how we design our products, how we build them, how we test them, how we advertise them, how we sell them, how we warrant them, how we repair them, the compensation we pay our employees, and even the prices we may charge our customers."[1]

This quotation may seem surprising in view of the general belief that utilities are the most closely regulated industry in the United States. To be sure, government agencies regulate the rates charged and terms of services supplied by electric, gas, and telephone companies. Yet, the basic design of the electric range or gas stove or telephone is a matter that is left to the discretion of private industry. This contrasts sharply with the government's involvement in determining standards for such basic items on the passenger car as engines,

---

[1] *1973 Report on Progress in Areas of Public Concern* (Detroit: General Motors Corporation, 1973), p. 88.

bumpers, headrests, seat belts, door latches, brakes, fuel systems, and windshields.

Regulation of automobile production is clearly an especially interesting case in the relations between business, government, and the public because public policy has proceeded beyond the initial stages of expanded regulation in response to public concerns. At times, the adverse effects of regulation have been so visible to the consumer—particularly in terms of higher fuel consumption (and concomitantly higher costs) and the increased inconvenience in operating the vehicle—that a dramatic response to policy has occurred. The unexpected and unintended side effects of the initial burst of safety and environmental legislation have led to several significant legislative and administrative changes in the nature of regulation. The most dramatic single change was the congressional reversal in 1975 of the requirement for the "interlock" system of seat belts, shoulder harnesses, and buzzers. On the other hand, the most extensive regulatory expansion has been the addition of ambitious requirements for energy efficiency, which in part offsets one of the key side effects of the environmental and safety regulations.

Although a great deal of attention has been given to the inconvenience involved in driving automobiles with federally mandated safety and environmental features, much less thought has been devoted to the higher cost of producing these vehicles, and hence the higher prices paid by American motorists.

THE EFFECT ON THE CONSUMER

The new devices that have been mandated for new model automobiles have, of course, contributed to lessened automotive injuries and deaths and to reduced levels of air pollution. Also, to a major extent, recent declines in motor vehicle accident and death rates can be attributed, at least in part, to the promulgation of lower speed limits (another form of regulation) in response to the changed energy supply situation in the United States.

As would be expected, however, the ever more complicated auto safety systems—as well as federally mandated pollution controls and energy usage goals—have simultaneously increased the price of motor vehicles. To comply with the Motor Vehicle Safety Act, nearly 900 items must be tested or checked on the standard, full-size automobile.[2] Accomplishing this task is no small matter.

[2] Henry L. Duncombe, Jr., and H. Paul Root, "Automobiles, Energy, and Product Planning Risks," *Journal of Contemporary Business*, March 1975, p. 40.

Table 3-1   Increase in retail price of automobiles due to federal requirements

Year of Regulation	Action	Estimated Current Cost (1978 Dollars)
1968	Seat and shoulder belts, standards for exhaust emissions	$ 48
1968-1969	Windshield defrosting and defogging systems, door latches and hinge systems, lamps, reflective devices, and associated equipment	15
1968-1970	Theft protection (steering, transmission, and ignition locking and buzzing systems)	13
1969	Head restraints	27
1969-1973	Improved side door strength	21
1970	Reflective devices and further emissions standards	15
1971	Fuel evaporative systems	28
1972	Improved exhaust emissions; seat belt warning system and locking systems on retractors	42
1972-1973	Exterior protection	95
1973	Reduced flammability of interior materials; location, identification, and illumination of controls improvements	9
1974	Improved exhaust emissions	133
1975	Additional safety features and catalytic converter	147
1976	Hydraulic brakes, improved bumpers	42
1977	Leak-resistant fuel system	21
1978	Redesign of emissions controls	10
	Total	$666

Source: Computed from data supplied by the U.S. Department of Labor, Bureau of Labor Statistics

Table 3-1 shows, for the typical new 1978 passenger automobile, the cost of the successive changes that have been required to meet federal standards. According to these data, the federally mandated costs averaged $666 per car.[3] With new-car purchases totaling about 10 million for the year 1978, American motorists paid approximately $6.7 billion extra for meeting government-imposed requirements in that one 12-month period. In addition, the

[3] Other figures on the cost of safety regulations are contained in U.S., National Highway Traffic Safety Administration, *The Contributions of Automobile Regulation, Preliminary Report* (Washington, D.C.: U.S. Government Printing Office, 1978).

added weight and complication of the mandated features increased the operating costs of the vehicles, particularly for fuel. The added weight to the auto, as will be seen, contributes to major problems in meeting the standards set by the government for automobile fuel economy.

To an economist, it is not only the magnitude of the resources that are important, but the alternatives to which they can be put — what is called the "opportunity cost." As Paul McCracken has stated the matter,

> . . . resources used in one direction are then not available to be used elsewhere. Whether they should be so used, therefore, depends not only on whether the intended use is "good," but on whether it is better than the uses to which the resources would otherwise be put.[4]

This statement permits us to see that the $6.7 billion that American motorists paid out in 1978 for the added features mandated by the federal government on new cars had a high "opportunity cost." We as a nation had to forego the opportunity to spend that considerable sum of money for other ways of reducing road accidents. To take one notable example, what would a portion of the $1 billion that was devoted to the now-discontinued "interlock" system have yielded if it had been applied to these useful safety alternatives?

1. Identifying and eliminating the serious hazards created by unclear or badly placed road signs, or placing signs where they are needed but now absent.
2. Providing more universal and more intensive driver instruction, including developing and testing simulators for use in training and licensing drivers. Simulators could be used to make driver tests more extensive and demanding. (The appendix to this chapter describes one such effort.)
3. Assessing costs and benefits of more thorough vehicle inspections. Perhaps expanded safety inspections could be combined with checkups on pollution-control equipment and engine operation. This would help to meet safety, environment, and energy conservation objectives simultaneously.[5]

Every benefit from regulation, to the customer or to the public, has a corresponding cost, and the car buyer ultimately must pay for those costs. In the case of tougher bumpers, for example, any saving in insurance premiums or reduced cost of car repair should be weighed

[4] Paul W. McCracken, "Will There Be an Economics in 2024?" *University of Michigan Business Review*, October 1974, p. 13.
[5] "The Bureaucrats Belt Us Again," *Fortune*, October 1973, p. 128.

against the additional cost of the bumper and the additional gasoline needed to move the cars made heavier by the new bumpers, the supporting frame, and related equipment. To illustrate: In 1971 the average bumper system weighed 104 pounds and cost the consumer approximately $140 per vehicle. The average weight of the bumpers on a 1975 car was 220 pounds and cost the car buyer $278.[6]

Though bumper standards, like the interlock system and the catalytic converter, may be relaxed or even reversed to some degree, the initial investments in technology and equipment to comply with these standards clearly cannot be recovered. The technological investment devoted to efforts to comply with government standards has been described in this way by Henry Duncombe and H. Paul Root of General Motors:

> To meet the certification requirements for our 1975 models, 284 test cars were driven more than 5 million miles and required that 2,734 separate emission tests be conducted, each taking more than 14 hours to complete. Nearly 500,000 gallons of gasoline were consumed in running these certification tests, and this procedure required the equivalent of 600 persons working an 8-hour day for one full year.[7]

What has happened in this one industry alone is a very considerable redirecting of manpower and revenue to regulatory compliance efforts.

AUTOMOBILE SAFETY REGULATION

Automobile safety regulation in the United States is characterized by great reluctance to interfere directly with individual behavior. It concentrates on the things people use, rather than on the *way* people use them. This is evident when we compare the softness in enforcing statutes on drunken driving with the stringent requirements imposed on manufacturers of motor vehicles for various safety-related components to be attached to their product. Because the great majority of automobile riders do not use seat belts, the federal government is moving to requirements for more expensive "passive" restraint systems, which, to be activated, do not require any action by the driver or other occupants of the vehicle.

[6] James E. Overbeke, "Washington Bumps Off Tough Bumper Rules," *Industry Week*, January 13, 1975, p. 61.
[7] Duncombe and Root, "Automobiles, Energy, and Product Planning Risks," p. 42.

In a related way, we might consider the neglected role of pedestrians. More than one out of three fatalities resulting from motor vehicle accidents are pedestrians and bicyclists, who do not benefit from air bags, interlock systems, and similar equipment required by federal safety regulation. One-third of auto-related deaths, therefore, lie *outside* the realm of government-mandated safety items installed in vehicles.

As will become apparent when we examine other types of government regulation of business, the federal agency tends to adopt a specific regulatory approach at the outset of its activities. Little, if any, attention is given to the basic *causes* of the public policy problem — highway injuries and fatalities, in this case — and to the analysis of alternate ways to deal with it. To illustrate this point, a recent study by the Institute for Research in Public Safety at Indiana University is revealing.

The institute made an in-depth study of 2,258 accidents during the years 1970 to 1975. The major cause, over two-thirds, turned out to be human factors — driver errors. So-called environmental factors accounted for less than one-fifth of the accidents. Examples of these factors included obstructed field of vision, slick road surfaces, and errors in design of roadways. Significantly, in last place, accounting for 4 percent of the accidents, were factors related to the vehicle itself. And most of these cases involved defective brakes and bald or underinflated tires.[8]

Evidently, then, the development of government regulation of industry, particularly in the safety area, seems to have at times lost sight of the important objective of seeking out the least costly way of achieving worthy objectives. Professor Roger L. Miller of the University of Miami has described the problem as follows:

> Now they seem to be insisting that Detroit should begin producing what amounts to overly expensive tanks without giving much thought to some alternatives that are just as effective, while less costly to society.
>
> Modification or removal of roadside hazards might eliminate as many as one quarter of all motor vehicle fatalities. Another 10 percent or so occur when automobiles collide with bridge abutments, or with pier supports or overpasses.[9]

---

[8] John Treat and Rickey Stansifer, "Vehicle Problems as Accident Causes" (paper prepared for the Society of Automotive Engineers, no. 770117, 1977), pp. 2-3.

[9] Roger L. Miller, "The Nader Files: An Economic Critique" (paper presented at a Conference on Government and the Consumer at the Center for Government Policy and Business, October 22-28, 1973), p. 3.

According to Miller, most of these safety hazards could be eliminated by better marking of poorly marked roads and intersections, the installation of breakaway traffic signs and light poles, and the padding of abutments and concrete pillars. The benefit of these particular actions also would go to owners and passengers of old cars, not just to owners of those newer models equipped with required safety features.

Moreover, 60 percent of drivers in fatal single-car crashes are drunk, as are 50 percent of the drivers at fault in fatal crashes involving two or more cars. A more cost-effective alternative to the mandating of auto safety features might involve more vigorous legal prosecution of drunken drivers and drunken pedestrians. In short, decreasing the number of drunks driving or walking may be more efficient than requiring every car-buying motorist to invest in expensive safety equipment.

But the government still has not taken this alternate route; it has concentrated on automotive "things" rather than on the persons who use autos. On June 30, 1977, the U.S. Department of Transportation mandated passive restraints as standard equipment in front seats for all passenger cars by 1984. The phase-in schedule starts with full-size cars in model year 1982, adds mid-size and compacts in 1983, and covers all cars in the 1984 model year. *Passive* is a term used here to describe a restraint that operates automatically, without action by the occupant. Examples include a belt that moves into place over the rider's body as the door is closed, or air bags that inflate in a frontal collision.

The impetus behind the passive restraint mandate is the low usage of seat belts by drivers and passengers. A 1978 study by the Department of Transportation revealed that only 14 percent of the nation's drivers use those belts. Discomfort and inconvenience were cited as the most common reasons for lack of use. So regulators have chosen to work around driver preferences by mandating automatic, passive restraints. But considerable controversy has been raised over the effectiveness of passive versus active restraint systems, especially by the people who do voluntarily use seat belts and shoulder harnesses.[10]

Another safety problem in the automotive field results from the interaction of the nation's various regulatory objectives. As will be discussed shortly, motor vehicle manufacturers are also being required to attain mandatory fuel economy standards. Reducing the weight

[10] "New DOT Study Finds Only 14% of Drivers Use Auto Safety Belts," *U.S. Department of Transportation News,* December 15, 1978, pp. 1-3.

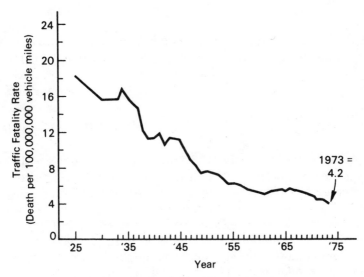

Figure 3-1   AUTOMOBILES AND TRAFFIC SAFETY

Source: James M. Dawson, *The Love Affair With the Automobile,* National City Bank, Cleveland, Ohio, July 5, 1974.

of the vehicle is a basic response by auto makers to this regulation. However, when two cars of different size collide, the safety advantage lies with the occupants of the heavier vehicle (this fact is in accord with the physical law of conservation of momentum).

It is difficult in a situation such as this one to determine which regulatory objective is superior. A more constructive approach may be to reconsider the nature of the standards. Professor Donald F. Huelke of the University of Michigan Medical School has criticized federal motor vehicle safety standards as having "been cast in bronze," leaving little room for change, even when research indicates that a standard has become ineffective or unnecessary. Thus, government regulatory activities can become more concerned with complying with the specific standards promulgated by a given agency than with attaining the original objectives of decreasing death and injury rates from automobile accidents.[11]

Although further reasonable improvements in automobile safety should be expected, it is informative to note that the traffic fatality rate in the United States had already been steadily decreasing prior to the introduction of federally mandated safety requirements (see fig. 3-1). Also, according to data supplied by the National Highway Traffic Safety Administration (NHTSA) for 1975, fatalities in

[11] James E. Overbeke, "Are the Standards 'Cast in Bronze'?" *Industry Week,* June 16, 1975, p. 85.

the United States (43 per 100,000 passenger cars) were lower than in other industrialized nations: Norway (58), Netherlands (69), Canada (72), West Germany (83), Belgium (89), and Spain (128).

AUTOMOBILE POLLUTION AND ENERGY USE

Actions taken by the U.S. Congress and the Department of Transportation in 1977 on pollution and energy will have a great influence on the nature of the American automobile for many years to come. In August 1977 Congress passed into law a new schedule of maximum allowable exhaust emissions, to be enforced by the Environmental Protection Agency. For example, allowable hydrocarbon emissions (expressed in grams per mile) were reduced from 1.50 for the model year 1978/79 to 0.41 in 1980 and beyond. Allowable carbon monoxide emissions were cut from 15.0 in 1978/79 to 7.0 in 1980 and 3.4 in 1981 and the years following. The NO_x (oxides of nitrogen) standard was set at 2.0 for 1980 and 1.0 for 1981 and thereafter. When the NO_x limit is lowered to 1 gram per mile, the existing emissions control systems in recent auto models — based on a single oxidizing catalytic converter — will no longer be adequate.

On the basis of the emission control systems imposed by EPA, the largest producer of cars (General Motors) expects about a 5-percent reduction from present fuel economy levels. Thus, the new pollution standards make it more difficult to achieve the new energy conservation standards. Also, the new emissions control system is estimated to cost about $200 more per vehicle than current equipment.[12]

Under the emissions certification process auto producers face a formidable task. A representative number of prototype cars must be driven through a fifty-thousand-mile "durability schedule" to establish the rate at which the effectiveness of an auto's emission controls can be expected to deteriorate over a given number of years (or miles). The manufacturers then have to design the actual production models so that they will meet more severe levels than those established in the initial formal standards, to compensate for the expected loss of the controls' effectiveness over time. Thus, General Motors's 1978 model cars achieved a hydrocarbon emission level 62 percent below the designated standard in order to make sure that the car will have a durable, long-term emission control.

[12] *General Motors Public Interest Report, 1977–78* (Detroit: General Motors Corporation, 1978), pp. 3–8.

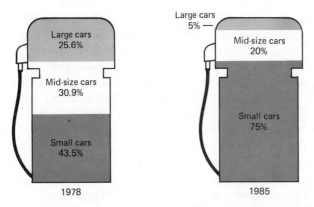

Figure 3-2 CHANGING COMPOSITION OF AUTOMOBILE PRODUCTION

Also in 1977 the Department of Transportation announced the schedule of automotive fuel economy requirements for model years 1981 through 1984. The Energy Policy and Conservation Act, passed in 1975, specifies that the average fuel economy for each motor vehicle manufacturer must be at least 20 miles per gallon in 1980 and 27.5 miles per gallon in 1985. Under the authority it obtained from this law, the department set standards for the intervening years — 22 in 1981, 24 in 1982, 26 in 1983, and 27 in 1984. The shift from production of large to smaller cars is the most obvious result of these standards (see fig. 3-2). Thus, meeting these new requirements is forcing a basic redesign of the American automobile. This change, too, is a formidable undertaking for the industry. In the words of Henry Ford II, of the Ford Motor Company, "Our strategy in the U.S. is plain and simple. It's dictated by government regulation."[13] Industry estimates show, moreover, that the savings in fuel costs are likely to be far exceeded by the additional capital investments required to achieve them (on the order of $10 billion by 1985).

Recent improvements in automotive fuel economy have thus far been the result of technical adjustments within existing technology. These have involved mainly upgraded designs of vehicles and some substitution of materials, such as using more plastics, aluminum, glass, and high-strength, low-alloy steel.[14] But to increase fuel economy even more, major innovations will be required, including development of an advanced engine and a new automotive drive train. On a more sweeping scale, in 1979 Secretary of Transportation Brock

[13] "Henry Ford II Leaves a Strategy for the '80s," *Business Week*, April 30, 1979, p. 69.

[14] D. Quinn Mills, "A Collision Course on Energy Policy," *The New York Times*, August 9, 1979, p. D-2.

Adams called upon the automobile industry to work with the federal government in designing a basically new car for the period beyond 1985. Proposed substitutes for the current mode of automobile transportation might be specialization of the car for the different tasks in which it may be used: mini-cars for neighborhood transportation and local shopping, a commuter car containing virtually no storage space, and larger models for longer family trips. (The last of these might be available for rental because of infrequent use.) Such specialization could result in very fuel-efficient and relatively low overall costs of transportation.[15] But transition to such an arrangement would certainly require much research, development, and investment by car manufacturers, as well as public-sector adjustments in highways, streets, and traffic rules.

As a result of the totality of governmental regulation, fundamental alterations are occurring in the nature of the automobile industry, and further changes in its structure are in the offing. According to a study done for NHTSA by the Cambridge consulting firm of Harbridge House, the length of the industry's product planning cycle has stretched to five or more years to meet regulatory standards, and traditional economies of scale are being magnified in the process. Meeting the government's fuel economy mandate places the smaller companies at a disadvantage. They have fewer resources available for other activities, such as product development and modernization of manufacturing facilities.[16] In commenting on the study, NHTSA stated, "In that respect, government regulations may have a disproportionately harsh impact on a small manufacturer."

Thus, the costliness of automotive regulation may show up not only in higher prices to the consumer but in a more concentrated structure of the automotive industry, notably larger market shares by the two industry leaders — General Motors and Ford. The latter result would, of course, be at variance with other regulatory policies — such as those administered by the Federal Trade Commission and the Justice Department to achieve a more competitive economy.

Alternatives to the current thrust of automotive regulations have been offered. For instance, Dr. Robert Crandall of the Brookings Institution has urged a very different approach to achieving a higher degree of fuel economy in motor vehicles. He advocates decontrol of oil and gasoline prices, a reexamination of safety standards which add weight to a car, and the substitution of pollution taxes

---

[15] Charles R. Day, Jr., "Detroit's Dilemma: Building the 21st Century Dream Machine," *Industry Week*, May 14, 1979, pp. 71–73.

[16] *Corporate Strategies of the Automotive Manufacturers* (Boston: Harbridge House, 1978).

for existing automobile pollution standards. Such policies might induce the manufacturers of motor vehicles to become more innovative. Crandall's approach also could achieve better trade-offs between the presently conflicting goals of automobile performance, fuel efficiency, safety, and pollution control.[17]

APPENDIX: DRIVER EDUCATION AS AN ADDITION TO SAFETY REGULATION*

Governmental regulation of the design and production of motor vehicles constitutes one method of attempting to achieve a reduction in road accidents. This appendix, however, describes another method, one that is not necessarily mutually exclusive. Improved driver instruction could contribute to more effective use of the automotive safety equipment mandated by the federal government.

This section describes an advanced driver education program developed at the General Motors Proving Ground. The program was designed around the concept of training drivers to handle specific driving emergencies. It was evaluated by comparing trained and untrained control groups. A significant reduction in both numbers of accidents and accident severity was indicated.

The Driver Study

The General Motors Proving Ground, which has the responsibility of testing the company's automotive products in the environment, analyzed 14 available accident causation studies. The data were then examined to isolate those causation factors primarily related to drivers. The researchers knew that it is difficult to isolate any particular factor as the only contributor to an accident. If, however, a careful study of the accident provided a strong possibility that the driver was a significant contributor, it was then tabulated by the probable driver error.

The following driver errors occurred with the greatest frequency:

[17]Robert W. Crandall, "Regulations and Regulators: The Best Laid Plans," *Policy Commentary*, December 1978, p. 6.

*This section draws on materials in U.S. Senate, Committee on Commerce, *Motor Vehicle Safety Oversight* (Washington, D.C.: U.S. Government Printing Office, 1975), pp. 383-92.

impaired judgment due to alcohol, misinterpretation of the driving task, and improper control of emergency situations.

The effect of alcohol on driving accidents presented a social problem beyond the scope of the project; the other two issues were not. The driving emergencies identified with a high degree of occurrence were improper off-road recovery, skids, improper evasive maneuvers, and improper braking. Using these specific problem situations and recognizing an obvious need to improve interpretation of the driving task and required driver reaction, the program designers developed a series of training exercises.

Off-road recovery. In normal driving a driver will often either deliberately or inadvertently drop two wheels off the road edge. Due to poor shoulder maintenance on many roads, this drop may be as large as four to six inches. The driver knows he or she should slow down and then return to the road surface. This is undoubtedly a correct approach, but there are several conditions that may prevent the driver from exercising this technique. The shoulder may be blocked by a disabled vehicle or some other obstacle, or the vehicle may be in a stream of high-speed traffic. Whatever the reason for difficulties, drivers do attempt to return the car to the road surface and often have problems.

The driver problem occurs because he or she tends to be cautious. The driver scrubs the tire on the road edge, and this action requires a very considerable amount of steering to enable the tire to climb the dropoff. When the tire does climb up under such circumstances, the vehicle rapidly crosses the traffic lane, possibly leading to a collision or to a difficult control situation. Exercises were developed to give the student practice in performing the maneuver properly. This requires a sharp input from a straddle position, with a quick return to the straight-ahead steering position at the moment of tire impact. In this maneuver, the momentum of the vehicle will carry it up on the road and it will still stay within the traffic lane.

Skids. The training of drivers in skid recovery long has been recognized as a desirable feature of advanced driver training programs. The common power skid, where the vehicle has lost rear wheel cornering traction due to overthrottle application on a slippery curve, is the most troublesome type of skid. It is the type the motorist identifies with the word *skid* per se. In the training exercise, this type of skid is simulated by momentarily locking the rear wheels to induce the skid on a wetted skid pad. Students are trained at speeds up to 35 miles an hour, progressing to more severe skids as they become more competent.

Evasive maneuvers. Many cases of a driver either failing to make or improperly performing an evasive maneuver led to the development of an instructive evasive exercise. A major driver deficiency, first of all, appears to be lack of awareness of the evasive capability of an automobile and overdependence on the brake as an emergency control. In addition, most drivers and many driving instructors are not aware that a locked tire cannot provide steering capability. These reasons led to the development of the evasive maneuver and the controlled braking exercise. In the evasive exercise, the student drives down a cone-marked lane, which is blocked at the end. At a predetermined point, he or she is cued to evade this barricade by making a left or right lane change without braking. Several cuing systems have been used, such as light, plastic curtains that close all but one lane, and vocal command. All appear to be equally effective. The major objective is for the student to become aware of and utilize the evasive capability of the automobile. The student is shown what can be done and then runs through the exercise at increasing speeds in proportion to his or her progress.

Controlled braking. It is important to brake a vehicle to reduce speed even in an evasive maneuver, but the driver must learn to break without locking the wheels so that he or she can maintain steering control. The controlled braking exercise also requires a lane change evasive maneuver. The student is told that the course is simulating his or her coming over the crest of a hill and, at the cue point, the student has just seen a disabled vehicle in his or her path. The student is first to get around this vehicle and then back into the original road lane because of the possibility of oncoming traffic, and at the same time he or she is to stop the car in the shortest possible distance. The student learns to modulate the brake and detect, as well as react to, wheel lockup. The maximum speed is generally 45 miles an hour for a 50-foot distance between the brake cue and the cone barricade.

Tire blowouts. Tire blowouts are infrequent occurrences today and account for few accidents, but drivers generally have a fear of what will happen if one occurs. The Proving Ground developed a blowout simulator, which is a pneumatic valve that allows the tire to be deflated through the rim in a time comparable to a sudden tire air loss. The device automatically reinflates the tire so that repetitive blowouts can be given on the same tire. (This unit has been licensed and is available to the general public.) Even though tire blowouts are not a major accident causation factor, the fear of a blowout, the ability to give a driver a simulated emergency, and the similarity of driver control response to other vehicle handling situations make it an effective training exercise. Both front and rear blowouts are given at speeds up to 60 miles an hour while operating in a straight line and on curves.

Serpentine course. Although not directly related to a specific emergency situation, a serpentine course is incorporated to develop proper hand positions, rhythm, and timing of steering inputs, and to increase the driver's ability to perceive the spatial relationship of his or her vehicle with respect to fixed obstacles such as cones.

The six foregoing exercises were used as a nucleus of the course with a classroom session consisting of the major topics in the following outline:

    I. Explanation of the driving system
        A. Driver
        B. Vehicle
        C. Road
        D. Interrelationships
   II. Discussion of driver's role
        A. Driver's role in the driving system
        B. Physical limitations of driver
  III. Discussion of importance of vehicle maintenance
  IV. Discussion of pretrip driver preparation
    V. Basic discussion of vehicle dynamics as related to the particular driving exercises
  VI. Discussion of tires as related to vehicle performance with emphasis on tire
 VII. Discussion of the elements of defensive driving and how they are used
        A. Sight habits
        B. Concentration
        C. Knowledge
        D. Judgment
        E. Skill

The Program and Its Evaluation

This entire program is designed to be conducted in a single 7½-hour period, with 1½ hours devoted to two classroom sessions and the remaining 6 hours on the driving exercises. Each exercise accommodates three students per car, so that the actual behind the wheel time is 2 hours per person, the remainder being observation time.

Having developed a course in advanced driving techniques, it was important to evaluate achievements of the first objective — does the course reduce accidents? A training program had been conducted using Proving Ground personnel, but the accident experience of this group is so low that no effective evaluation could be made in a reasonable length of time.

A local law enforcement agency, the Oakland County, Michigan, Sheriff's Department, had approached the Proving Ground in regard to a training program for its patrol officers. An experimental program was undertaken. A group of 60 officers was matched to provide two groups of as similar a makeup as possible. Thirty officers were put through the program and 30 were kept as a control group. The officers attended the 7½-hour program in October 1969.

Each officer in the program was evaluated by his instructor for each exercise, using a combined objective-subjective system. The evaluation consisted of such items as hand positions, number of cones knocked down, number of successful passes, speed of each run, lane position, number and types of improper responses, and the instructor's overall opinion of performance, attention, and attitude. At the conclusion of each day's workshop, the evaluation cards were collected, sorted, tabulated, and converted into percentile scores. Upon completion of the workshops, a percentile ranking was made for each exercise and an overall performance percentile ranking was tabulated for the entire trainee control group. The total performance scores ran from a high of 84.3 to a low of 67.8, with a median of 75.2

Utilizing the evaluation data plus the instructor's personal evaluation of each student, each officer was provided with a private composite analysis of his performance and a listing of his weak and strong areas. As of October 1971, the two groups had an accident record of 10 to 5 in favor of the trained group. The trained group showed a 50-percent reduction in accidents as compared with the untrained group. This relates to 13 and 11 accidents, respectively, for the equal time period preceding October 1969.

It is also useful to examine the severity of the accidents and examine factors relating to a good benefit-cost ratio. A following summary is provided of injuries, days lost, lost wages, and vehicle damage cost as per insurance company payment. It does not include the cost required to replace patrol cars damaged beyond repair or the cost of replacing the man on duty while he was off due to injuries.

These data indicate that the total costs for the untrained group were 10 times those of the trained group. The average cost per accident of the trained group was only 20 percent of that of the untrained group.

Although no formal benefit-cost analysis was performed, the available data are intriguing. A total of 30 officer-students participated in the pilot program, each undergoing a 7½-hour training program. Over a two-year period, the group had $13,300 less accident costs (in terms of lost wages and damage to vehicles) than the control group. Thus, the economic benefit of the program came to $59 per student per hour. Moreover, the accidents that did occur were less serious; no wages were lost and no vehicles were completely demolished.

Category	Trained Group	Untrained Group
Number of accidents	5	10
Injuries	0	2
Lost days	0	87
Lost wages	0	$ 3,500.00
Vehicle damage costs	$1,446.50	$11,247.10
Vehicles totaled	0	3
Total cost	$1,446.50	$14,747.10
Average cost per accident	$289.30	$ 1,474.71

Conclusions

Staff of the General Motors Proving Ground drew several conclusions from the study, as follows:

1. Prior to this study, it was anticipated that the officers might have a tendency to be more aggressive in their driving, since they were trained to handle more severe driving conditions. In fact, observation showed the opposite to be true. The trained group became more cautious in their driving. One could hypothesize that they had acquired a better understanding of the limits of their capabilities and, therefore, tended to stay within those limits.
2. The group, before the program, did not use restraint systems. Since the program, 29 of the 30 became conscientious restraint-device users. From their comments, it was concluded that they used the restraints not because of a fear of injury, but because they were better able to control the car if they are "belted" in the vehicle. This may indicate a more promising method of promoting restraint usage.
3. There appears to be a very rapid rise in the learning curve for this type of training, and a shorter course may be possible. And although General Motors is not in the position to undertake mass training programs for drivers, the company hopes to be able to provide assistance to those groups having this responsibility.

4

consumer product regulation

The actions of numerous federal agencies relate to consumer products, including those of the Food and Drug Administration, the Department of Agriculture, and the Federal Trade Commission. Yet it is the Consumer Product Safety Commission which has the most direct and explicit responsibility in this area. The Consumer Product Safety Act of 1972 created an independent regulatory agency "to protect the public against unreasonable risks of injury associated with consumer products." A five-member Consumer Product Safety Commission (CPSC) sets safety standards for consumer products, bans products presenting undue risk of injury, and in general polices the entire consumer product marketing process from manufacture to final sale.

In creating the commission, Congress adopted a "no-fault" view of accidental product injuries, involving a complex interaction between the consumer, the product, and the environment. Rather than stressing punitive action against the producers and distributors of unsafe products, the emphasis in the statute is on setting new product standards. Under this approach, products would be redesigned

Table 4-1   Selected Consumer Product Safety Commission reports of possible
             substantial hazards, fiscal year 1978

Product	Defect or Hazard	Action Taken
Amusement park ride	Potential failure in hydraulic cylinder caps	Company replaced all cylinder caps
Solid state AC adaptor	Possible shock hazard	Units embargoed in warehouse
Jack-in-the-box toy	Top box may separate	Company changed design
Portable baby strollers	Possible pinching of baby	Company repaired strollers
Sewing machine	Foot pedal may overheat	Engineering changes made
Portable hydrotherapy appliance	Risk of shock hazard	Company issued stop-sale order
Aluminum step ladder	Defective step	Company recalled all ladders
Burglar alarm	Possible fire hazard	Modified with smaller bulb
Gas valve for furnace	Valve may fail	Company replaced all units
Refrigerator	Uninsulated wire contacts	Company repaired all units
Scuba diver regulator	Potentially defective clamp ring	Company retrofitted all units
Thermostat relay	Relay may not function properly	Cause of defect undiscovered
Sweat shorts	Flammable	Recalled from retailers
Stereo receiver	Possible fire hazard	Defective module replaced
Coffee maker	Water leak creates possible fire hazard	Company recalled the product and refunded the customers
Christmas lights	Short circuit	Recalled; refunded or replaced
Gas furnace	Minute deposits of cadmium in coating	CPSC ruled not a substantial hazard
Sewer cleaning equipment	Fatigue in blade motors	Defective part replaced
Crib	Infant's head may get stuck	Manufacturer changed design

Source: U.S., Consumer Product Safety Commission, *1979 Annual Report*, part 2 (Washington, D.C.: U.S. Government Printing Office, 1979)

to accommodate to possible consumer misuse and ignorance of proper operation of the product. In the words of E. Patrick McGuire of the Conference Board, in describing this approach, "The most dangerous component is the consumer, and there's no way to recall him."

Specific functions of the commission include aiding consumers in the evaluation of product safety, developing uniform product safety standards, gathering medical data and conducting research on product-related injuries, and coordinating federal, state, and local product safety laws and enforcement. Consumers are assured the right to participate in the commission's activities, as "any interested person . . . may petition the commission to commence a proceeding for the issuance, amendment, or revocation of a consumer product safety rule."[1] Safety standards cover product performance, contents, composition, design, construction, finish, packaging, and labeling.

Powers of the commission extend to requiring manufacturers of products found to be hazardous to take corrective actions. These actions include refunds, recalls, public warnings, and reimbursements to consumers for expenses of the recall process. Any product representing an unreasonable risk of personal injury or death may, by court order, be seized and condemned. Under the Consumer Product Safety Act of 1972, the commission's jurisdiction extends to more than 10,000 products. Table 4-1 shows a sample of recent actions taken by the commission.

THE IMPACT ON CONSUMERS – BENEFITS AND COSTS

Important benefits to the public can be expected from an agency designed to make consumers more aware of product hazards and to require the removal from the market of products likely to cause serious injuries. Simultaneously, it must be noted that such actions also can generate large costs, which will be borne ultimately by the consumer. The consumer's total welfare is therefore maximized by seeking out the most economical and efficient ways of achieving safety objectives. Thus, banning products can be seen as one of a variety of alternatives. These can range from relabeling a product (so that the consumer becomes aware of a previously hidden hazard) to recalling and modifying an existing line of products.

At times, higher consumer product prices result from the commission's forcing expensive complexity on the manufacturers of consumer products. Poor, and even middle-income, families may thus be priced out of many markets for consumer products. A case in point is the four million electric frying pans for which the commission has ordered formal hearings to determine if they are hazardous. What is puzzling, however, is that, out of the four million pans, not a single injury has been reported by the commission.[2]

One way of looking at government-mandated product safety requirements is that they constitute a "tie-in sale." Every consumer, whether he or she wants or needs the new layer of protection, has to

---

[1] Consumer Product Safety Act, Public Law 92-573.
[2] "Some Fry Pans and Chain Saws May Be Unsafe," *St. Louis Post-Dispatch*, January 15, 1974, p. 8A.

accept and pay for it. As Walter Guzzardi puts it, "What is made safe for the village idiot will cost the man of common sense more."[3]

All this suggests that there should be some key considerations at work in the decision of a government agency to regulate a product's use. If the product hazard is *hidden*, the unknowing consumer is denied the freedom of deciding whether to risk using a product. But the risk in using a sharp knife is visible, and each individual may choose the degree of care in handling the instrument. Thus, there is little demand for regulation of that consumer product. Hazards, however, may be either unknown — such as the danger of cancer from exposure to asbestos, which was recently discovered — or unexpected — such as brake failure of a car while it is being driven. These hazards are not visible, and thus the consumer has little or no choice in whether or not he will expose himself to such hazards. So there may be a need for government intervention in the area of hidden hazards.

Usually, moreover, a consumer's choice of a product will also depend upon the *seriousness* of its hazard (assuming the hazard is known). In the area of product safety, it should be recognized that consumers have unequal tastes for safety as well as for other characteristics of product performance. Particularly where the safety hazard is minor (the occasional blister on a finger), policymakers need to realize that very large cost increases may merely deprive many consumers of the use of many products. This possibility of exclusion points to the importance of considering the cost of correcting safety hazards as well as the need to recognize trade-offs between safety and other criteria which are important to consumers.

For example, a power tool selling for $20 may not have the capability of being in use for more than an hour; the $500 piece of equipment may be safely used for a much longer period. Although the instructions on each tool may be very clear in this respect, some consumers may willingly buy the cheaper model and knowingly take the chance of burning it out. A policy of complete product safety would ban the cheaper item, thereby effectively depriving the low-income consumer (or the thrifty consumer) of buying a power tool. If equity is a social goal, then this is an example of increasing product safety at the expense of consumer welfare. Additionally, even if safety is considered paramount among consumers' criteria, the regulator may still be faced with a trade-off among product hazards.

One such trade-off can be seen in the following case. About one-fifth of the 16,000 injuries and 500 deaths a year due to burning clothes are caused by children's sleepwear catching fire. For this

[3] Walter Guzzardi, Jr., "The Mindless Pursuit of Safety," *Fortune*, April 9, 1979, p. 64.

reason, the Consumer Product Safety Commission requires children's pajamas to have a flame-resistant property. But since the National Cancer Institute established that Tris, one chemical used, may cause cancer, the commission was faced with the dilemma of reducing the chance of cancer by increasing the chance of fire injury or death. The commission chose to ban Tris.

Another example is that of the household ladder. The accidents which are associated with that household product have given rise to pressure for more detailed standards for its design and production. However, industry experts point out that if a ladder is made too difficult or too expensive to use, many consumers will wind up using a chair or a table instead. Those latter consumer products, which are not built for climbing, show incidence of far more accidents.[4]

The *probability of a hazard* actually occurring is also of prime consideration. This factor might often be determined in the laboratory. In testing whether TCE (trichlorethylene), a chemical used in decaffeinated coffee, might be a possible cause of cancer, the National Cancer Institute used a generous dose of the chemical on its test animals — the equivalent of a person drinking 50 million cups of decaffeinated coffee every day for an entire lifetime. Despite the doubtful relevance of this test, the coffee industry quickly changed to the use of a different chemical, fearing another ban such as that imposed on cyclamates.[5]

As Professor Max Brunk of Cornell University points out, it is not the industry which suffers the greatest burden of a regulatory action such as one of those just described, since "consumerism is aimed at the consumer . . . look what it does to the consumer who pays the cost and loses the benefits that a prohibited product or service could have provided."[6] Following this line of reasoning, business can better adjust to these controls than can the consumer, because it can pass on the added costs that result.

Brunk notes that it is interesting to observe that consumer advocates sometimes have as much difficulty convincing the consumer of his or her need for protection as in convincing a regulatory body

[4] Frederick C. Klein, "Setting Safety Rules for Products Proves Costly and Complicated," *Wall Street Journal*, August 11, 1977, p. 17.
[5] U.S., Food and Drug Administration, "Trichlorethylene (TCE) and Coffee," *FDS Talk Paper*, June 27, 1975, p. 1; "Memorandum of Alert: Trichlorethylene" (memorandum from associate director for carcinogenesis, DCCP, NCI, to Chairman, DHEW Committee to Coordinate Toxicology and Related Programs, March 21, 1975), p. 1 and attachments; Isadore Barmash, "General Foods Changing Sanka and Brim Solvent," *The New York Times*, July 17, 1975.
[6] Max E. Brunk, "Consumerism and Marketing," in *Issues in Business and Society*, 2d ed., ed. George Steiner and John F. Steiner (New York: Random House, 1977), p. 384.

to provide the protection. The Truth-in-Lending law is a cogent example. The compulsory requirement to show true interest costs has not slowed down the growth of consumer debt or the rise in interest rates. Since the passage of the act, the ratio of consumer debt to consumer income has reached an all-time high, and interest rates, for many reasons, have risen sharply. The average credit purchaser still seems to be more interested in the absolute amount of the monthly payment than in the rate of interest that is included in it. Similarly, despite the justification for unit pricing as a means of helping low-income families to stretch their dollars further, available surveys show that it is the high-income, well-educated customers who are most aware of this information.

A vast majority of Americans is concerned over product safety, and this concern has risen steadily since 1971. However, 87 percent of the adult Americans participating in a Harris survey blame consumers themselves for injury from products. Many believe that "most products are safe, but a lot of people do not read the directions or misuse products, so it is unfair to put all the safety blame on manufacturers." In the same survey a distinct opposition was shown to bans on products. Of the consumers surveyed, 73 percent believed that product safety objectives should be accomplished through publicity on product risks and dangers and by health warnings such as those required on cigarettes and drugs.[7]

A nationwide poll conducted in November 1978 by the Opinion Research Corporation showed that leaders of consumer organizations may not be thinking the same thoughts as the public. Fifty-three percent of the respondents agreed (and 33 percent disagreed) with the statement "Overall, the federal government has gone too far in its responsibility to protect the individual from himself by enacting laws and regulations concerning consumer goods and services." However, only 31 percent of the leaders of public-interest groups agreed, and 69 percent disagreed. A comment by David Pittle, member of the CPSC, however, suggests that regulators are beginning to sense the change in public attitudes: "Business people and consumers generally are feeling threatened by what they perceive to be increased governmental control over their lives." In this regard, the consumer response in early 1977 to the Food and Drug Administration's prospective ban on saccharin (subsequently postponed by Congress) is instructive. It is readily summed up by a newspaper headline, "A Run on Saccharin Here to Beat Ban."

_____

[7] Louis Harris, "Concern over Product Safety," *Washington Post*, June 1, 1975, p. F-2.

THE EFFECT ON BUSINESS

The record-keeping requirements imposed by the CPSC are substantial. It has called on every manufacturer, distributor, or retailer —upon learning that a product it sold "creates a substantial risk of injury"—to inform and provide the commission with a wide array of information, including

1. The number of products that present a hazard or potential hazard.
2. The number of units of each product involved.
3. The number of units of each product in the hands of consumers.
4. Specific dates when the faulty units were manufactured and distributed.
5. An accounting of when and where such products (and the number of units of each) were distributed.
6. The model and serial numbers affected.
7. A list of names and addresses of every distributor, retailer, and producer, if known.
8. A description of the effort made to notify consumers of the defect.
9. Details of corrective tests, quality controls, and engineering changes made or contemplated.[8]

The reporting requirement is not completed until the company submits a final report indicating that the "potential" product hazard has been corrected. Thus, the commission shifts to the company the responsibility and costs of determining and remedying potential product defects, with the possibility of criminal sanctions should the commission disagree with the company's decisions. Product safety reporting by companies is a necessary input to the commission's evaluation of potentially dangerous products. The reporting requirements are substantial and, therefore, costly. It is not, however, a question of whether or not companies should report information on product injuries, but of how much detail is needed for decision making.

An example of a questionable action on the part of the commission was its handling of the alleged hazards involving spray adhesives. The variety of factors involved in banning a consumer product can be seen in the appendix at the end of this chapter dealing with this case.

On the other hand, the commission has turned down the most extreme demands of consumer advocates. It rejected the petition of Ralph Nader's Health Research Group, which warned of the "im-

[8] *Federal Register*, 38, no. 149 (August 3, 1973).

minent hazard to the public health" represented by lead-wick candles. The petition asserted that small children might chew or swallow the candles, taking lead into their systems, and candlelit suppers would result in "meals literally bathed in lead." In a letter to the Nader group, Commissioner Laurence M. Kushner stated that the petition "was drawn either with abysmal ignorance of elementary physical science, colossal intent to deceive the public, or both. The calculations, in the petition, of possible concentrations of lead in air which might result from burning such candles, were based on assumptions that are physically impossible."[9]

The CPSC also declined to act favorably on a petition to declare mistletoe a hazardous product. The commission's research did reveal that 132 "ingestions" of mistletoe were reported in a four-year period and that five of the people involved developed symptoms, two of whom required hospitalization. Although we are left to surmise the reasons for the commission's actions, it may be reasonable to assume that CPSC was wary of creating a field day for cartoonists. It is easy to conjure up illustrations of a couple kissing under a sprig of mistletoe and the accompanying caption reading "The Federal Government Has Declared This Hazardous to Your Health." In any event, as good bureaucrats, the commission stated that denying the request should not "be construed as endorsement of the complete safety of these plants."[10]

Some indication of the specific areas that may receive the CPSC's special attention can be obtained by examining its tabulations reporting product-related injuries (see sample in table 4-2). Such data need to be interpreted with great care. The statistics indicate only that a product was "associated with" an injury. Richard O. Simpson, former chairman of the CPSC, frankly acknowledges the shortcomings of the data: "Note that I said injuries *associated* with consumer products and not necessarily injuries *caused* by products. Just how many injuries are caused by the products is anybody's guess."[11]

Nor does the list show the ratio of product-related injuries to the total number of products in use or whether the individual voluntarily and knowingly used a product that is inherently risky. Nevertheless, such data can be useful to company management by

[9] "Please Don't Eat the Candles," *Wall Street Journal*, January 16, 1974, p. 12.

[10] U.S., Consumer Product Safety Commission, *Briefing Paper on Poinsettia Plants and Mistletoe Sprigs* (Washington, D.C.: Office of Standards Coordination and Appraisal, December 17, 1975).

[11] "Producing Safe Products: An Interview with Richard O. Simpson," *ASTM Standardization News*, April 1975, pp. 8-9.

Table 4-2   Product injury tabulation, September 1, 1977–August 31, 1978

Products	Number of Injuries (in thousands)
Sports and recreation	
Football, baseball, and basketball equipment	1,153
Wrestling and gymnastics equipment	98
Soccer and volleyball equipment	145
Hockey and track and field equipment	53
Swimming and water skiing equipment	96
Bowling and horseback riding equipment	22
Tennis, badminton, and squash equipment	60
Table tennis, pool, and billiards equipment	13
Golf equipment and golf carts	20
Snow skiing equipment, toboggans, sleds, etc.	166
Skates, ice skates, skateboards	228
Snowmobiles, go-carts, motor scooters, mini-bikes, etc.	44
Bicycles and tricycles	442
Fishing equipment	53
Exercise equipment and trampolines	33
Playground and juvenile sports equipment	166
Camping trailers	9
Bleachers	9
Amusement rides	5
Skeet guns and gas, air, spring operated guns	19
Total	2,834
Toys	
Toy cars and trucks, nonflying planes, boats	9
Wagons and other ride-on toys	15
Fireworks and projectile toys	19
Toy houses and furnishings	7
Total	50
Child nursery equipment and supplies	
Baby carriages, walkers, strollers	11
Cribs, playpens, high chairs	20
Total	31
Home entertainment, sound, and hobby equipment	
Telephone and sound recording, reproducing, receiving, and transmitting equipment	20
Television sets	17
Total	37

(continued)

Table 4–2 (contd.)

Products	Number of Injuries (in thousands)
General household appliances	
Dryers and washers	17
Vacuum cleaners and other cleaning equipment	9
Irons and ironers	11
Electric fans	12
Grills	6
Sunlamps and heat lamps	8
Total	63
Kitchen appliances	
Refrigerators and freezers	16
Cooking ovens, ranges, etc.	28
Blenders, mixers, and general appliances	15
Total	59
Housewares	
Cookware, pots and pans	15
Drinking glasses	88
Tableware and flatware	59
Cutlery and knives	102
Pins and needles	40
Skewers, ice picks, toothpicks	10
Other products	30
Total	344
Household containers	
Glass bottles and jars	106
Cans	79
Wooden and pressurized containers	11
Total	196
Home maintenance products	
Bleaches, dyes, and cleaning agents	40
Paints, solvents, and lubricants	16
Miscellaneous household chemicals	29
Total	85
Home furnishings and fixtures	
Countertops, bars, bar stools	132
Glass doors, windows, and panels	186
Tables	176
Chairs, sofas, sofa beds, and other furniture	175

Table 4-2 (contd.)

Products	Number of Injuries (in thousands)
Home furnishings and fixtures (contd.)	
Electric fixtures and lamps	26
Beds	135
Desks, storage cabinets, and shelving	89
Carpets and rugs	24
Sinks, toilets, bathtubs	82
Ladders and stools	83
Other fixtures	63
Total	1,171
Personal use items	
Razors, shavers, razor blades	39
Hair accessories	9
Pencils, pens, desk supplies	39
Other items	37
Total	124
Home structures and construction materials	
Chimneys, fireplaces; bricks, concrete blocks	43
Lumber	48
Nails, tacks, screws	265
Wires, cords, and chains	43
Roofs and roofing materials	13
Floors and flooring materials	101
Walls	69
Doors	45
Window and door frames and sills	26
Stairs, steps, ramps, landings, and elevators	579
Porches, balconies; handrails and railings	62
Total	1,294
Home workshop tools and apparatus	
Home workshop saws	76
Workshop tools	36
Chain saws	48
Hammers, hatchets, axes, screwdrivers, drills	87
Batteries and automotive tools	28
Other items	37
Total	312

(continued)

Table 4-2 (contd.)

Products	Number of Injuries (in thousands)
Yard and garden equipment	
Power lawn mowers	69
Fences	70
Pruning and trimming equipment	19
Hand garden tools	34
Tractors and other motorized equipment	9
Garden hoses, nozzles, sprinklers	11
Total	212
Heating and cooling equipment	
Heating stoves and space heaters	10
Furnaces	7
Air conditioners	6
Miscellaneous heating systems	9
Hot water and steam pipes	24
Total	56
Other items	
Liquid fuels	23
Grocery and shopping carts, luggage carriers	16
Paper money and coins	11
Rope and string	8
Lockers	7
Total	65
Grand Total	6,933

Source: Consumer Product Safety Commission

indicating which products are receiving the attention of federal safety authorities. Thus, changes may be designed either to forestall or to meet possible future government regulatory requirements. As Simpson has further remarked, "Industry has a choice — either question the validity of our data or take actions that will result in the product in question moving further down the hazard index. This is the preferred approach."[12]

[12] Ibid., p. 10.

According to Chairman Arnold Elkind of the National Commission on Product Safety, whose recommendations led to the creation of the CPSC, "It's true that the CPSC may be the most powerful independent regulatory agency ever created . . . but it has to be. It has to have a wide choice of weapons to cope with the diverse range of situations it confronts."[13]

The commission does have an impressive array of powers, and at times it uses them in a fashion that could seem arbitrary, at least to some people. For example, in promulgating ban lists, the CPSC appears to have taken the position, perhaps unwittingly, that a company can be guilty until proved innocent. This surprising stand, which contradicts the basic notion of fairness in legal matters, seems implicit in the following statement in an issue of the CPSC's Banned Products List: "Articles not meeting the requirements of the regulation are to be considered as banned even though they have not yet been reviewed, confirmed as banned, and added to the Banned Products List by the Consumer Product Safety Commission."[14]

Taken literally, the commission's statement means that the responsibility for treating a product as being banned can fall entirely on the company involved, even in circumstances where the commission is not aware of the product's existence, much less of its supposedly hazardous characteristic.

The case of Marlin Toy Products of Horicon, Wisconsin, illustrates the dangers that can arise in the excessive use of the CPSC's great powers. Due to an "editorial error," the commission put Marlin's major products on its new ban list in 1973. When the error was called to its attention, the CPSC refused to issue a prompt retraction. As a result, Marlin was forced out of the toy business. (The appendix to Chapter 13 presents the details of this case.) Since the Marlin case the commission has suspended the issuance of ban lists, without providing any public explanation.

In recent years, moreover, the commission has encountered problems in determining the boundaries of its own jurisdiction. This was displayed by its involvement in the handgun controversy. In response to a request to ban handgun ammunition as a hazardous

[13] William H. Miller, "Consumer Product Safety Commission," *Industry Week*, October 29, 1973, p. 41.

[14] U.S., Consumer Product Safety Commission, *Banned Products*, October 1, 1973, p. 1.

substance, the commission was required by statute to ask for public comments. It received more than 130,000 cards and letters, all on an issue that four of the five commissioners believed they had no business investigating.[15]

To complicate matters, the CPSC has defined "consumer products" fairly broadly — a definition which even covers rides in amusement parks. Consequently, the commission worked out a consent agreement with Chance Manufacturing Company under which Chance altered the restraint system on cars it produces for amusement parks because the CPSC found the system inadequate. Walt Disney World Company, in contrast, is challenging in court the commission's jurisdiction in this area.[16]

It is apparent, overall, that government regulators experience great difficulty in choosing the product hazards which they regulate. Take, for example, the serious problem of residential fires. The emphasis in public policy to date has been on wiring standards. How important a hazard are they? According to the National Fire Protection Association, here are the major sources of fatal residential fires in the United States in recent years:

Smoking	56.0%
Heaters	13.8
Electrical	7.5
Cooking stoves	7.0
Arson	4.3
All other	11.4
Total	100.0%

The dominant cause of residential fires, smoking, is beyond the CPSC's jurisdiction. Thus, the agency concentrates on a relatively minor cause which accounts for less than 8 percent of fatal fires.

Expectations, either for private or public activities, should not be set too high. Considering the importance of the problems confronting the CPSC and the difficulties involved in solving them, perhaps the comments of writer Paul Weaver may provide the basis for an alternate approach:

In the end there is no such thing as a perfect safety regulation; in most

---

[15] Burt Schoor, "Consumer Product Safety Commission Finds Deep Hazards in Just Getting Itself Rolling," *Wall Street Journal*, May 6, 1975.

[16] Guzzardi, "The Mindless Pursuit of Safety," p. 54.

cases, in fact, even a fairly good one is hard to find. Thus there's nothing surprising or dishonorable about the failure of the Commission to issue perfect regulations in wholesale lots.

But the environment within which they work—the law, the expectations of Congress, the conflicting pressures from consumerists and industry, the nature of government, the climate of public opinion, the methods and ambitions of the staff, and above all the monumental complexity of the task—makes good judgment difficult. The scarcest ingredient in this marvelously intricate and rational system is the homely virtue of common sense.[17]

REGULATION VIA INFORMATION

The CPSC is not the only guardian of the consumer established by Congress. More traditional efforts have centered in the Departments of Agriculture and Health, Education and Welfare, where they have ranged from controlling the production and distribution of drugs to regulating the sale of pet turtles.

The governmental response to rising consumer pressures now often takes the form of stricter controls over product labeling. Rather than merely attractive coverings, packaging is required increasingly to contain information on the nutritional contents of the product and its usage. One court has held that the standard of clarity applicable to a package label is not what it says to "the reasonable consumer," but rather what it communicates to "the ignorant, the unthinking and credulous."[18] Figure 4-1 contains the old and new approach to labeling a can of green beans.

State and local governments are becoming more active in the area of product labeling. As a greater number of states and localities pass labeling legislation, the likelihood decreases that a nationally marketed product can have a single label that will meet the requirements of all the jurisdictions in which the company hopes to sell it. The General Foods Corporation reports that it has encountered such a problem in Massachusetts, Oregon, and New York City, which have enacted labeling restrictions in conflict with national regulations as well as the requirements in other local areas. The company has issued the following warning: "The result of this trend, if it continues un-

---

[17]Paul H. Weaver, "The Hazards of Trying to Make Consumer Products Safer," *Fortune*, July 1975, p. 140.
[18]"Social Issues Briefs," *Business Week*, May 18, 1974, p. 78.

PRE-REGULATION	POST-REGULATION
Size of Can .. No. 303 / Net Wt. ... 1 lb. / Cups .. Approx. 2	**Net Weight........ 16 oz. (1 lb.)** **Metric Weight ...... 454 grams** **Cups.................... Approx. 2**
Tender, young Blue Lake green beans, carefully selected for quality and sliced lengthwise to bring out the full delicate flavor of the beans.	INGREDIENTS: GREEN BEANS, WATER, SALT. NUTRITION INFORMATION—PER ONE CUP SERVING SERVINGS PER CONTAINER APPROX. 2

INGREDIENTS: GREEN BEANS, WATER, SALT

SUGGESTIONS FOR SERVING

Pour liquid into saucepan and boil rapidly down to one-half volume; add beans and heat quickly. Do not overcook. If desired, season with salt, pepper, butter or crisply cooked bacon bits. Add minced dill pickle or onion for a zippy flavor. Or serve with a sauce such as: horseradish, mustard, sour cream, tomato.

Nutritional information is available on request

CALORIES 40	CARBOHYDRATE 8gm
PROTEIN 2gm	FAT 0gm

PERCENTAGE OF U.S. RECOMMENDED DAILY
ALLOWANCES (U.S. RDA) PER ONE CUP SERVING

PROTEIN	2
VITAMIN A	25
VITAMIN C	10
THIAMIN (B_1)	4
RIBOFLAVIN (B_2)	6
NIACIN	2
CALCIUM	6
IRON	8
PHOSPHORUS	4
MAGNESIUM	6

For good nutrition eat a variety of foods.

Figure 4-1   TWO APPROACHES TO LABELING A CAN OF GREEN BEANS

Source: U.S. General Accounting Office.

checked, would be a severe impairment of the ability of food processors to distribute food efficiently and economically."[19]

"What's in a name?," asks the U.S. Department of Agriculture. It answers its own question: "Plenty, when a meat or poultry product bears the mark of federal inspection!"[20] And the USDA inspects a vast amount of products. The instructions to the producers of beef products are quite extensive. Products labeled "beef with gravy," for example, must contain at least 50 percent cooked beef. However, "gravy with beef" requires only 35 percent cooked beef. "Beef and dumplings with gravy" needs only 25 percent beef, as is the case for "Beef and gravy with dumplings." Beef and pasta in tomato sauce" can get down to as little as 17½ percent beef.

Meeting the poultry requirements, in contrast, is an exercise in straightforward arithmetic. The permutations and combinations are so numerous that they can be best presented in tabular form (see table 4-3 for the results). To the extent that consumers are unaware of these numerical distinctions, little benefit would seem to result from the imposition of such detailed requirements. Nevertheless,

[19] *The Impact of Government Regulation on General Foods* (White Plains, N.Y.: General Foods, 1975), p. 6.

[20] U.S., Department of Agriculture, *Standards for Meat and Poultry Products* (Washington, D.C.: Animal and Plant Health Inspection Service, 1973), p. 1.

Table 4-3   Federal standards for poultry

Item	Minimum Required Percent Poultry Meat
Poultry almondine	50 percent
Poultry barbecue	40 percent
Poultry paella	35 percent*
Poultry hash	30 percent
Poultry chili	28 percent
Poultry croquettes	25 percent
Poultry cacciatori	20 percent†
Poultry casserole	18 percent
Poultry chili with beans	17 percent
Poultry tetrazzini	15 percent
Poultry pies	14 percent
Poultry Brunswick stew	12 percent‡
Cabbage stuffed with poultry	8 percent
Cannelloni with poultry	7 percent
Poultry tamales	6 percent
Poultry chop suey	4 percent
Chop suey with poultry	2 percent

*Or 35 percent poultry meat and other meat (cooked basis); no more than 35 percent cooked rice; must contain seafood.
†Or 40 percent with bone.
‡Must contain corn.

Source: Computed from U.S. Department of Agriculture, *Standards for Meat and Poultry Products* (Washington, D.C.: Animal and Plant Health Inspection Service, 1973)

kept within reason, the case for accurate, informative descriptions of food products can be very convincing.

One of the most controversial new developments in consumer product regulation has been the effort of the Federal Trade Commission to limit advertising of products aimed at children. The commission's staff has developed three options:

1. A complete ban on advertising on programs aimed at children under eight years of age.
2. A ban on advertising on programs aimed at children under twelve for those sugar-coated products most likely to cause tooth decay.
3. A requirement that if advertising for heavily coated products appears on programs aimed at children under twelve, it be balanced by separate dental and nutritional announcements.[21]

[21] William Sklar, "Ads Are Finally Getting Bleeped at the FTC," *Business and Society Review*, Summer 1978, p. 44.

Congressional hearings on the proposals revealed a variety of viewpoints, ranging from the desire to protect children completely to leaving the responsibility on the parents to "turn the dial" on the radio or "pull the plug" on the TV set.

OUTLOOK

Although an upward trend in federal legislation related to consumer interests has been visible since the turn of the century, a rapid acceleration in the frequency of new control legislation has occurred since the mid-1960s. Not only have more laws been passed in recent times, but, as shown in chapter 1, the laws are also broader and more far-reaching. This trend shows little sign of slackening.

It is unlikely that this upward trend will slow unless the public comes to realize that regulation is only one method for promoting product safety among an array of possible policy alternatives. As described earlier, the provision of adequate information may be in many cases a satisfying alternative to outright bans or detailed standards — providing the agency is aware of the problem of "overloading" the individual with more details than he or she can or is interested in reading. It is curious to note, moreover, that the information route is the one used in the case of one of the most hazardous consumer products — cigarettes. That fact may illustrate the limited power of analysis when regulators are confronted with the greater forces of economic and political interests.

Another alternative to specific regulations is reliance on the judicial process by consumers who have been harmed by unsafe products. Fines and jail sentences may adequately deter producers and sellers of products with serious but infrequent hazards. But, perhaps more fundamentally, market competition might be allowed to play a more important role. Information on comparative safety may provide one firm with a competitive advantage over another. In this way, the market itself would produce safer products.

But ultimately, perhaps, it will be more widespread knowledge of the economic effects — and especially of the costs and benefits — of government intervention that will alter the current reliance on government-mandated standards for private-sector production and consumption. This will not be, however, an easily performed job of communication. The following lament of the director of government relations of the Public Interest Economics Group is noteworthy:

One of the most difficult problems faced in public interest lobbying is how to communicate basic economic principles without antagonizing consumer and other public interest groups who may not have taken them into consideration in formulating their position.[22]

This dilemma would appear to be at the heart of many of the problems in relationships between business, government, and the public.

APPENDIX: THE AEROSOL SPRAY ADHESIVE CASE*

On August 20, 1973, the U.S. Consumer Product Safety Commission banned certain brands of aerosol spray adhesives as an imminent hazard. The commission's decision was based primarily on the preliminary findings of a chromosome research study by Dr. J. Rodman Seely. Dr. Seely identified possible links between the use of certain brands of aerosol spray adhesives and chromosome damage and between chromosome damage and birth defects. After more extensive research and review and a medical panel's evaluation of this research, the commission determined that the ban should not continue, and withdrew it on March 1, 1974.

Background

Dr. Seely, an associate professor of pediatrics, biochemistry, molecular biology, and cytotechnology at the University of Oklahoma Medical Center, began his research in March 1973, after being asked to examine a child with multiple birth defects consisting of uncommon or nontypical abnormality patterns. Dr. Seely performed a chromosome analysis and found what he considered to be significant numbers of damaged chromosomes, which he defined as chromosome breaks and gaps. He examined the parents and found damaged chromosome patterns similar to their child's.

The parents participated in a hobby called "foiling" or "foil art"—attaching various designs of multicolored foil paper to posters

---

[22] "PIE Lobbying," *Public Interest Economics*, December 15, 1976, p. 6.
*The material in this case is taken from Comptroller General of the United States, *Banning of Two Toys and Certain Aerosol Spray Adhesives*, MWD-75-65. (Washington, D.C.: U.S. General Accounting Office, 1975), pp. 13-30; Ernest B. Hook and Kristine M. Healy, "Consequences of a Nationwide Ban on Spray Adhesives Alleged to Be Human Teratogens and Mutagens," *Science*, February 13, 1976, pp. 566-67.

and other objects, usually with aerosol spray adhesives. The exhibits were usually finished with spray paint. Dr. Seely directed his investigation to determine whether a possible link existed between foilers' use of aerosol spray adhesives and chromosome damage. He discounted the foilers' use of spray paint as a cause factor because it was used for only a short period of time, and chemical agents in spray adhesives were generally more subject to question by the medical community. Aerosol spray adhesives of various formulas have been commercially marketed since 1961.

Dr. Seely examined four other foilers who had been exposed to aerosol spray adhesives and found that their blood cells had chromosome damage similar to that found in the deformed child and parents. Also, in mid-July 1973, Dr. Seely examined another child with uncommon or unusual birth defect characteristics and found that the child and both parents had a high percentage of cells with damaged chromosomes. Both parents were foilers.

In total, Dr. Seely had examined 10 persons with what he considered to be a high percentage (about 9 percent) of damaged chromosomes — 2 deformed children, their 4 parents, and 4 other persons.

A complication in the study of these results is the fact that medical researchers are not sure what percentage of damaged chromosomes is normal, acceptable, or harmful and have not satisfactorily tied chromosome damage to birth defects. Dr. Seely examined 12 persons who were *not* spray adhesive users for possible chromosome damage. He found that 1.65 percent of the cells sampled showed chromosome damage, compared with 8.99 percent for exposed persons. He considered this 7.34-percent difference — a five-to-one relative difference — statistically significant. These findings reinforced his belief in a possible relationship between aerosol spray adhesives and chromosome damage, and suggested a relationship between chromosome damage and birth defects.

Dr. Seely attempted to identify a chemical agent he thought may have been responsible for the chromosome damage. He contacted the major manufacturer of the sprays the foilers used and obtained its formula. The products did not contain the chemical agent he thought was responsible. Dr. Seely was uncertain of the action to take but believed that a responsible federal agency should look at his preliminary findings and conclusions. On July 25, 1973, he contacted the U.S. Food and Drug Administration (FDA). FDA referred him to the Consumer Product Safety Commission's Bureau of Biomedical Science (BBS), which is responsible for the commission's laboratory reviews of potential hazards from chemical consumer products.

After the commission was given some preliminary information on the telephone, BBS and FDA respresentatives (an FDA researcher was assisting the commission in reviewing Dr. Seely's study) went to Oklahoma City on August 5, 1973, to meet Dr. Seely, establish his credibility, and review his research findings. At the meeting, the two representatives found Dr. Seely's data to be legitimate and adequately prepared and documented. They concluded that he was a responsible researcher.

One aspect of the study that they found particularly troubling was the fact that the second child's parents had stopped using aerosol spray adhesives several months before conception, yet both parents and the child had a high percentage of damaged chromosomes. This indicated that aerosol spray adhesives could be a hazard resulting in long-lasting chromosome damage that might remain in a person even after discontinuing the product's use and might affect future generations adversely through heredity. The BBS staff considered this condition critical and believed Dr. Seely's research had identified a link between aerosol spray adhesive use and chromosome damage.

On August 7, 1973, BBS and FDA representatives briefed the commission chairman and recommended that three brands of aerosol spray adhesives be declared an imminent hazard. Dr. Seely's data had been only verbally provided to the commission because he had not completed his research. The commission requested the two manufacturers whom Dr. Seely identified in his research — Minnesota Mining and Manufacturing Company (3M) and Borden, Inc. — to submit information on their spray adhesives, including formulas, sales data, and consumer complaints. Both companies complied.

Factors Considered before the Ban

The commissioners were concerned about Dr. Seely's preliminary research findings. One reason for the concern was the fact that his was the first study suggesting a link between aerosol spray adhesives and genetic problems. The potential severity of this hazard motivated the commission to act quickly.

On August 15, 1973, the commission informed 3M and Borden of its concern about the connection between their aerosol spray adhesives and potential health problems, and the possible need for quick regulatory action. Although the companies knew of the commission's prior interest in spray adhesives, this was the first indication they had of the possibility of the products being banned as an "imminent hazard" under the Federal Hazardous Substances Act.

The commission requested the two firms to provide any additional information that could refute Dr. Seely's findings and to discuss any action they planned to take as a result of the anticipated ban. The companies said they had not received Dr. Seely's written report (neither had the commission at that time) and asked for the opportunity to discuss his findings with him. Commission representatives accompanied 3M and Borden representatives to Oklahoma City on the following day to meet with Dr. Seely.

At that meeting the commission received Dr. Seely's report containing his preliminary research findings and conclusions. Although the companies did not receive copies of the report, Dr. Seely read it aloud at the meeting. Company representatives discussed with Dr. Seely the study's preliminary conclusions and the research methods and laboratory techniques used.

The commission's minutes of the meeting indicate that the company representatives questioned Dr. Seely on the possibility that other foiling materials may have contributed to the high damaged-chromosome readings. Company representatives expressed their concern about the organization of Dr. Seely's information and did not agree that the findings supported his conclusions. Neither company provided the commission with information substantiating their comments or otherwise refuting the findings. At the completion of these meetings a BBS representative told the companies that the commission might temporarily ban the products until the study was corroborated or disproved.

Representatives of 3M expressed their concern to the commission about Dr. Seely's research and conclusions and about the short time they were allotted to reply.

The 3M representatives told Dr. Seely and commission representatives that the company was concerned about possible subjective bias. That is, when analyzing blood samples for chromosome damage, Dr. Seely knew which samples were from exposed and nonexposed persons. They also said Dr. Seely was not fully objective in selecting and analyzing the nonexposed people. They did not believe these methods were consistent with good research techniques.

On the other hand, although 3M did not question Dr. Seely's data itself, it believed other factors, such as foilers' use of spray paint, could cause or contribute to chromosome damage. Also, 3M did not believe that the data adequately supported identifying its aerosol spray adhesives as the primary cause of chromosome damage and birth defects. It believed that Dr. Seely and the commission should have contacted medical specialists in mutagenics, genetics, and other related fields to discuss the research results and obtain comments on the preliminary findings and conclusions before taking regulatory action. A 3M toxicologist subsequently told governmental investigators that several such specialists he contacted said damaged chromosomes in the 4- to 8-percent range were common.

3M requested that the commission wait one to two weeks before deciding whether to ban the products because Dr. Seely's data were preliminary. This would have permitted the commission and 3M — working together, as they did after the ban — to look deeper into Dr. Seely's work and obtain the opinions of specialists before taking regulatory action.

Both companies recognized that a significant potential public health problem had been raised and that the commission had the authority to ban the products immediately as an imminent hazard. They also knew about the general lack of information linking aerosol spray adhesives and chromosome damage and recognized the potential seriousness of such a problem to future generations.

Therefore, knowing of the commission's intent to declare the products an imminent hazard, both manufacturers voluntarily stopped production and distribution of the aerosol spray adhesives in question on August 17, 1973 — the date the commission announced its intention to ban the sprays.

The commission banned the aerosol spray adhesives three days later, recognizing that certain aspects of Dr. Seely's research justified banning the products and, at the same time, recognizing that other aspects raised questions about the necessity of a ban. The commission did not have documentation showing whether and how it had considered all such questionable factors before the ban. The following information, therefore, was obtained primarily by interviews subsequently conducted by the U.S. General Accounting Office.

Factors supporting the ban. The CPSC considered Dr. Seely a credible researcher because of his credentials. He held M.D. and Ph.D. degrees, was a National Institutes of Health (NIH) grant recipient, and was widely published in the medical field. The CPSC officials believed that his research and test techniques showed good organization and investigative methods.

Dr. Seely's study identified two deformed children whose parents had used aerosol spray adhesives. The fact that this association did not have to be extrapolated from animal data added credibility to the research. Also, the fact that the second deformed child's parents had stopped using the products several months before conception illustrated potential long-lasting and hereditary effects of the hazard. The 5-to-1 ratio between damaged chromosomes in exposed persons and those in nonexposed persons was considered to be statistically significant.

Although the commission knew that little mutagenic testing had been previously performed, its staff believed Dr. Seely's research demonstrated an adverse relationship both between aerosol spray adhesive use and chromosome damage and between chromosome damage and birth defects. Additionally, neither the commission nor the manufacturers were able to produce any data assuring the products' safety or refuting Dr. Seely's research.

The commission's biomedical staff recommended, on the basis of discussions with Dr. Seely and its review of his preliminary research, that the aerosol spray adhesives be declared an imminent hazard. The commission also believed that enough alternative glue products were being marketed so that consumers would not be overly inconvenienced by the ban.

Factors raising questions. Because of the research procedures Dr. Seely used, he knew which blood samples came from exposed and nonexposed persons as he analyzed them. Such analyses are usually made without such knowledge to avoid subjective bias. Commission staff members were aware of such bias in Dr. Seely's research and of the need for additional study and review. However, the commission considered the percentage difference between damaged chromosomes in the two groups so significant that it did not want to take the time necessary to verify Dr. Seely's research before taking regulatory action.

Although researchers had studied the cause and effect of chromosome damage, its relationship to birth defects was relatively unresearched; little factual data existed at the time. The commission recognized that Dr. Seely's preliminary research findings were unique and that they addressed a subject not adequately explored by previous research. However, the commission, relying partly on BBS's review of Dr. Seely's research and laboratory practices, decided that the severity of the potential chromosome damage problem was overriding.

Dr. Seely's contacts with BBS were verbal. No written report was provided the commission until August 16, 1973, the day before it publicly announced its intention to ban the products. No peer group evaluation of Dr. Seely's research was conducted. Peer group evaluation is a corroboration tool that researchers use to help build confidence and credibility in research findings, especially in studies conducted in previously unresearched areas.

The commission has no stated policy, regulations, or procedures that provide guidance for coordinating its review of potential hazardous products. Before the banning of aerosol spray adhesives, a commission representative telephoned the National Library of Medicine and the Environmental Mutagen Information Center to determine if any chromosome damage studies had been performed on selected chemical formulations or aerosol spray adhesives. He was told that there were none.

Also, before the ban the commission contacted a pediatrician-epidemiologist at NIH to obtain his opinion of Dr. Seely's preliminary findings. The NIH physician did not believe Dr. Seely's preliminary research and findings were correct or that they could be adequately documented and supported. He offered the following comments:

1. The two deformed children had dissimilar abnormality characteristics, suggesting that the association with aerosol spray adhesives should not be considered seriously without further evaluations. Because of the dissimilarity, there was a good probability that the malformations were not caused by the same chemical agent and that aerosol spray adhesives were not the cause.

2. It is difficult to interpret the meaning of chromosome damage because little is known about causes and effects. An LSD study several years earlier tied chromosome damage to birth defects but was later proven inaccurate.

3. Because this was the first potential problem identified with aerosol spray adhesives, independent specialists should confirm Dr. Seely's findings by drawing and analyzing new blood samples before the taking of any regulatory action.

4. The commission should perform chromosome analyses for persons exposed to high concentrations of aerosol spray adhesives — such as industrial users — to ascertain if a problem exists. Industrial users would certainly be affected if the products were hazardous.

BBS discounted these comments because the doctor did not have a written report to review and therefore could not be expected to comment on the research's fine points. The NIH doctor provided the names of several specialists the commission could contact for views on Dr. Seely's preliminary findings. But commission representatives said they did not have time to contact other specialists before taking regulatory action.

Actions in Banning the Adhesives

The Federal Hazardous Substances Act permits the CPSC to ban immediately a product considered to be an imminent hazard by publishing a notice in the *Federal Register*. An imminent hazard determination does not require the same due process proceedings as do standard regulations, which generally need public hearings and advance notice before their effective date. However, normal regulation proceedings continue after the product is banned as an imminent hazard, and a manufacturer has the right to challenge the commission's determination in court. Neither 3M nor Borden challenged the ban.

Alerting the public. The commission wanted to alert the public immediately to the adhesives' potential danger but was not prepared to ban the products by publishing the required *Federal Register* notice. Therefore, on the basis of its intention to ban certain aerosol spray adhesives as an imminent hazard under the act, the commission issued a press release on August 17, 1973. The ban thus took effect initially via media publicity.

The press release stated that the commission was going to use all appropriate means to halt the production and sale of aerosol spray adhesives and was conducting a nationwide investigation to determine the extent of the problem. The commission believed the seriousness of the potential problem justified warning consumers before formal publishing of the ban. On August 20, 1973, the commission banned the three aerosol spray adhesive brands as an imminent hazard, with the appropriate notice in the *Federal Register*.

The commission drew criticism from the medical community because of the contents of the press releases. The commission's August 17, 1973, press release stated, ". . . there is concern about the genetic damage which may cause problems in subsequent offspring." In an August 27, 1973, announcement, the commission recommended that adults concerned about aerosol spray adhesive exposure "should consider delaying pregnancies" until further information was available. This announcement also warned pregnant women that the risk for the infant is not known and concern may be increased if both parents have been exposed to aerosol spray adhesives.

Practicing and laboratory medical professionals were concerned about the mental anguish these announcements inflicted on the public, especially pregnant women. Several physicians complained to the commission that Dr. Seely's findings were based on limited knowledge and were prematurely announced to the public. The commission's own medical director stated at a later date that because the aerosol spray adhesives case was a medical problem, medical opinions should have been obtained before imposing the ban.

The criticism of medical professionals about the CPSC's public announcements turned out to be prescient.

Commission Analysis of Dr. Seely's Research after the Ban

After banning the adhesives, the commission called on mutagenic and genetic specialists and other researchers to provide additional opinions. The studies were generally completed in about two months and reports transmitted to the commission in mid-November 1973.

Study A. This study was designed to check the chromosome damage rates of the persons included in Dr. Seely's research. Two researchers reviewed the blood samples Dr. Seely had taken from the patients in the original study. They analyzed different slides than Dr. Seely had analyzed for 12 (6 exposed and 6 nonexposed) of the original 22 persons. These two researchers did not find the same statistical difference between exposed and nonexposed persons that Dr. Seely had found and did not confirm his findings that aerosol spray adhesives adversely affected chromosomes.

Study B. In this study the doctors that performed Study A reviewed the *same* slides Dr. Seely had analyzed for 6 of the 12 persons examined in their initial study. Their analysis reaffirmed the results of Study A. There was no statistically significant difference in damaged chromosomes between exposed and nonexposed persons. The study did not confirm Dr. Seely's original conclusion of a relationship between aerosol spray adhesives and chromosome damage.

Study C. A medical researcher attempted to corroborate Dr. Seely's findings by analyzing new blood samples from several persons, most of whom were included in Dr. Seely's original study. The researcher studied new blood samples from 10 persons — 6 exposed and 4 nonexposed. This study's results conflicted with Dr. Seely's original findings because nonexposed persons showed a higher percentage of damaged chromosomes than did the spray adhesive users. The researcher questioned the objectivity of Dr. Seely's selection of nonexposed people because some worked in the medical field and others were his patients.

Study D. This study was directed at industrial and other heavy users of aerosol spray adhesives (although not necessarily the same brands as those banned). A comparative analysis of 14 aerosol spray adhesive users and 5 nonexposed persons failed to show the same statistically different percentages of damaged chromosomes that Dr. Seely found.

After reviewing the results of the studies, commission staff believed that continuing the ban was not justified and, in mid-November 1973, recommended that the commissioners withdraw it. The commission did not accept the staff recommendation, although it did consider the study results adequate to support an eventual withdrawal of the ban. Instead, the commission prepared a series of questions about the relationships between aerosol spray adhesives and chromosome damage and between chromosome damage and birth defects. It also established an *ad hoc* committee to review Dr. Seely's and the other studies.

The Ad Hoc Committee. The commission requested 11 medical researchers in genetics, pediatrics, epidemiology, and toxicology to give their professional opinions on the validity and significance of Dr. Seely's study and the other research performed. The committee members generally responded that Dr. Seely's original conclusions were not corroborated and that the research data failed to establish a relationship between spray adhesive use and chromosome damage.

Most committee members did not believe that the relationship between adhesive use and birth defects was adequately documented. The consensus was that the commission should withdraw the ban because Dr. Seely's conclusions were not adequately supported by data.

Withdrawing the Ban

The commissioners voted on January 18, 1974, to announce their intent to withdraw the aerosol spray adhesive ban on March 1, 1974. Waiting until March to withdraw the ban would give interested parties time to make other information available or to comment on the proposed action.

In a press release issued on January 25, 1974, the commission explained that subsequent research did not substantiate Dr. Seely's findings, and it alerted the public (again through press release) to the commission's intent to withdraw the aerosol spray adhesives ban on March 1, 1974, unless other information was presented affecting the case. The required *Federal Register* notice was published on January 28, 1974.

The commission received three written responses to its proposed ban withdrawal. A retail store chain said it planned to resume selling aerosol spray adhesives on March 1, 1974. One private citizen supported the commissions proposal to withdraw the ban. Another suggested that all aerosol sprays be banned. The ban was lifted on March 1, 1974.

But the commission did not publicly announce the ban's withdrawal at this later date. A press announcement was not considered necessary because the commission had issued the earlier press release and published the *Federal Register* notice. The news services did carry stories early in March reporting the ban's withdrawal. The commission's general counsel sent identical letters to 3M and Borden on March 4, 1974, informing them that the ban had been withdrawn.

Consequences

A follow-up study on the consequences of the CPSC's ban of the aerosol spray adhesives was performed in 1975 by two medical researchers in Albany, New York. They found that the ban, revoked after six months, and its publicity directed at pregnant women produced some unexpected and irrevocable results.

Responses to the researchers' questionnaires sent to medical genetic centers throughout the United States showed that more than 1,100 inquiries had been made about the spray adhesive ban and that 1,273 working days had been expended on this issue at the centers. No dollar estimates were given for the cost of this work, nor was the expense of work done by government or industry researchers estimated.

More important, however, the study showed that nine pregnant women who were exposed to the spray adhesive elected to have abortions. Eight of them did so without first undergoing a diagnostic test to determine any chromosomal damage to an unborn child. These abortions may reflect only the minimum impact of the CPSC ban and publicity, since these nine women were only those reported by genetics centers which replied to the questionnaires. There is no information as to whether other women who consulted private physicians about the "imminent hazard" may have had abortions.

The study, which attempted to illustrate some of the unexpected and unnecessary consequences that can arise from the false identification of an environmental agent as a mutagen or teratogen, concluded that there is a need to distinguish a suspicion of toxicity in a substance from clear evidence of toxicity, especially in cases involving nationwide publicity.

Conclusions

The commission's actions in banning the aerosol spray adhesives were directed at protecting consumers from potentially hazardous products and were within the legal provisions of applicable laws. Although the commission gave the two manufacturers an opportunity to refute its reasons for banning the products before the ban was effective, provisions for advance notice and public hearings were not applicable because the adhesives were banned as an imminent hazard. The commission responded in the manner that it believed most appropriate to inform the public of what it considered to be a hazardous product.

In an analysis prepared for Congress, the General Accounting Office stated that the basis for the commission's decision could have been strengthened and the controversy surrounding its public announcements minimized if the commission had coordinated its evaluation of the preliminary research with medical specialists before imposing the ban, and had relied less on undocumented verbal evidence and more on documented evaluations in reviewing the preliminary findings and conclusions. If the commission had documented its review on Dr. Seely's research and checked its evaluation with its own and other medical specialists, the decision and the press announcements could have indicated the limited evidence available and placed the decision in its proper perspective.

The General Accounting Office concluded that the commission has no formal policy for reviewing possible imminently hazardous products. It urged that a regular procedure be established, including documenting the basis for declaring a product an imminent hazard.

5

job safety regulation

The Occupational Safety and Health Administration (OSHA) was created in December 1970 "to assure so far as possible every working man and woman in the nation safe and healthful working conditions and to preserve our human resources."[1] Congress provided several means for OSHA to use in fulfilling this mandate:

1. Encouraging employers and employees to reduce hazards in the workplace and to institute and improve existing health and safety programs.
2. Establishing responsibilities and rights for both employers and employees.
3. Authorizing OSHA to set mandatory job safety and health standards.
4. Providing an effective enforcement program.
5. Encouraging the states to take responsibility for administering and enforcing their own job safety and health programs, which must be at least as effective as the federal program.
6. Reporting procedures on job injuries, illnesses, and fatalities.[2]

[1] Occupational Safety and Health Act, Public Law 91-596.
[2] *All about OSHA*, U.S. Department of Labor, OSHA 2056 (n.d.), p. 2.

Compliance with OSHA regulations is enforced through inspections. OSHA inspections may be triggered by serious or fatal accidents or employee complaints concerning a specific company or plant, they may be aimed at "target industries" or "target health hazards," or they may be randomly selected workplaces. Target industries are those with injury frequency rates more than double the national average, including longshoring, meat and meat products, roofing and sheet metal, lumber and wood products, and miscellaneous transportation equipment. Target health hazards are associated with the five most hazardous and most commonly used toxic substances: asbestos, carbon monoxide, cotton dust, lead, and silica.

If, upon inspection, an employer is found in violation of one or more OSHA regulations, the violation is to be placed in one of the following categories:[3]

De minimis. A condition having no direct or immediate relation to job health and safety (example: lack of toilet partitions).

Nonserious violation. A condition directly related to job safety and health but which is unlikely to cause death or serious physical harm (example: tripping hazard). A penalty of up to $1,000 is optional. Such a penalty may be reduced by as much as 50 percent, depending on the severity of the hazard, the employer's good faith, the history of previous violations, and the size of the business. Another 50-percent reduction occurs if the employer corrects the violation within the prescribed time.

Serious violation. A condition in which substantial probability of death or serious physical harm exists, and in which the employer knew or should have known of the hazard (example: absence of point-of-operation guards on punch presses or saws). A penalty of up to $1,000 is mandatory. This penalty also may be reduced up to 50 percent for good faith and so forth.

Imminent danger. A condition where there is reasonable certainty that the hazard can be expected to cause death or serious physical injury immediately or before the hazard can be eliminated through regular procedures. If the employer fails to deal with the violation immediately, OSHA can go directly to a federal district court for legal action as needed.

Although the OSHA program is designed to benefit both employers and employees, the bulk of the effort is aimed at the employer. It is the employer's responsibility to assure that safe and

[3] Ibid., pp. 13-14.

healthful conditions exist in the workplace, and to purchase equipment necessary to correct unsafe or unhealthy conditions. It is the employers who must make sure that the employees adhere to safety rules and safe practices. For example, if an employee is instructed to wear a particular piece of personal protective equipment, such as safety-toe footwear, but the employee fails to do so and ultimately sustains an injury as a result of this failure, the OSHA law requires that the citation and the proposed penalty, if any, be issued against the employer. Contributory negligence by the employee is no longer a defense for the employer.

REACTIONS TO OSHA

The Occupational Safety and Health Act of 1970 was passed by an overwhelming vote in the Congress — 83 to 3 in the Senate and 383 to 5 in the House of Representatives. These margins clearly indicate strong support for the bill on the part of the public's congressional representatives.

But aside from this fact, and despite the obvious worthiness of the agency's objectives (who is ever opposed to a safer workplace when one out of every 11 workers experience a job-related accident or illness each year?), the public reaction to OSHA generally has been negative. Almost from its inception the agency has been subject to a constant barrage of criticism from almost every quarter — business, labor, academic researchers, the media, and government itself. Corporate and trade association executives claim that the agency's standards are needlessly burdensome and costly. Union representatives complain that OSHA is spread too thin and is not tough enough. Cartoonists and columnists seem to have a field day pounding on the agency's shortcomings. Such widely syndicated columnists as Art Buchwald, James J. Kilpatrick, and George Will have written about OSHA on numerous occasions.

Economists contend that the agency is not effective in achieving its basic objective. The conclusions of a major study by Albert L. Nichols and Richard Zeckhauser of Harvard University are typical of academic reactions: "OSHA . . . has become a prominent symbol of misguided federal regulation. It accomplishes little for occupational safety and health, yet imposes significant economic costs."[4] President Carter's Interagency Task Force on Workplace Safety and

---

[4] Albert L. Nichols and Richard Zeckhauser, "Government Comes to the Workplace: An Assessment of OSHA," *Public Interest*, Fall 1977, p. 39.

Health reported in late 1978 that "OSHA knows little more about what works to prevent injury today than it did in 1971."[5] Yet, as we shall see, these varied criticisms may not be too inconsistent with one another. The basic shortcoming may be not so much with the manner in which the agency conducts its activities as with the nature of the basic congressional statute governing occupational safety and health.

Labor union representatives have criticized OSHA for "administrative ineptness, extended delays . . . elephantine pace [which] breeds a disrespect for the law."[6] The facts do seem to demonstrate that OSHA's bark may be worse than its bite. The average employer faces an inspection once in 66 years. The average OSHA fine was only $253 in fiscal 1975 for companies employing more than 25 workers and $165 for companies with 25 employees or fewer.[7] It would seem, therefore, that the agency has irritated business far out of proportion to the actual scope of its activities. Yet business complaints continue to mount, especially from smaller companies.

One small businessman in Indiana was ordered by OSHA to place exit signs over the 12-foot doors at the front and back of his small, seven-person shop. This was necessary, according to the OSHA inspector, "so in case of a fire, a newly hired employee could tell where the door was." The business owner's question was a logical one: "If the new employee could not see a 12-foot door, how was he to see a 12-inch sign?" Another business was ordered to have signs printed in both Spanish and English, since there was one employee of Spanish descent. The employee, however, only spoke English.[8]

Some of the most severe impacts may result from OSHA's inspection activities. The frustration experienced by small-business executives is exemplified by Irvin H. Dawson, a small businessman who closed his Cleveland operation for a day as a proclamation mourning "the loss of rights of [American] citizenry under the so-called OSHA."[9] This act of protest was precipitated by an OSHA inspection charging him for nonserious violations such as:

[5] Philip Shabecoff, "Job Safety Changes Are Sought," *The New York Times,* December 19, 1978, p. D-3.

[6] George Perkel, Research Director, Textile Workers Union of America, "Making It Safe to Work," *Viewpoint,* First Quarter 1975, p. 28.

[7] *Occupational Safety and Health Administration's Impact on Small Business* (Washington, D.C.: U.S. Occupational Safety and Health Administration, 1976).

[8] Tim Engel, *OSHA: An Overview* (Washington, D.C.: American Conservative Union, 1977), p. 10.

[9] Stanley J. Modic, "Are You a Coward?" *Industry Week,* November 4, 1974, p. 5.

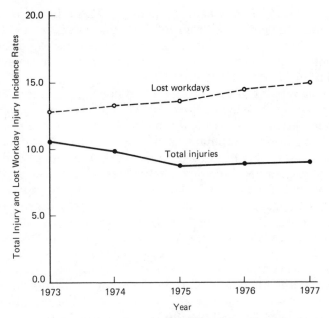

NOTE: Incidence rates represent the number of total injuries or lost
workdays per 100 full-time workers

Figure 5–1 OCCUPATIONAL INJURY INCIDENCE RATES IN THE
PRIVE SECTOR OF THE UNITED STATES, 1973–77

Source: Bureau of Labor Statistics, U.S. Department of Labor

Failing to post a copy of the act (which he never received).

Failure to maintain a separate OSHA folder even though he had all necessary records.

The presence of an "insufficiently" guarded fan, which was dust-covered, its cord wrapped around the base, without brushes, and obviously not in use.

OSHA activities produce more than frustration and irritation, however; it has had a significant impact on company capital investments. According to the McGraw-Hill Publishing Company, which conducts an annual survey on the subject, in 1978 business firms in the United States devoted $3.4 billion of plant and equipment outlays to meet OSHA requirements. That figure was 17 percent above the total for 1977 and represented 2.1 percent of private capital investment in 1978. But the fundamental criticism relates to OSHA's lack of effectiveness.

According to the U.S. Bureau of Labor Statistics, days lost due to work-related injuries have been rising despite OSHA's efforts (see fig. 5–1). For example, days lost rose from 51 per 100 workers in

1973 to 60 in 1977, a rise of 17 percent. The rate of job-related illnesses and accidents rose from 9.2 per 100 workers in 1974 to 9.3 in 1977. Other current statistics are not reassuring. Fatalities rose 20 percent during the most recent year for which data are available, from 3,940 in 1976 to 4,760 in 1977.[10]

The main point of these statistics, of course, is that the problem of workplace safety has not been solved and continued government involvement in this area is highly likely. Thus, some analysis of the underlying question of job hazards may be in order.

Researchers who have focused on workplace safety and health regulation, such as Nichols and Zeckhauser, almost uniformly conclude that the fundamental flaw in the OSHA approach is the decision by Congress at the outset to rely primarily on government-promulgated standards.[11] In theory, such a decision would only be made after an analysis of the causes of job injuries and illnesses and an evaluation of the alternative methods to reduce them. In practice, Congress followed the more traditional procedure which is not unlike that in the old comic routine, where the straight man reads off an answer and the comic is asked to infer what the question is. No attempt was made to analyze the causes and cures of occupational safety and health. In the drafting of the OSHA statute, no serious consideration was given to any approach other than regulation via the promulgation of standards.

Many safety professionals believe that OSHA's reliance on standards is misguided because its inevitable emphasis on capital equipment clashes with their belief that the worker's behavior is the prime determinant of accidents.[12] According to a study reported in the *British Journal of Industrial Medicine*, the lead exposures of employees working at almost identical jobs differed by ratios of up to 4 to 1. This was attributed totally to personal differences in working habits.[13] A number of other studies show that most accidents on the job do not involve violating standards. So, in short, even if full compliance were achieved, large numbers of job-related accidents would still occur.[14]

[10] "BLS Reports on Occupational Injuries and Illnesses for 1977," *U.S. Department of Labor News*, November 21, 1978, pp. 1–5.

[11] See also Robert Smith, *The Occupational Safety and Health Act* (Washington, D.C.: American Enterprise Institute, 1976).

[12] Nichols and Zeckhauser, "Government Comes to the Workplace," p. 40.

[13] M. K. Williams et al., "An Investigation of Lead Absorption in an Electric Accumulator Factory with the Use of Personal Samples," *British Journal of Industrial Medicine*, 26 (1969), 202–16.

[14] Walter Y. Oi, *On Evaluating the Effectiveness of the OSHA Inspection Programs*, May 15, 1975 (unpublished), pp. IX–X; James R. Chelius, *Expectations for OSHA's Performance: The Lessons of Theory and Empirical Evidence*, March 1975 (unpublished), pp. 22–23.

Two investigators attempted to determine if states with stiffer regulations and tighter enforcement had lower injury rates. Neither was able to show any significant effects. However, other studies show that inexperienced workers have high accident rates. The same applies to tired workers on long or varying shifts. Over the period 1942 to 1970, for example, a one percent decline in the national unemployment rate tended to generate a one-quarter of one percent rise in the work-injury rate. On reflection, those results should not be surprising.

At lower rates of output there is more time for maintenance and repair of equipment. During expansions, in contrast, there is more pressure on workers to produce and less time for maintenance of machinery. Moreover, new hires tend to be less experienced or their skills may be rusty if they have been out of work for some time.[15] Statistically, the turnover rate among employees may be the most important single factor in determining injury rates.

Under the circumstances there would seem to be an important role in workplace safety for training. And here OSHA may have been counterproductive. We should not forget that many companies have had professional safety departments long before the Occupational Safety and Health Act was enacted in 1970. In practice, however, OSHA may have diverted much of the focus of these safety units from their traditional task of training workers in safer procedures to following bureaucratic procedures — studying the regulations, filling out the forms, meeting with the inspectors, responding to their charges, and so forth.

Exactly how a safe and healthy work environment is achieved is a managerial matter. Some companies might reduce job hazards by buying new equipment. Others might initiate new work procedures. Still others might provide financial incentives to their employees — for example, paying them to wear earmuffs instead of spending much larger sums on so-called engineering noise containment.

In this vein, a U.S. District Court barred OSHA from barring Continental Can Company's use of "personal protection devices" instead of the more expensive engineering controls. The judge noted that the company's current program of earplugs and earmuffs was more effective than OSHA's preferred alternative. The judge's order stated:

> Defendants [OSHA and the Secretary of Labor] must leave plaintiff alone in this issue, unless or until the Secretary can specify and prove the feasibility of some engineering or administrative controls . . . which will do as

---

[15] Michael Gorham, "Bum Rap for OSHA?, *FRBSF Weekly Letter* (Federal Reserve Bank of San Francisco), January 19, 1979, pp. 1-3.

effective a job of employee protection as the present personal protection devices at comparable cost.[16]

Another example of the kind of thinking that results from this "managerial" concept in contrast to the standards approach is the findings of Donald L. Tasto, a clinical psychologist who was director of the Center for Research on Stress and Health at the Stanford Research Institute. According to Dr. Tasto, the data are very clear that people who rotate shifts have significantly more accidents than those who work permanent shifts.[17] They reported more stomach problems, cramps, colds, chest pains, fatigue, menstrual problems, nervousness, alcohol consumption, and use of sleeping pills and stimulants. Standards do not deal with this type of significant work environment problem.

COSTS AND BENEFITS OF JOB SAFETY CONTROLS

While it may be easy to identify the problems encountered in the regulation of job safety and health, the potential benefits from a less hazardous work environment should not be ignored. Although many of the potential benefits of improved occupational safety and health are often not quantifiable — at least without making numerous assumptions about the value of an arm, of hearing loss, or of life itself — it is useful to try to identify the various types of benefits that can be expected. The point being examined here is a subtle one. That is, the benefits of a safer workplace described in the following discussion may also constitute a strong incentive to business to minimize job-related hazards, even in the absence of government regulation. Tough enforcement of existing liability and a sophisticated notion of property rights may provide adequate incentive to management. Likewise, greater information on the hidden hazards on the job may result in greater attention to safe practices on the part of employees.

1. The greater productivity of those who would have sustained a job-related injury or illness in the absence of government regulation.
2. The greater enjoyment of life by those who thus avoided work-related disabilities.

[16] "Judge Issues OSHA Noise Decision," *Insight*, August–October 1978, p. 10.
[17] "Shift Workers' Health Suffers," *Investments in Tomorrow*, 8, no. 3 (1978), 7.

3. The resources that would have had to be used in the treatment and rehabilitation of victims of work-related injuries or illnesses which were avoided.
4. The resources that would have had to be used to administer workmen's compensation and insurance, and to train those who would have been needed to replace the sick or disabled.
5. The reduction in the private efforts to increase occupational safety and health, which are replaced or reduced by the government's efforts.
6. The consequent decrease in damage to plant and equipment.
7. The savings that result from less disruption of work routines caused by accidents plus potential improvements in the morale and productivity of the work force.[18]

But likewise, the estimates of current expenditures by various industries to meet government safety or other requirements are often no more than reasonable guesses. The results of surveys are not easy to interpret realistically. It is often difficult for a company to distinguish between investment to meet federal requirements and investment in production equipment, which would be purchased even in the absence of the government restriction.

Another important potential benefit of health and safety regulations has been cited in a study by MIT's Center for Policy Alternatives. Preliminary findings of the study indicate that in four Western European countries and Japan, which have health and safety regulations similar to those in the United States, these regulations tend to encourage technological innovation in firms by forcing firms to implement product or process changes. The regulations, the study contends, oftentimes incidentally shock companies out of a rather inflexible production system and thereby provide the catalyst for innovation to occur.[19]

At times, however, the lack of comparable benefits from a costly standard seem to be readily apparent. The case of the rubber gloves (used by electric utilities) is such an example. After reading complaints from industry that there was no need for OSHA promulgating a standard for electrical rubber gloves, the author requested details from a knowledgeable Missouri engineer who had worked for a half century in the electrical field. The reply in part follows:

> During all that period, I have never observed or heard of an accident due to failure of electrical rubber gloves *in service*. One must understand, I believe, the procedures, practices, and daily uses of these gloves to understand this record.

[18] Russell F. Settle, "Benefits and Costs of the Federal Asbestos Standard" (paper presented at the Department of Labor Conference on Evaluating the Effects of the Occupational Safety and Health Program, Washington, D.C., March 18, 1975), pp. 3-7.

First, each gloves is electrically tested by the manufacturer before ship-ment. Upon receipt of these gloves they are again electrically tested by the utility or a testing laboratory and stamped with a number. Then each lineman is issued at least two pair of gloves — and the numbers recorded. He uses one pair and before using it in his daily work he gives it an "air test," which is done by twirling the cuffs and forcing the entrapped air into the fingers. Obviously — if there is a hole — the air escapes. Mean-while, his second pair is on test and he changes gloves once every week or two weeks.

After usage — there are of course gloves that fail on test and are replaced. But it is the continual testing that I have described that prevents accidents while gloves are being used.

I hope this information may be of interest to you. I am sure you are aware that a leather protector glove is worn over the rubber gloves when in use.[20]

This testimony would seem to indicate that OSHA was promul-gating standards in an area where existing practices were adequate.

One final set of statistics should affect our thinking about OSHA's effectiveness. For many industries the lost time due to illnesses and injuries off the job far exceeds that due to on-the-job hazards. The medical director of Exxon, for example, states that nonoccupational diseases and injuries account for about 96 percent of the time lost due to disability.[21] The OSHA-mandated efforts are thus limited only to the remaining 4 percent of the disability-caused absenteeism in that large company. Along the same lines, B. F. Goodrich reported in one recent year that its employees suf-fered almost eight times as many injuries off the job as on and missed work more than four times as often from off-the-job injuries as from those that occurred at work.

ANNOUNCEMENT EFFECT

One unmeasurable impact of safety and other types of regula-tion is the announcement effect. For many years economists have identified what is termed an "announcement effect" of government spending or taxation. That is, potential government contractors may start preparing to bid on a project before Congress has appropriated funds for it. Similarly, consumers may increase their expenditures as soon as a tax cut is voted on or even while it is being considered.

[19] David Burnham, "U.S. Rules Called Spur to Industry," *The New York Times*, June 24, 1975, p. 17.

[20] Letter to the author, dated June 17, 1974, from Clarence H. LeVee, retired vice president of Engineering, A. B. Chance Company.

[21] N. J. Roberts, M.D., "Medicine at Work," *The Lamp*, Fall 1974, p. 21.

Government regulatory programs may have somewhat similar effects. In Illinois the very rumor of more stringent standards for migrant worker housing by the Occupational Safety and Health Administration caused strawberry farmers to reduce their production. Lester Pitchford, the largest grower in the Centralia area, was quoted as saying, "We don't know if OSHA is coming or not, but when it was even rumored, it put it [strawberry production] out."[22]

By OSHA directive, it is expected that farmers will have to provide 100 square feet of living space for each migrant (the present state standard is 60 square feet), flush toilets and showers in each room, as well as other amenities. Apparently, at least some Illinois strawberry farmers have concluded that the capital investments required cannot be justified for a two-week harvest.

According to James Mills, a sanitary official with the Illinois Department of Public Health, one of the basic problems in a case of this sort is the lack of distinction under OSHA regulations between long-term and short-term migratory farm worker housing. Centralia strawberry farmers, he was quoted as saying, "just can't compete, and if OSHA puts the pressure on them, they'll get out of the migrant business completely and go strictly U-Pick" (consumers pick the fruit for their own use for a fee).

OUTLOOK

OSHA surely seems to be having a difficult time in attempting to achieve its basic objective—a safer working environment. It is doubtful that there is an invariant, unique way of achieving that desirable result, although OSHA depends almost entirely on the setting of standards. Changes in equipment, variations in work practices, education and training of employees, and leadership on the part of management all may be practical alternatives for achieving the desired ends, at least in some circumstances. An economist would opt for the mix of methods that entails the least loss of productivity and output, and those combinations would probably vary both from plant to plant and over time.

But the trend toward more intensive and more expensive job safety and health regulation is likely to continue, even though OSHA eliminated in early 1979, with considerable fanfare, close to a thousand of what is called "those Mickey Mouse regulations"—dealing with the shape of toilet seats and the height of fire extinguish-

[22] Pamela Meyer, "Fear of OSHA Making Farmers Plow Under Strawberry Crops," *St. Louis Post-Dispatch*, June 11, 1974, p. 7C.

ers. Yet, virtually simultaneously, it issued a tentative ruling which could increase very substantially the total cost of complying with the agency's directives — its general proposal for identifying, classifying, and regulating all toxic substances posing a potential occupational carcinogenic (cancer-causing) risk.[23]

- *Category I* would be reserved for confirmed carcinogens — any substance found to cause cancer in humans, or in two mammalian species of test animals or in the same species if the experiment has been duplicated. A chemical placed in that category would trigger an emergency temporary standard by OSHA, reducing worker exposure as much as practicable. At the same time the agency would start proceedings on a permanent standard which would reduce exposure to the lowest feasible level or ban the material if OSHA determines there is a substitute.
- *Category II would encompass suspected carcinogens* — where evidence is only suggestive or from one animal species. Substances in this category would be subject to a permanent standard to reduce worker exposure to a level low enough to prevent acute or chronic toxic effects.
- *Category III* would be an alert area — to include other suspect substances which can't be placed in one of the first two categories because of insufficient data.

The regulatory procedure would go forward automatically and inexorably once data satisfying Category I are presented to OSHA. In determining whether a material is a carcinogen, OSHA says it will make no distinction between benign and malignant tumors. The proposed regulation assumes there is no safe level of exposure to a carcinogen and would mandate lowest feasible exposure without considering economics of a ban. Moreover, there are no criteria in the plan for evaluating proper substitutes should a ban be imposed.

Once a substance is assigned to a category, a fairly standard set of regulations would ensue. Category-I substances would first fall under an "emergency temporary standard," which would require companies to reduce exposures to minimum levels, warn workers, give them physicals, and begin monitoring their exposure. After six months full permanent standards would go into effect. If a suitable substitute could be found, worker exposure would be prohibited entirely.

The requirements for Category-II substances would be pretty much the same except that OSHA could prescribe a higher permissible level of exposure than "lowest feasible."

[23] U.S., Occupational Safety and Health Administration, "Identification, Classification, and Regulation of Toxic Substances Posing a Potential Occupational Carcinogenic Risk," *Federal Register*, October 4, 1977, pp. 54148–247.

The National Institute for Occupational Safety and Health (or NIOSH, a unit of the U.S. Department of Health, Education and Welfare) has projected that 1,870 substances are likely to be classified in OSHA's proposed Categories I and II. The engineering consulting firm of Foster D. Snell has estimated that to reduce the exposure level of a substance to ten parts per million would impose capital costs of $17 billion on American industry and annual operating costs of $10 billion.

If OSHA were to limit its enforcement efforts to only 38 high-volume substances so categorized by NIOSH, the Snell firm estimated the capital costs at $9 billion and the annual operating costs at $6 billion. However, if for those 38 substances, OSHA attempted to enforce a more stringent maximum exposure level of one part per million, the capital costs were projected at $23 billion and the continuing operating costs at $11 billion[24].

The possibility of a less costly approach to the setting of job safety and health standards, however, has occurred in the case of OSHA's benzene standard. In that instance, the U.S. Court of Appeals set aside major portions of the regulations which would have required employers to assure that no employee is exposed to airborne concentrations of benzene in excess of one part per million over an eight-hour day. The court stated that it took such action because OSHA had not shown that the costs being imposed bore a "reasonable relationship" to the benefits to be obtained.[25]

On balance, then, there remains the central issue in OSHA's regulatory activities posed by the agency's legislated requirement to set *standards*. Substantial improvement in this area of regulation may come only when Congress shifts the agency's mandate to analyzing actual causes of illness and injury and then evaluating and choosing among appropriate methods to eliminate them.

[24] *Preliminary Estimates of Direct Compliance Costs and Other Economic Effects of OSHA's Generic Carcinogenic Proposal on Substance Producing and Using Industries*, (Scarsdale, N.Y.: American Industrial Health Council, 1978); see also Tom Alexander, "OSHA's Ill-Conceived Crusade against Cancer," *Fortune*, July 3, 1978, pp. 86-87.
[25] American Petroleum Institute v. OSHA, no. 78-1253 (5th Cir., 10-5-78).

6

managing
the environment

During the 1970s federal legislation substantially enlarged the role of the government in regulating the environment and committed the nation to ambitious goals. The Environmental Protection Agency (EPA) was set up to pull together a variety of scattered activities and provide a unified ecological policy at the national level. EPA now administers programs relating to air pollution, water pollution, solid waste disposal, pesticide regulation, and environmental radiation, and it possesses an impressive arsenal of powers and duties.

THE ENVIRONMENTAL PROTECTION AGENCY

Activities of EPA center around the setting and enforcing of standards relating to environmental concerns. EPA defines a standard as "the product of fact and theory provided by scientists, and a public value judgment conditioned by the balance of risks against benefits, with a margin of safety on the side of public health and welfare."[1] EPA has several avenues of enforcement at its disposal. Upon finding a violation, it may seek voluntary compliance. If this approach fails, it may order compliance and take court action. Possible penalties for violation of EPA standards include fines and jail sentences. The largest and best-known EPA programs are those dealing with the control of air and water pollution.

Air Pollution Controls

The Clean Air Act of 1970 provides for a nationwide program of air pollution control, including provisions for setting and enforcing standards. Standards fall into the following categories:

Emergency Standards. EPA defines air pollution levels that pose an imminent and substantial danger to health. When these levels are reached, emergency actions are taken, which can include shutting down industrial polluters.

National Air Quality Standards. National air quality standards have been set for the six most common pollutants — sulfur oxides, particulates, carbon monoxide, photochemical oxidants, hydrocarbons, and nitrogen oxides. Regulations come in two parts. A primary standard, aimed at protecting public health, sets a limit on air pollution that is safe for humans. A secondary standard, designed to protect public welfare, establishes a level of pollution that is safe for vegetation, animals, and property.

National Emission Standards. For hazardous pollutants that "may cause, or contribute to, an increase in mortality or an increase in serious irreversible, or incapacitating reversible, illness," EPA must set national emission standards.

New Plant Standards. EPA is required to set "standards of performance for new stationary sources." The purpose is to require these plants to use the best available technology to control air pollution.

Motor Vehicle Emission Standards. Manufacturers of new or imported cars or engines must have their products certified by EPA that they comply with stated emission levels.

Fuel Standards. EPA can control or prohibit substances in motor vehicles that significantly hinder performance of emission control systems.

Violation of an implementation plan, a new source performance standard, or a hazardous emission standard is punishable by a fine of up to $25,000 a day and one year in prison. Subsequent violations can double both the fine and the jail term. If a manufacturer or dealer sells a car not certified by EPA or disconnects an emission control device, he can be fined up to $10,000 for each offending

---

[1] *Action for Environmental Quality* (Washington, D.C.: Environmental Protection Agency, 1973), pp. 1–4.

car or engine. A violation of EPA's motor vehicle fuel standards is punishable by a fine of up to $10,000 a day. As an indication of the pace of EPA's air pollution regulatory activities, in 1978 the agency promulgated 8 new source performance standards, issued 93 control technique guidelines, and performed 1,860 emissions certification tests.[2]

Pursuant to the Clean Air Act Amendments of 1977, EPA is accelerating the tempo of air pollution control. The amendments provide that, in any area where EPA's air quality standards have not been fully attained, new industrial plants cannot be built after July 1, 1979, unless the following conditions have been met:

- The state has adopted an air pollution control plan that will ensure "full compliance" by the end of 1982 (or 1987 in the case of photochemical oxidants).
- EPA has approved the plan.

Full compliance covers both emissions from stationary sources and from motor vehicles. Thus, even if industry is in full compliance, the plan must also include a statewide transportation plan that ensures motor vehicle compliance. Figure 6-1 shows the various steps that may be involved in meeting the clean-air standards for a new industrial facility.

Water Pollution Controls

A national effort to fight water pollution was launched under the Water Pollution Control Act of 1972. The law proclaims two major goals: By July 1, 1983, wherever possible, water should be clean enough for swimming and other recreational use, and for the protection of fish and wildlife; and by 1985, no more discharges of pollutants shall be made into the nation's waters. Under the law, EPA issues national effluent limitation regulations and national performance standards for industries and publicly owned waste treatment plants. No discharge of any pollutant into the waters is allowed without a permit. In 1978 EPA issued 240 major water discharge permits and assessed 844 administrative penalties.

Violators of the water pollution standards may be fined up to $10,000 a day. Willful or negligent violators can be fined up to $25,000 a day and sentenced to one year in prison; these penalties can be doubled for subsequent violations. EPA may enter and inspect

[2] *The Budget of the United States Government, Fiscal Year 1980* (Washington, D.C.: U.S. Government Printing Office, 1979), appendix, pp. 783–84.

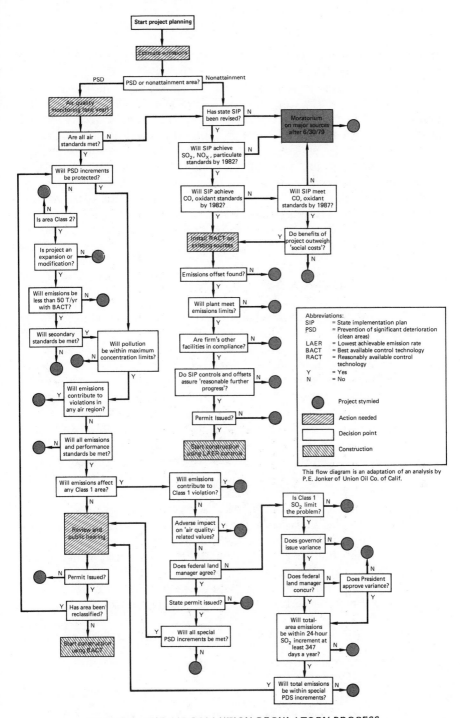

Figure 6-1 THE AIR POLLUTION REGULATORY PROCESS

Source: Industry Week, February 5, 1979, p. 71. Reprinted with permission.

any polluting facility to check its records and monitoring equipment and to test its discharges.

Failure to report the discharge of oil or other hazardous substances into the water can result in a fine of up to $10,000 and one year in jail. Expelling hazardous substances from a vessel can be punished with a fine of up to $5 million; also, cleanup costs of up to $14 million can be assessed to the polluter. Anyone discharging hazardous substances due to willful negligence or misconduct is liable for actual cleanup costs, no matter how high. Both the Clean Air Act and the Water Pollution Control Act empower citizens to bring suit against anyone violating these laws. Citizens can also take court action against EPA itself if it fails to perform any duty required by the two laws.

Hazardous and Toxic Substance Controls

EPA also administers several more specialized statutes. Under the Federal Insecticide, Fungicide, and Rodenticide Act, supplies are controlled to keep "hazardous" chemicals off the market and to prevent "unreasonable" adverse effects to humans or to the environment. Producers of new products must register with the agency. This procedure allows EPA to make a "rebuttable presumption" against registration of any pesticide which it believes violates the act.

The Resource Conservation and Recovery Act empowers EPA to regulate the disposal of what it considers to be hazardous wastes. The law requires generators of wastes to create a record-keeping system to track wastes from the point of generation to their ultimate disposal. Producers of more than 220 pounds a month of hazardous wastes are required to furnish information on the waste to transporters and to designate a permitted disposal or treatment facility to which the residues must be taken. Landfills must be lined with clay, plastic, or other material that would prevent waste from moving through the soil and reaching water sources.

The Toxic Substances Control Act (TSCA) gives EPA substantial power over the chemical industry, including the following:

- Authority to require selective testing of new and existing chemical compounds.
- Premanufacturing notices 90 days prior to the production of any new chemical or significant new use of an existing chemical.
- Power to control the manufacturing, processing, distribution, use, and disposal of any chemical substance.
- Required reporting, which covers each chemical produced by every chemical manufacturer.

Pursuant to TSCA, EPA is obtaining from manufacturers test data on 50 groups of chemicals. From that information it will be making in-depth risk assessments and developing control strategies and regulations on specific chemical substances.

Also, EPA sets standards for drinking water (under the Safe Drinking Water Act), regulates ocean dumping (via the Marine Protection, Resources, and Sanctuaries Act), limits "poisonous and deleterious" substances added to food (under the Food, Drug, and Cosmetic Act), establishes noise emissions standards for railroads and motor carriers (the Noise Pollution and Control Act), and sets standards for using nuclear materials to protect health and the environment (Atomic Energy Act of 1954).

In sum, the regulatory processes followed by EPA for controlling pollution involve five steps:

1. Deciding the levels of environmental quality desired.
2. Setting environmental quality standards.
3. Deciding on the abatement actions or methods of achieving the standards.
4. Monitoring compliance with the standards and abatement schedules.
5. Taking enforcement actions against violators.

THE COSTS AND BENEFITS OF A CLEAN ENVIRONMENT

Although, as we have seen, penalties for violation of pollution standards can be substantial, compliance is not inexpensive either. The U.S. Council on Environmental Quality (CEQ) estimates expenditures for pollution control at $40 billion in 1977, with a steady rise anticipated to $86 billion in 1986. From 1977 to 1986 public agencies and private companies will be spending over $645 billion to control and reduce all forms of pollution. But, as CEQ points out, people — as consumers and taxpayers — ultimately pay all the costs of cleaning up the environment[3] — and also receive the benefits that may ensue (see Table 6–1).

The Costs of Environmental Regulation

The impacts of these outlays on specific industries may be especially severe. In 1977 the paper industry allocated 14 percent of

---

[3] U.S., Council on Environmental Quality, *Environmental Quality* (Washington, D.C.: The Council on Environmental Quality, 1978), p. 446.

Table 6-1   Estimated pollution control expenditures (in billions of 1977 dollars)

Category	1977			1986			Cumulative – 1977-86		
	Operating Costs	Capital Costs	Total Annual Costs	Operating Costs	Capital Costs	Total Annual Costs	Operating Costs	Capital Costs	Total Annual Costs
Air pollution	6.8	7.3	14.1	14.6	19.1	33.7	111.8	136.1	247.9
Water pollution	6.4	11.2	17.6	15.5	23.5	39.0	109.5	182.0	291.5
Radiation	<0.05	<0.05	<0.05	<0.05	0.1	0.2	0.1	0.3	0.4
Solid wastes	6.7	1.4	8.1	8.6	2.5	11.1	77.1	17.0	94.1
Land reclamation	0.1	NA	0.1	0.8	NA	0.8	6.0	NA	6.0
Toxic substances	NA	NA	NA	0.2	NA	0.2	1.2	NA	1.2
Noise	NA	NA	NA	0.4	0.5	0.9	2.0	2.2	4.2
Total	20.0	19.9	39.9	40.1	45.7	85.9	307.7	337.6	645.3

NA = Not available

Source: Council on Environmental Quality

its capital expenditures to air and water pollution control equipment. An EPA study has estimated that from 1975 to 1983 this proportion could average as much as 27 percent, with $6.4 billion (in 1975 dollars) being invested over the eight years. These government-required outlays are expected to cause price increases of 5 to 7 percent.

Substantial capital cost increases in the paper industry relating to pollution investments are occurring for two major reasons. First, a higher technological cost is connected with the design of nonpolluting mills and with upgrading existing mills while maintaining an adequate return on this capital, which has a limited economic life. Second, additional costs have emanated from the shortages of capital goods caused by the insufficient capacity to provide all the pollution-free equipment demanded. For example, the foundries that manufacture parts for the capital equipment needed to eliminate or control pollution have themselves been affected severely by pollution regulations which require them to divert funds from investment in increased or even constant capacity. One private study estimates that meeting the pollution standards has cost the economy about 10 percent of its industrial capacity.[4]

In the case of the iron and steel industries the 1977 proportion of capital outlays devoted to pollution control was 19 percent. EPA estimates that 20 percent of the industry's plant and equipment outlays during the period 1975 to 1983 will be devoted to control equipment, increasing consumer prices by about 4 to 5 percent. In addition, CEQ acknowledges that capital availability will be a significant concern for the industry.

A study by Arthur D. Little, Inc., concluded that there will be little if any growth in copper smelting capacity in the United States through 1985 because of the lead time required for conversion to environmentally sound processes. Further, growth after 1985 is not assured because of unsolved problems with fugitive emissions and because of the large capital outlays required during the 1980s to meet state implementation plan limits on sulfur dioxide emissions.[5] In an effort to lessen the capacity constraints projected in the study, EPA is allowing limited increases in SO_x and particulate emissions at the four cleanest smelters after installation of control technology.

---

[4] Bruce R. Lippke et al., *The Impact of Pollution Standards on Shortages, Inflation, Real Income and Unemployment* (Tacoma, Wash.: Weyerhaeuser Company, 1975), p. 15.

[5] *Economic Impact of Environmental Regulations on the United States Copper Industry,* prepared for the U.S. Environmental Protection Agency (Acorn Park, Mass.: Arthur D. Little, 1978).

The most dramatic impacts on industry of environmental regulations are the forced closings of entire facilities. By court order United States Steel Corporation shut down its open hearth furnaces in Gary, Indiana, because of failure to comply with EPA pollution regulations. One cost of the plant closing is the loss of 2,500 jobs directly and another 1,500 at suppliers and supporting industries. The EPA, whose suit brought about the situation and who subsequently refused an extension, urged the company to follow an alternate strategy: Continue operating the plant while paying a fine of $2,300 a day.

The foundry industry has probably experienced some of the most serious impacts of environmental regulations. Between 1968 and 1974, 427 foundries were closed. Although a variety of factors was given for the terminations, including the added expense of meeting job safety requirements, the cost of compliance with environmental regulations was frequently cited as a factor in a sizable number of foundry failures. The greatest fatality rate occurred among the small foundries.[6] It would thus appear that one unintended side effect of these government regulations has been to achieve a more concentrated industry structure, in which a relatively few large firms tend to dominate the market.

In a more general survey of plant closures due to environmental regulation, CEQ stated that although the overall impact of pollution controls may not be large, the plant closures and the unemployment they cause can be significant for the communities they affect.[7] CEQ also points out that the closed facilities are usually older and smaller and only marginally profitable in the absence of the government standards. There is some geographic concentration of the plants which have closed, and many are located in older industrial towns already suffering relatively high unemployment rates (see fig. 6-2).

The Benefits of Environmental Regulation

The benefits achieved by government regulation are also worthy of attention.

As CEQ states in its annual report for 1978, "Comprehensive estimates of the benefits of environmental programs are still lacking."

[6] Robert E. Curran, *The Foundry Industry* (Washington, D.C.: U.S. Department of Commerce, Bureau of Domestic Commerce, 1975), p. 20.
[7] U.S., Council on Environmental Quality, *Environmental Quality*, p. 432.

	4 Plants	400 Employees

Region	Number of plant closings	Number of affected employees	Labor force (thousands)	Regional employment rate
I			5,871	8.4
II			7,830	9.2
III			13,906	7.4
IV			15,884	6.7
V			20,905	5.9
VI			10,251	5.6
VII			5,550	4.4
VIII			2,974	5.7
IX			12,242	8.5
X			3,443	8.5

Figure 6-2 PLANT CLOSINGS ALLEGEDLY RESULTING IN PART FROM POLLU-
TION ABATEMENT COSTS, APRIL 1978

Source: U.S. Department of Labor, *Bureau of Labor Statistics News,* June 12, 1978. Letter
from Douglas Costle, Administrator, U.S. Environmental Protection Agency to
Ray Marshall, Secretary of Labor, May 9, 1978.

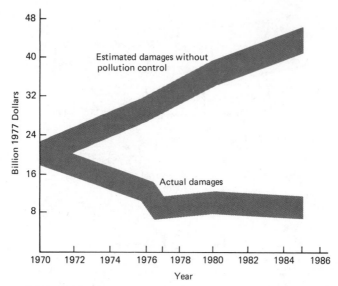

Figure 6-3 ESTIMATED   EFFECTS   OF   AIR   POLLUTION
            CONTROLS

Source: Thomas E. Waddell, "Preliminary Update and Projections of Selected Categories of
           Damage Cost Estimates," prepared for the Council on Environmental Quality, May
           1978

The agency does note that a very substantial portion, perhaps more
than half of all pollution control expenditures, is being made simply
to prevent the environment from becoming more degraded than it
already is.

Figure 6-3 illustrates this point with data on air pollution, prepared for CEQ. The chart shows that following substantial reduction
in damage costs from 1970 to 1977, no further overall improvement
is anticipated through 1985. That explains, of course, why it is
difficult to find many examples of cleaner air or purer water, despite
the massive outlays that have been made for those purposes.

Nevertheless, specific examples of improved ecology do exist.
A dramatic instance is the cleanup in Oregon which permitted the
salmon to run again (see appendix to this chapter, "Cleaning Up the
Willamette"). CEQ also has estimated that the overall trend in urban
air quality is toward continued improvement. Emissions of the most
troublesome pollutants in U.S. cities, photochemical oxidants and
carbon monoxide, dropped significantly between 1973 and 1976
in most cities which have had severe problems with them (and for
which data are available). The severity of pollution in major cities
has declined, as shown by a 29-percent drop during this four-year

period of the number of days when the Pollution Standard Index rose above 200 for all five "criteria" air pollutants in 43 cities.[8]

The lack of uniform water quality data has made it difficult for CEQ to characterize trends in that area, but encouragement has been found in (1) a decline in water bacteria levels in the United States in 1977; (2) gradual improvement in water quality downstream of 11 cities where major municipal and industrial treatment plants began operating between 1967 and 1975; and (3) significant drops in the ocean dumping of wastes in the two-year period 1976-77.[9] Also, outstanding success has been reported in the progress of the Great Lakes sport fisheries, especially those in Lake Michigan.

The Economics of Environmental Regulation

Examination of the costs and benefits of environmental regulation inevitably raises the more fundamental question of the economic rationale for this type of governmental intervention. As shown in Chapter 1, the promulgation of standards in only one of a variety of approaches that can be followed to correct the "externalities" of air and water pollution.

Until fairly recently, air and water (and the environment generally), if thought about at all, were viewed as common property, as "free goods." Individuals and organizations, both public and private, used the environment as a free dump — which, of course, is the act of polluters polluting. Private benefits were received by the polluters, albeit social costs to society in the form of dirtier air and water resulted. Excessive pollution was encouraged because, although the social costs of polluting may have, at times, exceeded the social benefits, the private benefits of polluting usually exceeded the private costs. People tend to pollute less if they have to pay for the cost of cleaning up.

To an economist the environment pollution problem essentially is one of altering people's incentives. The basic assumption is that people pollute not because they enjoy messing up the environment but because polluting is cheaper or easier than not polluting. Thus, from an economic standpoint, if prices of goods and services would reflect the costs imposed on the environment (perhaps as measured by cleanup costs), consumers would tend to shift to those less ex-

[8] Ibid., p. 1. See also pp. 4-19.
[9] Ibid., pp. 91-117.

pensive goods and services which embody lower environmental costs.[10]

The idea in this approach is not to punish polluters but to get them to change their ways because high-polluting products become more expensive than low-polluting products. Taxation (or effluent fees), in this regard, is a basic way of working through the price system. A tax or charge levied on high-polluting products alters relative prices in favor of low-polluting products. A low tax rate (a "revenue tariff") does not stop the act of polluting, but it may raise the revenue needed to pay for cleaning up. A high enough tax rate (a "protective tariff") would stop the pollution by totally discouraging the purchase of the high-polluting product — although it would not raise revenue.

In practice, we would expect an intermediate result. The pollution tax or effluent fee would shift some, but not all, demand to the lower-priced alternatives. Some, but not all, producers would have sufficient incentive to change to less polluting methods of production and distribution. Thus, producers would have more incentive than they now do to "economize" on pollution — an incentive similar to their developing methods of reducing labor and material costs. The basic idea, of course, is that the price of a product should reflect its cost to or burden on the environment.

As an illustration of this proposal, a detailed study of the Delaware Estuary showed that effluent fees, set at a high enough level to achieve the desired level of water purity, would cost approximately one-half as much as a conventional regulatory program requiring an equal percentage reduction by all polluters. To achieve the standard of two parts of dissolved oxygen per million, the estimated annual cost came to $2.4 million via an effluent charge, compared with $5.0 million for treatment of the pollution under a uniform regulation.[11]

In the real world, however, business and government tend to favor the customary approach that consists of government issuing uniform standards. This alternative is defended on the grounds of equity: All polluters are treated equally — all cars must meet the same air pollution rules, for example. The popularity of the regulatory approach may be explained in part by the fact that the majority of the members of Congress are lawyers. They are trained to think

----

[10] See Frederick R. Anderson, et al., *Environmental Improvement through Economic Incentives* (Baltimore: Johns Hopkins University Press, 1978).

[11] Allen Kneese et al., ed., *Managing the Environment* (New York: Praeger Publishers, 1971), appendix c.

in terms of rulings and litigations.[12] Consequently, much of EPA's staff resources have gone into defending the agency against more than a thousand lawsuits, brought both by environmentalists urging sterner enforcement and by companies seeking relief from what they regard as arbitrary interpretations.

But uniform standards are an expensive regulatory approach. It may cost a great deal to reduce the pollutants from one type of activity and very little from another. For example, it may be cheaper to redesign a new building still on the drafting boards than to totally revamp one that already is standing. This assertion certainly is obvious, and in late 1978, responding to the pleas of economists, EPA took important initial steps to accommodate the economic approach, as follows:

Under the "bubble concept," each plant complex is treated as if it were encased in a bubble, with EPA's attention focused on the total pollution, instead of each pollution source. Trade-offs among pollution sources are permitted if they are comparable in nature and in their effect on public health. EPA hopes that the "bubble concept" will encourage company officials to adopt innovative, less costly methods of pollution control.

A related new departure on the part of EPA is its "offset" policy. When any region of the country is not in compliance with clean-air standards, the agency refuses to permit construction of new facilities that will further reduce air quality. However, rather than arbitrarily banning all new industry or requiring a new plant to be pollution-free, EPA permits the new construction if the company will also clean up pollution produced by existing facilities. This cleanup effort by a new firm must more than offset the additional pollution which it causes. Consequently, some companies now advertise to sell their reducible pollution to firms needing "offsets."[13]

All in all, economic approaches to pollution problems, which involve reasonable trade-offs and discerning choices between appropriate (and efficient) alternative methods, can — and in fact do — produce results that are less costly both to business and to the public. In addition, economic approaches have the advantage of bringing about needed benefits for society — a cleaner environment — at the

---

[12] Russell F. Settle and Burton A. Weisbrod, "Governmentally Imposed Standards: Some Normative Aspects," in *Research in Labor Economics,* vol. 2, ed. Ronald G. Ehrenberg (Greenwich, Conn.: JAI Press, 1978), p. 160.

[13] Peter Nulty, "A Brave Experiment in Pollution Control," *Fortune,* February 12, 1979, p. 121.

same time that they reduce the costly, and often self-defeating, regulatory interventions by agencies such as EPA. In this regard, therefore, an interesting commentary on public policy formation in the United States has been made by the Washington representative of the Sierra Club, a major ecological organization which has been in the forefront of the conventional approach of government-promulgated environmental rules and regulations: "In retrospect, we would have accomplished more if we'd simply taxed pollution and then left compliance in the hands of businessmen rather than regulators."[14]

APPENDIX: CLEANING UP THE WILLAMETTE*

In one important respect the Willamette River in Oregon is now more like the river that Lewis and Clark saw in the early nineteenth century than the river was 10, 30, or even 50 years ago. What used to be one of the nation's most polluted waterways has been transformed once again into a clean river. Fifty years ago men refused to work at riverside construction because of the water's stench. Now thousands of people regularly swim, fish, water-ski, and boat on summer weekends.

The Setting

The Willamette Valley in the western part of Oregon is approximately 150 miles long and 25 miles wide. It is bordered by mountains on both sides. At lower elevations the mountains are heavily forested. Lakes, rock outcroppings, and meadows appear at the higher elevations in the Cascades. Most of the Willamette's water originates in the mountains and flows down into the river by way of its major tributaries. The valley itself is relatively flat. The main river begins at the confluence of several tributaries at the southern part of the valley and meanders northward for 185 miles. At Oregon City, the river plunges dramatically over the 41-foot Willamette Falls. From there to the Columbia, the Willamette is subject to ocean tides.

---

[14] Quoted in "Clean Air: The Job Industry Still has to Do," *Business Week*, October 11, 1976, p. 40F.

*The details of this section are drawn from U.S., Council on Environmental Quality, *Environmental Quality* (Washington, D.C.: U.S. Government Printing Office, 1973), pp. 43-70.

Near the mouth of the Willamette and stretching along both banks as far as the falls is the metropolitan area of Portland, with a population of 900,000. It is a major port and a center of industry and finance. Portland's suburbs stretch southward along both banks of the river as far as Willamette Falls. Salem, the state capital with a population of 75,000 lies 47 miles south of Portland. Above the falls, agricultural areas begin; the land on both sides of the river is cultivated. Lumbering and food processing are primary economic activities.

The residents of the basin make up 70 percent of Oregon's population. The river has always played a major role in the history of the valley. By the turn of the century Willamette Falls was harnessed to generate electric power. Sawmills were situated on the river in order to transport logs and finished products. With the advent of pulp and paper mills the river was also used to dispose of industrial wastes.

The hydrology of the Willamette is one of the river's important factors. Variability in flow is extreme. There is heavy precipitation in the winter months and very little in the summer. This pattern perennially led to extremely high water in the winter and early spring and extremely low water from July through October. Before the construction of storage reservoirs, the natural flow of the river ranged from an estimated maximum of 500,000 cubic feet a second during the flood of December 1861, to summer minimums of less than 2,500 cubic feet a second. These variations in flow were important to pollution control.

Water Quality Restored

Pollution — the early days. Pollution of the Willamette was a concern as early as the 1920s. In 1926 the Oregon State Board of Health organized an "Antipollution League," and in 1927 the Portland City Club was studying the pollution of the Willamette. Several water quality surveys were undertaken. The studies concentrated on measuring the amount of dissolved oxygen (DO) in the water. Specific concentrations of dissolved oxygen are needed to support not only fish and plant life but also the natural biological processes by which organic wastes are converted to stable inorganic materials by bacteria and other organisms. As a general rule DO concentrations of five parts per million are required if a river is to stay healthy.

The first comprehensive water quality survey was undertaken by the Oregon Agricultural College in 1929. The dissolved oxygen level was measured during the low summer flow from the headwaters to the Portland Harbor. DO was above eight parts per million for the first 130 miles. At Salem, DO dropped to seven parts per million and remained at that level as far as Newberg, 35 miles farther downstream. DO fell below five parts per million 15 miles above Willamette Falls and stood at four parts per million at the upper end of Portland Harbor. Considering the volume of wastes entering the river at Portland, the study concluded that DO was less than 0.5 parts per million where the waters of the Willamette reached the Columbia River.

The water was polluted simply because all bordering municipalities dumped their wastes into the river without treatment. Although the Willamette was able to absorb and stabilize the discharges of smaller communities, it could not handle the municipal loads from the larger communities such as Eugene and Salem. Of even greater consequence were the five pulp and paper mills in operation by the late 1920s. These plants produced pulp by using the sulfite process, which entails cooking wood chips under pressure and then separating the larger cellulous fibers which are used to produce paper. The residue, primarily wood sugars and smaller wood fibers, was discharged into the river. In decomposing, the wood sugars exerted an immediate and severe demand on dissolved oxygen. The wood fibers exerted their demand over a more extended period, and often they formed sludge deposits on the river bottom. During the low-flow summer months, the wood fiber deposits frequently surfaced as unsightly, foul-smelling floating rafts. As much as 80 percent of the total demand on the dissolved oxygen in the river stemmed from the effluents from pulp and paper mills.

When these waste flows reached Portland Harbor, the water quality situation became serious. The municipal wastes of the city, which by 1930 had 300,000 inhabitants, flowed untreated into the harbor through 65 separate discharge sewers. Tidal action and backflows from the Columbia generally kept the wastes in the deep harbor for an extended period during the low-flow summer months. The result during the summer was often a total absence of dissolved oxygen along stretches of the harbor.

Public concern over the river's condition increased in the 1930s. In 1933 the governor of Oregon called the mayors of the cities on the Willamette together for a conference "responsive to a statewide demand for abatement of stream pollution." The first technical study of the pollution generated by the pulp and paper industry followed that meeting. In 1935 the Oregon State Planning Board made a study of the water pollution laws. After identifying 35 separate state laws, the board determined that the existing statutes fostered administrative duplication and ineffectiveness, made it impossible to undertake ameliatory regulation, and provided for unacceptably severe, and therefore unenforceable, penalties. The board concluded that "promiscuous adoption of unrelated and uncoordinated nuisance and penal statutes . . . cannot form the basis of a concerted and direct effort to prohibit pollution of streams."

First plan. During 1937 the energies of those concerned about water pollution were directed at the state legislature. A bill passed that year was vetoed by the governor on the grounds that it would cause financial hardship for the cities and towns. In November 1938, through the efforts of the Izaak Walton League and other citizen groups, an initiative measure proposing the "Water Purification and Prevention of Pollution Bill" was placed on the election ballot. No arguments against the bill appeared in the official state *Voters Pamphlet.* The measure passed by a margin of 3 to 1. The act made it public policy to restore and maintain the natural purity of all the state's public waters. It authorized establishment of water quality standards and created a six-member State Sanitary Authority to develop a statewide control program and to enforce the new requirements.

The Sanitary Authority, organized in February 1939, decided as a first priority that the cities should be required to clean up their wastes. The authority determined that primary treatment and effluent chlorination would be sufficient to restore acceptable water quality. An important consideration in choosing this strategy, rather than one requiring higher levels of treatment, was the fact that several large multipurpose storage reservoirs were to be constructed by the Corps of Engineers on tributaries of the Willamette. These projects — authorized for flood control, hydroelectric power, irrigation, and navigation — would provide increased stream flows during the critical summer and fall months. Instead of natural low flows of 2,500 to 3,000 cubic feet a second at Salem, it was expected that a minimum flow of 6,000 cubic feet a second would be possible. The higher flows would provide a greater capacity to absorb wastes. The authority, therefore, directed the municipalities to construct primary treatment facilities.

World War II delayed the construction program. However, in 1944 Portland approved a $12 million bond issue to finance construction of necessary interceptor sewers to collect and carry wastes to a new primary treatment plant. After treatment the effluent was to be discharged into the Columbia River because its low summer flow was generally 40 times greater than the Willamette's. The first two municipal plants were completed in 1949. Portland's was placed in operation in 1951 and Salem's in 1952. By 1957 all cities on the Willamette had at least primary treatment. All construction costs were borne by the municipalities themselves.

In 1950, amid the improvements made in municipal sewage treatment, the Sanitary Authority faced a difficult problem. On the one hand, significant improvement in the Willamette's water quality depended on abatement by the mills. On the other hand, there appeared to be no available technology by which the mills could reasonably reduce the oxygen demand of their wastes.

The Sanitary Authority adopted what it saw as a stopgap solution. It formally ordered the five mills to halt, by July 1952, all discharges of concentrated sulfite waste effluents during the summer months of June through October. All the mills complied with the order. Three constructed storage lagoons in which their wastes were impounded during the summer months and released into the river during high-water periods. One mill at Willamette Falls was unable to find a site for an impoundment. It was granted permission to barge its wastes to the Columbia and release them into the larger river. The fifth mill changed to an ammonia-base sulfite process, which allowed the wastes to be concentrated by evaporation and spray drying for recovery of the solids as a salable by-product.

In 1953 and 1954 the two largest of the dams built by the Corps of Engineers began operating. The dams permitted a flow of between 5,000 and 6,000 cubic feet a second in the mid-1950s compared with the low flow of between 3,000 and 4,000 cubic feet a second in the 1940s.

The plan reexamined. In 1957 the Sanitary Authority assessed its original plan. Water quality was still poor. DO in Portland Harbor that summer was one part per million. Because of a tremendous increase in the sources of pollution since 1939 — particularly a 73-percent increase in the population served by public sewer systems and a 93-percent increase in industrial waste loads — water quality in the Willamette had not improved. It was clear that higher degrees of treatment were necessary. In early 1958 the Sanitary Authority initiated a new set of requirements.

The cities of Eugene, Salem, and Newberg were directed to install secondary treatment facilities. The growth in their populations was not the only reason for this action. There had developed in these areas a major fruit and vegetable processing industry, whose waste discharges coincided with the river's low-flow summer months. For the most part, this industry depended on municipal facilities for waste treatment services, thereby significantly increasing facility requirements.

The city of Portland was also lagging in its program to intercept discharges from its 65 outfalls. In 1959 the Sanitary Authority filed a lawsuit against the city council — one of the few times that the authority went to court during the entire course of the cleanup campaign. In 1960 the voters of the city approved an increase in the monthly public sewer charge sufficient to finance the completion of the interceptor project over a five-year period. In addition, the pulp and paper mills were directed to reduce their pollution discharges sufficiently to eliminate slime growths and sludge deposits and to maintain a minimum dissolved oxygen concentration of five parts per million. Finally, all municipalities downriver from Salem were directed to adopt secondary treatment.

Further actions. On the basis of an updated water quality evaluation, the Sanitary Authority issued even more stringent policies in 1964. All pulp and paper mills were ordered to adopt year-round primary treatment to remove settleable solids. The sulfite mills were directed to apply secondary treatment during the low-flow summer months, providing an 85-percent reduction in oxygen demand. In 1967 the secondary-treatment requirement was extended to cover the entire year. Secondary treatment for all other industries was also required, and the possibility was reserved of demanding still higher degrees of treatment in some cases.

This policy is still in effect. Secondary treatment is now universal in the Willamette Basin. The total oxygen demand of wastes has been reduced to one-fourth the 1957 level. Dissolved oxygen in Portland Harbor has remained above the standard of five parts per million every summer since 1969.

A living sign of the new health of the Willamette is the success the Chinook salmon have had in entering the river in autumn. Salmon had been successfully migrating upstream in the spring even during the 1940s and 1950s, because the pollution was not a hindrance given the high-water flow common at that time of the year. No autumn Chinook salmon run had existed on the Willamette due to low summer flows at Willamette Falls. Attempts to start autumn runs failed because of the extremely low DO levels in the lower river. But the situation has changed: Pollution has been abated, flows are higher, and a new fish ladder has been built at the falls. In 1965, 79 Chinooks were counted; in 1968, 4,040; in 1970, 7,460; and in 1972, 11,614. The outlook is for even larger numbers.

Evaluation

A series of factors was responsible for the success of the pollution control efforts in the Willamette Valley. First, the limited but steady progress made between 1939 and the 1960s set the stage for more comprehensive efforts. That the Sanitary Authority (now the Department of Environmental Quality) succeeded with limited resort to the courts is noteworthy. Without doubt the single major factor behind the cleanup of the Willamette was the strong concern of the people of Oregon. Citizen organizations worked hard for a cleaner river at all stages. The people of Oregon wanted "their river" cleaned up.

With broad public support, new state legislation was enacted in 1967 to strengthen the antipollution effort. The new law created a mandatory waste discharge permit program. This permit authority allowed the state to set legally enforceable limitations on the amount and concentration of wastes and to establish compliance schedules for each step in the cleanup process. The 1967 legislation also provided for state aid to local governments for sewage works construction and established a system of tax credits for industrial expenditures on pollution control.

The assumption by the federal government in 1965 of a stronger role in controlling water pollution was also important. Legislation enacted that year required each state to establish approved water quality standards for its interstate waters and to place industry and municipalities on schedules for building treatment facilities. The Willamette as far upstream as the falls was held to be interstate. In meeting the federal requirement, Oregon in 1967 reviewed and updated its water quality standards not only for the lower Willamette but for its other waters as well, and it was one of the first states to receive federal approval of its standards. The stronger role of the federal government was a spur, particularly for industry, which came to recognize that pollution control was inevitable and that the state of Oregon could deal firmly with industry without fear that jobs would be lost to another state. The federal government also gave financial assistance to municipalities for their waste treatment plants.

A final factor in the improvement of water quality was the achievement of a higher minimum flow through releases from the upstream reservoirs during the low-flow months.

Clearly, the cleanup effort was effective and the results all seem positive. Yet, further study of the Willamette River case shows that certain kinds of information necessary for broadly based evaluations and judgments are not available. For example, on the basis of the material presented in the case it is difficult to answer questions such as the following: What were the alternatives available to Oregon's public decision makers? What was the basis for their selection of alternatives in the cleanup? What were the costs involved in the cleanup? What was the overall benefit-cost situation in the Willamette Valley, and what was the incremental benefit-cost situation?

Given the obvious difficulty in measuring the benefits that accrued in cleaning up the river, perhaps the case involves more strictly a cost-effective approach. In that approach we can take as a given the fact that it was public policy to improve the environment. What then becomes important is the selection of the most economical and efficient way of cleaning up the river. In this case, however, and with this approach, still other important questions are posed as to the level of cleanup achieved in the valley overall. For instance, why were the pulp and paper mills directed to maintain a minimum dissolved oxygen concentration of five parts per million? Why not four? Or six? Also, how strict was the secondary treatment of wastes required of the municipalities downriver from Salem? And, finally, what was the cost to Oregon of the 11,614 Chinook salmon which ran in the Willamette in 1972?

7

regulation of energy

Energy is rapidly becoming one of the more regulated industries in the United States. Although the regulation of petroleum production goes back at least to the 1930s, it is only since the 1970s that the federal government has closely controlled price formation in oil and other petroleum products. Over 300,000 different companies are subject to federal energy regulatory requirements (see Table 7-1).

DEVELOPMENT OF ENERGY REGULATION

Federal subsidy of energy goes back at least to 1926, when Congress amended the Internal Revenue Code to provide that oil and gas producers receive tax-free 27.5 percent of the wellhead value of their oil and gas production. That is the system of "depletion allowances," which served to make oil production and exploration more profitable and also low priced. Subject to a limit of 50 percent of the net income from each property, the depletion allowance rules

Table 7-1   Number of firms subject to federal energy reporting and audit
requirements fiscal year 1977

Sector	Number of Firms
Importers (crude and product) other than refiners	600
Gathering systems between crude producers and refiners	200
Independent crude producers	15,000
Refiners (also some crude producers)	100
Natural gas liquids (propane/butane) (709 plants)	100
Wholesalers (resellers) other than propane	26,000
Retailers other than propane	268,000
Retailers of propane	8,000
Total	318,000

Source: Paul W. MacAvoy, ed., *Federal Energy Administration Regulation* (Washington,
D.C.: American Enterprise Institute, 1977), p. 40

remained in effect until 1969. In that year the Treasury Department
convinced Congress to reduce the percentage from 50 to 22. Subsequently, depletion allowances were phased out for the larger
companies.

In the 1930s the major oil-producing states introduced "prorationing." This limited the amount of oil that could be produced
domestically. It also raised prices, thus offsetting some of the results
of depletion allowances. Prorationing also led to domestic prices
being higher than world prices, thus contributing to rising imports of
foreign oil. To offset that effect, President Eisenhower in 1959,
via an administrative proclamation, introduced mandatory oil import
quotas. The quotas remained in effect until removed by President
Nixon in 1972.

Meanwhile, in 1954, the Federal Power Commission set wellhead prices for natural gas flowing into interstate commerce at levels
substantially below market prices. The FPC action encouraged more
domestic consumption of energy.

Thus, during the years of rapid economic growth that characterized much of the period following World War II, the United States
had available energy below world market prices. As a result of
government policy, therefore, this nation on balance consumed far
more oil and natural gas than would have been the case under a free
market situation.

The regulatory atmosphere began to change dramatically in the
1970s. In August, 1971 President Nixon imposed price controls on
the economy generally (exempting special sectors such as agriculture). In 1973-74 the controls were lifted on everything except

crude oil and petroleum products. Meanwhile, beginning in late 1973 and extending through part of 1974, the Organization of Petroleum Exporting Countries (OPEC) embargoed the shipment of oil to many nations, including the United States, and when it lifted the embargo, it quadrupled world oil prices. This situation led to the establishment of a Federal Energy Administration and a series of actions by the federal government to increase domestic energy supply and reduce demand. However, those efforts were restricted by pressures both to limit price increases to American consumers and to contain "windfall" profits on the part of American oil producers.

In December 1975 President Ford signed the Energy Policy and Conservation Act. The law provided for price controls on crude oil ranging from a low of $5.25 a barrel on "old" oil (oil from fields in operation in 1973) to $11.28 a barrel for "new" oil. At the time, the world price of oil delivered to the United States was $13.50 a barrel. Under this act refiners were required to make cost-equalizing payments to one another — so-called "entitlements." These resulted in each refiner paying the same average price for a barrel of oil, regardless of whether it was classified as "old" or "new," or whether it was produced domestically or imported. The average price established by the combination of price controls and entitlements was below the imported price. Each company importing foreign oil in effect receives a subsidy from American producers to cover the difference between the higher world price and the lower and controlled price. In May 1979 that subsidy came to $2.56 a barrel.

In the fall of 1977 Congress established a permanent Department of Energy, thus making it clear that federal intervention in this area of the economy was not a transient matter, limited only to short-term factors such as the OPEC embargo.

In November 1978 Congress passed a substantially modified version of President Carter's energy plan. The new law gave the President authority to phase out price controls on oil over an extended period of time. Under this approach, a growing proportion of oil from "old" wells could be sold at "new" prices. Thus, by December 1979 an "old" well producing 100 barrels of oil a day could sell 12 barrels at "new" prices; by December 1980 it could sell 54 barrels at the higher price. Moreover, the price of "new oil" is being phased up to the world price during the period January 1, 1980 to October 1, 1981.

As of May 1979, however, about 40 percent of domestic oil was subject to the "old oil" cap of about $6 and another 30 percent to a maximum of about $13. The world price was $15.80 a barrel at the time. The new law was more ambivalent on natural gas, extending price controls to cover previously exempt intrastate gas. In general, the 1978 act contained price escalation provisions which permitted increases only at the general rate of inflation. Three exceptions were provided: (a) new gas, (b) high-cost gas produced from depths of 15,000 feet or greater, and (c) small wells (so-called stripper well production). These latter categories were allowed additional price increases of 3½ to 4 percent a year.

The 1978 law provided partial decontrol of natural gas in the following manner: In November 1979 the price of new high-cost gas was decontrolled. Moreover, on January 1, 1985, three more categories are to be decontrolled, including gas produced from wells drilled after February 19, 1977, and at least two-and-a-half miles from the nearest existing well or at least 1,000 feet below the deepest well within two-and-a-half miles. On July 1, 1987, decontrol is provided for new wells from depths of 5,000 feet or less. The prices for all other categories of natural gas will continue to be controlled permanently. Table 7–2 shows the complexity of federal regulation of natural gas pricing.

Table 7-2   How Congress is decontrolling the price of natural gas

Type of Production	Price as of Jan. 1979 (per million BTUs)	Date of Deregulation
Stripper well	$2.24	Not deregulated
New outer continental shelf leases (after 4/20/77)	2.10	1/1/85
New onshore wells	2.10	1/1/85
New onshore reservoirs	2.10	1/1/85
Gas from reservoirs discovered after 7/26/76 on pre-4/20/77 shelf leases	2.10	Not deregulated
Production from below 15,000 feet from wells drilled after 2/19/77	2.10	Deregulated on effective date of FERC incremental pricing rule
Onshore — below 5,000 feet	1.98	1/1/85
Onshore — above 5,000 feet	1.98	1/1/87
Interstate commerce gas — before enactment — wells started 1/1/75–2/18/77	1.64	Not deregulated
Prudhoe Bay — Alaska gas or gas not otherwise covered	1.64	Not deregulated
Interstate commerce gas — before enactment — wells started 1/1/73–12/31/74		
Small producer	1.39	Not deregulated
Large producer	1.06	Not deregulated

(continued)

Table 7-2 (contd.)

Type of Production	Price as of Jan. 1979 (per million BTUs)	Date of Deregulation
Sales under "rollover" contracts — intrastate	1.00 or more	1/1/85 if > $1.00
Replacement contract or recompletion — small producer	.78	Not deregulated
Interstate rollover contracts — small producer	.72	Not deregulated
Interstate rollover contracts —large producer	.61	Not deregulated
Replacement contract or recompletion	.60	Not deregulated
Certain Permian Basin gas — small producer	.47	Not deregulated
Certain Rocky Mountain gas — small producer	.47	Not deregulated
Certain Permian Basin gas — large producer	.41	Not deregulated
Certain Rocky Mountain gas — large producer	.40	Not deregulated
Certain Appalachian Basin gas — north sub area — contract after 10/7/69	.37	Not deregulated
Other contracts	.35	Not deregulated
Minimum rate gas — all producers	.20	Not deregulated
Sold under existing intrastate contract	Contract price	1/1/85 if > $1.00; not deregulated if lower than $1.00

Source: Natural Gas Policy Act of 1978

IMPACTS OF ENERGY REGULATION

As in earlier periods, the political and economic crosscurrents tend to generate government energy policy which is internally inconsistent and which makes it difficult to achieve the national goal of reduced dependence on foreign sources. As former Secretary of the Treasury W. Michael Blumenthal stated in testimony to Congress in May 1979, "If ever a federal program deserved to be called a 'bureaucratic nightmare,' the regulation of U.S. oil prices has earned that distinction."

Price Regulations

What Secretary Blumenthal alluded to was the fact that since the OPEC-generated explosion of oil prices in 1973 the United States has been operating programs that encourage oil consumption and imports but discourage domestic oil production and the development of new energy sources. Although these policies were adopted in the name of protecting the consumer, they tend to have the opposite effect. The policies put upward pressure on world oil prices by discouraging investments in domestic oil production and in developing alternate energy sources, by enlarging the U.S. trade deficit and weakening the dollar, and by tightening world oil markets.[1]

Energy Economics

The basic economics of energy are straightforward. As pointed out by a variety of sources, including the Energy Policy Project of the Ford Foundation, people will tend to use more energy when it is cheaper and less when it is expensive. Conversely, those who produce energy will generally have greater incentive to produce more at higher prices than they will at lower prices. Changing prices provide signals to both producers and consumers of energy. The reaction to these signals may vary in speed and extent, but so long as they exist at all, they provide a basis for automatic market adjustment and permit the individual consumer and producer some freedom of choice in the process.

On occasion, this adjustment process may not be as rapid as we would like. On the demand side, consumers may own heavy "gas-guzzling" automobiles and houses with little insulation and large glass windows. Thus, the demand for energy may be relatively inelastic to price changes in the short run. Over the longer run, however, when equipment and energy-consuming habits can be modified more substantially, demand is more responsive to price.

On the supply side, too, the response to price movements may be relatively slow at first. Long lead times may be involved in developing new energy sources which become commercially attractive at higher prices. But those adjustments do occur and work to equilibrate the demand for and supply of energy.[2] Certainly, historical evidence shows that price increases do provide incentives for the development of energy supply. In Sutton and Edwards counties, Texas, total gas completions were raised from less than 10 to 240

---

[1] *Statement of the Honorable W. Michael Blumenthal, Secretary of the Treasury, before the Committee on Ways and Means* (Washington, D.C.: U.S. Treasury Department, 1979), pp. 4–5.
[2] *Exploring Energy Choices, A Preliminary Report of the Ford Foundation's Energy Policy Project* (Washington, D.C.: Ford Foundation, 1974), p. 12.

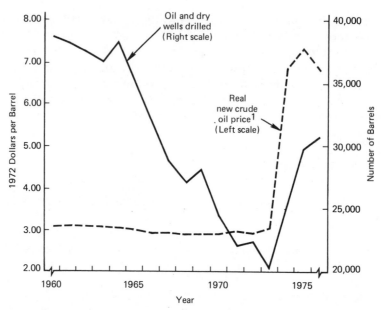

[1]Nominal price deflated by wholesale price index for finished goods.

Figure 7-1 NEW CRUDE OIL PRICES AND DRILLING ACTIVITY

Source: Department of Energy, Department of Labor, and American Petroleum Institute

in the period 1968 to 1974 while the price of natural gas rose from 14.0 cents per million cubic feet to $1.40 per million cubic feet. In eastern Ohio total gas completions rose from 200 to 1,400 during the same period.[3]

The aggregate pattern of supply response in terms of oil wells drilled is clearly shown in Figure 7-1. The number of wells drilled in the United States tended to decline while real prices of crude oil were static, and drilling activity expanded sharply when the real price level rose.

Effects of Regulations on Incentives

Other impacts of energy regulation are less dramatic but also contribute to high costs and economic inefficiency. One such example is the so-called Small Refiner's Bias included in the entitlements program. Under this special provision a refiner with a capacity less than 175,000 barrels a day is required to purchase proportion-

[3] James M. Collins and H. A. Merklein, "An Assessment of the Supply Effects of Natural Gas Deregulation," in *Energy Perspective*, ed. Milton R. Copulos (Washington, D.C.: Heritage Foundation, 1978), p. 38.

ately fewer entitlements and the large refiners proportionately more. Payments under the Small Refiners Bias amount to about $700 million a year. Approximately 140 refiners are classified as small, including some who make the *Fortune* list of the 500 largest industrial corporations.[4]

The Department of Energy also has established an Exceptional Relief Program to provide help to small refiners adversely affected by its regulations. A refiner may become eligible for such relief if the estimated profits are projected to fall below historical levels — regardless of the cause. Poor business decisions thus may be subsidized by the federal Treasury. Approximately 20 refiners receive benefits under the Exceptional Relief Program, estimated to total about $300 million a year. In one month the bias varied from 10 cents a barrel for refineries with 100,000 barrels a day to $1.81 for those refining 10,000 barrels a day or less. Not surprisingly, the number of small refiners has grown during the life of this program. Eighteen new refining companies have been created by "spinoffs" from individual refineries. Most of the 23 new refineries built have capacity of 50,000 barrels a day or less; the industry rule of thumb is that a refinery needs a capacity of about 175,000 barrels a day to be efficient, which is the level at which the small-refiner bias phases out. A task force of President Ford's Domestic Council concluded that the small-refiner bias encourages excessive use of small refineries and makes the petroleum industry less able to alter the product mix desired at the lowest possible cost achievable with economies of scale in refinery equipment.[5]

Federal energy regulations simultaneously have reduced the incentive to build large new refineries. This occurs because the price controls on product sales, unlike limits on crude oil, are imposed on sales margins. Thus, most cost increases can be passed on to the consumer on a dollar-for-dollar basis. A refiner who invests in new facilities can pass through the costs of interest on its borrowed funds and the cost of depreciation, but *not* a return on its investment. A refiner, therefore, cannot adjust product prices to maintain the rate of return it has been obtaining on its existing investments. Thus, the regulations withdraw the basic economic incentive to expand refining capacity.[6]

[4] John B. Boatwright, "Regulation of American Business: The Petroleum Industry" (lecture at Washington University, Center for the Study of American Business, February 8, 1979), p. 13.

[5] Paul W. MacAvoy, ed., *Federal Energy Administration Regulation* (Washington, D.C.: American Enterprise Institute, 1977), p. 66.

[6] Ibid., pp. 13–14. See also *Draft Environmental Impact Statement, Motor Gasoline Deregulation* (Washington, D.C.: U.S. Department of Energy, 1978), p. III-2.

The negative incentive to investment in new refineries has especially affected the production of unleaded gasoline, which requires more expensive processing than leaded gasoline. The demand for unleaded gasoline, which results in good measure from federal environmental regulations, has risen from 13 percent of total gasoline consumption in 1975 to 42 percent in 1979. This was precisely the period most seriously affected by the federal restrictions on refiners' profit margins. During that period the demand for unleaded gasoline frequently outstripped available supplies at prices prevailing under federal regulations.[7]

Other federal energy policies also have had negative consequences unanticipated by policymakers. In May 1979 the U.S. Department of Energy announced that it would provide a $5-a-barrel subsidy for imported heating and diesel oil to build up inventories that the department believed were at "unusually low levels." During the next few days the spot price for middle distillate oil (essentially heating or diesel fuel) rose from $45.47 to $51 a barrel, or more than the amount of the $5 subsidy. The energy commissioner of the European Common Market quickly issued a vigorous protest to the American ambassador, stating that the subsidy resulted in undesirable upward pressure on world oil prices.[8]

Many specialists in energy economics believe that probably no combination of domestic energy policies can reduce significantly the dependence of the United States economy on Middle Eastern oil before 1990. They doubt that new domestic energy sources — such as solar energy or synthetic fuel — will become available at prices lower than those established by OPEC. Thus, it appears that the United States is going to have to adjust to a relatively high volume of high-cost oil imports.[9] The longer that the prices of domestically produced oil and gas are kept below world market levels, the more difficult that adjustment will be, both because of the encouragement to consumption and the discouragement to alternative high-cost domestic energy sources.

Clearly, the lower the price of existing fuel sources is kept, the less attractive becomes the prospect of developing new domestic energy alternatives. To those concerned that rising energy prices will be inflationary, it should be noted that inflation is not curbed by holding down individual prices (the classic way to create a shortage).

---

[7] "Tank Queues," *The New Republic*, May 26, 1979, pp. 7–11.
[8] J. P. Smith, "Imported Heating Oil Subsidy Program Backfires," *Washington Post*, June 1, 1979, p. A–2.
[9] Lecture notes by Professor Arlon R. Tussing at the Brookings Institution, Washington D.C., January 28, 1976.

The basic method to reduce inflationary pressures is through appropriate macroeconomic policies, such as a moderate growth in the money supply and a reduction in the government's budget deficit.

Interaction with Environmental Regulations

The interrelationships between energy and environmental policies are numerous and significant. Virtually every new energy project has been delayed via such actions as challenges to the environmental impact statement (EIS) or legal disputes over the process through which the cognizant federal agency has considered the environmental aspects. One major study of the effects of the EIS described it as an instrument of "legal and political warfare." The authors concluded, "There can be no doubt that a major effect of the EIS requirement has been to give environmental groups a legal and political instrument to cancel, delay, or modify development projects that they oppose."[10] (See appendix to this chapter on the Kaiparowits case for an example of an energy project which was canceled during the lengthy review process.)

A task force of the President's Energy Resources Council analyzed the regulatory problems that would be faced in developing a domestic synthetic fuel industry. They specifically evaluated the effects of the environmental impact statements (EIS) required by the National Environmental Policy Act of 1969 (NEPA). The task force stated:

> . . . the major uncertainty under NEPA is not whether or not the project will be allowed to proceed, but rather the length of time it will be delayed pending the issuance of an EIS that will stand up in court. The cost of such delays (construction financing and inflated raw materials and labor costs) is an obvious potential hazard to any synfuels project. . . .
>
> In summary, the cost and delay occasioned by NEPA constitute a substantial disincentive, aggravated by the fact that in dealing with new processes it is very hard to anticipate what the EIS requirements will be and on what grounds the EIS may be attacked. The general guidelines offered by the Council on Environmental Quality (40 CFR Part 1500) provide a drafting framework but no assurance of compliance.

The Presidential Task Force also identified 14 major regulatory

---

[10] Eugene Bardach and Lucian Pugliaresi, "The Environmental Impact Statement vs. The Real World," *Public Interest*, Fall 1977, p. 23.

constraints which would be faced in developing a new synthetic fuel project:

- Preparing an environmental impact statement, as required by the National Environmental Policy Act of 1969.
- Meeting new source performance standards for air quality, under the Clean Air Act Amendments of 1970.
- Meeting the hazardous pollutant emission standards, under the Clean Air Act Amendments of 1970.
- Meeting the state air-quality implementation plans required by the Clean Air Act Amendments of 1970.
- Obtaining necessary point source discharge permits, under the Water Pollution Control Act Amendments of 1972.
- Meeting state water quality standards and water quality management plans, as promulgated under the Water Pollution Control Act Amendments of 1972.
- Complying with limitations applicable to "underground injections," under the Safe Drinking Water Act of 1974.
- Complying with the regulation of interstate pipeline transmissions, under the Interstate Commerce Act.
- Complying with the prohibition against a carrier transporting its own products, under the Interstate Commerce Act.
- Complying with the allocation of railroad cars transporting coal, under the Interstate Commerce Act.
- Complying with the regulation of interstate transmission of synthetic gas once it is mixed with natural gas, under the Natural Gas Act.
- Obtaining necessary plant and mine leases, from the U.S. Bureau of Land Management.
- Obtaining necessary water allocations, from the U.S. Bureau of Reclamation.
- Complying with the Coal Mine Health and Safety Act of 1969.

The task force's conclusion is noteworthy: "In summary, some of these requirements could easily hold up or permanently postpone any attempt to build and operate a synthetic fuels plant."[11]

Interaction with Other Regulatory Programs

Although petroleum and natural gas are the two major types of energy currently available in the United States, other sources are or can become available. Conventional supplies include coal and atomic energy. Unconventional or potential new energy sources range from solar to shale oil to synthetic fuel from coal gasification. As it turns

[11] President's Energy Resources Council, Synfuels Interagency Task Force, *Recommendations for a Synthetic Fuels Commercialization Program*, vol. 1, (Washington, D.C.: U.S. Government Printing Office, 1975), p. 134.

out, regulatory requirements, directly or indirectly, are major obstacles to the development of these alternate supplies.

The United States possesses a great abundance of coal, yet numerous regulations inhibit the production and use of it. The passage of the Coal Mine Health and Safety Act of 1969 provides a dramatic example. In 1969 coal production averaged 19.9 tons per man per day; this figure had been rising steadily in the preceding seven years. By 1976, however, seven years after the new law, coal production averaged only 13.6 tons per man, a 32-percent decline. There is widespread agreement that the basic cause of this drop in productivity was the changes in mining procedures made by the coal companies to comply with the 1969 legislation.[12] Strip mining, moreover, is now closely circumscribed by the rules promulgated under the Surface Mining Control and Reclamation Act. But the greatest restrictions on coal arise from the operations of the Clean Air Act, which limits severely the use of coal.

Nuclear power plants, in contrast, are subject primarily to the jurisdiction of the Nuclear Regulatory Commission. The NRC issues licenses for all civilian reactors, nuclear fuel storage facilities, and radioactive waste disposal, and it regulates their siting, construction, operation, and security. However, other government agencies also have jurisdiction over aspects of nuclear power, especially federal, state, and local environmental and safety authorities.

A number of citizen groups have utilized the review processes of the various regulatory agencies to delay most new nuclear projects. The Clamshell Alliance, in successfully opposing the nuclear power plant at Seabrook, New Hampshire, issued a Declaration of Nuclear Resistance, which stated that "the supply of energy is a natural right and should in all cases be controlled by the people. Private monopoly must give way to public control."[13] Clearly, the issue raised goes beyond the question of nuclear power and illustrates some of the difficulties involved in the development of energy by the private sector. An analysis of the Seabrook case yielded a conclusion which goes far beyond questions of technological feasibility and operational safety:

> The current uncertainty which surrounds the nuclear licensing process is a major factor contributing to the deferral of many utilities' decisions to

[12] Edward F. Denison, "Effects of Selected Changes in the Institutional and Human Environment upon Output per Unit of Input," *Survey of Current Business* (January 1978).

[13] Quoted in Milton R. Copulos, *Confrontation at Seabrook* (Washington, D.C.: Heritage Foundation, 1978), p. 39.

build such facilities. Due to the lead time necessary for planning bulk power facilities and the vast amounts of capital involved, it is not surprising that utilities are increasingly apprehensive about making a commitment to a nuclear plant as long as there is no certainty that it will ever be licensed.[14]

The availability of new, unconventional energy sources is also influenced by governmental regulatory activity, though the impacts may be more indirect. Many observers are concerned that in the absence of special government assistance automatic market forces will not be strong enough to stimulate production of substitutes in sufficient quantities before the supplies of petroleum and natural gas are exhausted.

There are strong reasons, however, to believe that the feared hiatus between the exhaustion of fossil fuels and the commercialization of more exotic fuels will not occur. For example, Professor W. N. Peach of the University of Oklahoma reminds us that a century and a quarter ago the world was worried about running out of trees (then used for both construction and fuel). Coal production at the time was low. But coal quickly became the major source of inanimate energy for most of the world until about the middle of the twentieth century.[15] During that period there were also times when engineers and geologists lamented the catastrophes that would follow the imminent exhaustion of coal.[16]

Historically, the notion of absolute resource exhaustion is difficult to support. The typical pattern has not been to "run out" of any specific resource but for market forces to shift demand to substitutes. The original resource continues to be available, typically at a lower level and higher price. The first American switch from exhaustible resources to synthetic fuels and back to exhaustible resources occurred in the nineteenth century. In 1800 illumination in America was provided mainly by candles and oil lamps, the fuel for the latter coming from whale oil. The gradual exhaustion of whale oil caused prices to soar, from a low of 23¢ a gallon in 1832 to $1.45 in 1865.[17]

As prices increased, consumers switched to substitutes such as coal gas, camphene distilled from vegetable oils, and lard oil. In the

[14] Ibid., p. 44.
[15] W. N. Peach, *The Energy Outlook for the 1980s, Joint Economic Committee Print* (Washington, D.C.: U.S. Government Printing Office, 1973), p. 9.
[16] C. Robinson, *The Energy "Crisis" and British Coal*, Hobart Paper no. 59 (London: Institute of Economic Affairs, 1974).
[17] W. Phillip Gramm, "Energy Crisis in Perspective," *Wall Street Journal*, November 30, 1973, p. 8.

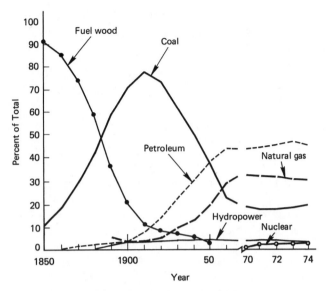

Figure 7-2 ENERGY SOURCES IN THE UNITED STATES,
1850-1974

Source: U.S., Congress, House, Committee on Interstate and Foreign Commerce, *Basic Energy Data,* 94th Congress, 1st session, 1975, p. 87

1850s coal oil (kerosene) came to dominate the residential market for illumination.[18] The success of coal oil, however, was followed by its equally meteoric decline. This abrupt shift occurred as the result of competition from a new fuel that had appeared on the market: crude oil (petroleum), discovered in 1859. As crude oil production swelled, its price fell, from $18 to $20 a barrel in early 1860 to 10¢ a barrel in late 1861. By 1863 virtually all coal oil refineries had shifted to crude oil refining, and much new refining capacity appeared.

Thus the innovations leading to the development of camphene, lard oil, coal gas, coal oil, and eventually crude oil resulted from an increase in the price of the basic source of illumination, whale oil. As shown in Figure 7-2, there have been frequent shifts in the course of American history in the relative importance of different fuels. The implications for current policy would seem to be clear: The sooner government frees conventional energy sources from artificial price restraints, the sooner will new unconventional energy sources become commercially competitive. Conversely, the continuation of price controls on petroleum and natural gas will delay the time when solar

[18] Harold F. Williamson and Arnold R. Daum, *The American Petroleum Industry: The Age of Illumination, 1859-1899* (Chicago: Northwestern University Press, 1959), p. 13.

energy or synthetic fuels will come into widespread use without government subsidies—to offset the negative influence of government regulation![19]

APPENDIX: THE KAIPAROWITS POWER PROJECT CASE*

In April 1976 a consortium of western electric utilities abandoned plans to build a coal-fired power plant on the Kaiparowits Plateau in southern Utah. This decision came thirteen years after the companies first joined in the project, during which time numerous delays in the siting, planning, and building of the plant increased construction costs sevenfold—from $500 million in 1962 (for a 5,000-megawatt plant) to $3.5 billion in 1975 (for a 3,000-megawatt plant). Construction of the plant was supported by the state government of Utah and by residents in the southern part of the state; it was opposed by environmental groups.

Background

The Kaiparowits Plateau, whose name derives from a Paiute Indian word meaning "mountain of many people," is a massive, dun-colored mesa situated in an unpopulated area in the middle of southern Utah near the Arizona state line. Deep canyons formed by wind and water erosion slash through rolling terrain which is covered with hardy desert vegetation. The plateau is surrounded by numerous national recreation areas and national monuments: Zion National Park, Bryce Canyon National Park, Capitol Reef and Canyonlands National Parks, and the Glen Canyon National Recreation Area (which includes Lake Powell). Further south, in Arizona, are the Marble Canyon and Grand Canyon National Parks.

---

[19] Murray L. Weidenbaum and Reno Harnish, *Government Credit Subsidies for Energy Development* (Washington, D.C.: American Enterprise Institute, 1976), pp. 4–8.

*The details of this case are drawn primarily from William R. Gould, "The Kaiparowits Decision," *Electric Perspectives* (April 1976), pp. 12–18. Other sources include James M. Rock, "No Boomtown on the Kaiparowits Plateau: Who Made the Decision and Why?" *Intellect*, (February 1977), pp. 248–50; "Defeat for Kaiparowits," *Time*, April 26, 1976, p. 39; John L. Dotson, Jr., "Duel in the Sun," *Newsweek*, October 27, 1975, p. 10; "The Power Plant War on a Utah Plateau," *Business Week*, January 19, 1976, p. 22.

Kane County, Utah, the site of the Kaiparowits Plateau, is about twice the size of Delaware. It was originally settled by Mormons, who were the first to discover and use the vast deposits of coal which lay exposed in steep canyon walls. Since the 1930s Kane County has been losing population; in 1970 the figure stood at 2,421. In 1976 the county had the lowest average wage rate in Utah. Unemployment rates in the southern part of the state ranged between 10 and 15 percent in the mid-1970s.

In 1931 a geologist reported to the U.S. Geological Survey the coal deposits from which the Mormons had already been picking by hand. Subsequent drilling and surveying revealed the existence of approximately 500 million tons of low-sulfur, recoverable coal. It has been estimated that this amount of fuel could power a large, modern steam-electric generating station for 35 to 40 years.

The Power Companies

In late 1962 and early 1963, following issuance of coal prospecting permits, a group of western utility companies entered into an agreement for the Kaiparowits Coal Project. Southern California Edison, the project manager, had 40 percent interest; San Diego Gas and Electric had 23.4 percent; Arizona Public Service had 18 percent; and the Salt River Project had 10 percent. Remaining interest was unsold.

The utilities favored the project for several reasons. At the time, new electric generating capacity could not be added to the South Coastal Air Basin of California. The supply of coal in Utah, in contrast to projected supplies of oil and natural gas, was reliable. While construction costs of the facility in the mid-1960s ($500 million for a 5,000-megawatt plant) were high, the fuel cost was low. Cooling water for the station was also readily available in Utah.

The companies' first action on the project was to secure water rights to Lake Powell and the Colorado River. After meetings with Utah's water conservators and after public hearings, they were authorized to withdraw 102,000 acre-feet of water a year. From the filing date to the time of authorization, 21 months elapsed. Plans for the project were made public in 1965: Kaiparowits would be the nation's largest coal-fired generation facility, and its total construction time would be a period of 10 years. Electricity would be transmitted along 1,500 miles of overhead cable to cities such as Los Angeles, San Diego, and Phoenix.

Utah's governor was enthusiastic about the project, since it would mean an end to economic hardship in southern Utah. A town of nearly 15,000 people would be created at Kaiparowits, and the state would benefit from the creation of 3,000 jobs, payrolls of approximately $100 million, and tax revenues estimated at $28 million a year.

But because the Colorado's water came under federal jurisdiction, application for its use had to be made to the U.S. Department of the Interior. The utilities did so in 1965. At that point, construction for the plant was scheduled to begin in 1970, with the first power to be produced in 1975.

A year later the Secretary of the Interior announced he would grant water rights if the federal government retained control over the Colorado's flow, in order to ensure water supplies to downstream users. The state of Utah argued it could allocate water as it pleased. Negotiations continued for three years, until a new Secretary of Interior granted the water rights in 1969. At this point, the utilities had to ask the state of Utah for an extension of the water rights to 1975, and this was granted.

During this time, inflation had driven the project's cost upward from $500 million for the 5,000-megawatt plant to $750 million for a 3,000-megawatt plant. Equipment and labor costs were rising — but so were the prices of fuels other than coal. The utilities still considered the project feasible. In fact, they began to participate with other energy companies in plans to build other coal-fired generators at Four Corners, New Mexico, and at the Navajo Plant near Page, Arizona.

The Kaiparowits group authorized the Bechtel Corporation in 1969 to review work on the project, to drill and define coal deposits more exactly, and to collect environmental data. In 1970, however, the Interior Department announced a delay on all decisions on further power plant construction until a task force had studied all factors involved in energy development in the Southwest. This action in effect placed a one-year moratorium on the Kaiparowits Project. Each further month of delay in project approvals was now costing the utilities an estimated $6 million.

The Interior Department and Environmentalists

In August 1965 the president of the Sierra Club attacked the proposed building of dams on the Colorado River, indicating that coal plants on the Kaiparowits Plateau would produce electric power for half the price of power generated by dams. But in 1970 the same organization sought an injunction that would bar federal cooperation with power plant developments in the Southwest until the Interior

Department would agree to comply with the provisions of the National Environmental Policy Act of 1969. This act required the filing of environmental impact statements for projects having major ecological effects. A U.S. District Court judge dismissed the Sierra Club suit in early 1972.

In 1971 the U.S. Senate began public hearings on power generating projects in the Southwest. The outcome was a two-year study which concluded there was no alternative to the construction of some coal-fired plants to meet growing energy needs, but it left the final decision regarding their construction to the Interior Department. The utilities were satisfied with these findings and had already begun studies on engineering and environmental impacts.

The first environmental report on the Kaiparowits Project was one month away from submission when the Interior Secretary denied project applications for environmental reasons. Engineering work stopped on June 14, 1973. Eventually, however, the Secretary reconsidered the report. A siting study conducted by the participants in the project suggested moving the plant from its original site on the plateau, Nipple Bench, near Lake Powell, to Four Mile Bench, 15 miles further north. This site selection was based on a variety of economic, engineering, and environmental concerns. The move to the new location would cost the project $131 million.

In December 1973 the Interior Department accepted the renewed applications for the project and directed its Bureau of Land Management (BLM) to conduct new environmental reviews for the site relocation. The utilities proceeded with preliminary engineering studies. The estimated cost of the project had now more than tripled ($1.7 billion) and generating capacity had been reduced to 3,000 megawatts. At this time the Arab oil embargo had inflated the cost of low-sulfur fuel oil to nearly eight times its pre-1970 price. Coal-fired electric power still seemed to be a good alternative.

Engineering plans for Kaiparowits included the latest equipment in emissions control. It would remove 99.5 percent of particulates and 90 percent of sulfur dioxide in the emissions. The Southwest Energy Study had contemplated only 20-percent removal of the latter pollutant when the Interior Secretary had turned down the project. The mining of coal would be accomplished through use of deep underground mines, not strip pits, located very near the plant itself. The coal conveyor system would be covered, and dust would be suppressed.

Plans for a new community of 13,000 to 14,000 people were being made in cooperation with local, county, state, and federal governments. A permanent community rather than a trailer town was being provided for. At the same time, plans were being made for a school for miners in order to employ many of southern Utah's unemployed. The city would be the largest population center between Provo, Utah, and Flagstaff, Arizona.

In mid-1975 the Salt River Project withdrew its 10-percent interest in the Kaiparowits Project after reviewing its generating resources options. Talks with potential new partners began, but costs for Kaiparowits by September 1975 had reached $3.5 billion.

Environmental Impacts

The Bureau of Land Management's draft of the required environmental impact statement (EIS) was submitted to the Council on Environmental Quality in 1975, four months later than expected. It suggested that although 12.2 tons of soot, 34.3 tons of sulfur dioxide, and 250 tons of nitrogen dioxide would be emitted into the air daily from Kaiparowits, visibility would be only "minimally affected." These data would appear to be consistent with the utilities' claim that, even under worst-case conditions, the plant would generate less than 17 percent of the pollution allowed under the strictest regulations then in force. On the other hand, the same EIS predicted that plant and animal life in the area would be reduced and, over a long period, sport fishing would be jeopardized in the 186-mile-long Lake Powell.

Public hearings on the draft EIS began in September 1975 in five western cities to receive public comment. The utilities were not encouraged to participate in the hearings. Critics of the project were concerned about increased water salinity in the lower Colorado River Basin, "people pollution" in southern Utah caused by the proposed new city, and the impact of more energy coming to southern California — hence causing more people and more pollution.

Environmental organizations requested and received a 45-day extension on the hearings to review the EIS. During the following two months nine legal motions, petitions, and protests were filed against the project. These included two major actions. The Escalante Wilderness Committee in Utah, supported by the Sierra Club and the Environmental Defense Fund, asked the Utah state engineer to continue hearings on an extension of water rights for Kaiparowits and asked for a delay on this matter until Utah had adopted a state water-use plan. Also, the Sierra Club petitioned the California Public Utilities Commission to issue an order compelling Southern California Edison and San Diego Gas and Electric to obtain a certificate of public convenience and necessity prior to commencing construction for the project. This action was intended to give the California commission jurisdiction over the generating station in Utah.

The utilities at this time were on the verge of committing large amounts of money for plant equipment, including $600 million for environmental controls. But on December 30, 1975, they called a one-year halt to any further financial outlays, although they stated that they would continue to seek the necessary government approvals for the Kaiparowits Project.

In March 1976 the National Park Service reported that mercury emissions from Kaiparowits into Lake Powell would cause adverse effects on the game fishery there. It also stated that air pollution from the plant would cause an aesthetic intrusion and substantially reduce visitor appreciation of scenic resources within 60 miles of the plant site. Also in March the actor Robert Redford appeared on the CBS television program "60 Minutes" and argued, on the part of the Environmental Defense Fund, for the preservation of the wilderness area in southern Utah. Utility spokesmen also appeared on the program. Lawsuits were proposed in early 1976 by environmental groups, in the event of the project's approval, as a means of bringing on further delays.

During 1976 the Environmental Protection Agency said it would advise the Secretary of the Interior to reject the project, stating that the utilities had failed to document a need for the electric power. Meanwhile, Congress was considering revisions of the 1970 Clean Air Act, which could have placed tighter restrictions on air emissions. The Interior Secretary announced he would visit the site on April 21, 1976, and that he would make public his decision the following week.

Abandoning the Project

On April 14, 1976, the utility companies assessed their situation and informed the Secretary and the governor of Utah that they had decided to abandon the Kaiparowits Power Project. This information was leaked to the press, and government officials accused the companies of a lack of faith in the way the announcement was made. The companies gave as reasons for their decision delays in regulatory approval, excessive project costs, and uncertainty about future legal and regulatory developments. They estimated that between 1963 and 1976 $20 million had been expended on a project that had never actually gotten underway.

The following weekend, a Utah group, the American League for Industry and Vital Energy (ALIVE), burned in effigy Robert Redford, other environmentalists, politicians, and government officials. Southern Utah residents voiced concern over economic hardship and the belief that benefits from industry would outweigh any damages. The director of the Sierra Club stated that Kaiparowits was a project undertaken at the wrong time and in the wrong place.

Chronology of Events

1963 • Participants enter into project agreement.
1965 • After twenty-one months of study, Utah grants water rights to project; but, Interior Department requires review, too, before final approval can be granted.
1969 • Interior Department approves use of Colorado River water.
• Bechtel Corporation to review project work, determine coal reserves, and begin collecting environmental data.
1970 • Interior Department study of energy developments in Southwest will halt project planning for one year.
1971 • Senate opens hearings on power projects in Southwest. Outcome: two-year study that finds need for some coal-fired plants, but leaves ultimate decisions on construction to Interior Department.
1973 • Project group submits first environmental report to Interior Department.
1975 • In July, Bureau of Land Management completes draft version of environmental impact statement on Kaiparowits Project. In September public hearings on EIS begin.
• Several legal motions, petitions, and protests are filed against the project.
• Salt River Project withdraws as participant.
• National Park Service to conduct three-month environmental impact study.
• Participants call for one-year halt to new financing.
1976 • Bureau of Land Management completes final EIS.
• Congress considering tighter provisions for 1970 Clean Air Act.
• In April participants vote to abandon Kaiparowits Project.

Cost Projections versus Time

1962 $500 million for 5,000-megawatt plant
1969 $750 million for 3,000-megawatt plant
1973 $1.7 billion for 3,000-megawatt plant
1975 $3.5 billion for 3,000-megawatt plant ($600 million of this sum was projected for plant environmental controls, alone)
1961-1976 $20 million expended by participants over entire life of project.

Evaluation

Over a total of fifteen years (1961 to 1976) in which the western electric utilities planned and developed the Kaiparowits project, five groups were involved: the utilities themselves, the state government of Utah, the people of southern Utah, a variety of environmentalists, and federal agencies. It may be seen that the first three of these formed a group aligned in an opposition of sorts to the last two.

This group classification is illustrative because it points to major reasons for the eventual abandonment of the project. On the one hand, the utilities were concerned with safe and efficient generation of coal-fired power for a large area of the Southwest over a long term; the government of Utah and much of the population of the southern part of the state were interested in revitalizing the depressed economy of that region and relieving unemployment. On the other hand, environmental groups were concerned with the project's overall environmental impacts on a wilderness area which contains a host of public recreation areas; the Interior Department, in conjunction with the National Park Service and the Environmental Protection Agency, was concerned with these same environmental issues and with maintaining standards for air quality, water quality, and natural resources.

The opposition brought about regulatory delays almost from the start of the project. These delays were increased in number and exacerbated by tactical actions taken by private environmental groups. Assertions made by the National Park Service and the environmentalists about air quality impacts appear to have conflicted with both the findings of Interior's EIS and the engineering data of the utilities. These disagreements led to a further round of delays. Meanwhile, inflation drove up project costs with each passing year until the utilities, responsible both to shareholders and power rate payers, found Kaiparowits no longer financially viable. In the end, after the project was cancelled, the opposition led to considerable hostility and bitterness on the part of the southern Utah population against environmentalists (who felt they had scored a victory) and government officials (who were responding in large part both to environmentalists and government regulations).

A variety of important issues was at stake in the controversy: (1) the need for more electric power in the Southwest, considered especially in the light of demands for fuels other than coal and the rise in costs of those other fuels; (2) the desire for an economic revitalization of southern Utah through jobs and revenues created by the electric plant; (3) the desire to preserve a large wilderness and recreation area and protect it from forms of pollution; (4) the data about levels of pollution to be caused by the plant—with estimates provided by the utilities, the Department of the Interior, and the National Park Service; (5) the resource management (mining of coal) by the utilities and its proposed impacts; (6) the strategy of delays used by environmental groups and the impacts of those delays; (7) the effect of inflation on project costs over a 13-to-15-year period; and (8) the questions concerning the transmission of power generated in Utah to adjoining states.

As for the first of these issues, the 1979 annual report of Southern California Edison projected that 650,000 new customers would be added to its power system in the years 1979 to 1989. It is possible, therefore, in light of the continued increases in the cost of alternative power sources, that the electricity that could be generated by the coal at the Kaiparowits site could become both necessary and economically competitive sooner rather than later.

Alternatively, should the California utilities, having abandoned the Kaiparowits Project, find it necessary to build more nuclear power plants to meet energy needs, such a move would probably also be opposed by environmental groups.

8 ‖

regulation of
personnel practices

In a great variety of ways federal legislation influences the hiring, pay, promotion, firing, pension plans, and other personnel practices of private industry. Regulation of work force policies affects a wide spectrum of business operations.

Affirmative action programs are the most conspicuous and, in recent years, most controversial government influences on company personnel policies. These federal programs are directed by two major government agencies: the Department of Labor and the Equal Employment Opportunity Commission. In addition, many other agencies, ranging from the Internal Revenue Service to the National Labor Relations Board to the Pension Benefit Guarantee Corporation, play important parts in the setting and enforcement of work force regulations. In the broad picture, the personnel area is a key example of the public's unwillingness to accept the impacts on society that result from the unregulated workings of the free market.

Government responsibility for ending job discrimination rests primarily with two federal agencies — the Equal Employment Opportunity Commission (EEOC) and the Office of Federal Contract Compliance (OFCC) in the Labor Department. Table 8-1 indicates how these government units go about enforcing federal antidiscrimination laws and directives.

The most familiar of these agencies, the EEOC, was created by Title VII of the Civil Rights Act of 1964 to prohibit job discrimination on the bases of race, color, religion, sex, or national origin in all employment practices, including hiring, firing, layoffs, promotion, wages, training, disciplinary actions, and other terms, privileges, conditions, or benefits of employment. Those covered by the act are firms and labor unions with 15 or more members, joint labor-management committees for apprenticeship and training, employment agencies, educational institutions, and state and local governments.[1] In July 1979 President Carter transferred from the Labor Department to EEOC the responsibility for enforcing the Equal Pay Act and the Age Discrimination in Employment Act.

EEOC conducts its enforcement through the following procedure: A person who believes that he or she has been discriminated against files a charge of discrimination (see fig. 8-1). After receipt of the charge, EEOC investigates it to determine if sufficient evidence of discrimination exists. If so, EEOC tries to persuade the employer to remedy the situation voluntarily. If the conciliation attempts fail, the EEOC files suit in federal court. In the words of the commission, "Court ordered compliance with Title VII often results in large expenses to the employer, usually exceeding the cost of effective voluntary affirmative action. Widespread voluntary compliance is by far the most desirable method for eliminating job discrimination."[2] Expensive settlements are at least partly a result of the retroactive liability of the employer. Companies are held liable for back pay for two years prior to the filing of the charge, and if two additional years were required to settle the case, the employer would be liable for four years' back pay.

Aside from the significant legal influence of its enabling legislation, the commission's power is also exemplified by its growing budget and staff. The federal budget for fiscal year 1970 allocated

[1] *EEOC at a Glance* (Washington, D.C.: U.S. Equal Employment Opportunity Commission, 1974), p. 1.
[2] Ibid., p. 2.

Table 8-1   U.S. laws against job discrimination

Executive Orders 11246 and 11375, Vietnam Veterans Readjustment Act, and the Rehabilitation Act	Title VII of the Civil Rights Act of 1964 as Amended by Equal Employment Opportunity Act of 1972	Equal Pay Act of 1963 as Amended by the Education Amendments of 1972 (Higher Education Act)
Which employers are covered?		
All employers with federal contracts over $10,000.	All employers with 15 or more employees.	Most employers.
What is prohibited?		
Discrimination in hiring, upgrading, salaries, fringe benefits, training, and other conditions of employment, on the basis of race, sex, color, religion, or national origin.		Discrimination in salaries (including most fringe benefits).
Who enforces the provisions?		
Office of Federal Contract Compliance (OFCC) of the Labor Dept.	Equal Employment Opportunity Commission (EEOC).	Equal Employment Opportunity Commission (EEOC).
How is a complaint made?		
By letter to OFCC.	By a sworn complaint form, obtainable from EEOC.	
Who can make a complaint?		
Individuals or organizations on own behalf or on behalf of aggrieved individual(s). In the case of the EEOC, members of the commission may also file charges.		
Can investigations be made without complaints?		
Yes.	No.	Yes.
Can the entire establishment be reviewed?		
Yes.	Yes.	Yes.
Record-keeping requirements and government access		
Employer must keep and preserve specified records relevant to the determination of whether violations have occurred. Government is empowered to review all relevant records.		
Enforcement power and sanctions		
Government may delay new contracts, revoke current contracts, and debar employers from eligibility for future contracts.	If attempts at conciliation fail, EEOC or the U.S. Attorney General may file suit. Aggrieved individuals may also sue. Court may enjoin respondent from engaging in unlawful behavior, order appropriate affirmative action, or order reinstatement of employees and award back pay.	
Is harassment prohibited?		
Employers are prohibited from discharging or discriminating against any person because he/she has made a complaint, assisted with an investigation, or instituted proceedings.		

(continued)

Table 8-1 (contd.)

Executive Orders 11246 and 11375, Vietnam Veterans Readjustment Act, and the Rehabilitation Act	Title VII of the Civil Rights Act of 1964 as Amended by Equal Employment Opportunity Act of 1972	Equal Pay Act of 1963 as Amended by the Education Amendments of 1972 (Higher Education Act)
	Notification of complaints	
Notification of complaints has been erratic in the past.	EEOC notifies employers of complaints within 10 days.	
	Confidentiality of names	
Individual complainant's name is usually given to the employer. Investigation findings are kept confidential by the government but can be revealed by the employer. Policy on government disclosure of investigations and complaints has not yet been issued. Aggrieved party and respondent are not bound by the confidentiality requirement.	Individual complainant's name is divulged when an investigation is made. Charges are not made public by EEOC, nor can any of its efforts during the conciliation process be made public by EEOC or its employees. If court action becomes necessary, the identity of the parties involved becomes a matter of public record. The aggrieved party and respondent are not bound by the confidentiality requirement.	

approximately $12 million to the EEOC; the 1980 budget contained an appropriation of $124 million, or ten times the earlier level of support. In 1980 EEOC employed 3,600 people in 22 district and 37 area offices — as compared with a total staff of 780 in 1970.

The Labor Department's Office of Federal Contract Compliance (OFCC) examines the antidiscrimination programs of companies with federal government contracts of $50,000 or more and 50 or more employees. These companies must have affirmative action plans listing the specific goals and timetables for the hiring of women and minorities. Even if only one division of a company has a government contract of $50,000 or more, the entire firm must participate in the required affirmative action program. The agency's jurisdiction was broadened by the Vietnam Veterans Readjustment Act and the Rehabilitation Act Amendments of 1973.

The OFCC indirectly provides incentives as well as punishments to government contractors. Robert L. Malcolm, vice-president of Rockwell International Corporation, contends that Rockwell's

(PLEASE PRINT OR TYPE)

CHARGE OF DISCRIMINATION	EEOC CHARGE NO.	FORM APPROVED OMB NO. 124-R0001

INSTRUCTIONS

If you have a complaint, fill in this form and mail it to the Equal Employment Opportunity Commission's District Office in your area. In most cases, a charge must be filed with the EEOC within a specified time after the discriminatory act took place. IT IS THEREFORE IMPORTANT TO FILE YOUR CHARGE AS SOON AS POSSIBLE. *(Attach extra sheets of paper if necessary.)*

CAUSE OF DISCRIMINATION

☐ RACE OR COLOR ☐ SEX
☐ RELIGIOUS CREED
☐ NATIONAL ORIGIN

NAME *(Indicate Mr. or Ms.)* — DATE OF BIRTH

STREET ADDRESS — COUNTY — SOCIAL SECURITY NO.

CITY, STATE, AND ZIP CODE — TELEPHONE NO. *(Include area code)*

THE FOLLOWING PERSON ALWAYS KNOWS WHERE TO CONTACT ME

NAME *(Indicate Mr. or Ms.)* — TELEPHONE NO. *(Include area code)*

STREET ADDRESS — CITY, STATE, AND ZIP CODE

LIST THE EMPLOYER, LABOR ORGANIZATION, EMPLOYMENT AGENCY, APPRENTICESHIP COMMITTEE, STATE OR LOCAL GOVERNMENT WHO DISCRIMINATED AGAINST YOU *(If more than one, list all)*

NAME — TELEPHONE NO. *(Include area code)*

STREET ADDRESS — CITY, STATE, AND ZIP CODE

OTHERS WHO DISCRIMINATED AGAINST YOU *(If any)*

CHARGE FILED WITH STATE/LOCAL GOV'T. AGENCY ☐ YES ☐ NO — DATE FILED — AGENCY CHARGE FILED WITH *(Name and address)*

APPROXIMATE NO. OF EMPLOYEES/MEMBERS OF COMPANY OR UNION THIS CHARGE IS FILED AGAINST — DATE MOST RECENT OR CONTINUING DISCRIMINATION TOOK PLACE *(Month, day, and year)*

Explain what unfair thing was done to you and how other persons were treated differently. Understanding that this statement is for the use of the United States Equal Employment Opportunity Commission, I hereby certify:

I swear or affirm that I have read the above charge and that it is true to the best of my knowledge, information and belief.

DATE — CHARGING PARTY *(Signature)*

Subscribed and sworn to before this EEOC representative.

DATE — SIGNATURE AND TITLE

NOTARY PUBLIC

SUBSCRIBED AND SWORN TO BEFORE ME THIS DATE *(Day, month, and year)*

SIGNATURE *(If it is difficult for you to get a Notary Public to sign this, sign your own name and mail to the District Office. The Commission will notarize the charge for you at a later date.)*

EEOC FORM JUN 72 5 — Previous editions of this form may be used.

U.S. GOVERNMENT PRINTING OFFICE : 1973-728-451/1250
GPO 871-168

Figure 8-1

success in meeting affirmative action goals was "a definite factor" in winning the $2.6-billion space shuttle contract.[3]

The statutes governing antidiscrimination guidelines are numerous and complex. Individual or class action suits can be filed against a firm under any one, or any combination, of the following laws or directives:

- The Fifth and Fourteenth Amendments to the Constitution
- The Civil Rights Acts of 1866, 1870, and 1871
- The Equal Pay Act of 1963
- Titles VII and IX of the 1964 Civil Rights Act
- The Age Discrimination in Employment Act of 1967, as amended in 1978
- Executive Order 11246, as amended by 11375
- Executive Order 11478, Equal Employment Opportunity in the Federal Government
- The State and Local Fiscal Assistance Act of 1972
- The Equal Employment Opportunity Act of 1972
- The Comprehensive Employment and Training Act of 1973
- 1973 Amendments to the Omnibus Crime Control and Safe Streets Act
- The Rehabilitation Act of 1973
- The Vietnam Era Veterans Readjustment Assistance Act of 1974
- The Pregnancy Discrimination Act of 1978

A problem that has developed in eliminating discrimination against minorities is the fact that these regulations in the aggregate cover a majority of the population, including:

- All females
- All blacks
- All those of Spanish, Asian, Pacific Island, American Indian, or Eskimo ancestry.
- All Vietnam-era veterans
- All those handicapped
- All workers between the ages of 40 and 64 (and most of those between 65 and 70)
- Members of religious and ethnic groups such as Jews, Catholics, Italians, Greeks, and Slavic groups

These categories overlap, of course, but it is estimated that since females constitute over half the population, a majority of American citizens falls into protected categories. Some civil rights lawyers are concerned, therefore, that the growth of the legal "minority" into a majority has undermined the statutory goal of protecting cer-

[3] "Acting Affirmatively to End Job Bias," *Business Week*, January 27, 1975, p. 94.

tain groups in the society against majority prejudice.[4] To complicate the matter further, affirmative action programs cover most but
not all of the forementioned categories. Government contractors
must maintain such special efforts to recruit, train, and promote
members of the following designated groups: blacks, females,
Spanish-surnamed Americans, handicapped, and Vietnam veterans.
Other companies have been required to set up affirmative action
programs when the courts have found them to have discriminated.
Other employers have established affirmative action programs voluntarily.[5] (See appendix to this chapter for a landmark case establishing an affirmative action program in the construction industry).

THE FEDERAL GOVERNMENT
AND PERSONNEL PRACTICES

The importance given equal employment opportunity considerations, perhaps at the expense of employee productivity, is often
evident in the statements of federal officials involved in the regulation of personnel practices. For example, in 1974 the deputy director
of the Equal Opportunity Program of the U.S. Treasury Department
in a speech to a group of commercial bankers listed the following
item in a ten-point "overall strategy for identifying and correcting
EEO problems": "10. Refuse promotions or substantial wage increases to those who do not produce satisfactory EEO results, no
matter what other performance results they achieve." In contrast,
the ninth point in the "overall strategy" conveys a sense of balance
among a variety of important objectives: "Make each line manager
and personnel manager accountable for, and rewarded in terms of,
equal employment opportunity results in his or her unit as well as
other performance measures."[6]

Likewise, the head of EEOC has promised an even stronger
push within the agency to search out and eliminate patterns of job
discrimination, using such powerful tools as lawsuits, back pay

---

[4] T. R. Reid, "Rules to Protect Minorities' Rights Guard a Majority,"
Washington Post, March 18, 1979, pp. A-1, A-16. See also Robert Reinhold,
"Government 'Minority' Category Growing to Include More Groups," *The New
York Times*, July 30, 1978, pp. 1, 33.

[5] U.S., Equal Employment Opportunity Commission, *Affirmative Action
and Equal Employment, A Guidebook for Employers* (Washington, D.C.: U.S.
Government Printing Office, 1974).

[6] Inez S. Lee, "Current EEO Regulations" (address to the Pennsylvania
Bankers Association, Philadelphia, February 20-21, 1974), p. 12.

awards, and the loss of government contracts. Eleanor Holmes
Norton stated that "beginning in 1979 a very substantial part" of
the EEOC staff will put "an unprecedented amount of its work"
into class action suits against companies. She also stated that penalties of various kinds have already cost business "hundreds of millions" of dollars, and added: "There's not an employer who hasn't
seen somebody in his community pay $500,000 in back pay."[7]

The EEOC has previously stated, moreover, that it is concentrating on the nation's largest and most visible corporations to get
the results it wants. In the words of former Commission Chairman
John H. Powell, Jr., "Once we get the big boys, the others will soon
fall in line."[8]

The agency has followed this procedure with considerable force
and effect. American Telephone and Telegraph signed a widely
publicized $38-million settlement in 1973 which obligated the com-
pany to make sweeping changes in its hiring and promotion practices
in order to raise the number (a "target" or "goal," or in effect a
"quota") of women and minorities it employs in all areas of its
operations. The total cost of AT&T's compliance was large, not only
in terms of back pay to employees but also in terms of legal costs,
increased training expenses, and the staffing of 750 people in its
equal employment opportunity office. Don Liebers, AT&T's director
of equal employment and affirmative action, has remarked, "Virtually every decision that's made of a personnel nature has an EEO
consideration in it."[9] This situation has led to an important concern
about the corporation's operating efficiency: To the extent that
AT&T has found it necessary to hire and promote people other than
those who are the best available, it has not been able to operate as
efficiently as it would have otherwise.

AT&T is not alone among the so-called "big boys" in this
regard. In 1978 alone, three large discrimination settlements were
reached: General Electric Company settled an EEOC complaint by
agreeing to spend over $32 million on benefits to workers and af-
firmative action plans for women and minorities; Chase Manhattan
Bank paid $1.8 million to settle a suit; and *The New York Times*
terminated a suit charging sex discrimination against women by
paying $250,000 and an additional $100,000 in legal fees. Nationally, government figures show that business paid out in 1978 nearly

[7] Jerry Flint, "Washington Plans Affirmative Action Push in '79," *New York Times*, December 24, 1978, pp. 1, 2.
[8] Gerald R. Rosen, "Industry's New Watchdog in Washington," *Dun's Review*, June 1974, p. 83.
[9] Carol J. Loomis, "AT&T in the Throes of 'Equal Employment,'" *Fortune*, January 15, 1979, p. 56.

$30 million in awards of back pay for equal pay violations and age discrimination.

The irony inherent in these facts and figures is that the large, national corporations often have the best civil rights record in industry. At the time it was sued by the EEOC, General Motors Corporation had a work force that was 17 percent black and 15 percent female. The same comparatively favorable record was true of Sears, Roebuck and Company. Colston A. Lewis, then a commission member, remarked: "Sears has the best damn affirmative action program in the country. . . . The Commission is harassing Sears and GM, because this is the way the chairman can get headlines."[10]

Sears's view of affirmative action, in fact, does not stop with an effort in the area of jobs and promotions but is extended to minority economic development. Ray Graham, the head of Sears's affirmative program, stated, "We sell more than anyone else in the world, but we manufacture nothing. Obviously we have to buy a lot, and our buying creates a lot of business opportunities." Sears is trying to pass some of these opportunities along to minority businesses.[11]

Many large companies seem to have decided that the most practical course is to agree to EEOC's demands. Adverse publicity may be considered too high a price to pay for possible ultimate vindication in the courts. The resultant agreements often involve the companies' consent to hire a stipulated quota, such as that implemented by the nine major steel companies who agreed to fill one-half of the openings in trade and craft jobs with minority and women employees.

However, once the quota system has been set in place in a corporation, large firms tend to report substantial progress in the hiring of minorities. Montgomery Ward and Company, the Bell System, Inland Steel, Southern California Gas and Electric, and General Motors all showed large increases in the percentage of women and minorities in their work forces in the mid- to late 1970s. The director of employment relations at GM explained the auto maker's affirmative action policy this way: "Essentially we divide the work force into job groups, and where we determine there are fewer minority or women in the job group [than there should be] we set a goal," which results in "recruitment, hiring, development, and training."[12]

The "quota" systems implemented by business, or the rules on

---

[10] Rosen, "Industry's New Watchdog in Washington," p. 83.

[11] William Raspberry, "Action on Affirmative Action," *Washington Post,* July 30, 1975, p. A-15.

[12] Flint, "Washington Plans Affirmative Action Push," p. 2.

"employment selection procedures," can be both burdensome and costly. They can mean the hiring of minimally qualified rather than best-qualified people, which, as has been mentioned, can result in operational inefficiency. Moreover, they mean a large paperwork burden covering job descriptions, hiring tests and techniques, complicated procedures for "validating" the relevance of a job test to job performance, and considerations of alternative testing methods that result in the hiring of more women and minority employees. The entire area of job advertisements, job applications, and standardized tests for jobs has led to considerable wariness, if not confusion, on the part of businesses seeking new hires.[13]

This tendency was enforced by a decision of the Supreme Court in *Griggs* v. *Duke Power Company* in 1971 which made clear that job requirements must be related directly to job performance. The decision struck down a North Carolina power company's requirements of a high school education and general aptitude tests for job applicants, because these stipulations screened out a disproportionate number of black applicants. The outcome of this case has set an important legal precedent for personnel practices in firms throughout the country by substantially restricting the sorts of qualifications a company can ask for in its new hires.

IMPACTS OF AFFIRMATIVE ACTION PROGRAMS

Two other major Supreme Court cases, the Alan Bakke decision in 1978 and the *Weber* v. *Kaiser Aluminum and Chemical Corporation* case in 1979 have dealt with what has come to be called "reverse discrimination." In brief, the issue is concerned with the advancement or "unfair" advantages had by minorities over white nonminority applicants or employees.

In the latter of these two cases, a white employee at Kaiser Aluminum's Gramercy, Louisiana, plant filed a complaint which challenged the selection of black employees with less job seniority for an apprenticeship training program. A collective bargaining agreement had set aside half the craft openings for blacks until the percentage of minority craft workers reflected that of blacks in the area work force.[14] The white employee unsuccessfully charged that this practice constituted a racial preference (favoring blacks and

---

[13] See Vivian C. Pospisil, "What Can You Ask a Job Applicant?" *Industry Week,* March 1, 1976, pp. 24–28.

[14] See *Fair Employment Practices* (Washington, D.C.: Bureau of National Affairs, 1978), no. 354 (September 28, 1978), p. 1.

setting whites at a disadvantage) forbidden by Title VII of the 1964 Civil Rights Act. The EEOC has issued guidelines designed to protect company affirmative action programs from complaints of reverse discrimination. In effect, this requires those who believe that the programs discriminate against them to pursue the matter on their own in the courts without help from the commission.[15]

According to Professor George C. Lodge of Harvard University, the old idea of equality of opportunity has been replaced by equality of result or equality of representation:

> You've got to have so many men telephone operators, so many women vice-presidents. You've got to have minority groups spread up and down the corporate hierarchy, roughly in proportion to their numbers in the community. That's a very new idea radically different from the old way.[16]

The difficulties inherent in a reliance on a quota system to increase the proportion of certain groups in the labor force are described by Professor Richard Posner of the University of Chicago Law School:

> The problem of remedy becomes acute if the law is interpreted to require that the employer have some minimum number or percentage of black employees regardless of whether he or his white employees have been guilty of discrimination. To comply, the employer must lay off workers or, what amounts to the same thing, favor black over white job applicants for as long a period of time as is necessary to attain the quota. In either case white employees untainted by discrimination are made to bear a high cost in order to improve the condition of black workers. The result is a capricious and regressive tax on the white working class.[17]

Even more sweeping changes in employment policy have been proposed by U.S. District Judge Albert V. Bryant, Jr. To remedy job discrimination at a Richmond, Virginia, tobacco plant, he ordered:

> A flat ban on hiring anyone but blacks and women as foremen, assistant foremen, or their white-collar counterparts until the percentage of women and blacks in these occupations equals their percentage of the population in the surrounding area. A white male can be hired only if no other qualified person can be found.
>
> A "bumping" system where any black or woman can replace any produc-

[15] "EEOC Issues Guidelines to Aid Resolution of Reverse Discrimination Suits," *EEOC News*, December 21, 1977, pp. 1-2.

[16] "Recovery and Beyond," *Saturday Review*, July 12, 1975, p. 25.

[17] Richard A. Posner, *Economic Analysis of Law* (Boston: Little, Brown, 1973), p. 306.

tion-line employee with less seniority. No skill requirements may be imposed by the company, but the new worker may be removed if he or she cannot perform the job competently in a reasonable time.[18]

All in all, the EEOC itself presses business firms to agree to sex and minority hiring goals "voluntarily," or, in other words, without resorting to federal court suits or the cancellation of federal funds or contracts. Employers are asked to make what are viewed as good faith efforts. They are not asked to treat their minority hiring "goals" as mandatory "quotas," yet the commission expects companies to take the kinds of actions that will enable them to reach the goals. Figure 8-2 (a page from EEOC's employer guidebook, *Affirmative Action and Equal Employment*) lists the specific aspects stressed by the commission.

The spirit of quotas, if not the letter, does persist, however. According to the EEOC's long-range goals, the only way a company can satisfy the commission completely is if its work force reflects the minority group situation in the area in which it is located. Commissioner Ethel Walsh stated, "Each plant should reflect the percentages of minority people that make up the labor force in its locality."[19] A plant in Alaska, for example, should employ a high percentage of Eskimos; a plant in Oklahoma should have a high proportion of Indians.

The possibility, of course, arises that the strategy could backfire. A company could avoid the entire problem by locating its new plants in largely white communities, making it more difficult for minority group applicants to obtain jobs. In such an event, the EEOC's actions would hurt the very people it is trying to help. There is some evidence to support this concern.

The St. Louis office of the EEOC is reported to follow standards that, whatever their intention, serve to discourage prospective employers from locating in the central city, where most of the area's black population resides. This situation results from the EEOC setting up a county (not metropolitan area) standard whereby it will infer discrimination has taken place if a firm's work force contains a smaller percentage of blacks than the county as a whole. Thus, if a company locates in the city limits of St. Louis (about 42 percent black), it has to work under a far more severe personnel restraint than if it locates in suburban St. Louis County (16 percent black). Not too surprisingly, the opposition to the EEOC position did not

---

[18] "A Sweeping Remedy for Job Discrimination," *Business Week*, February 3, 1975, p. 21.
[19] Ibid., p. 85.

EEOC AFFIRMATIVE ACTION PROGRAM GUIDELINES

AFFIRMATIVE ACTION – RESULTS

The most important measure of an Affirmative Action Program is its RESULTS.

Extensive efforts to develop procedures, analyses, data collection systems, report forms and fine written policy statements are meaningless unless the end product will be measurable, yearly improvement in hiring, training and promotion of minorities and females in all parts of your organization.

Just as the success of a company program to increase sales is evaluated in terms of actual increases in sales, the only realistic basis for evaluating a program to increase opportunity for minorities and females is its actual impact upon these persons.

The essence of your Affirmative Action Program should be:

- Establish strong company policy and commitment.

- Assign responsibility and authority for program to top company official.

- Analyze present work force to identify jobs, departments and units where minorities and females are underutilized.

- Set specific, measurable, attainable hiring and promotion goals, with target dates, in each area of underutilization.

- Make every manager and supervisor responsible and accountable for helping to meet these goals.

- Re-evaluate job descriptions and hiring criteria to assure that they reflect actual job needs.

- Find minorities and females who qualify or can become qualified to fill goals.

- Review and revise all employment procedures to assure that they do not have discriminatory effect and that they help attain goals.

- Focus on getting minorities and females into upward mobility and relevant training pipelines where they have not had previous access.

- Develop systems to monitor and measure progress regularly. If results are not satisfactory to meet goals, find out why, and make necessary changes.

Figure 8-2 EEOC AFFIRMATIVE ACTION PROGRAM GUIDELINES

Source: U.S. Equal Employment Opportunity Commission

arise in the suburbs but was led by two St. Louis city aldermen who claimed that the policy contributed to the exodus of business to the suburbs.[20]

One of the basic problems encountered in the administration of any national regulatory program is the inevitable shortcomings that result from a bureaucratic, do-it-by-the-numbers approach. In the case of the equal employment opportunity program, this would appear to be a problem in terms of the substantive issues as well as the detailed administration. In July 1974 the Department of Labor gave final approval to its Revised Order 14, with reference to the procedures that federal agencies must use in evaluating affirmative action programs by government contractors.[21]

As mentioned earlier, all prime contractors or subcontractors who have fifty or more employees and a contract of fifty thousand dollars or more are required to develop written affirmative action programs for each of their establishments. They must now list each job title as it appears in their union agreements or payroll records. Listing only by job group, as was formerly required, is no longer acceptable. The job titles must be listed from the lowest paid to the highest paid within each department or other similar organizational unit.

If there are separate work units or lines of progression within a department, separate lists must be provided for each such unit, or line, including unit supervisors. For lines of progression, the order of jobs in the line through which an employee can move to the job must be indicated. If there are no formal progression lines or usual promotional sequences, job titles must be listed by departments, job families, or disciplines, in order of wage rates or salary ranges. For each job title two breakdowns are required—the total number of male and female incumbents, and the total number of male and female incumbents in each of the following groups: blacks, Spanish-surnamed Americans, American Indians, and Orientals.

The wage rate or salary range for each job group at the facility, with an explanation if minorities or women are currently being underutilized in any group, also is required. Underutilization means "having fewer minorities or women in a particular job group than would reasonably be expected by their availability." Separate utilization analyses must be prepared for minorities and women. Clearly, these requirements will necessitate a significant increase in the amount and costs of record keeping and reporting required of federal

[20] Marsha Canfield, "U.S. Minority Hiring Guides Here Called Unfair," *St. Louis Globe-Democrat*, December 1, 1973, p. 3A.
[21] "Revised Order No. 14 Clarifies Rules," *NAM News*, July 29, 1974, p. 5.

contractors. Matters are made more difficult for federal contractors because compliance is administered by 15 separate agencies, each with its own approach. Todd Jagerson, president of EEO Services, a New York based consulting firm, provides a vivid description of actual practice:

> I've got a client who deals with six compliance officers for a single, 25,000-employee plant. No two of them will accept the same affirmative action program, so the company has six, with the required 170 items for each program. And that's small potatoes. Some big corporations with plants all over the U.S. may have 100 programs.[22]

A positive effect of OFCC affirmative action pressures has been the reexamination of requirements for certain positions. For example, the availability of black and women engineers traditionally has been small. For this reason, Westinghouse reanalyzed its entry-level professional and managerial positions to identify those jobs where a liberal arts degree would do as well as the engineering degree required previously. The very real and serious lingering effects of past discriminatory practices, whether intentional or not, surely provide the continued impetus for substantial efforts to promote equal employment opportunity. Nevertheless, a Gallup poll conducted after the Alan Bakke reverse discrimination decision had been handed down by the Supreme Court indicated that "by an overwhelming 83-to-10 percent vote, the American public believes ability, as determined by examination, not preferential treatment to correct past discrimination, should be the main consideration in selecting applications for jobs or students for college admission."[23]

EQUAL OPPORTUNITY VERSUS SENIORITY

Periods of economic recession have forced many employers either to erase gains in the employment of women and minorities or to turn their backs on the seniority system. When job layoffs are prevalent, blacks and women, often the last hired, are frequently slated as the first to be let go. If this occurs, affirmative action gains may be drastically reduced or negated completely. The position of employers resembles that of being in the middle of a triangle, threat-

[22] "Acting Affirmatively to End Job Bias," *Business Week*, p. 102.
[23] Thomas A. Johnson, "White Majority Found to Favor Affirmative Action for Blacks If Quotas Are Not Rigid," *The New York Times*, February 19, 1979, p. A-12.

ened from three sides at once, with the forces including women's rights organizations, organized labor, and the civil rights enforcement agencies.[24]

EEOC asserts that minority and women workers warrant special consideration and protection from layoffs as compensation for past discrimination. Former EEOC Chairman John Powell described the position of the EEOC during the recession of 1974–75: "Contrary to letting up, we're going to tighten up. We intend to use the full panoply of enforcement powers through the courts."[25] Many employers, especially those bound by union agreements, have used seniority as the basic determinant of who gets the pink slip. One survey of companies that experienced layoffs failed to find a single employer who openly flouted seniority to retain minority or women workers.[26]

Numerous layoff decisions have been tested in the courts, with differing and conflicting opinions from judges. In a case involving the Harvey, Louisiana, plant of Continental Can, using seniority as the guidelines meant that 48 of 50 black employees were laid off. One federal district judge stated, in a ruling prohibiting the use of the seniority approach:

> The company's history of racial discrimination in hiring makes it impossible now for blacks (other than the original two) to have sufficient seniority to withstand layoff.
>
> In this situation, the selection of employees for layoffs on the basis of seniority unlawfully perpetuates the effects of past discrimination.[27]

NEW DEVELOPMENTS IN EQUAL EMPLOYMENT OPPORTUNITY

Since 1967 business personnel practices have come to be regulated by a variety of new laws. The Rehabilitation Act of 1973 mandated that firms doing business with the federal government under a contract of $2,500 or more must take affirmative action for handicapped persons in the areas of hiring, job assignments, promo-

[24] Ernest Holsendolph, "Layoff and the Civil Rights of Minorities," *The New York Times*, January 29, 1975, p. 17.
[25] Marilyn Bender, "Job Discrimination, 10 Years Later," *The New York Times*, November 10, 1974, p. F-5.
[26] "Seniority Squeezes Out Minorities in Layoffs," *Business Week*, May 5, 1975, p. 66.
[27] Holsendolph, "Layoff and the Civil Rights of Minorities," p. 17.

tions, training, transfers, working conditions, terminations, and other aspects of employment. This legislation affects almost one-half of the 6 million businesses in the United States.[28]

Other laws forbidding job discrimination against handicapped workers are in effect in many states as well as in the federal government. There are important benefits, both public and private, to be achieved from the productive utilization of the skills of handicapped workers. Savings in unemployment or welfare payments accrue to the society, as well as the increased output of the goods and services that they produce. Moreover, handicapped individuals benefit from increased income as well as having the satisfaction of holding productive jobs. Yet, the cost to the employer of compliance with these regulations can be substantial. A number of the laws require employers to make architectural adjustments around the requirements of workers or applicants with physical handicaps. Under federal law an employer could also be required to restructure work schedules to meet the needs of the handicapped. The significance of this regulation should not be understated. The government has, for the first time, made an affirmative action program a direct cost to employers — the employer must pay to make it possible for an employee to do the job for which he or she was hired.

In April 1972 the EEOC established new advisory guidelines for maternity leave among women employees, stating that benefits from health insurance plans for sickness or temporary disability must be given to women disabled by pregnancy, miscarriage, abortion, or childbirth. The commission's revised guidelines led immediately to union suits charging companies such as General Electric, AT&T, General Motors, Ford, and Chrysler with violations in this area. In 1978 the Pregnancy Discrimination Act was signed into law, making clear that discrimination in employment based on pregnancy, childbirth, or related medical conditions constituted unlawful sex discrimination under Title VII. Though a study conducted at the Federal Reserve Bank of Boston concluded that the costs incurred by these guidelines would be minimal,[29] some firms employing large numbers of women could pay significant sums in sick pay and disability benefits to comply with this law.

In 1967 the Age Discrimination in Employment Act was enacted, providing the basic federal statute prohibiting discrimination on the basis of age in virtually all areas of employment policy. This

---

[28] See James M. Goldberg et al., *Employer's Handbook of Federal Employee Regulations* (Washington, D.C.: London and Goldberg, 1978), pp. 47–48.

[29] Carol Greenwald, "Maternity Leave Policy," *New England Economic Review* (January–February 1973), pp. 13–18.

law was amended in 1978, banning mandatory retirement before the age of 70 (with a few exceptions, such as workers in high-risk jobs and highly paid executives). The age limitation for retiring federal employees was eliminated entirely.

Though it is impossible to estimate how many people will work until age 70, it is conceivable that a trend of older workers remaining in the work force will reduce the number of job opportunities for the unemployed young, as well as drive up the cost of employment through greater administrative expenditures. Robert M. Macdonald of the Amos Tuck School of Business Administration has further described the effects of the law in this way:

> It will affect individuals, organizations, and activities unevenly, reducing efficiency and redistributing rights and rewards within the society. It proposes to extend freedom of choice by restricting freedom of contract — and indeed, by voiding contracts entered into voluntarily and in good faith.[30]

MINIMUM WAGE LAWS AND UNEMPLOYMENT

An amendment to the Fair Labor Standards Act in 1977 scheduled new increases in the federal minimum wage from $2.65 an hour in 1978 to $3.35 an hour in 1981, a rise of nearly 26 percent over the four years. See Table 8-2 for data on the historical growth of this regulatory activity.

Raises in the minimum wage are generally popular because low-income people seem to be getting more generous incomes. But something like the reverse is the practical result. The increase in labor costs not only is inflationary but it contributes to the country's unemployment rate, especially for minority teen-agers.[31]

A survey by the National Restaurant Association found that after the 1978 minimum wage increase, 95 percent of its 2,000 members raised prices, 78 percent reduced man-hours, 63 percent laid off workers, and over half invested in equipment that would help reduce their labor force. The president of the Marriott hotel and restaurant chain, which employs some 20,000 workers, has

---

[30] Robert M. Macdonald, *Mandatory Retirement and the Law* (Washington, D.C.: American Enterprise Institute, 1978), p. 28.
[31] See Steven P. Zell, "The Minimum Wage and Youth Unemployment," *Federal Reserve Bank of Kansas City Economic Review*, January 1978, pp. 3-16. For a contrary view, see Sar A. Levitan and Richard S. Belous, *More Than Subsistence: Minimum Wages for the Working Poor* (Baltimore: Johns Hopkins University Press, 1979).

Table 8-2   Minimum wage rate changes

| | Nonfarm Workers | | |
	Covered	Newly Covered	Farm Workers*
October 24, 1938	$0.25	$ —	$ —
October 24, 1939	0.30	—	—
October 24, 1945	0.40	—	—
January 25, 1950	0.75	—	—
March 1, 1956	1.00	—	—
September 3, 1961	1.15	1.00	—
September 3, 1963	1.25	—	—
September 3, 1964	—	1.15	—
September 3, 1965	—	1.25†	—
February 1, 1967	1.40†	1.00	1.00
February 1, 1968	1.60	1.15	1.15
February 1, 1969	—	1.30	1.30
February 1, 1970	—	1.45	—
February 1, 1971	—	1.60	—
May 1, 1974	2.00	1.90	1.60
January 1, 1975	2.10	2.00	1.80
January 1, 1976	2.30	2.20	2.00
January 1, 1977	—	2.30	2.20
January 1, 1978	2.65	2.65	2.65
January 1, 1979	2.90	2.90	2.90
January 1, 1980	3.10	3.10	3.10
January 1, 1981	3.35	3.35	3.35

*Not all farm workers are covered by the minimum wage.
†All job categories covered prior to the 1966 amendments were raised to $1.40 per hour in February 1967.
Source: U.S. Department of Labor, Bureau of Labor Statistics

described the effect of the wage law on jobs and prices in the industry. With the compulsory wage rise in 1979 the Marriott chain stopped hiring at many locations and thus cut its work force by 2 to 3 percent. The higher wage costs coupled with higher food costs forced the chain to raise prices in some restaurants by as much as 10 percent. The company president remarked, "Unfortunately, as we raise prices, we often lose customers; it's axiomatic. . . . And as we serve fewer customers, we lay off more people."[32]

[32] "How the Minimum Wage Destroys Jobs," *Fortune*, January 29, 1979, p. 101.

REGULATION OF PRIVATE PENSIONS

The 1974 pension reform law, the Employee Retirement Income Security Act of 1974 (ERISA), has added and will add substantially to the cost of private pension plans. ERISA is widely considered to be one of the most complicated laws ever enacted. It is estimated that 90 percent of all private pension plans have had to be rewritten to comply with this law.[33] Basically, the pension law establishes seven areas of requirements to be met. Compliance is required for a company's pension plan to be acceptable to IRS, thus allowing the contributions and earnings on the plan to be tax-exempt.

Eligibility. An employee must be eligible to participate in the retirement plan when he or she is 25 and has worked for one year.

Vesting. Explicit regulations are established on the time it takes for an employee to earn the right to a pension. Once vested, the employee has a right to a pension at retirement even if he or she is not working at the company at the time.

Surviving-Spouse Benefit. In the event of the retired employee's death, the surviving spouse must receive at least 50 percent of the pension benefit.

Funding. Employers must fully fund the annual cost of the retirement program. They must also contribute an additional amount to amortize existing liabilities over a designated period of time.

Fiduciaries. Fiduciaries, those who manage or administer a pension plan or those who give investment advice for a fee, are more widely defined and are placed under strict rules of conduct. Under the law, they must act as a "prudent man" would in similar circumstances. Fiduciaries are personally liable for violations of this responsibility.

Plan Termination Insurance. The U.S. Pension Benefit Guaranty Corporation (PBGC) was chartered to guarantee the payment of pension benefits should a plan be terminated with insufficient assets to pay pension liabilities. Initially, annual premiums for employers are one dollar for each participant for single-employer plans and 50 cents for each participant in multiemployer plans. Firms are liable for up to 30 percent of their assets if they terminate a pension plan that is not fully funded.

[33] Vivian C. Pospisil, "The New Law and Your Pension," *Industry Week*, March 3, 1975, p. 24.

Reporting and Disclosure Requirements. Extensive reports on benefits are required of all employers, including a detailed plan description, a summary plan description understandable to the laymen, and an annual report.

The Labor-Management Services Administration, a division of the Labor Department, is responsible for enforcing the law with regard to disclosure and fiduciary standards. Civil penalties may be invoked and criminal penalties may apply to disclosure violations. The Internal Revenue Service enforces the provisions regarding vesting, funding, and participation.

The paperwork requirements of the new pension law is hitting small businesses hardest. Moreover, "the act requires that plans be communicated in layman language, and then proceeds to make such requirements on what the plan summary should include that they've got to be very difficult to understand," says Peter Biggins, corporate benefits manager of Xerox Corporation. Xerox solved the problem through a dual communications system. One publication explains the program in layman's language and another in technical, legal language that will satisfy the law.

Standard Oil of California has at least 102 pension plans covering 30,000 employees and 9,000 annuitants. Fifty of the plans were a result of merger and are no longer operative except to pay out old benefits. If Standard Oil has to meet all the reporting and disclosure rules for each plan, costs, according to Robert Maggy, benefits manager, could reach $2.5 million to initiate the statistical system with ongoing costs of operation rising an additional $750,000 a year.[34]

The total effect of all the provisions of the 1974 pension reform law (ERISA) is to raise annual pension costs 10 to 15 percent for the average employer, according to Robert D. Paul, president of Martin E. Segal Company, an actuarial consulting firm. The initial result in the first half of 1975 was the termination of pension plans at three times the normal rate—plans which covered primarily small companies employing an average of 30 people. PBGC reported that in the three years following ERISA's enactment, 16,500 plans were terminated, while an estimated 11,000 new plans were established. Approximately 350,000 participants lost pension coverage, but more than double that number gained coverage under new plan formations (see fig. 8-3). ERISA was reported to be the reason for many of the plan terminations.[35]

---

[34] "Pension Reform's Expensive," *Business Week*, March 24, 1975, p. 149.
[35] Pension Benefit Guaranty Corporation, *Analysis of Single Employer Defined Benefit Plan Terminations, 1977* (Washington, D.C.: U.S. Government Printing Office, 1978), p. 1.

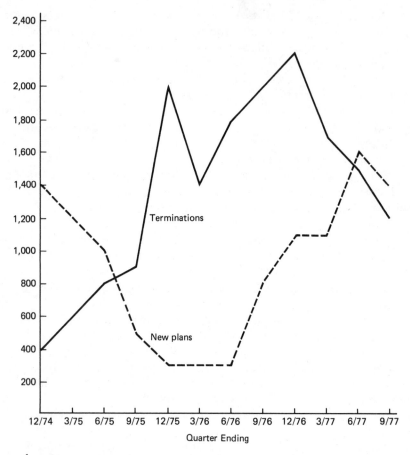

[1] Estimates of new plan formations based on IRS data on determinations of qualification. Plans covered under Title IV for termination insurance are estimated to account for 75 percent of all defined benefit plans.

Figure 8-3   POST-ERISA PLAN FORMATIONS AND TERMINATIONS COVERED BY TERMINATION INSURANCE[1]

Source: Pension Benefit Guaranty Corporation

PBGC has also reported that about 10 percent of multiemployer pension plans, which cover about 1.5 million workers, are experiencing financial difficulties that could end in terminations by 1988. If this were to happen, the cost under the government's current termination insurance program would be an estimated $4.8 billion. It would require an annual premium of approximately $80 for each employee covered by an existing pension plan to raise that amount.

All things considered, ERISA is likely to lead to a reduction in the overall use of corporate pension plans.[36]

FUTURE TRENDS

An interesting trend in regulation of personnel practices is a rising sense of expectation seen by scholars among workers, professionals, and executives for more participation in decision making and greater protection of individual rights in the workplace. David W. Ewing of the Harvard Business School, among others, advocates an employees' bill of rights which would cover a worker's freedom of speech, conscientious objection, security and privacy, choice of outside activities and associations, and due process of grievances. Ewing also favors the reinforcement of an employer's rights in the areas of confidential business information, personal accusations, disruption of workplace morale, and certain aspects of everyday work decisions.[37]

Five states — California, Maine, Michigan, Oregon, and Pennsylvania — have passed laws giving employees the right to examine their personnel files and specifying other rights of confidentiality in the handling of personnel records by employers. In July 1977 the U.S. Privacy Protection Study Commission made 34 recommendations for rules of fair employment information practices that it called on employers to adopt voluntarily.[38]

APPENDIX: EQUAL EMPLOYMENT OPPORTUNITY IN CONSTRUCTION*

United States Court of Appeals, Ninth Circuit,
May 17, 1971, No. 26048 *United States
of America, Plaintiff-Appellee* v. *Ironworkers
Local 86 et al.,* Defendants-Appellants

Action wherein government charged unions and joint apprenticeship and training committees with having denied equal employ-

[36] Pension Benefit Guaranty Corporation, *Multiemployer Study Required by P.L. 95-214* (Washington, D.C.: U.S. Government Printing Office, 1978), pp. 1-2; Dennis E. Logue, *Legislative Influence on Corporate Pension Plans* (Washington, D.C.: American Enterprise Institute, 1979), pp. 106-9.
[37] Albert L. Kraus, "Next Item on the Civil Liberties Agenda: Freedom inside the Work Organization," *Money Manager,* August 22, 1977, p. 2.
[38] Alan F. Westin, "Message to CEOs — About Employee Privacy," *Across the Board* (June 1979), pp. 8-13.
*This section contains excerpts from the law case upholding the federal government's affirmative action efforts in the construction industry, the so-called Philadelphia Plan.

ment opportunities to blacks in violation of Civil Rights Act. The United States District Court for the Western District of Washington entered judgment in favor of government, and all but one defendant appealed. The Court of Appeals held that finding that building construction unions and joint apprenticeship and training committees associated with them had engaged in a pattern or practice of discriminatory conduct with respect to equal employment opportunities for blacks was not clearly erroneous when well documented with statistical evidence showing a distinct absence of black membership in unions and committees, failure of union hiring halls to grant black referrals, many overt acts of discrimination on part of unions and committees, and many facially neutral employment practices, which had a differential effect on blacks.

On October 31, 1969, the attorney general of the United States brought an action in the United States District Court for the Western District of Washington against five building construction unions, located in Seattle, Washington, and three joint apprenticeship and training committees associated with them. The complaint alleged that the named unions and joint apprenticeship and training committees had denied employment opportunities to blacks on account of their race and that certain policies, practices, and conduct, described therein, constituted a "pattern or practice" of resistance to full employment of blacks in violation of Title VII of the Civil Rights Act of 1964. The district court found that all the named unions and joint apprenticeship and training committees had pursued a pattern or practice of conduct that denied blacks, on account of their race, equal employment opportunities in the construction industry; two judgments and decrees followed. All but one of the defendants have joined in the instant appeal.

Many of the basic facts were largely undisputed and were stipulated by the parties. Appellant building trades unions are labor organizations that represent a large number of workmen employed in the construction industry in and about Seattle, Washington. Through the union hiring halls, appellant unions effectively control a large percentage of the employment opportunities in the construction industry in that area. Under the bargaining agreements entered into between the contractor-employers and the unions, the unions must be given first opportunity to fill positions. Contractors may not employ nonunion workers unless the positions are not filled by the unions within a period of time stipulated under the bargaining agreement.

The joint apprenticeship and training committees who join in this appeal are entities legally separate and distinct from the specific unions with which they are associated. The committees consist of members representing both the unions and the employers, and are formed to oversee and run the apprenticeship programs whose purpose is to train apprentices to become journeymen in the respective trades. Once an applicant is accepted into the program, he becomes indentured to the joint apprenticeship and training committee for a period of years and participates in a program consisting of both on-the-job training and classroom instruction. It is through this program that participants gain admission to the union as journeymen, thereby obviating the necessity of taking the avenue of direct admission, which demands that an applicant meet certain requirements such as a specified number of years of experience, being within a given age range, having letters of recommendation, and passing a journeyman's examination.

The court found appellant unions and joint apprenticeship and training committees to have engaged in a pattern or practice of discrimination that denied blacks employment opportunities in the construction industry. It based its conclusions on specific findings of discrimination, which included (1) the employment of tests and admission criteria that had little or no relation to on-the-job skills and that had a differential impact upon blacks, operating to exclude them from entrance into the unions or referrals to available jobs; (2) the active recruitment of whites, at the same time giving little or no publicity to information concerning procedures for gaining union membership, work referral opportunities, and the operation of the apprenticeship training programs in the black community; (3) the granting of preferential treatment to friends and relatives of existing members of the unions; and (4) the differential application of admission requirements, often bypassing such requirements in cases of white applicants. In addition, several instances were shown where black workers who sought referrals were turned away without reason or after being given a spurious reason in support of the action; and in some cases, unions refused to place blacks on the referral lists, thus assuring their inability to secure work.

The relief granted by the court took the form of two judgments and decrees: the first related to the unions and the second related to the joint apprenticeship and training committees. In the first, the court enjoined the unions from engaging in future discrimination with respect to referrals for employment and the acquisition or retention of union membership. It ordered that the unions keep detailed records of their operations and actively disseminate information in the black community describing the operation of the referral systems, membership requirements, and available job opportunities. Specific relief was granted by the court to certain individuals or groups of persons ordering the unions to offer them immediate construction referrals in response to the next contractor requests for workers and to open their membership application lists to these persons. The court retained jurisdiction for such further relief as it deems necessary or appropriate to effectuate further equal employment opportunities.

The committees were enjoined from all future discrimination against applicants for apprenticeship on account of race. It further ordered the committees to disseminate information concerning the requirements and procedures for admission to the apprenticeship programs so as to apprise blacks within the geographical area of available opportunities. The respective committees were ordered to consider all applicants who met the standards set out by the court in the decree. In addition, an affirmative action program was included in the decree in the hope of eradicating the vestiges of past discrimination. Among the provisions under this program were the creation of special apprenticeship programs designed to meet the special needs of average blacks with no previous experience or special skills in the trade, or black applicants who have some previous experience or special skills in the trade but do not meet journeymen standards. The court also retained jurisdiction over the committees in order to grant such further relief as it deems necessary.

Findings of Fact. We are confronted initially with the appellants' contention that the "clearly erroneous" rule should not govern our review of the findings of fact made by the district court. They reason that the rationale underlying the rule is that an appellate court should defer to the judgment of the trial court because the trial judge has access to demeanor evidence and could readily assess the credibility of the witnesses. Hence, where, as they allege, "large reliance" is placed upon written instruments and depositions, they claim the rule does not apply as demeanor evidence played a small part in the trial judge's decision.

Appellants' characterization of the proceeding below as one in which the trial judge placed "large reliance" on documentary evidence and depositions ignores the fact that over 55 witnesses testified, many of whom were deponents prior to trial. Even if "large reliance" was placed on written evidence, the clearly erroneous rule would still apply. We examined this problem in *Lundgren v. Freeman*, 307 F.2d 104, and found the better rule to be that the clearly erroneous rule does apply, even where the factual issues are decided on written evidence alone. Appellants would have us review the evidence de novo and freely substitute our judgment for that of the trial judge. We decline to do so. The well-established rule is that we "may not substitute our judgment if conflicting inferences may be drawn from established facts by reasonable men, and the inferences drawn by the trial court are those which could have been drawn by reasonable men."

Appellants further contend that the district court's findings were based on evidence which it had previously excluded. Prior to trial, the attorney general examined the application forms found in the files of the joint apprenticeship and training committees. At trial, appellants objected to the introduction of charts which were made from information found in the application forms on the ground that they did not qualify for admission under the business records exception to the hearsay rule. The court, sustaining, in part, appellants' objection, held this evidence was inadmissible to prove the truth of the matters contained therein, but was admissible as evidence of the type of information sought by the committees and relied upon by them in reaching their evaluative decisions.

The contention of appellants is unsupportable, given the limited purpose for which the information contained in the applications was used, as we noted in *Phillips* v. *United States*, 356 F.2d 297, 307, where a similar argument was raised.

The purpose of that section (Business Records Act, 28 U.S.C. 1732 as amended, 28 U.S.C. 1732) is to provide, in the case of business records, an exception to the hearsay rule, and to provide an acceptable substitute for specific authentication of each business record. We are not here concerned with the hearsay rule because the letters and requests contained in exhibits 968 and 984 were not offered in proof of the statements contained therein. They were introduced only to show defendants had knowledge that such statements had been made. Nor are we concerned with authentication since the authenticity of the documents need not be established where the only purpose of the documents is to show notice. As in Phillips, supra, the information contained in the applications was not proffered to prove the statements therein, but to show what information was sought by the apprenticeship committees in the applications and relied upon by them in making their decisions. The application form information was properly admitted for this purpose.

The district judge's duty was to consider the evidence, reach all reasonable inferences therefrom, and make specific findings of fact and conclusions of law. This task was necessarily a difficult one and involved the review of extensive oral testimony, many depositions, and a great amount of accompanying documentary evidence. Its proportions are reflected in the size of the reporter's transcript, which alone numbers 20 volumes. In his carefully written and excellent opinion, covering some 50 pages, Judge Lindberg made separate findings of fact as to each party, carefully analyzing the supportive

evidence found in the record. In these findings of fact Judge Lindberg has pointed out by page reference to the record, the testimony,
stipulations, admitted facts, and exhibits upon which his findings
were based. It would serve no purpose to repeat such references in
this opinion. It is not our duty to relitigate the facts at this time.
Having reviewed the findings below and the record before us, we
are fully convinced that the findings are amply supported by the
evidence.

Conclusions of Law. At the outset, appellants contest the use
of racial statistics to prove a "pattern or practice" of discrimination
as a matter of law. They categorize this mode of proof as a statistical
"numbers game," incapable of proving a violation of Title VII. We
believe this argument is without support as the use of statistics is well
established in recent Title VII cases.

In the district court's opinion, a separate statement was made as
to each appellant concerning the racial composition of its membership. As to appellate unions, it was stated: Ironworkers Local 86
had approximately 920 members in January 1970, only one of
whom was black. Sheet Metal Workers Local 99 had approximately
900 members in its construction division, only one of whom was
black; Plumbers and Pipefitters Local 32 had approximately 1,900
members in its construction classification, only one of whom was
black. In addition, with respect to the appellant joint apprenticeship
and training committees, the court noted: Sheet Metal Workers
JATC had 100 apprentices indentured in its program and seven were
black; Plumbers and Pipefitters JATC had 104 building trades apprentices and none were black.

The district court also made a specific finding applicable to all
parties concerning the racial composition of the city of Seattle where
the main offices, hiring halls, and training facilities of the appellants
are found. Approximately 42,000 blacks reside in the city, constitut-
ing roughly seven percent of the population. This information came
from an expert witness, a demographer, called to testify by the
attorney general.

Since the passage of the Civil Rights Act of 1964, the courts
have frequently relied upon statistical evidence to prove a violation.
This judicial practice has most often taken the form of the use of
such data as a basis for allocating the burden of proof. On the basis
that a showing of an absence or a small black union membership in
a demographic area containing a substantial number of black workers
raises an inference that the racial imbalance is the result of discrimination, the burden of going forward and the burden of persuasion is
shifted to the accused, for such a showing is enough to establish a

prima facie case. In many cases the only available avenue of proof is the use of racial statistics to uncover clandestine and covert discrimination by the employer or union involved. One court, in *Parham* v. *Southwestern Bell Telephone Co.*, 433 F. 2d 421, 426 (8th Cir. 1970), held as a matter of law, without other supportive evidence, that the statistics introduced showing an extraordinarily small number of black employees, notwithstanding a small number who held menial jobs, established a violation of Title VII. Of course, as is the case with all statistics, their use is conditioned by the existence of proper supportive facts and the absence of variables, which would undermine the reasonableness of the inference of discrimination which is drawn. It is our belief that the often-cited aphorism, "statistics often tell much and courts listen," has particular application in Title VII cases.

Here, even if we were to accept appellant's assertion that statistics alone cannot show as a matter of law that there has been a violation, it would not command our overturning of the conclusions of law reached by the district court. We are not faced with a situation where a court has relied upon statistical data alone. On the contrary, in its findings the district court cited specific instances of discrimination on the part of the unions and apprenticeship committees. Thus the statistical evidence is complementary rather than exclusive. We see no merit in appellants' complaint regarding the use of statistics.

Appellants next argue that the conclusions reached by the court that appellants engaged separately in a "pattern or practice of resistance" are wholly unsupportable. They equate the phrase "pattern or practice" with "uniformly engaged in a course of conduct aimed at denying rights secured by the act." We feel that such an interpretation is overly restrictive and does violence to the meaning intended by Congress to be accorded the phrase. Moreover, it is our firm belief that the conclusions reached by the district court are not clearly erroneous and must be affirmed.

The phrase is not defined in Title VII, but some guidance is offered by an examination of the legislative history of this and other Civil Rights Acts employing the same words. Commenting on the meaning to be accorded the phrase in the debates on the Civil Rights Act of 1964, Senator Humphrey stated: "Such a pattern or practice would be present only where the denial of rights consists of something more than an isolated, sporadic incident, but is repeated, routine or of generalized nature."

In testimony before the House Judiciary Committee on the Civil Rights Act of 1960, Deputy Attorney General Walsh said: "Pattern or practice have their generic meanings. In other words, the court finds that the discrimination was not an isolated or accidental or peculiar event; that it was an event which happened in the regular procedures followed by the state officials concerned."

In *United States* v. *Mayton*, 335 F.2d 153, 158 (5th Cir. 1964), an action under the Civil Rights Act of 1960, in which the court found that racial discrimination in the voter registration process was pursuant to a "pattern or practice," the court addressed itself to defining the words and concluded that they "were not intended to be words of art." With respect to the phrase, Senator Keating commented that "[t]he 'pattern or practice' requirement means only that the proven discriminatory conduct of defendants was not merely an isolated instance of racial discrimination."

We are firmly convinced that it was the intent of Congress that a "pattern or practice" be found where the acts of discrimination are not "isolated, peculiar, or accidental" events. The words were not intended to be words of art. Applying this definition in the instant case, we are compelled to concur with the district court's findings that appellants engaged in a "pattern or practice" of discrimination. The findings are well documented with statistical evidence showing a distinct absence of black membership in the unions and the apprenticeship programs; the failure of the union hiring halls to grant black referrals; many overt acts of discrimination on the part of appellants; and many facially neutral employment practices, which had a differential effect upon blacks. We are not concerned with isolated or accidental acts by appellants but a "pattern or practice" or resistance by them, which has had an effect of denying black workers equal job opportunities in the Seattle area.

Therefore, we hold that the conclusions reached by the district court finding appellant unions and joint apprenticeship and training committees to have engaged in a pattern or practice of discriminatory conduct with respect to employment opportunities in the construction industry are not clearly erroneous.

Relief Granted. Appellants finally contend that the district court violated section 703(j) of the act in ordering appellant unions to offer immediate job referrals to previous discriminatees, and ordering appellant apprenticeship and training committee to select and indenture sufficient black applicants to overcome past discrimination, and to also meet judicially imposed ceiling requirements in apprenticeship program participation. This they condemn as "racial quotas" and "racial preferences." We cannot agree.

The act vests in the attorney general and the trial court power to eliminate both the vestiges of past discrimination and terminate present discriminatory practices. Under sections 706(g) and 707(a) unlawful employment practices may be enjoined by the court and such affirmative relief granted as the court may deem appropriate. The only statutory limitation on the availability of relief is the anti-preferential treatment provision of section 703(j).

There can be little doubt that where a violation of Title VII is found, the court is vested with broad remedial power to remove the vestiges of past discrimination and eliminate present and assure the nonexistence of future barriers to the full enjoyment of equal job opportunities by qualified black workers. On the basis of this broad equitable power, the courts have allowed a wide range of remedial relief.

In Vogler, supra, 407 F.2d at 1053-1055, the district court ordered, in addition to an injunction against future discrimination and the immediate admission of four discriminatees, that the union develop objective criteria for membership and union size. As here, it was contended that the order established a "quota system to correct racial imbalance in violation of section 703(j)." Rejecting this argument, the court held the district court did "no more than ensure that the injunction against further racial discrimination would be fairly administered" Id. at 1054. The Vogler court succinctly stated that "where necessary to insure compliance with the act, the district court was fully empowered to eliminate the present effects of past discrimination." Similarly, in International Brotherhood of Electrical Workers, Local No. 38, supra, 428 F.2d at 149, the court felt that such an interpretation of section 703(j) "would allow a complete nullification of the purposes of the Civil Rights Act of 1964."

We therefore reject appellants' contention. The district court neither abused its discretion in ordering the affirmative relief, nor did it in any way establish a system of "racial quotas" or "preferences" in violation of section 703(j).

The judgment of the district court is affirmed.

Reflections on the Case

Many of the basic facts of the case were largely undisputed by the parties: (1) the building trade unions represented a large number of workers employed in the construction industry in Seattle; (2) through the union hiring halls the unions effectively controlled a large part of the employment opportunities in the construction industry in that area; (3) under existing union contracts the unions had to be given the first opportunity to fill job positions; and (4) no nonunion workers could be hired unless the positions could not be filled by the unions within a specified time period.

The union position on the discrimination charge was that a statistical "numbers game" was being played. The Court of Appeals, however, reiterated in its decision the statistical facts which showed that black membership in the unions and the apprenticeship and training programs ranged from 0 to 7 percent.

Furthermore, the statistics were bolstered by references to many specific discriminatory actions on the part of the unions and the committees. These supported the conclusion that the unions were not engaging in isolated or incidental acts of discrimination but were indeed following a "pattern or practice" of discriminatory conduct. Thus, the landmark Seattle case rested neither on overall statistics alone nor on selected instances of individual discrimination. Rather, the case relied on the mutual reinforcement of the two approaches.

9

regulation via government procurement

While many business executives and scholars continue to debate the desirability of companies becoming more socially responsible, the debate may be largely over for an important sector of the American economy. For companies that do business with the federal government, the very act of signing the procurement contract forces them to agree to perform a wide variety of socially responsible actions. These requirements range from favoring disadvantaged groups to showing concern for the quality of life and the environment.

The magnitude of the government's procurement outlays, and particularly their importance to government-oriented firms, creates opportunities for implementing a host and variety of government economic and social aims through the contract mechanism.

THE NATURE OF THE GOVERNMENT MARKET

The federal government currently is the world's largest buyer of goods and services. Its military and civilian installations purchase goods and services ranging from complex space vehicles to paper clips. and from janitorial services to studies of genetics. Thus, because of the unique market basket of goods and services that government departments and agencies purchase, and the detailed laws and regulations that they must adhere to, a government market structure has developed that differs in many ways from normal commercial procurement.

A Monopsonistic Market in Large Part

In a procedural way, the government market (federal, state, and local) is a buyer's monopoly (*monopsonistic*), in that prospective contractors must do business the government's way. If they do not, either they are violating the law or they do not get the government's business. In the case of many purchases related to national security (aircraft carriers, nuclear submarines, supersonic bombers, ICBMs, space exploration systems), the federal government is indeed the single customer. (Purchases by "friendly" foreign governments are channeled through the Department of Defense.) Because the market is so completely subject to the changing needs of this one customer, the relationship between buyer and seller differs fundamentally from the one existing in the commercial sector of the economy. Particularly in the military segment of the market, the government, by its selection of contractors, controls entry into and exit from the market, determines the growth patterns of the firms participating, and imposes its ways of doing business.

A contract is awarded as the result of negotiation with suppliers whom the government buyer believes are in a position to undertake the magnitude of research, development, and production required. This single-customer market makes for an extremely keen but novel type of either-or competition. A company generally is not competing for a share of the market for a given product, but for all or none of the market. Boeing and General Dynamics both competed for the F-111 aircraft program. General Dynamics won and produced all of this type of aircraft. Similarly, McDonnell-Douglas builds all of the F-15 aircraft, as the result of a design competition it won against Rockwell International and Fairchild-Hiller. The volatility in the roster of major defense contractors is shown in Table 9-1.

The military buyer, in the restless search for ever more sophisticated weaponry, assumes many of the risks that in more normal business activities are borne as a matter of course by the seller. Along with greater assumption of risk, the federal government also

Table 9-1   Shifts in positions of major defense contractors, fiscal years 1977–
78

Rank			Contracts Awarded (billions)	
1978	1977	Company	1978	1977
1	8	General Dynamics Corporation	$ 4.2	$ 1.4
2	1	McDonnell-Douglas Corporation	2.9	2.6
3	3	United Technologies Corporation	2.4	1.6
4	2	Lockheed Corporation	2.2	1.7
5	5	General Electric	1.8	1.5
6	16	Litton Industries, Inc.	1.6	.6
7	4	Boeing Company	1.5	1.6
8	9	Hughes Aircraft Company	1.5	1.1
9	11	Raytheon Company	1.3	1.0
10	7	Grumman Corporation	1.2	1.4

Source: U.S. Department of Defense

has been taking on increased operating responsibility for its suppliers' internal operations. (This is a point to which we will return.)

In the one-third of government purchases that are for defense and space programs, potential contractors' past records of technical achievement are often a dominant factor in awarding a contract. Whether a particular program will reach the production stage depends largely on the technical capability displayed during the research and development stage. In many cases the military is not a buyer of products — frequently the products do not yet exist at the time of purchase — but of research and design capacity and the ability to convert research and development into fully developed weapon systems. For the other two-thirds of government procurement, mainly at the state and local level, bidding occurs generally among civilian-oriented firms that are merely offering standard commercial products.

For most civilian government agencies price is all-important. Sealed bidding is the order of the day. No weight is given to conscientiousness of prior performance, as long as bidders are considered to be "responsible." For military and space systems, as pointed out, technical capability is given much greater weight. Since the significant competition for high technology systems frequently occurs before the final product is completely designed, estimates of total cost are tentative and of limited reliability or real usefulness. The seller's previous cost performance and demonstrated capabilities may be given much greater weight than the price estimate it offers.

There may be little if any advertising done in the government markets. On military work the "allowable" costs, such as for advertising, are strictly regulated. Very limited marketing and distribution capabilities are needed. Often the manufacturer ships directly to the government purchaser, who may not necessarily be the actual user. Thus, it is the government rather than the private supplier that maintains the internal distribution system, be it General Services Administration warehouses or Air Force supply depots or a state purchasing department. The flow of material from the seller to central warehouses to the operating command and on to the final user is analogous in the commerical economy to the flow from manufacturer to wholesaler to retailer and on to the final customer. Given this distribution setup, many government contractors have developed only very limited marketing capabilities. At times, this has inhibited their ability during declines in military sales to shift their merchandising efforts to the civilian economy.

Government contractors generally do not need to devote as much attention as do civilian contractors to standard economic and industrial market forecast techniques. Concern focuses instead on sociopolitical trends and forces that influence the size and composition of public disbursements.

THE COMPOSITION OF THE GOVERNMENT MARKET

As shown in Table 9-2, government expenditures are only a starting point in analyzing the public-sector market. Transfers, interest payments, and subsidies must be deducted. Account also must be taken of the fact that more than half of the category of "government purchases of goods and services" consists of wages, salaries, and fringe benefits paid to government employees; these items can be expected to rise steadily as a result of their statutory tie to expanding wage costs in the private economy. Less than one-third of total government expenditures account for actual purchases from the private sector.

When the total of such purchases is broken down, it can be seen that the aggregate of federal procurement is less than the combined purchases of state and local governments, albeit a portion of the latter is financed by federal aid. Also of interest is the fact that durable goods and construction outlays account for a third of total government purchases of goods. This is a basically different pattern

Table 9-2   Composition of the government market, 1977

Category	Billions of Dollars	Percent
Government expenditures*	622	100
Less: Transfers, interest payments, and subsidies	228	37
Equals: Government purchases of goods and services	394	63
Less: Compensation of government employees	208	33
Equals: Government purchases from the private sector	186	30

Breakdown by Customer			Breakdown by Type of Purchase		
Level	Billions of Dollars	Percent	Level	Billions of Dollars	Percent
Federal	79	42	Durable goods	24	13
State and local	107	58	Nondurable goods	39	21
			Construction	37	20
			Services	86	46
Total	186	100		186	100

Detail of Government Purchases (billions of dollars)				
	Construction	All Other	Total	Percent
Military	2	49	51	27
Other federal	5	23	28	15
Total federal	7	72	79	42
Education	5	23	28	15
Other state and local	25	54	79	43
Total state and local	30	77	107	58
Total	37	149	186	100

*National income accounts basis.
Source: U.S. Department of Commerce data

from that in the consumer-oriented private sector, with its heavier emphasis on services and nondurables. More detailed breakdowns are available for military procurement. In the fiscal year 1978, the Department of Defense awarded $52.6 billion in procurement contracts to business firms for work in the United States, primarily for aircraft, missiles, ships, and other weapon systems. Table 9-3 shows the size and relative importance of the various items that the military establishment buys from the private sector, ranging from tanks to textiles.

Table 9-3   Product composition of the military market fiscal year 1978

Category	Amount (in millions)	Percent of Total
Major weapon systems:		
Aircraft	$ 10,976	20.9
Electronics and communications equipment	6,911	13.1
Missiles and space systems	6,560	12.5
Ships	5,441	10.3
Tanks and automotive vehicles	2,011	3.8
Ammunition	1,580	3.0
Conventional weapons	843	1.6
Total, major weapon systems	34,322	65.2
Other manufactured commodities:		
Fuels and lubricants	$ 2,880	5.5
Subsistence	1,126	2.1
Textiles — clothing and equipage	680	1.3
Medical supplies and equipment	222	.4
Production equipment	147	.3
Materials handling equipment	131	.2
Construction equipment	98	.2
Photographic equipment	81	.2
Building supplies	70	.1
All other supplies and equipment	1,257	2.4
Total, other commodities	6,692	12.7
All other purchases:		
Services	$ 4,554	8.7
Construction	2,385	4.5
Procurements of less than $10,000	4,663	8.9
Total, all other	11,602	22.1
Grand total	$ 52,616	100.0

Source: U.S., Department of Defense, *Military Prime Contract Awards*, fiscal year 1978

TYPES OF REGULATION

The federal government requires that firms doing business with it maintain "fair" employment practices, provide "safe" and "healthful" working conditions, pay "prevailing" wages, refrain from polluting the air and water, give preference to American products in their purchases, and promote the rehabilitation of prisoners and the severely handicapped. Table 9-4 contains a sample listing of such ancillary duties required of government contractors. From this book's viewpoint, we are concerned about the important extent to

Table 9-4   Special social and economic restrictions on government contractors

Program	Purpose
Improve Working Conditions	
Walsh-Healey Act	Prescribes minimum wages, hours, age, and work conditions for supply contracts
Davis-Bacon Act	Prescribes minimum wages, benefits, and work conditions on construction contracts over $2,000
Service Contract Act of 1968	Extends the Walsh-Healey and Davis-Bacon Acts to service contracts
Convict Labor Act	Prohibits employment on government contracts of persons imprisoned at hard labor
Favor Disadvantaged Groups	
Equal Employment Opportunity (Executive Orders 11246 and 11375)	Prohibits discrimination in government contracting
Employment Openings for Veterans (Executive Order 11598)	Requires contractors to list suitable employment openings with state employment systems
Prison-made supplies (18 U.S. Code 4124)	Requires mandatory purchase of specific supplies from federal prison industries
Blind-made products (41 U.S. Code 46–48)	Requires mandatory purchase of products made by blind and other handicapped persons
Small Business Act	Requires "fair" portion of subcontracts to be placed with small businesses
Labor Surplus Area Concerns (32A Code of Federal Regulations 33)	Requires preference to subcontractors in areas of concentrated unemployment or underemployment
Favor American Companies	
Buy American Act	Provides preference for domestic materials over foreign materials
Preference to U.S. Vessels (10 U.S. Code 2631; 46 U.S. Code 1241)	Requires shipment of all military goods and at least half of other government goods in U.S. vessels
Protect the Environment and Quality of Life	
Clean Air Act of 1970	Prohibits contracts to a company convicted of criminal violation of air pollution standards
Care of Laboratory Animals (ASPR 7-303.44)	Requires humane treatment by defense contractors in use of experimental or laboratory animals
Humane Slaughter Act (7 U.S. Code 1901–1906)	Limits government purchases of meat to suppliers who conform to humane slaughter standards
Promote Other Government Objectives	
Use of Government Facilities (ASPR 7-104.37)	Requires defense contractors to purchase jewel bearings from government facility
Use of Government Stockpile (ASPR 1-327)	Requires defense contractors to purchase aluminum from national stockpile

Source: Murray L. Weidenbaum, "Social Responsibility Is Closer Than You Think," *Michigan Business Review,* July 1973

which this required "social responsibility" reduces the discretion of private management and increases the costs of the goods and services that government agencies, as well as others, purchase from the private sector.

HISTORICAL DEVELOPMENT OF REQUIRED
SOCIAL RESPONSIBILITY

One of the earliest attempts to bring about social change through the government procurement process was the enactment of the Eight-Hour Laws, a series of statutes setting standards for hours of work. In 1892 the eight-hour work day was first extended to workers employed by contractors and subcontractors engaged in federal projects.[1] President Theodore Roosevelt, by an executive order issued in 1905, prevented the use of convict labor on government contracts. This order was based on an 1887 statute prohibiting the hiring out of convict labor.

The use of the government contract as a means for promoting social and economic objectives became widespread during the depression of the 1930s. In the face of high unemployment and depressed wages, Congress passed the Buy American Act and most of the current labor standards legislation governing public contracts, including the Davis-Bacon Act and the Walsh-Healey Public Contracts Act.

The economic mobilization during World War II gave further impetus to this use of the government purchasing process. Executive orders requiring nondiscrimination in employment by government contractors were justified by the need to encourage maximum use of the nation's scarce manpower and other resources. A similar concern during the Korean War led to a provision encouraging the placement of government contracts and subcontracts in areas of substantial labor surplus.

Rarely have these social provisions been eliminated or scaled down, even when the original depression or wartime conditions that led to them were no longer present. Rather, the trend has been to extend their application. In 1964, for example, an amendment to the Davis-Bacon Act broadened the prevailing wage concept to include certain fringe benefits as well as actual wages.[2] The Service Contract Act of 1965 extended to service employees of contractors the wage and labor standards policies established by the Davis-

---

[1] These statutes have been superseded by the Work Hours Act of 1962, 76 Stat. 357. See Murray L. Weidenbaum, "Social Responsibility Is Closer Than You Think," *Michigan Business Review*, July 1973, pp. 32–35.
[2] Public Law 88–349, 78 Stat. 238.

Bacon Act and the Walsh-Healey Public Contracts Act. In 1969 the Contract Hours Standards Act was amended to give the Secretary of Labor authority to promulgate safety and health standards for workers on government construction contracts.

Federal contractors are being compelled to follow energy conservation measures that remain voluntary for all other companies. These restrictions include keeping heating levels in buildings and facilities down to 68 degrees and reducing indoor lighting standards.

The federal procurement process has been utilized as the cutting edge of the effort to reduce barriers to the employment of minority groups. In 1970 the hiring of apprentices and trainees was required on federal construction projects. In 1971 all government contractors and subcontractors were required to list job openings with state employment service offices.[3] This was especially intended to help Vietnam veterans reenter civilian labor markets. The Vocational Rehabilitation Act of 1973 extended the equal employment opportunity programs of government contractors to include handicapped personnel. As shown in Chapter 8, the coverage of many of the federal government's personnel regulations is limited to firms who hold government contracts. This is especially true in the case of affirmative action programs.

The advantages of using government contracts to promote basic social policies are quite clear. Important national objectives may be fostered without the need for additional, direct appropriations from the Treasury. Because restrictive procurement provisions seem to be costless, the government has been making increasing use of them.[4] Any disadvantages, being more indirect, receive less attention.

Although aimed at worthwhile social objectives, those special provisions are not without costs to the government procurement process. They increase overhead expenses of private contractors and federal procurement offices alike. Many of the provisions also exert an upward pressure on the direct costs incurred by the government. The basic concern of government buyers should be to meet public needs at lowest cost. Yet special provisions such as the Davis-Bacon Act have tended to increase the cost of public construction projects through government promulgation of wage rates higher than those that would have resulted if the market were allowed to operate without impediment.[5]

[3] *Weekly Compilation of Presidential Documents,* 376 (1970), article III, sec. B4; Executive Order 11598, 3 CFR 161 (Supp. 1971).

[4] See *Report of the Commission on Government Procurement,* 1, 1972, pp. 110-24.

[5] John P. Gould, *Davis-Bacon Act* (Washington, D.C.: American Enterprise Institute for Public Policy Research, 1971).

Because it has been examined most intensively, some attention to the effects of the Davis-Bacon Act may be appropriate. Several studies have demonstrated that the act tends to increase the costs of the construction projects that the federal government finances or subsidizes. It directs the Department of Labor to set "minimum" rates for construction workers on these projects. Although the law stipulates that the minimums be set at the level prevailing in "the city, town, village, or other civil subdivision of the state in which the work is performed," in practice these rates are rarely the average of those paid all construction workers in the area.

In a study of the Davis-Bacon Act, the General Accounting Office interviewed several private contractors, who stated that they would not bid on federally financed construction projects because of the high wages they would have to pay, even though the added costs would be covered by the government contract. They believed that paying the higher wage rates, as required by the Department of Labor, would disrupt their operations because the workers on federally financed construction would receive more generous wages than the workers on the company's other construction projects. The general contractor for a low-rent public housing project in Lancaster, Pennsylvania, offered to reduce its price by $114,000 if the Davis-Bacon clause were omitted from its contract.[6]

"Minimum" wage rates set under the Davis-Bacon provision are usually at least as high as the local union rates and, in some instances, higher. Contractors who want to bid on these projects must agree to pay at least these rates. Professor Yale Brozen of the University of Chicago reports that in many cases the Labor Department has set minimum rates above the union scale found in the area in which the work is performed. Higher union rates in some other area, 50 or 70 miles from where the work is to be done, are frequently used instead of local rates, despite the instruction in the law to the contrary. More than 50 percent of the time, the Labor Department has used union rates from a county other than that in which the work was done.[7]

Davis-Bacon minimum wage rates in western Pennsylvania, for example, are based on the Pittsburgh construction union scale. When the common labor rate for building construction in Pittsburgh was $6.75 an hour, plus 80 cents in fringe benefits, the prevailing wage

---

[6] Cited in Armand J. Thieblot, Jr., *The Davis-Bacon Act* (Philadelphia: University of Pennsylvania, The Wharton School, 1975), p. 104.

[7] Yale Brozen, "The Law That Boomeranged," *Nation's Business*, April 1974, pp. 71-72.

for common labor in depressed Appalachia was only $3 an hour. As a consequence, local contractors did not bid for water, sewage, and school projects. The "minimums" forced on them for these projects would have raised their wage scales so high that they would have been unable to compete for nongovernmental projects.

The temporary suspension of the Davis-Bacon Act in 1971 provided an opportunity for measuring the effect of this legislation. Several construction contracts were awarded during that period, which provide a direct comparison of the cost with and without the influence of this federal regulation. A contract to install government-supplied generators in a veterans hospital was to be awarded just before the suspension. The low bid, using the "prevailing" wage determination of Davis-Bacon, was $28,884. After the suspension the contract was rebid. The new low bid, without Davis-Bacon, dropped to $22,769, submitted by the original low bidder. The work was completed at this price, a 21-percent saving.

A federally assisted hospital under construction in the Northeast let a contract during the suspension for one phase of construction work. The result was a 23-percent saving over the cost of a similar phase that was subject to the Davis-Bacon Act. In Florida a contractor submitted two bids for the same work on a public housing project, the higher one under the Davis-Bacon procedure and the lower one without the restriction. The difference was $18,000, or a 6-percent saving. In the Midwest an electrical company was awarded two separate contracts for similar-size phases of work on a college building being built with federal support. The phase that was not subject to Davis-Bacon cost 10 percent less than the phase that was.[8]

ADVERSE EFFECTS ON DEFENSE PRODUCTION

Many of these provisions that accompany government procurement contracts reflect the notions of an earlier age. For instance, the prohibition against convict labor was enacted because of the concern over "chain gang" workers, which was a live public issue several decades ago. Changing attitudes on rehabilitation since then, however, have cast doubt on the validity of the negative approach. In fact, under another and more recent statute, federal prisoners may work for pay in local communities under work-release programs.

---

[8] Chamber of Commerce of the United States, *Why Davis-Bacon Must Go* n.d., p. 1. See also U.S., Comptroller General, *The Davis-Bacon Act Should Be Repealed* (Washington, D.C.: U.S. General Accounting Office, 1979).

The greatest shortcoming of the use of government contracts to foster unrelated economic and social aims is the cumulative impact they have on the companies themselves. Since they are forced to take on so many of the concerns and attitudes of government agencies, it should not be too surprising that the more government-oriented corporations have come to show many of the negative characteristics of government bureaus and arsenals. Consequently, the advantages of innovation, risk taking, and efficiency may be lost to the public and private sectors alike. That may be a high price to pay for legislating social responsibility.

Some appreciation of the adverse consequences of government requiring companies to be "socially responsible" can be gained from examining the area of the industrial economy where government control over production is most intensive and of longest standing — the defense industry.

In its long-term dealings with those companies or divisions of companies that cater primarily to the military market, the Department of Defense gradually has taken over decision-making functions that are normally the prerogatives of business management. A new type of relationship has been created in which the military establishment, as the buyer, makes many of the management decisions about policy and detailed procedures within the companies or divisions of companies that sell primarily to the military, management decisions that in commercial business would be made by the companies themselves.[9]

The government's assumption of, and active participation in, private business decision making takes three major forms: virtually determining the choice of products the defense firms produce, strongly influencing the source of capital funds that they use, and closely supervising much of their internal operations.

By awarding billions of dollars of contracts for research and development (R&D) each year, the Department of Defense strongly influences which new products its contractors will design and produce. The government customer thus directly finances the R&D efforts and assumes much of the risk of success or failure of new-product development. In the commercial economy, in contrast, the R&D costs are not borne by the buyer, but by the seller, who only recovers the investment if it results in the sale of profitable products.

The Defense Department also uses its vast financial resources to supply much of the plant and equipment and working capital used by its major contractors for defense work. Military contractors hold

[9] See Murray L. Weidenbaum, *Economics of Peacetime Defense* (New York: Praeger Publishers, 1974), chap. 6.

over $8 billion of outstanding "progress" payments (government payments made prior to completion of the contract and while the work is still in progress).

The most pervasive way in which the military establishment assumes the management decision-making functions of its contractors is through the procurement legislation and regulations governing the awarding of these contracts. The military procurement regulations require private suppliers to accept, on a "take it or leave it" basis, many standard clauses in their contracts that give the government contracting and surveillance officers numerous powers over the internal operations of these companies.

The authority assumed by the government as purchaser includes power to review and veto company decisions as to which activities to perform in-house and which to subcontract, which firms to use as subcontractors, which products to buy domestically rather than to import, what internal financial reporting systems to establish, what type of industrial engineering and planning system to utilize, what minimum as well as average wage rates to pay, how much overtime work to authorize, and so forth. Thus, when a business firm enters into a contract to produce weapon systems for the military, it tends to take on a quasi-public nature. This is given implicit recognition by requiring the firm to conduct itself in many ways as a government agency, to follow the same Buy American, equal employment, depressed area, prevailing wage, and similar statutes.

The following is just a sample of the authority over the private contractor that the Armed Services Procurement Regulation gives to the military contract administration office:[10]

Personnel
Review the contractor's compensation structure.
Monitor compliance with labor and industrial relations matters.
Remove material from strikebound contractor's plants.
Administer the defense industrial security program.

Production
Screen, redistribute, and dispose of contractor inventory.
Review the adequacy of the contractor's traffic operations.
Review and evaluate preservation, packaging, and packing.
Evaluate the contractor's request for facilities.
Evaluate and monitor reliability and maintainability programs.
Perform quality assurance.

[10] Sec. 1-406 of the Armed Services Procurement Regulation; Seymour Melman, *Pentagon Capitalism* (New York: McGraw-Hill, 1970), pp. 38-42.

Maintain surveillance of flight operations.

Assure compliance with safety requirements.

Research and Development

Provide surveillance of design, development, and production engineering efforts.

Review engineering studies, designs, and proposals.

Review test plans.

Evaluate the adequacy of engineering data.

Monitor value engineering programs.

Evaluate and perform surveillance of configuration management systems.

Evaluate the management, planning, scheduling, and allocation of engineering resources.

Purchasing

Review, approve or disapprove, and maintain surveillance of the contractor's procurement system.

Consent to the placement of subcontracts.

Assure compliance with small business and labor surplus area mandatory subcontracting.

Finance

Manage special bank accounts.

Review the contractor's insurance plans.

Monitor the contractor's financial condition.

Assure timely submission of required reports.

Determine the allowability of costs.

Negotiate overhead rates.

On occasion, the attempt to regulate in detail the operations of defense contractors can be self-defeating. For example, one section of the procurement regulations seeks to encourage prime contractors to subcontract as much of their work as possible to small business. Another section, however, attempts to prevent prime contractors from realizing large profits on the work that is subcontracted. In essence, the contractor is told that he will be given favorable treatment if he subcontracts to small business but that his profits will be less than if he does the work himself — an odd combination of incentives.

Government policymakers in the area of military contracting rarely consider the cumulative and long-term effects on company initiative and entrepreneurship. Viewed as a totality, these restrictions represent substantial government regulation of industry. This regulation is not accomplished through a traditional independent regulatory agency, such as the Interstate Commerce Commission, but rather through the unilateral exercise of the government's dominant market position.

Despite the talk from time to time about reducing the degree of government regulation of the defense firms, the trend and the stated policy go the other way. One senior Pentagon official described enthusiastically his visit to a large defense contractor: "I was impressed with the complete interrelationship of the service/contractor organizations. They are virtually colocated. . . . The service is aware of and, in fact, participates in practically every major contractor decision. Both parties join in weekly management meetings."[11]

The same official recalled an earlier visit with the chief executive of a major public utility, during which the executive was asked about the government controls to which he was subject. The answer was a short pamphlet. In striking contrast, a comparatively minor support contractor for the military has over 450 major specifications, directives, and instructions to comply with, weighing in the aggregate several hundred pounds. The Pentagon official's conclusion may not be widely appreciated, but it is amply borne out by the facts: "The reality is that there are infinitely more controls in the so-called free enterprise environment of the major weapons systems contractor than there are in the controlled environment of the public utility."[12]

It is hard to avoid concluding that the current environment for defense work attenuates the normal entrepreneurial characteristics associated with private enterprise. It is not surprising, therefore, that the design and production of weapon systems for the military establishment have been frequently characterized by cost overruns, technical shortcomings, and time delays. A comprehensive report on this subject by the General Accounting Office in January 1977 covered 147 military systems with a total cost estimated in excess of $244 billion. When the 147 projects first went into development, it was estimated that they would cost $149 billion. An increase of $95 billion occurred in the intervening period, or an average overrun of more than 64 percent.[13] Thus, it is hard to avoid the conclusion that a great deal of the taxpayers' money is wasted.

It is not inevitable, of course, that the wave of government regulation of the private sector described in earlier chapters will lead firms in other industries to experience effects now being felt by government contractors. Yet, the ineffective nature of the detailed regulation of defense production provides a clear warning.

[11] Barry J. Shillito, "How to Implement Our Sound Weapons System Acquisition Policies," *Defense Management Journal*, Fall 1971, p. 26.
[12] Ibid.
[13] U.S., Comptroller General, *Financial Status of Major Acquisitions, June 30, 1976*, Report PSAD-77-62, January 18, 1977, p. 4.

10 ‖

government as financier

The arsenal of government power over the private sector is extensive, including the authority to tax, the ability to spend the proceeds of that taxation, and the capability of issuing rules and regulations determining or prohibiting private behavior. One of the lesser known components of that arsenal is the government's power to provide credit to various individuals and organizations. Over the years, many programs to extend credit have been established by the federal government. Since most of these activities do not appear in the federal budget, they seem to be a painless way of achieving national objectives. In the main, the federal government is "merely" guaranteeing private borrowing or sponsoring ostensibly private institutions, albeit with federal aid. Existing examples include the Export-Import Bank and the Federal National Mortgage Association. Serious proposals have been made in recent years to revive that credit instrument of the 1930s — the Reconstruction Finance Corporation.

Is this use of the federal government's credit power a variation of the proverbial "free lunch"? As will be demonstrated, upon closer inspection we find that the government's extending credit results in substantial costs to business as well as to taxpayers; furthermore, it generates opportunities for the application of federal controls over private economic activity — credit serving as the sweetener for the recipient of the added regulation. On the other hand, substantial benefits may accrue from these programs in achieving various national priorities. The advantages of the use of government credit power arise from its effectiveness in channeling more credit — and ultimately additional real resources — to specific groups of the society. In each case Congress has passed a law stating in effect that it believes the national welfare requires that the designated groups receive larger shares of the available supply of credit than would result from the operation of market forces alone.

What may not be apparent are the costs and other side effects that result from the expanded use of government credit programs. In terms of their overall economic impact, they do little to increase the total pool of capital available to the economy. They result literally in a game of musical chairs. By preempting a major portion of the annual flow of savings, the government-sponsored credit agencies reduce the amount of credit that can be provided to unprotected borrowers — mainly consumers, state and local governments, and private business firms.

During periods of tight money it is difficult for unassisted borrowers to attract the financing they require. They are forced to compete against the government-aided borrowers. Federal loan guarantees reduce the riskiness of lending money to the insured borrowers. The result of that uneven competition is still higher interest rates. More detailed analysis of the phenomenon of federal credit programs is warranted because, over the years, substantial numbers of credit programs have made their way through the legislative process of the federal government. These programs emerged on an *ad hoc* basis, with each program directed toward providing assistance in overcoming a specific problem at hand. As a result of this gradual but very substantial accretion, federal credit program subsidies are now provided to many various sectors of the American economy — housing, agriculture, transportation, health, education, state and local governments, small business — as well as to foreigners.[1] As shown in Table 10-1, there are three major uses of the federal government's credit power.

---

[1] Detailed information on individual credit programs is presented in *Special Analyses, Budget of the United States, Fiscal Year 1980* (Washington, D.C.: U.S. Government Printing Office, 1979), pp. 132-82.

Table 10–1 Major federal credit programs, fiscal year 1978 (new commitments, dollars in millions)

Category and Agency	Direct Loans On Budget	Direct Loans Off Budget	Guaranteed Loans	Government-Sponsored Enterprises	Total
Aid to Business					
Commerce	$ 289	—	$ 696	—	$ 985
Interior	33	—	7	—	40
Energy	—	—	32	—	32
National Credit Union Admin.	14	—	—	—	14
Transportation	263	—	43	—	306
Export-Import Bank	1,499	—	5,489	—	6,988
Small Business Admin.	3,093	—	4,258	—	7,351
U.S. Railway Association	735	56	—	—	791
Subtotal	5,926	56	10,525	—	16,507
Aid to Farmers					
Agriculture	21,318	1,326	12,991	—	35,635
Farm credit agencies	—	—	—	29,536	29,536
Subtotal	21,318	1,326	12,991	29,536	65,171
Aid to Local Governments					
Housing and Urban Development	1,327	—	—	—	1,327
Treasury	729	—	—	—	729
District of Columbia	133	—	—	—	133
Subtotal	2,189	—	—	—	2,189

Source: Special Analyses, Budget of the United States Government for Fiscal Year 1980 (Washington, D.C.: U.S. Government Printing Office, 1979)

Aid to Individuals

Health, Education and Welfare	664	—	1,568	—	2,232
Housing and Urban Development	2,172	—	30,133	—	32,305
Veterans Administration	601	—	12,223	—	12,824
Federal Home Loan Bank System	38	—	—	30,294	30,332
Federal National Mortgage Assoc.	—	—	—	18,014	18,014
Student Loan Marketing Assoc.	—	—	—	332	332
Subtotal	3,475	—	43,924	48,640	96,039
Aid to Foreign Governments					
Security Assistance	1,873	—	1,584	—	3,457
Development Assistance	413	—	161	—	574
Subtotal	2,286	—	1,745	—	4,031
Miscellaneous	38	—	752	—	790
Grand total	$ 35,232	$ 1,382	$ 69,937	$ 78,176	$184,727

187

TYPES OF GOVERNMENT CREDIT PROGRAMS

Direct loans by federal departments and agencies. These, such as the loans made by the Rural Electrification Administration, generally involve significant subsidies because the funds usually are loaned at rates below those available in the private sector. In many cases, the government also absorbs the administrative expenses and losses arising from loan defaults, thus further increasing the amount of the subsidy. Although not formally considered a federal credit program, the generous progress payments made by the Department of Defense represent interest-free provision of working capital to government contractors on a very large scale. Direct loans have become a less important form of federal credit aid, in part because they require unequivocal use of federal money.

Loans guaranteed and insured by federal departments and agencies. These account for the greatest share of the current expansion in federal credit subsidies, largely because the loans are made by private lenders and thus excluded from the federal budget. Also, there has been a substantial increase in the federal payments of part of the interest on insured loans for such programs as low-income housing. Technically, all the government does is assume a contingent liability to pay the private lender if the private borrower defaults. When there is little collateral in connection with the guarantee, the government may be assuming relatively high risks. For example, how could the federal government take over its "collateral" should New York City default on its debt?

Loans by federally sponsored agencies, such as the Federal National Mortgage Association, the Federal Home Loan Banks, and the farm credit agencies. These involve relatively little direct subsidy. However, these ostensibly privately owned agencies have various tax advantages and are able to borrow funds in the market at low interest rates because of the implicit government backing of their debentures and other issues. Loans made by these sponsored agencies have increased sharply since the mid-1960s. They now comprise the dominant form of federal credit assistance to the private sector.

IMPACTS ON TOTAL SAVING AND INVESTMENT

The conclusions of the empirical literature on the impacts of federal credit programs on the total flow of saving and investment in the American economy are clear. These programs do little if anything to increase the total flow of saving or investment. They mainly change the share of investment funds going to a given industry or sector of the economy and, in the process of doing so, exert upward pressures on interest rates as investment funds are bid away from other sectors.

In commenting on existing programs of federally assisted credit to the private sector, Dr. Henry Kaufman, distinguished economist with the investment house of Salomon Brothers, has written: "Federal agency financing does not do anything directly to enlarge the supply of savings. . . . In contrast, as agency financing bids for the limited supply of savings with other credit demanders, it helps to bid up the price of money."[2] In referring to borrowing by the federal government and its agencies, Dr. Albert Wojnilower has made a similar observation: "Because these governmental borrowers need have few if any worries about creditworthiness or meeting interest payments, they can preempt as much of the credit markets as they choose. As a result, the federal sector has become one of the most relentless sources of upward pressures on interest rates."[3]

In a comprehensive study of federal credit programs for the prestigious Commission on Money and Credit, Warren Law of Harvard University concluded that the programs have created inflationary pressures in every year since World War II.[4] Professor Patricia Bowers has noted what she terms "costs" of federal credit programs. One cost arises from the fact that given the availability of funds, an increase in credit for housing means lesser amounts for other borrowers. The other two borrowing groups most adversely affected by tight credit are state and local governments and small businesses. A further cost is created when the operations of the federal credit agencies tend to increase the level of interest rates above the level that would have prevailed if they had not entered the credit markets.[5]

This phenomenon occurs for a variety of reasons. The total supply of funds is broadly determined by household and business

[2] Henry Kaufman, "Federal Debt Management: An Economist's View from the Marketplace," in *Issues in Federal Debt Management* (Boston: Federal Reserve Bank of Boston, 1973), p. 171.
[3] Albert M. Wojnilower, "Can Capital-Market Controls Be Avoided in the 1970s?" in *Containing Inflation in the Environment of the 1970s*, ed. Michael E. Levy (New York: Conference Board, 1971), p. 42.
[4] Warren A. Law, "The Aggregate Impact of Federal Credit Programs on the Economy," in *Federal Credit Programs*, ed. Commission on Money and Credit (Englewood Cliffs, N.J.: Prentice-Hall, 1963), p. 310.
[5] Patricia F. Bowers, *Private Choice and Public Welfare* (Hinsdale, Ill.: Dryden Press, 1974), pp. 494-96. See also Alan Greenspan, "A General View of Inflation in the United States," in *Inflation in the United States* (New York: Conference Board, 1974), p. 4.

saving and the ability of banks to increase the money supply. This is the basic limit on the availability of funds referred to by Bowers. The normal response of financial markets to an increase in the demand for funds by a borrower, such as is represented by a federal credit program, is an increase in interest rates so as to balance out the demand for funds with the supply of saving. But the federal government's demand for funds is "interest-inelastic" (the Treasury will generally raise the money that it requires regardless of the interest rate), and the interest elasticity of saving is relatively modest. Thus, weak and marginal borrowers will be "rationed" out of financial markets in the process, while the Treasury and other borrowers pay higher rates of interest.

Important insight into the effects of federal credit programs on capital markets has been provided by Bruce MacLaury, president of the Brookings Institution and a former deputy undersecretary of the Treasury:

> The more or less unfettered expansion of federal credit programs and the accompanying deluge of agency direct and guaranteed securities to be financed in the credit markets has undoubtedly permitted Congress and the administration to claim that wonder of wonders — something for nothing, or almost nothing. But as with all such sleight-of-hand feats, the truth is somewhat different.[6]

MacLaury goes on to point out that there are extra costs associated with introducing new government credit agencies to the capital markets, selling issues that are smaller than some minimally efficient size and selling securities that only in varying degree approximate the characteristics of direct government debt in terms of perfection of guarantee, flexibility of timing and maturities, "cleanness" of instrument, and so on. He points out that, as a result of such considerations, the market normally charges a premium over the interest cost on direct government debt of comparable maturity. That premium ranges from one-quarter of one percent on the well-known federally sponsored agencies, such as Federal National Mortgage Association, to more than one-half percent on such exotics as New Community Bonds. In general, if cost of financing were the only consideration, it would be most efficient to have the Treasury itself provide the financing for direct loans by issuing government debt in the market.

Reduced efficiency occurs in the economy by providing a

---

[6] Bruce K. MacLaury, "Federal Credit Programs — The Issues They Raise," in *Issues in Federal Debt Management*, (Boston: Federal Reserve Bank of Boston, 1973), p. 214.

federal "umbrella" over many credit activities without distinguishing their relative credit risks. A basic function that credit markets are supposed to perform is that of distinguishing different credit risks and assigning appropriate risk premiums. This is the essence of the ultimate resource-allocation function of credit markets. As an increasing proportion of issues coming to the credit markets bears the guarantee of the federal government, the scope for the market to differentiate credit risks inevitably diminishes. Theoretically, the federal agencies issuing or guaranteeing debt would perform this role, charging as costs of the programs differing rates of insurance premiums. In practice, all of the pressures are against such differential pricing of risks.[7] This is a hidden cost of federal regulation via credit programs.

IMPACTS ON SECTORS OF THE ECONOMY

The very nature of federal credit assistance is to create advantages for some groups of borrowers and disadvantages for others. The literature provides clear answers on who will tend to be rationed out in the process. It is unlikely to be the large, well-known corporations or the United States government. It is more likely to be state and local governments, medium-size businesses, private mortgage borrowers not under the federal umbrella, and consumers, thereby contributing to additional economic and financial concentration in the United States.

The competition for funds by the rapidly expanding federal credit programs also increases the cost to the taxpayer by raising the interest rate at which the Treasury borrows its own funds. As shown in Table 10-2, there has been a massive expansion in the size and relative importance of federal government credit demands over the past decade. In 1960 the federal share of funds raised in private capital markets, using the Federal Reserve System's flow-of-funds data, was 12.7 percent. By 1970 the government's share had risen to 18.1 percent, and has continued to grow.

Virtually every session of Congress in recent years has enacted additional federal credit programs. Since 1960 the Federal National Mortgage Association (Fannie Mae) has been joined by the General National Mortgage Association (Ginnie Mae), Student Loan Marketing Association (Sally Mae), and the U.S. Railway Association (Fannie Rae). In 1978 Congress authorized 23 new or expanded

7 Ibid., p. 217

Table 10-2   Impact on credit markets of federal and federally assisted borrowing (fiscal years, dollars in billions)

Category of Credit	1960	1965	1970	1975	1978
A. Federal borrowing	$ 2.2	$ 4.0	$ 3.8	$ 50.9	$ 59.1
B. Federally assisted borrowing (off-budget)*	3.3	6.8	12.6	13.9	35.4
C. Total federal and federally assisted borrowing (A + B)	5.5	10.8	16.4	64.8	94.5
D. Total funds advanced in credit markets	43.4	69.6	90.5	177.9	366.9
E. = (C) ÷ (D)	12.7%	15.5%	18.1%	36.4%	25.8%

*Obligations issued by government-sponsored agencies or guaranteed by federal agencies.
Source: U.S. Treasury Department, Federal Reserve System

credit programs, including loan guarantees for demonstration projects for new types of fuel, help for small business in acquiring solar energy equipment, and coverage of a portion of New York City's debts. In view of the financial problems faced in raising sufficient funds for the extremely capital-intensive energy industry, proposals are now being seriously advanced for federal credit guarantees for the development of new domestic energy sources. In the summer of 1979 President Carter urged Congress to set up an Energy Security Corporation, with a charter to provide up to $88 billion of government credit for the promotion of a domestic synthetic fuel industry. Clearly, then, the upward trend has not leveled off.

RELATION TO GOVERNMENT CONTROLS

An examination of existing programs of federal guarantee of private credit reveals how the credit assistance is often accompanied by various forms of government controls of influence over the recipients of the credit. For example, federal credit guarantees for shipbuilders are part of a broader program whereby the federal government requires the builders to incorporate various "national defense" features into the vessels.

It is instructive to examine the largest federal program for guaranteeing private credit, that administered by the Federal Housing Administration (FHA), to observe the extent to which controls accompany the credit assistance. The FHA conducts an inspection of each residence to determine whether the builder has abided by all of the agency's rules and regulations governing the construction of the homes that it insures. There are four separate "veto" points facing a builder applying for FHA insurance of mortgages for a new project: (1) affirmative marketing to minority groups, (2) environmental impact, (3) architectural review, and (4) underwriting.

Because of the division of responsibilities among the various federal housing offices, considerable confusion and delay can arise. For example, after the underwriting has been approved, which gives an appraised value high enough to cover the builder's costs, additional requirements may be imposed by the environmental impact office or by the architectural review. These actions substantially raise the cost of the project. If this occurs, the builder must return to the first office and attempt to obtain a revised underwriting.

Miles Colean, distinguished analyst of the housing industry, has commented on the deleterious effects on the housing industry of the increasing array of government controls that has been imposed via the FHA program: "The complications of FHA operations, by introducing numerous requirements irrelevant to the extension of mortgage credit, placed the market-oriented activity of FHA at a competitive disadvantage."[8]

In October 1972 the National Center for Housing Management contracted with the Department of Housing and Urban Development to study HUD's housing programs. The Center drew on a distinguished group of experts in the area of housing. In analyzing the requirements added in recent years to the FHA processing format — "such matters as affirmative marketing, environmental protection, and project selection" — the Center's report stated:

> . . . the task force feels that HUD has not proceeded in the most logical fashion in dealing with these new requirements. It has tended to add them on to the process without even analyzing the effect that they would have on that process. . . . The end result has been that the constant imposition of new socially useful requirements for FHA processing has produced a substantial loss of competitive status for FHA's single-family programs.[9]

Thus, the implicit credit subsidy to the FHA in effect is being absorbed to a large extent by the social objectives. The current cost of attempting to implement these social policies may be quite high compared with more direct alternatives. Once an industry has become dependent on the federal financial assistance, that situation

[8] Miles L. Colean, "Quarterly Economic Report," *Mortgage Banker*, March 1974, p. 63.
[9] *Report of the Task Force on Improving the Operation of Federally Insured or Financed Housing Programs* (Washington, D.C.: National Center for Housing Management, n.d.), pp. 69-70.

can be used to impose additional controls, which may be unrelated to protecting the government's investment or contingent liability.

SUMMARY

Contrary to the popular view, government credit programs are not costless, either to the Treasury or to citizens in general. Three distinct costs of these government programs can be identified:

1. *The economic cost.* Since they do little if anything to increase the total supply of investment funds in the economy, government credit programs take credit away from other potential borrowers. These unsubsidized borrowers might have produced more for society than the recipients of the government-supported credit. This can be the situation when the presence of federal credit encourages individuals or organizations to incur expenditures that they would forego in the absence of the federal subsidy.
2. *The initial fiscal cost.* To the extent that government credit programs increase the total size of government-related credit, they cause an increase in the interest rates that are paid in order to channel these funds away from the private sector. Some increase, therefore, results in the interest rates paid on the public debt, which is a direct cost to the taxpayer.
3. *The ultimate fiscal cost.* When defaults occur on the part of the borrowers whose credit is guaranteed by the federal government, the Treasury winds up bearing the ultimate cost of the credit. In such cases government credit programs become a form of back-door spending whereby federal expenditures are incurred in the absence of direct appropriations for the purpose.

Boiled down to its essence, federal guarantees of bonds issued by business and other institutions really involve putting "the monkey" on someone else's back. They do not increase the amount of investment funds available to the economy. Rather, to the extent they succeed, they mainly move capital funds to some sectors of the economy by taking those funds away from other sectors, and they lead to similar requests for aid by those latter sectors. These government guarantees also tend to raise the level of interest rates in the economy, both for private as well as for government borrowers. They thus increase an important element of business costs.

Since a growing proportion of private saving is being borrowed by governments, the inelasticity of demand of the money and capital markets has been rising. That is, governments elbow private borrowers out of the capital markets simply because the federal government and its agencies are willing to pay whatever interest rates are required to cover their financial needs. Private borrowers are restricted by competitive pressures and the limits of their own resources.

The pressure on interest rates forces the Federal Reserve System to increase the reserves of the banking system to supply financing to the private sector. This, in turn, contributes to the general inflationary condition of the economy. Federal credit programs therefore tend to raise the private cost of production in two ways: (1) by causing an increase in interest rates, and (2) by resulting in a higher general rate of inflation.

Several concepts have been suggested to deal with the various problems that arise with the expansion of federal credit programs. One general approach is to require that all proposals to create new federal credit programs or to broaden existing ones be accompanied by an appraisal of the relation between the interest rate charged in the program, the rate which would be charged by competitive and efficient private lenders, and the rate necessary to cover the government's costs.

A more detailed method is to establish controls over the total volume of federally assisted credit. Even though no immediate impact on the federal budget may be visible in most cases, the influence on the allocation of resources — on the composition of income and employment — may be very considerable. At present, many of these federal credit programs tend to have virtually a blank check on the nation's credit resources. Under this second method, they would no longer be treated as a "free good."

One way of controlling federal credit programs is to impose a ceiling on the total borrowing of federal and federally sponsored credit agencies, both those "in" and those "out" of the budget. In addition, Congress could enact a ceiling on the overall volume of debt created under federal loan guarantees. It would be important to establish procedures to permit review of commitments far enough in advance to permit evaluating their likely impact when the commitments become actual loans.

A third method of controlling federal credit programs more effectively is to require these programs to be reviewed and coordinated along with other federal programs in the preparation of the government's annual budget and economic plans. At the present time, numerous federal credit programs — guaranteed and insured loans, and loans by federally sponsored enterprises — escape regular budget and program review.

Perhaps the most fundamental proposal does not deal with federal credit programs at all, but with the underlying conditions of which they are symptoms. Hence, if we can create an economic climate more conducive to private saving and investment, that will reduce the need for private borrowers to seek federal credit assistance. The creation of that climate may require a tax system that tilts in favor of saving rather than consumption and a fiscal policy that avoids the large Treasury deficits whose financing competes with private borrowers. Until these fundamental changes are achieved, continued expansion of federal credit programs seems to be likely.

11

the paperwork burden

Judging from statements of business executives, the major source of government intrusion is the paperwork burden imposed by the many agencies of federal, state, and local governments. Without minimizing the problem, the paperwork requirements should be seen in perspective. First of all, the burden is primarily a result of federal regulation. Government agencies demand a wide range of data from industry for the simple reason that they require a large amount of information to conduct their regulatory operations. That burden is, therefore, not an "autonomous" phenomenon in the relations between business and government but an effect or an ancillary aspect of regulation.

Second, however, much of the paperwork is generated not because the specific information is needed, but because agencies may feel the need to learn more about business operations — and possible violations of laws and regulations. The regulatory agencies, which usually are dominated by lawyers, often want exhaustive information, rather than samplings or selections of data. This method of information gathering is what one economist calls "the blunderbuss approach."[1] Moreover, the paperwork requirements are at times imposed by agencies as a reaction to the demands of a variety of special-interest groups which want close monitoring of business actions—often as a prelude to new or more detailed regulation. (A case in point here are the voluminous environmental impact statements which must be submitted to the Council on Environmental Quality—and which the CEQ itself has criticized as overblown.)

In addition, much of the paperwork burden is a result of non-regulatory functions of government, notably tax collections. Moreover, some of the paperwork results from voluntary acts of business: applying for loans and other credit assistance, bidding for government contracts, and requesting statistical data and other government information.

Surely the paperwork burden is costly. It is expensive and time consuming to process and submit reports, make out applications, fill out questionnaires, reply to orders and directives, and make appeals in courts for rulings and regulatory opinions.

In the 1970s complaints from businesses, both large and small, rose to a high pitch. In October 1976 the National Commission on Federal Paperwork began a detailed study of the problem; it made public its recommendations in late 1977. The commission estimated that the cost of the burden nationally amounted to more than $100 billion a year, or about $500 for each person in the United States. Less than half the cost is borne directly by the federal government. An estimated $25 billion to $32 billion is spent by private industry. In fact, the ten thousand largest firms in the country on the average spend over one million dollars each a year on paperwork.[2]

THE RANGE OF PAPERWORK REQUIREMENTS

An estimated ten billion sheets of paper are filled out each year by business organizations, occupying file space in the federal government that in fiscal year 1976 totaled 12.6 million cubic feet.[3]

The required reports and documents take a variety of forms. The General Accounting Office categorizes them broadly as applica-

[1] Frederic M. Scherer, "Statistics for Government Regulation," *American Statistician*, February 1979, p. 3.
[2] U.S., Commission on Federal Paperwork, *Final Summary Report* (Washington, D.C.: U.S. Government Printing Office, 1977), p. 5.
[3] Testimony of Senator Thomas J. McIntyre, Cochairman, Commission on Federal Paperwork, before Senate Committee on Government Operations, May 3, 1976.

tions (for benefits or grants, etc.), program evaluations, management reports, statistical surveys, and record keeping to assure compliance with the law. Under these headings the federal government requires filings of over 5,000 types of documents. Nearly half of these are applicable to business alone.[4] Eighteen of the 50 most burdensome requirements are concentrated in six regulatory agencies: the Interstate Commerce Commission (ICC), the Nuclear Regulatory Commission (NRC), the Office of Surface Mining Reclamation and Enforcement (in the Interior Department), the Federal Communications Commission (FCC), the Federal Trade Commission (FTC), and the Equal Employment Opportunity Commission (EEOC). The Departments of Labor and Commerce also contributed significantly to the paperwork burden.[5]

The great majority of government information requests is recurrent in nature (rather than one-time-only reports), and these requests fall into six broad categories.[6] The first is *statistical information* that is sent, for example, to the Bureau of the Census or the Bureau of Labor Statistics. Such information consists of summaries of plant operations, turnover, wages and working hours, and so forth.

Financial information can take a variety of forms, such as reports filed with the Securities and Exchange Commission, the Federal Trade Commission, the Labor Department, and the Internal Revenue Service. The best known of these is a business's general annual report, or the 10-K report, filed with the SEC. Other required financial information can relate to a company's personnel operations and benefits programs, including data on a company's pension plan (required in detail under the Employee Retirement Income Security Act), affirmative action plans that are required of government contractors (filed with the Office of Federal Contract Compliance), and equal employment reports which show the number of women and minorities employed in various occupational categories.

Types of *environmental information* required of a company will vary according to the firm's operations. If a company discharges substantial amounts of pollutants into the air or water, it must file reports with the Environmental Protection Agency. Other reports apply to drinking-water supplies and the manufacturing of a wide range of chemicals. Numerous reports, especially those related to product labels, must be made for the manufacture of pesticides and

4 *Federal Paperwork: Its Impact on American Business* (Washington, D.C.: U.S. General Accounting Office, 1978), p. 15.
5 Ibid., p. 12.
6 See Rogene A. Buchholz, *Corporate Cost for Compliance with Government Regulation of Information*, Working Paper no. 43 (St. Louis: Center for the Study of American Business, Washington University, 1979).

agricultural chemicals in particular. These are required under the Toxic Substances Control Act (TSCA) of 1976, enforced by EPA. Inventories of toxic chemicals must be kept current and filed with the government, and companies must continue to report detailed scientific data on all new chemicals that are developed.

In the area of *occupational safety and health*, information relating to occupational injuries and illnesses must be maintained at each plant or workplace of a company. Though it is not sent directly to a federal agency, the Occupational Safety and Health Administration requires, as a matter of law, that these safety and health records be kept current. OSHA inspectors can levy penalties against a firm if information is found to be deficient.

Since the creation of the Department of Energy in 1977, requirements for *energy information* have increased the paperwork load. This information often is very complex and can take the form of reports on energy conservation, domestic crude oil purchases, and domestic natural gas reserves. Public utilities regulated by the Federal Energy Regulatory Commission are faced with extensive requirements for their accounting and reporting procedures. Many energy companies must submit additional reports relating to energy to the U.S. Geological Survey and the Bureau of Mines, both in the Interior Department.

Finally, a variety of miscellaneous reports is required of businesses by federal agencies such as the Bureau of Alcohol, Tobacco and Firearms (in the Treasury Department).

All in all, the average large corporation in the United States can be subject to the paperwork requirements of as many as 14 different federal departments and agencies and their subsidiary units. These requirements are the result of a wide array of legislation designed either to monitor or to regulate business operations. The Office of Management and Budget estimated that the reporting burden imposed on American business by the federal government increased by 50 percent between December 1967 and June 1974.[7] Major new programs were the principal source of the increase — occupational safety and health activities, medicare and medicaid, environmental protection regulations, and equal employment opportunity compliance. Just keeping track of new reporting requirements can be difficult. Many firms rely on trade association publications and external consultants and lawyers to keep them advised of changes or new legislation or regulation pertaining to their business (see chapter 16).

One of the problems seems to be that the various levels of gov-

---

[7] *Statement of Robert H. Marik, Associate Director for Management and Operations, Office of Management and Budget, before the House Committee on Government Operations, 93d Cong., 2d sess., September 12, 1974, p. 5.*

ernment view proposed forms solely from the viewpoint of government, rather than from the vantage point of the private respondent. The Office of Management and Budget, which has the responsibility for minimizing the paperwork burden at the federal level, was unable to tell a congressional committee exactly the number of forms or which forms a typical small business might be required to fill out each year.

In spite of the efforts of the Commission on Federal Paperwork to limit or decrease the paperwork burden, the amount imposed by government regulatory agencies on private industry has remained the same, or has increased, simply because of more congressional action. As a result of a rider attached to the Alaska pipeline bill (Public Law 93-153), the authority to review proposed questionnaires of federal regulatory commissions has been shifted from the Office of Management and Budget to the General Accounting Office (GAO). In the process, the power to disapprove unnecessary reports has been converted merely to issuing advisory opinions to the agencies, who now have the final power to decide whether the report burdens that they impose on the private sector are necessary. Unlike OMB, GAO cannot now rule on "the necessity of the information." In the past, the value of the data requested was compared with the trouble and cost required to gather it, before the questionnaires were approved.

Governmentwide efforts to reduce the enormous range of paperwork requirements have not, to date, met with success. The General Accounting Office reported in 1978, at the time the Federal Paperwork Commission concluded its work, that the burden placed on large and small businesses, state and local governments, educational institutions, and individuals had reached "astounding dimensions" and was still growing. One effort to reduce the public reporting burden, a program initiated by President Ford in 1976 for executive agencies subject to the Federal Reports Act of 1942, yielded a reduction of 644 forms but an *increase* in the reporting burden of 3.6 million hours. The additional burden was the result of only three new forms (one for the settlement of real estate transactions and two for employee pensions under ERISA).[8]

THE COSTS AND OTHER EFFECTS OF PAPERWORK

The filing of documents for federal agencies would appear, on the surface, to be a relatively harmless requirement. But the filling

[8] *Data Collected from Non-Federal Sources — Statistical and Paperwork Implications* (Washington, D.C.: U.S. General Accounting Office, 1978), p. 4-1.

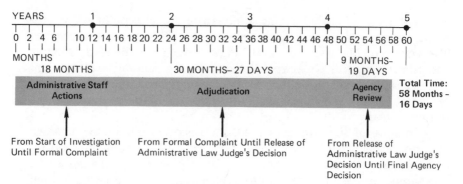

Number of Years, Months and Days That Elasped in Disposition of the Median Restraint-of-Trade Case

Figure 11-1 PROCESSING TIME ANALYSIS OF THE FEDERAL TRADE COMMISSION
Source: David Burnham, "Regulatory Agencies Scored on Delays," *New York Times,* June 15, 1974.

out and filing of forms and the providing of detailed reports to government agencies impose tremendous costs on businesses, both large and small, and consequently on the consumer.

Some federal regulations enacted to protect the customer also involve additional paperwork costs and not necessarily with altogether beneficial effects. The Real Estate Settlement Procedures Act of 1974 is designed to provide greater disclosure of home mortgage closing costs and possibly help consumers save money on settlement charges. The new law requires lenders to disclose all closing costs to buyers at least 12 days before settlement. In practice, this has meant lengthening the time that it takes to complete a purchase of a home. Moreover, one bank estimates that the cost of the added paperwork required by the 1974 law comes to about $50 a loan.[9] Although lenders are not permitted to charge directly for the extra documents required under the law, it is likely that they ultimately are compensated for the additional expense, notably in the form of higher loan fees.

Added costs of paperwork are also incurred by the length of time taken in handling and acting upon information. The extended process of decision making by federal agencies inevitably produces a "regulatory lag," a delay that can run into years and can be an encumbrance to private managerial decision making. For example, the Federal Trade Commission averages nearly five years to complete a restraint-of-trade case[10] (see fig. 11-1). Thirty percent of the electric utility rate cases decided in 1973 extended for more than one year, some of them taking more than two years to be settled.[11]

[9] "Business Bulletin," *Wall Street Journal,* July 3, 1975, p. 1.
[10] David Burnham, "Regulatory Agencies Scored on Delays," *The New York Times,* June 15, 1974, p. 10.
[11] Murray L. Weidenbaum, *Financing the Electric Utility Industry* (New York: Edison Electric Institute, 1974), chap. 5.

It took the Federal Power Commission (now reorganized into the Department of Energy) eleven years to determine how to regulate the price of natural gas all the way back to the wellhead.[12] Prior to the 1962 amendments to the food and drug law, the Food and Drug Administration processed an average new drug application in seven months. The more stringent regulation has resulted in increasing the regulatory lag to two and one-half years.[13]

Impacts on Small Business

Regulatory delay and government-required paperwork can be particularly costly for small businesses. A firm employing not more than 50 people is required to fill out as many as 75 to 80 different types of forms in the course of one year.[14] The lack of understanding which at times occurs between the regulators and those they regulate is conveyed in the interchange reported by a small manufacturer who attended a meeting to discuss the paperwork burden. When he was advised to have his staff complete the forms, he replied, "When I attend this meeting the staff is right here with me. It's me."[15]

Two employees working half time to fill out government forms may not sound particularly burdensome to a small enterprise employing 75 people until you consider that it might substantially reduce the plant's productivity increase for the year. In contrast, a plant employing 5,000 people can much more easily afford to employ a staff of 10 working full time to meet federal requirements. Figure 11-2 contains one of the shorter federal forms that accompany regulatory functions. It is the weekly one-page report on meat inspection that processing plants are required to submit to the Department of Agriculture.

Approximately 1,100 permits were required to build the Alaska pipeline. To obtain approval for a new drug, a 64-volume application, 10 feet tall, was submitted by one pharmaceutical company.[16] A small, 5,000-watt radio station in New Hampshire reported that it spent $26.23 to mail its application for license renewal to the Federal Communications Commission. An Oregon company, operating three small television stations, reported that its license renewal application

---

[12] Floyd G. Lawrence, "Can Industry Develop a Five-Year Strategy?" *Industry Week,* January 6, 1975, p. 43.
[13] Sam Peltzman, *Regulation of Pharmaceutical Innovation* (Washington, D.C.: American Enterprise Institute for Public Policy Research, 1974).
[14] U.S., Congress, Senate, Select Committee on Small Business, *The Federal Paperwork Burden,* 93d Cong., 1st sess., 1973, p. 2.
[15] Ibid., pp. 3–4.
[16] Lawrence, "Can Industry Develop a Five-Year Strategy?" p. 43.

- 205A -

FORM MI-404 (11-1-67)	U.S. DEPARTMENT OF AGRICULTURE CONSUMER AND MARKETING SERVICE MEAT INSPECTION	WEEK CODE NO.	MONTH	DAY	MONTH	DAY	YEAR	FORM APPROVED BUD. BUR. NO. 40-R2039
	PROCESSING OPERATIONS AT OFFICIAL ESTABLISHMENTS	TO: OFFICER IN CHARGE	From		To	CIRCUIT		EST. NO.

PART 1 - MEAT AND MEAT FOOD PRODUCTS *(Express in pounds)* This part is required under 9 CFR 320.3 and 21 U.S.C. 89.

	CODE NO.	POUNDS		CODE NO.	POUNDS
CURED OR PLACED IN CURE			LOAF; HEAD CHEESE; CHILI; JELLIED PRODUCT	1410	
Beef Briskets	1012		STEAKS; CHOPS; ROASTS; BONELESS CUTS	1420	
Beef - Other	1019				
Pork	1020		SLICED PRODUCT		
Other Meats	1030		Bacon	1440	
SMOKED OR DRIED			Other (Sausage; loaves; ham; luncheon meat)	1450	
Hams - Regular	1122				
Hams - Water added	1123		HAMBURGER	1460	
Hams - Boneless	1124		GROUND BEEF	1465	
Picnics - Regular	1125		MISCELLANEOUS MEAT PRODUCT	1470	
Picnics - Water added	1126		FROZEN FOODS - Dinners; Entrees; Meat Pies; Specialties	1480	
Pork Butts	1127				
Bacon	1121		LARD - Rendered	1510	
Pork - Other	1129		LARD - Refined	1520	
Beef	1110		EDIBLE TALLOW	1540	
Other Smoked or Dried Meats	1130		PORK FAT - Rendered	1550	
COOKED MEAT			PORK FAT - Refined	1560	
Hams	1224		COMPOUND CONTAINING ANIMAL FAT	1570	
Pork - Other	1229		OLEOMARGARINE CONTAINING ANIMAL FAT	1580	
Beef	1210				
Other Cooked Meats	1230		CANNED PRODUCT - Commercial	1590	
SAUSAGE			CANNED PRODUCT - Government	1595	
Fresh finished	1310		BEEF - BONED (Manufacturing)	5350	
Dried or Semi-dried	1320		PORK CUT	5360	
Franks/Wieners	1330		OTHER MEAT - BONED	5370	
Bologna	1335				
Other Smoked and/or Cooked	1340		HORSE MEAT PRODUCT	6910	

PART 2 - BREAKDOWN OF CANNED PRODUCT TOTAL *(Express in pounds of finished product. Do not include product canned for governmental agency. The following section of this report will be used for statistical purposes. It is not required by law.)*

	LUNCHEON MEAT		CANNED HAMS			BEEF HASH		CHILI CON CARNE		VIENNAS	
	40 OZ. OR OVER	UNDER 40 OZ.	UNDER 3 LB.	3 to 6 LB.	OVER 6 LB.	40 OZ. or OVER	UNDER 40 OZ.	40 OZ. OR OVER	UNDER 40 OZ.	40 OZ. OR OVER	UNDER 40 OZ.
WEEKLY TOTAL CODE NO.	2611	2612	2621	2622	2623	2631	2632	2641	2642	2651	2652

	FRANKS, WIENERS IN BRINE AND SAUCE	DEVILED HAM	OTHER POTTED OR DEVILED MEAT FOOD PRODUCTS	TAMALES		SLICED DRIED BEEF	CHOPPED BEEF		MEAT STEW (All products)	
				40 OZ. OR OVER	UNDER 40 OZ.		40 OZ. OR OVER	UNDER 40 OZ.	40 OZ. OR OVER	UNDER 40 OZ.
WEEKLY TOTAL CODE NO.	2660	2670	2680	2691	2692	2710	2721	2722	2731	2732

	SPAGHETTI MEAT PRODUCTS (All types)		TONGUE (Other than Pickled)	VINEGAR PICKLED PRODUCTS		SAUSAGE	HAMBURGER; ROASTED or CORNED BEEF, MEAT AND GRAVY		SOUPS	
	40 OZ. OR OVER	UNDER 40 OZ.		40 OZ. OR OVER	UNDER 40 OZ.		40 OZ. OR OVER	UNDER 40 OZ.	40 OZ. OR OVER	UNDER 40 OZ.
WEEKLY TOTAL CODE NO.	2741	2742	2750	2761	2762	2770	2781	2782	2791	2792

	SAUSAGE IN OIL		TRIPE	BRAINS	CANNED LOINS AND PICNICS	ALL OTHER WITH MEAT AND/OR MEAT BY-PRODUCTS				HORSE MEAT (All kinds)
						20% OR MORE		LESS THAN 20%		
	40 OZ. OR OVER	UNDER 40 OZ.				40 OZ. OR OVER	UNDER 40 OZ.	40 OZ. OR OVER	UNDER 40 OZ.	
WEEKLY TOTAL CODE NO.	2811	2812	2820	2830	2840	2851	2852	2861	2862	6940

NAME OF FIRM	BY	TITLE	APPROVED BY INSPECTOR

Figure 11-2

weighed 45 pounds. These small stations apparently were required to fill out the same forms as the multimillion-dollar radio and television stations operating in major metropolitan areas.[17]

One small businessman, James Baker, president of Gar-Baker

[17] U.S., Congress, *The Federal Paperwork Burden*, p. 10.

Laboratories in New York City, lamented the number of government forms his five-man firm must fill out:

1. Thirty-seven filings on 12 different federal forms, ranging from tax reports to data for the Census Bureau to registration with the Food and Drug Administration.
2. Twenty-six sets of data for nine different New York State agencies, including employee and tax records, an alcohol permit, and information on disability-benefits insurance.
3. Twenty-five forms for 12 different city departments, including a variety of tax records, a chemical permit from the fire department, two refrigerator permits, and one deep-freeze permit.[18]

A corporation with about 40,000 employees reports that it uses 125 file drawers of backup material just to meet the federal reporting requirements in the personnel area. The equivalent of 14 full-time employees is required to staff the personnel reporting activity. The personnel manager estimates that one-third of his staff could be eliminated if there were no federal, state, or local reporting requirements.[19]

The National Association of Food Chains, working with the Commission on Federal Paperwork, compiled a list of federal forms a typical food chain is required to submit (see table 11-1). The forms totaled 99, many of which are requested more than once a year. The head of the association's paperwork task force commented that "not counting tax filings, we estimate a typical supermarket chain spends 13,700 hours a year filling out federal forms. At an average wage of $7.50 an hour, the direct cost to the chain for labor only is $100,000 per year." These costs, which rise in proportion to employee wage increases, cover only the processing of *federal* forms.[20]

Some of the reporting requirements of the newer federal regulatory agencies may result in a relatively heavy burden on small business. To illustrate, the Graymills Corporation, which employed 120 workers in 1972, compiled a list of the 40 different government forms that it is required to fill out (see table 11-2). Some of these forms must be filled out several times a year and others must be completed for each employee.

The ability to fill out these forms may require more educated, and hence more expensive, workers than are assigned to producing the company's products. Some of the frustration on the part of the

[18] "Smothered in Paper Work — Businessmen Are Fed Up," *U.S. News and World Report*, April 29, 1974, pp. 57–58.

[19] Letter to the author, dated July 17, 1974.

[20] "Chains Struggle with Government," *Chain Store Age Executive*, October 1976, p. 36.

Table 11-1   Annual federal forms for a typical food chain

Agency	Number of Filings a Year	Estimated Annual Time Needed (hours)
Dept. of Agriculture	725	4,664
Dept. of Commerce	108	495
Dept. of HEW		
Food and Drug Administration	7	111
Dept. of Justice	460	1,875
Dept. of Labor	193	4,840
Dept. of Transportation	25	25
Dept. of Treasury		
Internal Revenue Service	42,642	6,068
Other	12,002	1,010
Environmental Protection Agency	57	355
Equal Employment Opportunity Commission	1	320
Federal Trade Commission	5	5
International Trade Commission	1	5
Securities and Exchange Commission	77	1,023
Total	56,303	20,796

Source: National Association of Food Chains

small business executives, who are burdened with the growing array of federal forms, can be gleaned from the correspondence received by the Small Industry Committee of the Illinois Manufacturer's Association:

> The bureaucrats can't seem to comprehend that we out of the government have to work for a living and that these papers detract from our productive time. . . .
>
> I have no argument with the policies of EEOC, OSHA, Corps of Engineers effluent controls, etc. But not enough thought has been put on minimizing unnecessary data and reports, in my opinion. In a small plant of 75 people, we have two men working half time on programs with attendant detailed plans and reports which were not necessary 2-3 years ago. . . .
>
> Our greatest concern is the changing of forms each time they become due. Especially in small businesses where it is necessary for one person to take care of several phases of the work, we find we are having to spend many hours keeping informed of changes made on the forms, and studying all the fine print. . . .[21]

The depth and breadth of the paperwork burden's impact on

[21] U.S., Congress, Senate, Select Committee on Small Business, *Hearings on the Federal Paperwork Burden,* part 1, 93d Cong., 1st sess., 1973, pp. 122-23.

Table 11-2   Government forms required of Graymills Corporation

Agency	Form or Subdivision	Form Number
Federal		
Department of Commerce	Census of Manufactures	MC-35M
Office of Equal Employment Opportunity	Employer Information Report EE0-1	265-41
Federal Trade Commission	Division of Financial Statistics	MG-1
Department of Labor	Log of Occupational Injuries and Illnesses	100
Department of Labor	Supplementary Record of Occupational Injuries and Illnesses	101
Department of Labor	Summary — Occupational Injuries and Illnesses	102
Department of Labor	Wage Developments in Manufacturing	BLS 2675b
Department of Labor	Employee Welfare or Pension Benefit Plan Description	D-1
Department of Labor	Employee Welfare or Pension Benefit Plan Description Amendment	D-1A
Department of Labor	Employee Welfare or Pension Benefit Plan Annual Report	D-2
Department of Labor	Information on Employee Welfare or Pension Benefit Plan Covering Fewer than 100 Participants	D-3
Department of Treasury	Federal Tax Deposits-Withheld Income and F.I.C.A. Taxes	501
Department of Treasury	Unemployment Taxes	508
Department of Treasury	Employers Annual Federal Unemployment Tax Return	940
Department of Treasury	Employee's Withholding Exemption Certificate	W-4
Department of Treasury	Reconciliation of Income Tax Withheld from Wages	W-3
Department of Treasury	Report of Wages Payable Under the Federal Insurance Contributions Act	941a
Department of Treasury	Return of Employee's Trust Exempt from Tax	990-P
Department of Treasury	U.S. Information Return for the Calendar Year 1971	1099
State of Illinois		
Industrial Commission	Application for Adjustment of Claim — Notice of Disputed Claims and Memorandum of Names and Addresses	None
Industrial Commission	Employer's Report of Compensable Injury	None
Industrial Commission	Memorandum of Names and Addresses for Service of Notices	None
Industrial Commission	Notice of Filing Claim	77

(continued)

207

Table 11-2 (contd.)

Agency	Form or Subdivision	Form Number
Employment Service	DOL-BES Form	None
Division of Unemployment Compensation	Notice of Possible Ineligibility	UC (I11.) Ben-22
Division of Unemployment Compensation	Employer's Contribution Report	UC-3D
Department of Revenue	Retailers' Occupation Tax, Use Tax, County, Municipal Service Occupation, and Service Use Tax Return	RR-1A
Department of Revenue	Employee's Illinois Withholding Exemption Certificate	I1-W-4
Department of Revenue	Monthly State Income Tax Payment Form	I1-501
Department of Revenue	Application for Renewal of Resale Certificate Number	RR-4904
State of Illinois	Report of Accident	C174
State of California		
Department of Business Taxes	State, Local, and District Sales and Use Tax Return	BT 401C
State of New Jersey		
Division of Taxation	Resale Certificate	SF-3
Division of Taxation	Blanket Exemption Certificate	1786 AC
City of Chicago		
Commission on Human Relations	Contractor Employment Practices Report	None
Metropolitan Sanitary District	Industrial Waste Surcharge Certified Statement	FI-235
Metropolitan Sanitary District	Report of Exemption Claim or Estimate of Liability for Surcharge	FI-236
Metropolitan Sanitary District	Computation of Initial Estimate of Liability for Surcharge	FI-236A
City of Los Angeles		
Department of Building and Safety	Application and Agreement for Testing Electrical Equipment	B&S E-147
Department of Building and Safety	Application for Approval Labels	B&S R9

Source: U.S., Senate, Subcommittee on Government Regulation of the Select Committee on Small Business, *Hearings on the Federal Paperwork Burden*, Part 1 (Washington, D.C.: U.S. Government Printing Office, 1972)

small business is similarly evident in several other examples. Rothenbuhler Engineering in Sedro-Woolley, Washington, employs 40 to 50 people in the manufacturing of safety equipment for the logging industry. The firm's head accountant has remarked, "Approximately 40 percent of my time is being utilized for recordkeeping for governmental agencies." When reporting deadlines are not met, he adds, "penalty assessments are made." Consequently, "faced with the burden of this paperwork, small businesses are eliminating some programs — like pension plans — so that reporting requirements are no longer necessary."[22]

A member of the Oklahoma City Motor Car Dealers has estimated that the paperwork burden adds from $50 to $75 to the price of each car sold. And finally, the office manager of a Midwest manufacturing company with 72 employees has perhaps summed up the general feeling of American small business: "I find myself devoting more than 50 percent of my time to filing reports pertaining to OSHA, ERISA, Census Bureau, Pollution Abatement, BLS, State and Federal EPA reports, EEO reports, and so on — the value of which is questionable at best."[23]

Impacts on Large Companies

Even large corporations with highly specialized staffs have difficulty at times in understanding federal regulations. Standard Oil of Indiana reported in 1975 that its phone calls to Washington for interpretation and clarification of new federal regulations had risen to approximately 27,000 a year, from 1,300 annually five years before.[24] The chairman of Standard Oil commented that the company spends $21 million a year on government-mandated paperwork and that the number of man-hours involved in this task would be more than sufficient to operate its fourth-largest refinery.[25]

The large pharmaceutical manufacturer, Eli Lilly and Company, fills out 27,000 government forms a year at a cost of $15 million. This cost is supplemented by an annual $1 million in research necessary to back them up. Lilly's chairman stated, "We spend more man-hours filling out government forms or reports than we do on research

[22] "Winning the War against Paperwork," *Nation's Business* (January 1978), p. 72.
[23] "The Drive to Cut Paper Work: One Step Forward, Two Steps Back," *U.S. News and World Report*, April 18, 1977, p. 51.
[24] James Carberry, "Red Tape Entangles Big Petroleum Firms in Complying with Federal Regulations," *Wall Street Journal*, September 3, 1975, p. 30.
[25] "The Drive to Cut Paper Work," p. 51.

for cancer and heart disease combined."[26] In a particular instance, the company's application to the Food and Drug Administration (Department of Health, Education and Welfare) for the manufacture of a drug for arthritis consisted of 120,000 pages, not including the duplicate and triplicate copies. About one-fourth of the pages contained information that was important to the FDA's evaluation of the actual drug.[27] Only one of over 200 applications the FDA receives every year, the material weighed 2,038 pounds and repeated much of the paperwork Lilly had originally submitted in requesting permission to test the drug.

The proliferation of paperwork, and its resultant costs, can be seen in a variety of other major industries. In 1972 the Chrysler Corporation received from the Environmental Protection Agency 140 pages of regulations for auto exhaust emissions. Chrysler's written response to the guidelines consumed 774 pages. In 1975 the EPA regulations spanned 242 pages, plus another 167 pages to explain their meaning. Chrysler's compliance report subsequently spanned 8,758 pages of detailed explanations. (Compliance with the emission standards cost the corporation an estimated $43 million and more than 1,000 man-years in the mid-1970s, and the expense was passed on to car buyers.) This paperwork was, moreover, only that required by *one* federal agency. A Chrysler executive remarked that it was "tougher and more expensive to follow the regulations to prove we've solved a problem than it was to solve the problem in the first place."[28]

In another sector of the economy the Joseph Schlitz Brewing Company estimated its one-year cost of compiling reports to regulatory agencies at $719,864. This paperwork does not include any data which Schlitz considers necessary for its own use, such as "financial information required for internal control and proper and complete reports to stockholders."[29]

Without disputing the merits of the suit itself, we can note the substantial paperwork costs involved in a Justice Department antitrust suit against one of the nation's corporate giants. American Telephone and Telegraph Company estimates the government demands for documents in relation to its antitrust suit could cost $300 million and 20,000 man-years of effort, including a search of seven billion pages of material.[30] One Justice Department request from AT&T

[26] Ibid.

[27] "Winning the War against Paperwork," p. 72.

[28] Glenna McWhirter, "242-Page EPA Regulation Sparks 8,758-Page Reply," *St. Louis Globe-Democrat*, November 13, 1976, p. 10A.

[29] "Winning the War against Paperwork," p. 72.

[30] "Data Would Cost $300,000,000, AT&T Says," *St. Louis Post-Dispatch*, February 20, 1975, p. 12A.

included every piece of paper "prepared, sent, or received since January 1, 1930, which relate or refer in whole or in part to, or which constitute instructions, directives, or suggestions regarding the purchase by AT&T or any Bell Company of telecommunication equipment from Western Electric."[31]

Similarly, in the Justice Department's antitrust case against IBM, charging that the company had achieved a monopoly in the data processing field, IBM supplied the government with over 4 million pages of documents. Additionally, the department's Antitrust Division had access to another 60 million pages produced by IBM for a host of civil suits. The case came to trial in January 1969, and three years later the transcript ran to 64,500 pages — with only government witnesses having testified. In June 1979 a federal district court affirmed a Justice Department data request that the company said will involve the copying of more than 5 billion pages of documents scattered in over 120 countries. It could take 62,000 manyears of work to meet the request at an estimated cost of over $1 billion. A verdict in the case is not expected until 1983, and an appeals process could take an additional five years.[32]

THE FUTURE OF PAPERWORK

At roughly the same time that the Federal Paperwork Commission began hearing complaints on the paperwork burden, the Federal Trade Commission (FTC) began mailing out large packages of documents to over 400 of the nation's largest manufacturing corporations. These firms were ordered to break down their assets, sales, operating costs, media and advertising expenses, operating income, and other expenses — all according to what the FTC calls "lines of business" (LB). In order to define these lines of business, the agency gives corporations 274 categories to choose from, ranging from "agricultural production — crops," to "woodworking machinery."[33]

According to the FTC, the purpose of the LB report is to examine the extent and effectiveness of competition in the United States economy and to supply return on investment data as guides to investors.[34] The FTC, in arguing for the LB reports, claimed they

---

[31] "'Great Paper War' Begins in Lawsuit of U.S. and AT&T," *Wall Street Journal*, January 20, 1975, p. 14.

[32] "The Antitrust Case They Never Should Have Started," *Fortune*, January 30, 1978, p. 75; N.R. Kleinfield, "IBM Fails to Quash Subpoena," *The New York Times*, June 27, 1979, p. D-1.

[33] George J. Benston, "The Baffling New Numbers Game at the FTC," *Fortune* (October 1975), p. 1974.

[34] Robert K. Mautz and W.G. May, "The FTC Line of Business Reporting Program," *Financial Executive*, January 1975, pp. 15–16.

would be useful to other federal agencies as well. But when the Office of Management and Budget asked several agencies how they would use the information, they replied that no use was planned because they did not view the data as sufficiently reliable.[35] Despite the costs and questionable value of the information, the General Accounting Office issued the following statement as part of its evaluation of the LB program: "The FTC and business respondents [should] get on with the task of developing reliable line-of-business information, recognizing that the initial information collected will be unreliable at best, and may be seriously misleading."

Dr. Betty Bock, director of antitrust research for the Conference Board, after studying the FTC categories for their correspondence to recognizable markets, concluded that 88 percent of them contain such a heterogeneous mix of products that the LB information will merely baffle any businessman or regulator who tries to make use of it.[36] In addition, the FTC reports merely duplicate the information that is collected by the Census Bureau's census of manufactures — information which, in contrast with that of the FTC, is obtained confidentially so that the credibility of the data can be guaranteed.

The commission's staff believes that the costs of the program will be "modest in relation to the substantial benefits" resulting from the additional information.[37] This conclusion is reached on the basis of their cost estimates from a sample of 25 major companies, which, on the average, figure the "setting-up costs" of providing the new information at $548,000 (see table 11-3).

Assuming that the $548,000 figure is representative, this means that the total initial cost of this single report from the 345 companies expected to fill out the form will be about $190 million. This sum would appear to be a substantial overhead cost that ultimately will be passed on, in good measure, to the customer.

Government can, of course, take actions to reduce the burden of reporting that it imposes on the private sector — when it becomes concerned with its costs. For example, the Interstate Commerce Commission eliminated 19 reports and trimmed back others in 1977, reducing the annual paperwork burden by over 700,000 hours. In June 1979 the Federal Home Loan Bank Board shifted from lengthy and detailed semiannual reports by member savings and loan associa-

---

[35] Shirley Scheibla, "Illegal Search and Seizure," *Barron's*, February 17, 1975, p. 18.

[36] Benston, "The Baffling New Numbers Game," p. 175.

[37] U.S., Congress, Senate, Subcommittee on Budgeting, Management, and Expenditures of the Committee on Government Operations, *Hearings on Corporate Disclosure*, 93d Cong., 2d sess. (1974), p. 924.

Table 11-3 Estimated start-up costs for FTC line of business reports

Company	Estimated Mean Start-Up Costs (thousands)
American Metal Climax	$ 75
Anaconda	1,000
Combustion Engineering	100
Crown Zellerbach	100
Deere	1,000
Dow Chemical	400
DuPont	500
Ex-cell-o	350
Exxon	1,000
General Instrument	100
Inland Steel	100
Lear Siegler	400
McGraw-Hill	45
Mobil	500
Nabisco	100
Northrop	300
Outboard Marine	100
R. J. Reynolds	1,000
Singer	500
Standard Oil, California	800
Union Carbide	1,100
U.S. Steel	2,000
Varian Associates	63
Westinghouse	2,000
Westvaco	75
Total	$13,708
Mean	548

Source: U.S., Congress, Senate, Subcommittee on Budgeting, Management, and Expenditures of the Committee on Government Operations, *Hearings on Corporate Disclosure*, 93d Cong., 2d sess., 1974

tions to a significantly reduced and shortened quarterly reporting system. The board also reduced the required monthly reporting to a sample of one-fourth of the industry. These changes account for a 50-percent reduction in reporting requirements and a 36-percent cut in overall data items filed with the board. The savings to the thrift associations are estimated at $4 million to $5 million a year.[38]

On the other hand, much of the reduction in paperwork is being

[38] *Highlights of Bank Board Reporting Requirement Reduction Proposals* (Washington, D.C.: Federal Home Loan Bank Board, 1979).

offset by increases in new or expanded requirement areas, such as the following:

- EEOC requirements for separate files on every applicant for a job in a company with more than 100 employees.
- Strip-mining regulations which the GAO estimates will add at least 10 million hours of reporting burden.
- Resource Recovery and Conservation Act requirements which are estimated to amount to at least one-eighth of all the burden now imposed on businesses by agencies subject to the Federal Reports Act, and which will involve 1 to 2 million hours of reporting.
- New Energy Department regulations which could add millions of reporting hours.[39]

All in all, therefore, the paperwork burden is not likely to disappear. Federal departments and agencies require a substantial amount of information to carry out their statutory objectives. Standardized reports are often the most efficient way of obtaining this information. Thus, it is irrelevant to attack the general notion of business and other private individuals and organizations reporting to government agencies. Rather, the useful questions relate to minimizing the time and costs incurred by business, government, and the public in meeting the government's information needs.

[39] "More Paperwork in the Mill," *Regulatory Action Network: Washington Watch*, June 1, 1979, p. 5.

Part Two

THE ADAPTATION
BY BUSINESS

12

impacts on top management

OVERVIEW OF BUSINESS REACTIONS

Three basic patterns of reaction to government controls over business are being followed by companies. In practice, a company will utilize a blend of these three approaches to regulation, varying its responses with external conditions, the capabilities of its management, and the nature of the firm. All of the changes tend either to increase the overhead costs of doing business or to deflect management and employee attention from conventional business functions.

Passive. Some corporate managements simply react to each new or expanded federal control. They may criticize the development or they may attempt to postpone its effects through litigation and administrative appeals. But, sooner or later, they gear their firm's operations to meet the new government requirements.

Anticipatory. Other corporate managements rely on their planning capability to estimate in advance likely changes in federal controls over business. Thus, for example, prior to congressional passage of restrictions on the use of private land, they will reorient their construction projects to minimize the likelihood of subsequently running afoul of new federal regulations. They also voluntarily may take socially responsible actions to make the initiation of more government controls less likely. Some food retailing chains have put nutritional information on private brand products and have instituted unit pricing systems, even when not required by law to do so. One major financial institution has appointed an executive vice-president to take charge of the company's action programs in such areas of social policy as consumer problems, minority affairs, and environmental protection.

As corporate managers become more sensitive to evolving social demands, they consider response to at least some of the public's expectations as being a normal aspect of conducting business. To the extent that this development occurs voluntarily, businesses themselves provide an important constraint on the degree of political pressure that social action interests can effectively exert against them.

Active. Still other business executives attempt to head off or shape the character of government intervention by playing a more active role in the development and enactment of public policies. Thus, some companies are strengthening their Washington offices to deal with pending legislation and new regulation, or are setting up such operations if they do not exist. Trade associations that are active on Capitol Hill are being supported more strongly. Despite the growing restrictions on political contributions and practices, many businessmen and businesswomen — as individuals — attempt to exercise leverage on government decision making by participating more actively in the political process. Business is seeking means of participation in the political process in addition to the conventional route of campaign contributions. Some business executives take leaves of absence to run for office or to work actively in election campaigns.

Business firms are making more extensive use of in-house publications, communications to shareholders, and other media to raise the public awareness of political issues that affect the future of the business community. Businessmen and businesswomen increasingly serve on government committees and participate more actively in public hearings. Professor Douglas North, of the University of Washington, believes that the key margin of decision making in the nation has become access to government influence. The predictable result is "to shift the locus of the investment of resources into attempts to favorably influence" the strategic government official or to prevent the enactment of government policies that will adversely affect a group's interest.[1] North's point probably is overstated. Many more opportunities for profitable private undertakings still exist. Moreover, the adverse public reaction to massive use of business resources in politics would, at least under present circumstances, be overwhelming. Nevertheless, he is indicating an important emerging development, especially in the case of the largest and most visible organizations.

An improved knowledge of the public policy process enables business and its representatives to affect, in entirely legal and legitimate fashion, the formulation of new and revised government policies toward the private sector. Often the most effective form of influence is making available to government decision makers prompt, knowledgeable, and detailed analyses of the various impacts of proposed legislation, in contrast to the traditional methods of "political" pressure.

IMPACTS ON TOP MANAGEMENT

Internal Monitoring

The growing array and increasingly serious effects of governmental intervention are changing the role of top management, in some ways expanding and in other ways restricting it. The result is important shifts in the entire corporate structure.

Operating management is increasingly more directed toward the internal corporate functions, because so much more attention needs to be devoted to such matters as hiring and promoting practices, personnel safety, product evaluation, and developing and reporting new types of information. With these pressures on his or her time, the chief operating officer (usually the president or the most senior executive vice-president) has less time for such matters as public and industry meetings and the external reactions to the company's activities. Such functions increasingly are becoming the primary responsibility of the corporation's chief executive officer (either the board chairman or the president) and his or her immediate associates. Thus top management itself monitors these externally oriented functions much more closely.[2]

---

[1] Douglas C. North, "Structure and Performance: The Task of Economic History," *Journal of Economic Literature*, September 1978, p. 969.

[2] "The Top Man Becomes Mr. Outside," *Business Week*, May 4, 1974, pp. 38–42.

The outlook of some of the modern corporation's key executives is shifting from primary concern with conventional production and marketing decisions to coping with a host of external and often strange policy considerations that frequently are those of ecological or consumer groups with nonbusiness and noneconomic priorities. Members of the senior management may become as attuned to the desires of those new interests as they are to their traditional accountability to shareholders. A survey by the Conference Board revealed that 43 percent of the chief executives of major American companies devote one-fourth or more of their time to external relations and that 92 percent devote more time to that activity than they did three to five years earlier.[3]

Consequently, a type of chief executive quite different from the traditional figure is emerging. William Agee, chairman of the Bendix Corporation, described the emerging outlook of the chief executive of a major corporation: "Companies today are accountable not only to their shareholders and their employees, but also to what is amorphously called the public, which may mean anything from the Sierra Club to the Federal Trade Commission or a congressional committee."[4]

Reginald H. Jones, chief executive of General Electric, told a meeting of company officials that public policy is no longer a "spectator sport" for GE managers. He went on to elaborate: "It is no exaggeration to say that for most managers, the main problems — the main obstacles to achieving their business objectives — are external to the company."[5]

Liabilities and Restrictions

Senior corporate officials are devoting more attention to government because the newer regulatory agencies are placing greater responsibility on top management. The courts increasingly are rejecting the traditional interpretation of *mens rea* (end intent) and placing blame at the top. As noted by Professor S. Prakash Sethi of the University of Texas at Dallas, the new presumption is that a vigilant executive will make certain that subordinates are obeying govern-

[3] Phyllis S. McGrath, *Managing Corporate External Relations* (New York: Conference Board, 1976), p. 49.
[4] William M. Agee, "The Moral and Ethical Climate in Today's Business World," *MSU Business Topics*, Winter 1978.
[5] D. J. Watson, "The Changing Political Involvement of Business: The General Electric Experience," in *Business and Its Changing Environment*, ed. George A. Steiner (Los Angeles: UCLA Graduate School of Management, 1979), p. 200.

ment laws and regulations. If those subordinates are in violation, it may be proof that the executive was not properly vigilant. The government's assumption here is that a manager is far more inclined to take a regulation seriously if he or she has a personal stake in the company's compliance with it. Thus, the executive's criminal liability may accrue solely from the fact that he holds a responsible position in the corporation.[6]

The Consumer Product Safety Commission (CPSC) requires that the chief executive officer of the company sign and certify the information sent to the commission. If the authority is delegated to a subordinate, the chief executive must so notify the commission in writing. The chief executive, in the words of the Occupational Safety and Health Administration, "must be willing to accept the responsibility for occupational safety and health as an integral part of his job."[7] He or she is charged with setting the company's safety policies and stimulating an awareness of safety in others.

The official responsible for the equal employment opportunity program in one utility, an officer of the company, states flatly, "No Affirmative Action program will ever work without active and strong support from a company's top management . . . the whole process is tied together. If the support for EEO didn't exist at the top, every other person involved in an EEO effort would be hard put to make any real progress."[8]

In another pronouncement with similar overtones, one federal court decision levying an unusually high antitrust fine cited as the reason for the severity of the penalty the failure of the company's top executives to exert sufficient pressure on subordinates to obey an earlier antitrust order.

The Supreme Court ruled in 1975 that chief executives are personally responsible for making certain that their firms are in compliance with pure food and drug standards. In that landmark case Acme Super Markets pleaded guilty to charges that its food shipments had been exposed to rodent contamination in a warehouse, and the company president, John R. Park, was convicted for the offense (his fine was $250). Park contended that he had consulted company officials responsible for sanitation and that he was

---

[6] S. Prakash Sethi, "Who, Me? Jail as an Occupational Hazard," *Wharton Magazine*, Summer 1978, pp. 22–23.

[7] U.S., Occupational Safety and Health Administration, *Guidelines for Setting up Job Safety and Health Programs* (Washington, D.C.: U.S. Government Printing Office, 1972), p. 1.

[8] "The Meaning behind the Words," *Continental System Communicator*, June 1975, p. 10.

informed that corrective action was being taken; thus he did whatever he could have "constructively" done.

The court disagreed, stating that persons in supervisory positions are not only required by the Food, Drug, and Cosmetic Act to seek out and remedy violations, but also "to implement measures that assure that violation will not occur. . . . The requirements of foresight and vigilance imposed on responsible corporate agents are beyond question demanding and perhaps onerous." But the court stated that the public had a right to expect that from executives of companies distributing products affecting health. Thus, proof of wrong action was not needed in the Park case. According to the Supreme Court, the act dispenses with the conventional requirement for criminal conduct—the awareness of some wrongdoing by the person found guilty.[9]

Individual business executives face stiff fines and jail sentences for violating various government statutes. Under the antitrust laws an individual may be fined as much as $100,000 and be jailed for up to three years. The maximum corporate penalty is a $1-million fine and divestiture. The top personal penalty under the Securities Act is a $10,000 fine and two years in prison, while the top corporate punishment is a $10,000 fine and an injunction prohibiting the activity. The Foreign Corrupt Practices Act, designed to curb illegal overseas payoffs, provides for maximum penalties of $1 million for corporations and $10,000 in fines and five years in jail for officers and directors.

With the growth of government regulatory activities, the grounds on which a member of a corporate board can be sued range far beyond traditional matters, and include the following matters:

- Conflict of interest.
- Mismanagement of corporate affairs.
- Misrepresentation in SEC registration statements.
- Antitrust violations.
- Insiders' trading of stock.
- Corporate failure to comply with pollution laws.
- Illegal campaign contributions.
- Misleading proxy material.
- Failure to include in proxy statement material requested by stockholders.[10]

An important segment of illegal corporate conduct is highly technical in nature. As Professor Sethi has pointed out, only after

[9] U.S. v. Park, 43 LW 4687–4695.
[10] John M. Nash, *Corporate Directors' Guide* (Washington, D.C.: Financial, Government, and Public Affairs Communicators, 1976), p. 5.

the courts have spoken can one say whether or not a law or regulation has been violated.

The Investor Responsibility Research Center has urged companies to take specific steps to prevent unethical or illegal behavior on the part of their officials. These include the following:

1. Adopting a statement of practices to be avoided. The statement should make clear that severe disciplinary measures will be invoked against any employee who engages in such practices.
2. Putting into effect controls to monitor the behavior of employees. A useful model might be the systems that many companies use to monitor the activities of purchasing officers. Such systems often require an annual written affirmation by personnel with purchasing authority that they have paid no more than fair market value for goods and services and have not accepted any bribes or kickbacks.
3. Monitoring the conduct of senior corporate officers through a group of outside directors (who are not themselves officers of the company).
4. Making public the information that would assure those interested that the company had done nothing improper. To be most helpful the public disclosures should include a brief description of the company's policies and monitoring practices and a statement describing any improper transactions that had been detected or noting that there had not been any such transactions.

The adoption of these measures may not eliminate the possibility of illegal or unethical corporate behavior. However, the Center believes that voluntary good faith implementation of systems of this sort would prove far more effective than the whole range of existing government enforcement efforts in deterring corporate officials from engaging in those kinds of transactions.[11]

Some major corporations have gone to great lengths to spell out the rules governing acceptable business conduct. McDonnell-Douglas Corporation (MDC), a leading aerospace contractor, issued to its employees a long tabulation of orders and prohibitions. These range from a simple statement on illegal payments ("No bribes, kickbacks, or other illegal payments are made by or on behalf of MDC, directly or indirectly") to spelling out the nature of bona fide consultant agreements. Exxon has gone to the length of publishing an entire booklet for its employees on avoiding conduct which would violate the antitrust laws (see fig. 12-1 for an excerpt).

Internal and External Communication

As chief executive officers become more personally liable to the government for the actions of their subordinates, and as they find

[11] Elliott J. Weiss, *The Corporate Watergate* (New York: Investor Responsibility Research Center, 1975).

Rules to Avoid Suspicion of Violation:

In *per se* situations it makes no difference that apparently sound business considerations may be involved: for instance, an industry effort to "stabilize" prices by buying up "distress" gasoline. There is no excuse, or any such thing as being a little bit guilty. Therefore,

1. There must be no conversations or communications of any kind with competitors concerning prices, territories, customers, suppliers or production except in strict accordance with rules established by the Law Department. If one of these subjects comes up in a gathering attended by a Company employee or during contact with a competitor, he has two choices: either to see that the subject is immediately dropped, or to leave the gathering or otherwise terminate the contact. He should report the incident to the Law Department at once, so that the Company can take steps to preserve a record of its and the employee's non-involvement. (This rule applies, of course, to gatherings or contacts of any kind, including those at trade association meetings and at meetings of government-sponsored groups.)

2. When the Company buys from or sells to someone with whom it also competes, special problems are presented, and great care should be used to limit any communications on prices to those actually required for the buyer-seller transaction at hand.

3. Do not discuss with a customer the prices the Company will charge others or the class of business to which each will or will not sell.

4. Do not discuss with anyone from outside the Company whether to do business with a third person, much less make commitments in that regard. For instance, do not discuss with one dealer whether to terminate another dealer.

5. Remember that once the Company sells a product it cannot control whether the buyer uses or resells it, or where, to whom or at what price he resells. While Company representatives may counsel or advise individual dealers to aid them with their business problems, care must be taken to ensure that each independent dealer is allowed to run his own business, and to decide what products he will sell and what his prices shall be. He must clearly understand that advice is merely that. No coercion or threats of any kind should ever be used.

Figure 12-1

Source: Exxon Company, USA, *Abiding by the Antitrust Laws*, 1974.

their managerial prerogatives curtailed, there is a growing incentive to become involved in the government and political arenas, where the requirements that limit management are initially established. Mobil Oil Corporation has assumed this role in its campaign to educate the public and politicians to its view of the energy situation. It has placed full-page advertisements in leading magazines and newspapers but has thus far been blocked in attempting to relay its message via television. The television networks have the right to refuse controversial commercials, and they have exercised this option in Mobil's case despite the corporation's offer to buy time for critics to reply.

Government relations are becoming a major concern of company boards of directors and, in particular, of full-time chairmen or chairwomen. More members of top management, particularly from well-known companies, frequently are speaking out on public affairs as part of their basic function. Important new positions are developing in the planning, legal, and government relations divisions in response to the added duties imposed by government regulatory activities. The array of interest groups with which corporate executives can expect to interact continues to grow rapidly. Figure 12-2 lists a sampling of "corporate activist" organizations. Their activities range from introducing politically oriented resolutions at annual meetings of companies (e.g., doing business in South Africa) to organizing boycotts of company products to testifying before congressional committees in favor of additional government controls over the business system.

There is a growing realization that senior corporate executives increasingly are placed in situations where their images and speaking abilities are crucial to public, and therefore consumer, reaction to their companies and products. As Carl Gerstacker, former board chairman of Dow Chemical Company, stated: "We are quickly approaching the point when it must be asked of candidates for executive posts in major corporations, 'How does he come across on television?'" Gerstacker went on to explain this relatively new function of top management:

> Too often, we who represent business are competing today in a situation where the opposition are pros and we are amateurs. The public, therefore, sees us in a bad light, doesn't understand and doesn't buy our point of view. Yet it is safe to assume that at some point in his career, the senior corporate executive might well have to cope with an audiovisual situation involving George Meany, Evelyn Davis, Ralph Nader, Clergy and Laymen Concerned, Philip Hart, or the Symbionese Liberation Army.[12]

Thomas A. Murphy, board chairman of General Motors, describes the "inescapable fact" that today's chief executive must be a public figure. "He must be ready to assume all of the risks and all of the difficulties that up-front visibility entails," Murphy reported to the 1978 annual meeting of the Business Roundtable, an organization of CEOs of major corporations.

Consequently, a new breed of consultants has originated to cater to this concern among business executives. These consultants

[12] "Grooming the Executive for the Spotlight," *Business Week*, October 5, 1974, p. 57.

VARIETIES OF CORPORATE ACTIVIST GROUPS

ADVOCACY AND TESTIMONY

    Coalition for a New Foreign and Military Policy
    Consumer Federation of America
    Federation of American Scientists
    Friends Committee on National Legislation
    Sierra Club

BOYCOTTS

    Infant Formula Action Coalition

LEGAL ACTION

    Action on Smoking and Health
    Center for Auto Safety
    Consumers Union of United States
    Environmental Defense Fund
    Natural Resources Defense Council
    Sierra Club

SHAREHOLDERS' RESOLUTIONS

    Infant Formula Action Coalition
    Interfaith Center on Corporate Responsibility

RESEARCH

    Action for Children's Television
    Agribusiness Accountability Project
    Center for Auto Safety
    Center for Defense Information
    Center for Science in the Public Interest
    Consumers Union of United States
    Council on Economic Priorities
    Exploratory Project for Economic Alternatives
    Friends of the Earth
    Health Policy Advisory Center
    Health Research Group
    Investor Responsibility Research Center
    Natural Resources Defense Council
    Public Interest Economics Center
    Sierra Club

Figure 12-2

instruct corporation officers on such specifics as the type of clothing to wear and the tone to take in public announcements. Such outside assistance has been utilized particularly by companies suffering the greatest criticism from consumer groups, environmentalists, and political figures. As a president of Shell Oil Company and an alumnus of a Dialog Telecommunications Development Course stated the matter: "I enrolled because I am not a natural to appear on the television set or to be publicly interviewed. This business of communicating has become as important as finding more oil."

But, as pointed out by Elisha Gray II, former chairman of the Whirlpool Corporation and chairman of the Council of Better Business Bureaus, "We have got to establish the public's confidence in the marketplace before we can establish our credibility." Thus, more fundamental than speaking out to overcome misconceptions about their activities, businesses must correct mistakes and shortcomings. According to Kenneth Schwartz, vice-president of Opinion Research Corporation, "Performance is more important than rhetoric."

C. Jackson Grayson, Jr., who served as chairman of the Price Commission during the 1971 to 1973 period of federal wage and price controls, concluded that many business executives, consciously or unconsciously, are adding to the probability of more government control over the economy by seeking ways to reduce competition. To illustrate this point, he quoted letters sent to him by various businessmen:

> We need government protection because we can't compete against the big companies.
>
> We must have minimum milk prices if we are to have an orderly market.
>
> If we allow liquor prices to fluctuate freely, competition will be ruinous and the Mafia might move in.[13]

Government and Corporate Governance

Increased interest has developed in recent years in the "governance" of the corporation. A number of public-interest groups are advocating the use of such government power as granting charters to change the basic organization of the corporation. Harold Williams, chairman of the Securities and Exchange Commission (SEC), has urged limiting the board of directors to only one company officer, the president. All other board members, including the chairman, would be chosen from outside the company. Williams's concept of outside directors excludes those bankers, lawyers, and consultants having business dealings with the company. In his view, outside-dominated boards could do a better job of representing the public interest as well as the concerns of the shareholders than could the executives responsible for day-to-day management.[14]

A more modest set of proposals has been presented by a distinguished group of business, academic, and professional leaders

---

[13] C. Jackson Grayson, Jr., "Let's Get Back to the Competitive Market System," *Harvard Business Review*, November–December 1973, p. 104.

[14] Harold M. Williams, "Corporate Accountability" (address to the Fifth Annual Securities Regulation Institute, San Diego, California, January 18, 1978).

convened by the American Assembly. That group urged that the majority of board members should come from outside the company management and be unencumbered by relationships which limit their independence. The report specifically recommended, however, that key inside managers, in addition to the chief executive, remain eligible to serve, but not as chairman of the board. Inside officers bring special strengths to a board's deliberations, including a detailed understanding of the people who are going to carry out the board's policies. The Assembly's report stated that business managers must be made more aware of their various publics, more sensitive to shifting expectations, and more alert to new claimants for corporate attention and service.[15]

A far more radical set of proposals has been offered by Ralph Nader and his associates to achieve what he terms the "popularization" of the corporation. He advocates the assumption by the federal government of the chartering power now held by the states. Under the Nader proposals the federal government would broaden the disclosure requirements of the SEC to cover "the whole impact of the corporation on society." He also has advocated for corporations beyond a "certain" size or having a "dominant" position in a market, that one-fourth of the board of directors be chosen in national elections. He also has urged a mandatory mail plebiscite of shareholders on all "fundamental" transactions. He seems to have softened some of these proposals in his more recent writings.[16]

Although none of these proposals for reform of corporate governance may be adopted in their present form —either Williams's or the American Assembly's or Nader's —it would not be surprising if some changes in corporate boards of directors would be made either by force of government action or voluntarily. A significant shift already is occurring in the composition of the boards of directors of larger corporations in the United States. In the case of the 500 largest industrial corporations (the *Fortune* 500), the number of outside directors rose from 3,049 in 1967 to 3,436 in 1977, although the total number of directors declined. The number of current executives on those corporate boards dropped from 2,868 to 2,332 during the decade, as did retired managers, from 277 to 227.[17]

---

[15] American Assembly, *Corporate Governance in America* (New York: Columbia University Press, 1978).

[16] Ralph Nader et al., *Taming the Giant Corporation* (New York: W. W. Norton & Co., Inc., 1976); Eileen Shanahan, "Business Change: Nader Interview," *The New York Times*, January 24, 1971, sect. 3, pp. 1-3. For a contrasting view, see Robert Hessen, *In Defense of the Corporation* (Palo Alto, Calif.: Hoover Institution Press, 1979).

[17] Lee Smith, "The Boardroom Is Becoming a Different Scene," *Fortune*, May 8, 1978.

IMPACTS ON CORPORATE PLANNING

Traditional market research tends to miss the effect of government on business and markets. Corporate planning departments are devoting more attention to analyzing factors that may result in changes in government regulatory policies and practices. On the whole, planning is becoming a more difficult function because of the conflicts among different government policies — for example, the desire to reduce the use of energy while avoiding the pollution of the environment, to produce safer products under healthier working conditions and avoid large price increases.

In addition to covering traditional economic and market trends, planning staffs are beginning to focus in detail on government regulations that can limit or greatly influence company managements in selecting new products, production processes, and/or marketing methods. They also now are giving more weight to government controls in forecasting future markets and product sales. Their approach is multifaceted, since government activities can either create new derivative markets or reduce the demand for existing products. For example:

> Energy allocations limit the availability of fuel but also encourage exploration and development of new energy sources.
>
> More stringent environmental controls are leading to the curtailment of the use of coal, and simultaneously are creating increased demands for devices to reduce pollution.
>
> Job safety and health regulations impinge on production processes declared unacceptable, but they also open new opportunities for companies to supply safety equipment and alternative methods of production.

IMPACTS ON RESEARCH AND DEVELOPMENT

Some of the most fundamental impacts of government intervention in business decision making are discernible in the corporate research and development area, although the ramifications are likely to unfold only over a long period in the form of a reduced rate of product and process innovation. According to a report of the House of Representatives Committee on Science and Technology, "in most situations, uncertainty in policy and regulatory practices serves as a barrier to innovation. Conflicting regulations constrain industrial R & D." This point can be seen in the opening statement of the Toxic Substances Control Act, where the language states that the regulations are intended "not to impede unduly or create unnecessary economic barriers to technological innovation while fulfilling the primary purpose."

Increasingly, business is operating in an environment in which the application of the fruits of science and engineering to products and services is coming under public scrutiny in advance of their widespread use. Government controls are having their impact at every major stage of the product cycle. Tightening federal standards for product safety are resulting in increased attention to original product design, because this is the phase where safety can be improved with minimum changes in existing production equipment. Thus, design staffs are improving their understanding of a product's intended operating environment—especially because legal liability may depend in part on whether or not the manufacturer could have foreseen the product's safety hazard. In addition, the OSHA rules need to be considered when R&D develops new manufacturing processes.

To the extent that existing products and processes do not meet new, more stringent government standards, R&D departments are facing different, but not necessarily reduced, demands for their function. For example, in the automobile industry some innovative engineering efforts have shifted from such traditional areas as style to bumper designs, emission improvements, and devices to prevent drunken drivers from being able to start their cars. The intense efforts of one automobile company to meet, and perhaps anticipate, federal emissions standards is demonstrated by the fourfold increase in personnel employed in its emissions-control research and development function during a recent five-year period.[18]

A rising share of company research and development budgets is being shifted to "defensive" research—which refers not to keeping up with the business competition but with meeting the requirements of government regulatory agencies. This trend is most advanced in the automotive industry, where the head of the General Motors research laboratory has stated, "We've diverted a large share of our resources—sometimes up to half—into meeting government regulations instead of developing better materials, better manufacturing techniques, and better products."[19]

It is discouraging to the innovative instincts of business firms, however, to undergo experiences like the recent one of Monsanto, a

[18] Harold W. Henry, "Pollution Control: Corporate Responses," *AMA Management Briefing*, 1974.
[19] "How GM Manages Its Billion-Dollar R&D Program," *Business Week*, June 28, 1976, p. 56.

major chemical company, with its Cycle-Safe plastic bottle for soft drinks. According to Monsanto's CEO, John W. Hanley, shoppers in the test markets liked the product because it was lightweight and shatter-resistant. It also was recyclable. But the Food and Drug Administration banned the new product because it was made with acrylonitrile (a chemical that had been used in food contact applications for more than 30 years). The regulators say that if the bottles were filled with acetic acid and stored for six months at 120° F., an infinitesimal amount of the chemical could leach into the solution. Monsanto has had to close down all plants making Cycle-Safe bottles.[20]

The adverse effect of regulation on innovation is likely to be felt more strongly by smaller firms, and thus also have an anti-competitive impact. According to Dr. Mitchell Zavon, president of the American Association of Poison Control Centers:

> We've got to the point in regulatory action where it's become so costly and risky to bring out products that only the very largest firms can afford to engage in these risky ventures. To bring out a new pesticide you have to figure a cost of $7,000,000 and seven years of time.

With the expanding activity of the congressional Office of Technology Assessment, federal requirements for technology assessment may increase.[21] One result would be more overhead expenses for corporate R&D departments. Another will be personnel or organizational shifts. If some form of technology impact statement should become common practice, corporate laboratories will require personnel with such nontraditional capabilities as evaluating social and economic effects of proposed new products. Alternatively, this function may be handled elsewhere in the corporation; because inputs will come from R&D and other departments, this type of assessment will be a difficult interdisciplinary task.

The cost pressures resulting from more stringent regulation of product safety, energy use, and ecological effects are affecting product design, especially by limiting product variety. More uniform, standardized, and conservatively and expensively designed products are often the result. For example, power tools that are less likely to burn out from extended use are usually the more expensive items in a producer's product line. In the pharmaceutical area a slowdown in the pace of innovation is apparently linked to the more stringent

---

[20] John W. Hanley, "The Day Innovation Died," *Vital Speeches of the Day,* November 1, 1978, pp. 55-58.
[21] Herbert Fore, "The State of the Art of Technology Assessment," *Astronautics and Aeronautics,* November 1974, pp. 40-47.

regulations in the United States governing the introduction of new drugs. According to Professor William Wardell of the University of Rochester Medical School, the United States was the fifteenth country in which the antiinflammatory drug indomethacin was marketed, the fifteenth for the diuretic ethacrynic acid and the antidepressant protriptyline; the twenty-second country for the antiinflammatory drug fenoprofen; the thirty-ninth country for the first oral cephalosporin, cephalexin; and the fortieth country for the antitubercular antibiotic capreomycin.[22]

SUMMARY

All in all, the top levels of business have undergone tremendous changes since the beginning of the 1970s. In some respects, this change — brought about by increased public intervention in the private sector — has spurred business to be much more aware of its actions and more wary of intentional or unintentional wrongdoing. Simultaneously, however, government oversight of the top management of companies has hampered business operations and has made both the day-to-day and the long-term tasks harder to perform efficiently.

Feedback effects surely will be important. Anticipatory actions by management will obviate, at least in some circumstances, further government intervention. In other cases prompt response to formal regulations may engender a more sympathetic reaction by government officials. In yet other instances business may succeed in modifying the often hostile environment in which public support is developed for increasing government control. Thus, the directions taken by top management may favorably affect the scope and nature of that changing and difficult environment in which the American business firm continues to operate.

[22] William M. Wardell, "Drug Regulation and Pharmaceutical Innovation," *Regulation*, September–October 1979.

13 ‖

impacts on company operations

Government regulations affect the production and distribution of goods and services in many ways. These requirements can change the methods by which some products are made and they can increase the cost of others. The range of company operations affected by government can include work procedures, manufacturing processes, marketing methods, and markets served.

MANUFACTURING FUNCTIONS

Changing Production Processes

A major impact of federal regulation on manufacturing is in the form of increased production expenses. As long as Congress does not directly impute to industry the costs stemming from legislated controls but concentrates primarily on the intended social benefits of the regulations, this situation can be expected to continue.

One result of the pressures for production processes to meet government environmental and safety requirements is that a rising share of company investment is being devoted to these required social responsibilities rather than to increasing output. This situation is leading to a significant decline in the long-term growth of productivity, at least as it is conventionally measured.[1]

Although regulations generally result in cost increases, some companies are finding that, in the long run, their adaptations to certain requirements can result in cost savings. Better process operation and control may be a consequence, in addition to improved "housekeeping," such as fewer leaks, more reprocessing of wastes, recycling of water and raw materials, energy conservation, and so forth. Although existing facilities often will require the addition of expensive pollution controls, new structures at times can be designed with less expensive pollution devices at the outset.

One example of cost reduction resulted from government efforts to standardize packaging, fostered by the Fair Packaging and Labeling Act of 1966, which led to less variety in package sizes. Between 1966 and 1974 the number of different types of toothpaste packages decreased from 57 to 5.

Various other impacts occur as a result of government regulation of production processes. To meet increasingly specific consumer product safety standards, many industries have been changing their materials mix.[2] Some manufacturers of sleepwear for children, for example, are using a higher proportion of cotton for thermal underwear to increase fire-retardant properties. Certain positive benefits result for companies that have successfully produced lines of flame-resistant clothing. This relatively new capability can be used to diversify into other areas of textile production, and the fire-retardant characteristic is also a promotional asset.

The Location of Production

According to John Quarles, former deputy administrator of the Environmental Protection Agency (EPA), recently enacted environment laws (especially the 1977 Clean Air Act Amendments) are transferring ultimate control over the location of industrial development from private corporations to public agencies. In general, he

[1] Edward F. Denison, "Effects of Selected Changes in the Institutional and Human Environment upon Output per Unit of Input," *Survey of Current Business*, January 1978.
[2] U.S., Consumer Product Safety Commission, *CPSC Issues Final Standard for Children's Sleepwear, Sizes 7 to 14* (Washington, D.C.: 1974), pp. 1-3.

Table 13-1   New source performance standards issued under clean air act

(Industries Affected)	
Asphalt concrete plant	Phosphate fertilizer
Coal cleaning plant	Primary aluminum reduction plant
Ferroalloy production	Primary copper smelter
Grain elevators	Primary lead smelter
Iron and steel mill	Primary zinc smelter
Kraft pulp mills	Portland cement plant
Lignite-fired steam generators	Secondary brass & bronze smelter
Lime plants	Secondary lead smelter
Municipal incinerator	Sewage treatment plant
Nitric acid plant	Steam generator
Petroleum refinery	Sulfuric acid plant
Petroleum storage	Sulfur recovery plants and refineries

Source: John Quarles, *Federal Regulation of New Industrial Plants* (Washington, D.C., 1979).

notes, the obstacles to approval of new factories are much greater than for expansion of existing plants. Thus, companies are being encouraged to acquire or expand existing facilities rather than to build new ones.[3]

Table 13-1 lists the new source performance standards which have been issued under the Clean Air Act by the beginning of 1979. If a standard applies to a particular plant, EPA regulations require that the company give advance notification to the state government before beginning construction and again before actual start-up of the plant. Also, operating data must be supplied thereafter.

The lead time required to build new manufacturing capacity is being increased substantially as the result of the need to conform to the Clean Air Act Amendments of 1977 (see chapter 6 for detail). The principal new elements of lead time now include the following steps which must occur after initial planning and plant design but before construction begins:

- Identification of legal requirements and data needs.
- Conduct of pollution monitoring program and collection of other supporting information.
- Preparation and submission of application to environmental regulatory agency.
- Response to any deficiencies identified in initial comments.

[3] John Quarles, *Federal Regulation of New Industrial Plants* (Washington, D.C.: Author, 1979), pp. 2–3.

- Processing by EPA, including public hearings if requested.
- Judicial review, which can be initiated by any interested person.[4]

Multiple approvals usually are required for a given plant. Discharges into rivers or other public waters, for example, require permits under the Federal Water Pollution Control Act. To accommodate water pollution control engineering into the design and construction of a new plant, a company would apply for a permit several years in advance of the date when the discharges would begin. However, since water pollution permits have a maximum term of five years, an approval issued at the beginning of the design period might expire shortly after the plant begins operation. Meanwhile, EPA or state requirements may have been tightened, increasing the uncertainty attached to the company's capital investment.

Frequently, a large industrial plant will operate some type of waste treatment, storage, or disposal facility on its premises. If hazardous wastes are involved, it has to obtain a permit and comply with the requirement set under the Resource Conservation and Recovery Act. In John Quarles's view, the siting of hazardous waste disposal facilities may prove to be one of the most insoluble environmental problems presented in planning future industrial plants in the United States.[5]

Furthermore, new factories located beside major bodies of water may be subject to special regulations designed to protect wetlands or to control development within the coastal zone. The views of locally elected officials and other community leaders may be especially influential; the permit-granting agency, the Army Corps of Engineers, has broad legal discretion to decide whether the permit would be in the "public interest." Moreover, project modifications designed to meet the objections of one regulatory agency may make it more difficult to win the approval of another.

The regulatory experience of an existing chemical plant is instructive. Dow's facility in Pittsburg, California, must file 563 separate permit applications each year to cover its direct "emissions" into the air. In addition, the company must obtain 370 permits for the "sources" that originate the materials that escape through the emission point.[6] As shown in table 13-2, the bulk of the cost that Dow Chemical Company incurs to meet regulatory requirements arises in the manufacturing and distribution area. The rapid expansion in these costs in recent years is also apparent.

[4] Ibid., pp. 44–45.
[5] Ibid., p. 148.
[6] *1978 Annual Report* (Midland, Mich.: Dow Chemical Company, 1979), p. 2.

Table 13-2 Estimated costs of meeting federal regulations, Dow Chemical Company, 1975–77 (in millions of dollars)

	Environment			Transportation			Health and Safety			Other			Total		
	1975	1976	1977	1975	1976	1977	1975	1976	1977	1975	1976	1977	1975	1976	1977
Corporate and other administration	1	4	7	10	10	12	2	2	2	9	8	6	22	24	27
R&D and product development	10	14	16	–	6	4	10	15	18	2	2	4	22	37	42
Manufacturing and distribution	52	64	140	35	35	29	9	13	19	6	10	10	102	122	198
Marketing	–	2	–	–	–	–	1	–	–	–	1	1	1	3	1
Total	63	84	163	45	51	45	22	30	39	17	21	21	147	186	268

Source: Dow Chemical, USA

237

Employer Responsibility for Safety

Many manufacturing departments have been revising their procedures to conform to the expanding occupational safety and health regulations pertaining to air, noise, and heat. Asbestos producers are now required to meet strict minimum operating requirements, and numerous other areas of manufacturing are being studied by the National Institute for Occupational Safety and Health to determine if additional standards should be promulgated. The often substantial cost to the manufacturer of complying with the new array of health and safety standards is shown in table 13-3. Although the cost of compliance rises, on the average, with size of the company, it is apparent that the increases are not proportional. Hence, the smaller firms tend to bear a disproportionately large share of the expenses that arise from employee safety and health regulation.

Organizational changes are also a consequence of the stepped-up pace of federal regulation. An interdepartmental work safety committee is becoming a common mechanism for responding to rising government and public concern with job safety and health (see table 13-4). Depending on the size of the company and the geographic dispersion of its activities, such safety committees may be set up at the plant, division, or corporate levels. Their role may vary from coordination to staff assistance to actual line authority over the safety aspects of production activities.

The Occupational Safety and Health Administration's (OSHA) approach to safety regulation is based on the notion that employers can best prevent accidents and disease. As stated by the U.S. Occupational Safety and Health Review Commission, "the [OSHA] law exhorts employees to comply with job safety and health standards, but its enforcement procedures are directed solely at employers." In a series of cases before the commission testing this question, the employers were given the onus for unsafe acts of their employees. The commission ruled that the employers should have done more than merely make protective equipment available. It was held that employers must establish an effective policy to ensure that the equipment is used and must continually monitor the program to make certain that their employees are complying with it.[7]

There are limits, however, to the company's responsibility for lack of safety consciousness by its employees. In one case (*Secretary of Labor* v. *Standard Glass, Inc.*) where the evidence demonstrated

[7] *The President's Report on Occupational Safety and Health* (Washington, D.C.: U.S. Government Printing Office, 1973), pp. 92-93.

Table 13-3   Estimated average cost of OSHA compliance

Company Size	Estimated Expense		
(Number of Employees)	(Weighted Average)		
	Safety	Health	Total
0- 100	$ 24,000	$ 11,000	$ 35,000
101- 500	50,500	23,000	73,500
501-1,000	141,100	209,600	350,700
1,001-2,000	272,000	58,600	330,600
2,001-5,000	552,000	278,000	830,000
over 5,000	2,226,500	2,455,000	4,681,500

Source: Occupational Safety and Health Management Research Survey, National Association of Manufacturers, 1974

Table 13-4   Functions of a company health and safety committee

1. Establishing procedures for handling suggestions and recommendations of the committee.
2. Inspecting a selected area of the establishment each month for the purpose of detecting hazards.
3. Conducting regularly scheduled meetings to discuss accident and illness prevention methods, safety and health promotion, hazards noted on inspections, injury and illness records, and other pertinent subjects.
4. Investigating accidents as a basis for recommending means to prevent recurrence.
5. Providing information on safe and healthful working practices to the foremen.
6. Recommending changes or additions to improve protective clothing and equipment.
7. Developing or revising rules to comply with current safety and health standards.
8. Promoting safety and first aid training for committee members and other employees.
9. Promoting safety and health programs for all employees.
10. Keeping records of minutes of meetings.

Source: U.S. Occupational Safety and Health Administration

that the employer had done all that could reasonably be required to assure that employees used their protective equipment, the commission ruled that their isolated failures to use it were not a violation by the employer. The commission held that the employer could not be expected to guarantee that all employees would observe good safety practices at all times.

In contrast to the bureaucratic approach fostered by OSHA — if the company follows the agency's standards, it will not get into trouble — some business firms have been taking a more positive, results-oriented attitude to occupational safety and health. DuPont, for example, sets formal safety goals for all supervisors in terms of lost-time injuries per million hours worked; line supervisors are held responsible for the safety of all work in their areas. Safety professionals are only used in an advisory capacity.

Once a DuPont manufacturing department, in cooperation with the company's Laboratory of Toxicology and Industrial Medicine, determines that a substance it is handling may be toxic, a number of crucial steps are taken. The first is initiating a program to safeguard the health of employees, which may include revision of work practices, requirements for additional protective equipment, changes in production processes, or other improved engineering controls.

Next, a program for monitoring and measuring exposure levels is instituted, along with an examination of employee medical histories to determine any possible adverse effects on health. Medical surveillance procedures, as well as the recording of employee exposures, are also undertaken. Depending on the circumstances, a variety of groups may be notified of the actions taken; these may include employees, customers, government agencies, other producers, and the media. If safe production cannot be assured, it is company policy to shut down production and halt sales of the items involved until adequate safeguards can be developed.

To deal with the possibility of accidents occurring while a product is in shipment, DuPont has developed a Transportation Emergency Reporting Procedure (TERP); this activity keeps track of company materials in transit. In the event of an accident, TERP can provide the carrier and local police and fire personnel with immediate advice, and often it follows with technical people to assist. TERP ties in with the Chemical Transportation Emergency Center (CHEMTREC), which the company helped to set up. CHEMTREC provides round-the-clock assistance throughout the United States in any transportation emergency involving chemicals.[8]

DuPont reports that its injury rate has dropped from 3 per million worker-hours in 1935 to 0.16 in 1972. The company estimates an annual saving of about $27 million compared with the average all-industry injury experience. In fact, the company receives a modest amount of income from the fees that it receives from other companies for the evaluation and review done for them by the DuPont occupational safety and health group.

A 1979 study of successful private industry safety programs concluded that they place great emphasis on training, education, and awareness programs. About three-fourths schedule safety meetings for workers. Half of the companies have ongoing safety training

---

[8] Edwin A. Gee, "Report on Safety," *DuPont Context*, 1 (1975), 7; Paul F. Jankowski, "Report on Safety: DuPont's Long Record," *DuPont Context*, 1 (1975), 14.

programs for supervisors and new hires. Several firms offer specialized training in jobs where accident data reveal specific hazards. When unsafe conditions or procedures are discovered at specific job sites, some firms issue safety alerts warning managers of other divisions with similar working conditions. In job safety, as in other areas, information thus seems to be a more widely used tool in voluntary private safety programs than in government regulatory efforts.[9]

QUALITY CONTROL FUNCTIONS

As a result of the stepped-up activities of the various federal regulatory agencies, many companies are finding it necessary to expand their quality control departments. In the process, some companies have been separating quality control operations from production, so that the two departments report to different vice-presidents. The establishment of such independent quality control units is further upgrading the function, in some cases resulting in the promotion of the chief quality control official to vice-presidential rank.

Those involved in quality control function are finding it especially necessary to focus on prevention of increasingly expensive, time-consuming, and publicly embarrassing product recalls. Many companies require a safety analysis of each of their products and of the ingredients that go into them. The resultant "safety profiles" enable the company to correct potential problems before their products reach the marketplace.

In the Whirlpool Corporation, the product safety audit is a formal product review. It is usually led by the engineering laboratory group charged with the responsibility for the total product evaluation program. It never is conducted by the engineers who did the product design work in the first place. Attendees at a product safety audit include the director of engineering of the operating division responsible for the product; the director of engineering for the product under review; the engineering director of a totally unrelated product; personnel from design, testing, manufacturing, and quality control; a representative of the reliability group; and people from the customer assurance and service departments.

The Whirlpool product audit covers the following subjects:

Shipping containers and shipping performance.
Provisions for handling the packed product.

[9] U.S., Comptroller General, *How Can Workplace Injuries Be Prevented? The Answers May Be in OSHA Files* (Washington, D.C.: U.S. General Accounting Office, 1979), pp. 33-35.

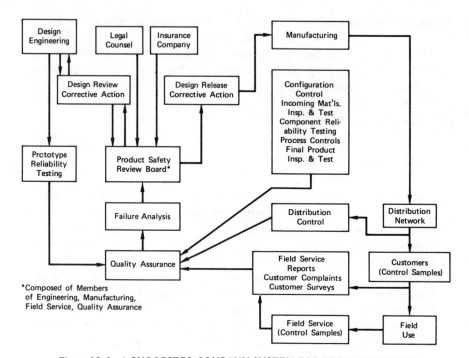

Figure 13-1   A SUGGESTED COMPANY SYSTEM FOR PRODUCT SAFETY

Source: James P. Kuhn, "How to manage product safety," *Industry Week,* April 22, 1974.

Unpacking procedures and instructions.
Product identification on the carton.
Product installation.
Instructions, cautions, and labels.
All performance characteristics.
Electrical, chemical, and construction standards.
Reliability of the product.
Serviceability, including access to parts.
Disposal of the product.[10]

Some firms are retaining outside experts to perform "product audits" with the purpose of having an independent authority review the firm's quality control procedures to verify both compliance with government regulations and the authenticity of company advertising claims. The product auditor also can act as an expert witness before federal regulatory bodies or in court cases. Although use of such

[10] Howard E. Brehm, "How to Establish a Product Safety Program," *Quality Progress,* February 1975, pp. 28–29.

independent experts is not new, it has become more important as a result of government programs of product safety, increased enforcement of truth-in-advertising, and the trend toward placing the burden of proof for safety on the manufacturer.

As a result of federal requirements, quality control departments, as well as company health groups, are receiving added responsibilities for testing the physical environment in which production takes place. As the pressures from government safety agencies increase, many companies are setting up product safety review boards responsible for monitoring and taking corrective action on all phases of the product development cycle (see fig. 13-1). Such interdivisional organizations are composed of representatives of quality control, engineering, manufacturing, marketing, and legal departments — and may be assisted by the company insurer. These boards can directly or indirectly influence a large share of company expenditures and potential liabilities — ranging from product liability costs to liability insurance premiums and legal fees to expanded outlays for risk prevention through product testing, certification, quality assurance, and product service.

MARKETING FUNCTIONS

The possibility of intermittent but direct federal intervention in company pricing decisions is one of the more significant areas of government regulation affecting marketing. Overall, long-term market planning needs to take account of the likelihood of the imposition of price (and wage) standards or controls or some form of federal influence over private industry pricing for one or more periods in the years ahead. Typically, the federal intervention coincides with periods of high and rising inflation in the economy as a whole (as in 1971 to 1973 and 1978-79).

Virtually every traditional aspect of the marketing function is also being affected by government, ranging from the advertising to distribution to servicing. "Caveat emptor" (buyer beware) is a concept being relegated to the business history books. Stepped-up enforcement by the old-line regulatory agencies, such as the Federal Trade Commission, and the establishment of newer activities (notably in the product safety area) mean that the seller must be aware of the dangers of inadequacy of his or her product. As the marketing departments are feeling the brunt of this aspect of government control, they are gradually undergoing a broadening of their outlook and a curtailment of their discretion as staff offices, notably the corporate legal and insurance staffs are more heavily involved.

More of the marketing department's efforts are now geared to reviewing and criticizing the internal product development efforts of the company prior to the products reaching the marketing stage, where the company may find itself in conflict with unofficial or formal consumer advocate agencies. According to Professor G. David Hughes of the University of North Carolina, the growing regulations and court decisions explain why many marketing managers spend most of their time dealing with matters related to the federal government.[11] Increasingly, government regulations are restricting the options available to the marketing manager.

At times, however, regulatory activities can serve to generate new or increased markets for business firms. The pollution control industry, for example, averaged a sales growth of nearly 20-percent a year from 1972 to 1974, compared with a 9-percent annual growth rate for all manufacturing companies. A new computer firm began successful operations in Michigan in 1976 to help automobile companies reduce the weight of various parts in order to produce lighter and hence more fuel-efficient cars.

Product Recalls

As a result of expanding government regulation and enforcement of existing controls, marketing departments are increasingly responsible for provisions for "reverse distribution"—product recalls. In addition to the highly publicized cases of motor vehicles and tires, growing numbers of nonautomotive products are recalled, including adhesives, bicycles, computers, deodorants, drain cleaners, electric shavers, epsom salts, gas ovens, heart monitors, lawn mowers, power drills, safety helmets, soup bowls, television sets, and toys. Voluntary recalls, of course, predate the new wave of government regulation. In 1903 Packard recalled its Model K when it realized that the car's drive shaft had a habit of popping out of its housing.[12]

Many companies, especially those catering to consumer markets, are introducing numerous modifications in their operating procedures to reduce the expense and anxiety associated with recall situations. For example, a coded identification number for each product or batch of products can expedite product recalls. Com-

[11] G. David Hughes, "Regulation and Marketing Strategy," *Executive*, 4, no. 3 (1978), 10.
[12] Mark Levenson, "Recalls: Tracing Them Back to the Turn of the Century," *Dun's Review*, January 1979, p. 117.

puters keep track of the numbers throughout the distribution chain. The minimum identification includes the labeling of each shipping package and container with a code indicating item, batch or period, day, month, year, and plant. In the example of grocery manufacturers, the following records and actions have been recommended by their trade association to facilitate locating a product subject to recall:

> A record of the cases, by identification code, packed in a batch so that a reconciliation with total shipments can be quickly accomplished if needed.
>
> Shipping specific batches of goods to defined distribution regions, rather than scattering them across the country.
>
> Retain documents at each shipping point to show the codes and number of cases for each item shipped.
>
> Keeping these documents until it is certain that the product has gone through the grocery marketing system, but not less than two years. Record retention for perishable products, however, may be limited to six months.
>
> Where practical, shipping only one batch of each item for each order.
>
> Where practical, reconditioned merchandise should not be packed with more than one batch to a case. Cases containing mixed codes should be clearly marked.
>
> Instructing each public warehouse to follow predetermined product recall procedures.
>
> In those cases where the stock is taken beyond the distributor warehouse, encouraging subsequent warehouses to follow similar identification procedures.[13]

Postage-paid, detailed warranty cards are a method of providing the manufacturer with the names and addresses of purchasers of certain types of products. Some companies have conducted "dry runs" of recall procedures. As part of its annual plant audit, Pillsbury Company selects a product at random and launches a "trace" to find out specifically where an entire production run may be in the distribution pipeline. Often, a single executive is assigned recall responsibilities, with the authority to halt production and to begin notification of dealers and customers. An example of a possible action plan, resulting from a situation that may require a product recall, is shown in Figure 13-2.

The stepped-up emphasis within the marketing function on the recall problem is resulting in a number of visible changes. For example, a major expansion is under way in record keeping so that the holders of the recalled products — final purchasers as well as

---

[13] *Guidelines for Product Recall* (Washington, D.C.: Grocery Manufacturers of America, 1974), pp. 57-58.

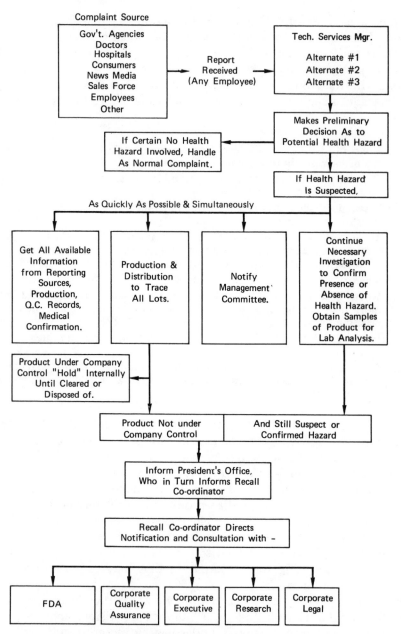

Complaint Source

Gov't. Agencies Doctors Hospitals Consumers News Media Sales Force Employees Other	Report Received (Any Employee)	Tech. Services Mgr. Alternate #1 Alternate #2 Alternate #3

Makes Preliminary
Decision As to
Potential Health Hazard

If Certain No Health
Hazard Involved, Handle
As Normal Complaint.

If Health Hazard
Is Suspected,

As Quickly As Possible & Simultaneously

Get All Available
Information
from Reporting
Sources,
Production,
Q.C. Records,
Medical
Confirmation.

Production &
Distribution
to Trace
All Lots.

Notify
Management
Committee.

Continue
Necessary
Investigation
to Confirm
Presence or
Absence of
Health Hazard.
Obtain Samples
of Product for
Lab Analysis.

Product Under Company
Control "Hold" Internally
Until Cleared or
Disposed of.

Product Not under
Company Control

And Still Suspect or
Confirmed Hazard

Inform President's Office,
Who in Turn Informs Recall
Co-ordinator

Recall Co-ordinator Directs
Notification and Consultation with –

FDA	Corporate Quality Assurance	Corporate Executive	Corporate Research	Corporate Legal

Figure 13-2 A PRODUCT RECALL CONTINGENCY PLAN

Source: Guidelines for Product Recall (Washington, D.C.: Grocery Manufacturers of America, 1974), pp. 28–29.

If After Consultation and Analysis, the Complaint Is A Confirmed
Hazard The Recall Co-Ordinator Shall Direct As Follows.

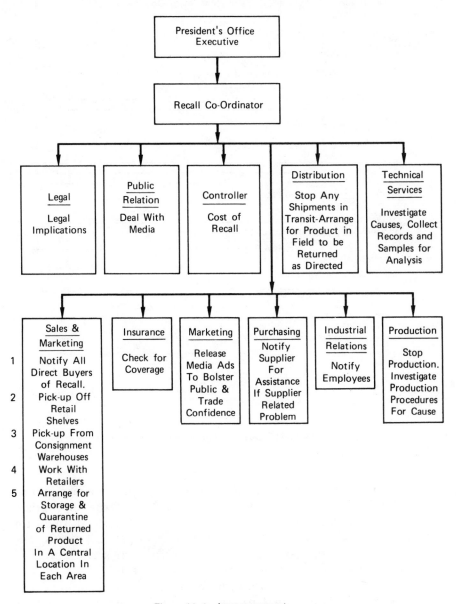

Figure 13-2 (CONTINUED)

This outline is intended to assist the affected Division in supplying the information necessary for company designee, such as Recall Coordinator of Corporate Affairs, to notify FDA.

I. PRODUCT INVOLVED

Give product, product code, labeling, packaging and description

_____
_____
_____

II. PRODUCTION CODE DATES

List all production code dates in full (include plant designation).

_____
_____
_____

III. ESTIMATED AMOUNT ON MARKET

Total amount produced _____
Indicate best estimate of product as yet unconsumed
Area of country affected _____

IV. REASON FOR RECALL
Describe precisely the reason for recall _____

_____

V. INJURIES, DEATHS

Furnish a statement, even if negative

_____
_____

VI. RECALL COMMUNICATIONS

Furnish a copy of the recall telegram sent to the trade.

Figure 13-3   AN FDA NOTIFICATION FORMAT FOR A PRODUCT RECALL

Source: Guidelines for Product Recall (Washington, D.C: Grocery Manufacturers of America, 1974), p. 43.

wholesale and retail distributors — can be promptly notified and so that the required information can be furnished to the appropriate government agency. Figure 13-3 contains a proposed format for notifying the Food and Drug Administration of product recalls. The necessity often arises of establishing a network of service firms to replace substandard parts or substitute new products.

Corporations are devoting more attention to correspondence from consumers than has been the case in the past. Such response also can be used as evidence of the company's acting in good faith should a product subsequently be declared hazardous.

The cost of a recall varies with the number of products sold;

the amount of time and effort required to track down purchasers; the percentage of products that require repair, replacement, or refund; and the cost per unit to remedy the problem. It cost one motor vehicle manufacturer $3.5 million for postage alone to notify by certified mail, as required by law, the 6.5 million owners of cars with questionable motor mounts. The cost of the recall may far exceed the price of the product itself. One company estimated that it cost on the average $5 to recall each defective 19-cent item. The costs included notifying each user by return receipt letter or personal call; locating, taking inventory, removing and disposing of suspect items at various locations; redesigning the item; overtime manufacturing of new items, printing labels and instructions, packing, shipping, installing, and testing new items; recording and reporting the actions taken; and the cost of medical and legal fees in connection with consumer complaints — all in addition to lost sales.[14]

As the trend toward more product recalls and greater liability continues, companies indeed are likely to produce safer, albeit more expensive, products. They will do much more testing, and because absolute safety is unattainable, they are also likely to increase their liability insurance coverage. The experience of Firestone Tire & Rubber Company with its "500" steel-belted radial tire surely illustrates the great stakes involved. After an acrimonious public battle with the National Highway Traffic Safety Administration the company was forced to recall 13 million of those tires — the largest product recall in history.[15] The damage to the company's sales and reputation was so substantial that for a while it operated in the red and was a candidate for a takeover effort.

Warranties

The Magnuson-Moss Warranty and Federal Trade Commission Improvement Act, which took effect July 5, 1975, for the first time sets standards for what must be incorporated in a product warranty and how the warranty must be worded. The law is bringing sweeping changes in product warranties. Some companies are simply dropping the entire warranty procedure to avoid the federal controls. Other companies, which continue issuing warranties as part of the competitive "package" offered to customers, are making theirs less com-

---

[14] Richard M. Jacobs and August B. Mundel, "Quality Tasks in Product Recall," *Quality Progress*, June 1975, pp. 16–17.

[15] "NHTSA and the Firestone 500," *Regulation*, May–June 1979, p. 12; Stuart A. Feldstein, "How Not to React to a Safety Controversy," *Business Week*, November 6, 1978, p. 65.

prehensive because they find it easier and cheaper to meet the requirements for a "limited warranty" than the more onerous "full warranty." Although the act regulates the nature of warranties, it cannot require any company to give a full warranty or any warranty at all. The major provisions of the act include the following:

> Warranties shall "fully and conspicuously disclose in simple and readily understood language the terms and conditions of such warranty." The complex legal language previously used in many warranties is no longer permissible.
>
> Warranty information shall be made accessible to consumers to aid in their decision to buy. The burden of education seems to be on the manufacturer, who should encourage, or demand if possible, that retailers pass the information on to buyers.
>
> Companies must label the warranty either "full" or "limited." If a warranty is labeled full it must meet minimum standards, including the company's pledge to repair any defects within a reasonable time and without charge. After a reasonable number of attempts at repair (the Federal Trade Commission defines "reasonable"), if the product still does not work it must be replaced or the full purchase price refunded; this is the so-called lemon provision. If the warranty does not meet these prerequisites, it must be conspicuously promoted as a "limited" warranty, in which case the customer may pay for parts or labor.[16]

Packaging and Labeling

Some of the emphasis in consumer product packaging is shifting from merely decorative coverings to informational labeling. Increased government response to consumer concerns is leading to expanding amounts of information on labels, as well as on supporting product literature and catalogues. The product contents and usage of components are more and more frequently being described. For example, the Federal Trade Commission forces detergent producers to list all ingredients so that buyers can avoid allergy-causing chemicals.[17]

The Food and Drug Administration requires companies that enrich foods or make nutritional claims about them to include nutritional information on the package.[18] The Consumer Product Safety Commission has the authority to set standards for packages containing hazardous substances. (see fig. 13-4 for an example). The CPSC

---

[16] George D. Webster and Arthur L. Herold, "Federal Trade Commission Issues Consumer Product Warranty Rules," *Association Management*, February 1976, pp. 20-22.

[17] U.S., Federal Trade Commission, *Care Labels*, Buyer's Guide no. 10 (Washington, D.C.: U.S. Government Printing Office, 1972).

[18] U.S., Food and Drug Administration, *The New Look in Food Labels*, DHEW publication no. FDA 74-2036 (Washington, D.C.: U.S. Government Printing Office, 1974).

Front panel

Front panel

TOILET BOWL CLEANER

POISON

CAUSES SEVERE BURNS—VAPOR HARMFUL
Read carefully cautions on back panel

DRAINPIPE CLEANER

POISON

CAUSES SEVERE BURNS
Read carefully cautions on back panel

Back panel

Back panel

Contains Hydrochloric Acid

Keep away from skin and eyes

Do not mix with chlorine type bleaches
or other household chemicals

First Aid: External: Flush with water for 15 minutes.

Internal: Drink large quantities of water or milk.
Follow with milk of magnesia, beaten eggs
or vegetable oil.

Call Physician immediately.

Eyes: Wash with water for 15 minutes and get
prompt medical attention.

KEEP OUT OF THE REACH OF CHILDREN

Contains caustic soda (Sodium Hydroxide)

Avoid contact with skin, eyes, mucous membranes
and clothing.

First Aid: External: Flush with water for
15 minutes then wash with vinegar.

Internal: Give large quantities of water or milk.
Follow with citrus juice or dilute vinegar.

Call Physician immediately.

Eyes: Flush with water for 15 minutes and get
prompt medical attention.

KEEP OUT OF THE REACH OF CHILDREN

Figure 13-4 EXAMPLES OF LABELS MEETING REQUIREMENTS FOR PRODUCTS
CONTAINING HAZARDOUS SUBSTANCES

Source: Lawrence E. Hicks, "Product Labeling and the Law," *AMA Management Briefing,*
1974, p. 21.

also regulates packaging so that products containing harmful substances cannot be opened easily by children under age five.

The federal government has ordered manufacturers to label household appliances regarding their annual energy costs to users. The costs of running the appliances are determined by standardized tests developed by the Department of Energy. The Federal Trade Commission, which has jurisdiction over the labeling, has extended the requirement to cover dishwashers, refrigerators, freezers, clothes washers, and air conditioners and has provided the alternative of showing energy efficiency ratings. Each label must give estimates of the highest and lowest energy costs or efficiency ratings for similar size products. A table showing estimated annual cost figures at different utility rates and for different levels of use is also required on the labels. The labels become a positive marketing device — that is, they may help overcome consumer resistance to buying a more expensive model, provided that it is more economical in terms of energy usage.

The regulation of labeling at times may have serious feedback effects on other company functions. For example, should a baking company list the full chemical names of product ingredients on bread wrappers — such as sodium aluminum pyrophosphate instead of baking powder — it would have to print up new labels each time it used a different type of baking powder. According to Gordon F. Bloom of MIT, the cost of nutritional labeling is especially heavy on those categories of products — baby food, candy, frozen fruits, and pickles — characterized by extensive variety and relatively small volume.[19]

Advertising

Advertisers are finding the government to be a greater influence both in terms of prescribing types of advertising — motor vehicle producers must include mileage ratings — as well as restricting the claims that are made. In recent years the Federal Trade Commission has shifted the burden of proof regarding the validity of advertising claims to the advertiser, even requiring documentation of product claims prior to running the ad.

If a claim is not substantiated because the product has not been tested, that may be an automatic violation. That is a marked shift from the earlier approach when the test of fairness or deception lay only in the literal truthfulness of the claim.[20]

Writers of copy are frequently being instructed about the product's liabilities — as well as its attributes. Advertisers and advertising agencies, spurred by federal action, are displaying a greater awareness of consumer safety in product advertising. Advertising copy prepared with an awareness of safety can provide such tangible benefits as enhancing product acceptability and reducing the possibility of unfavorable publicity and safety-related lawsuits.[21]

Some companies that are heavy advertisers in consumer markets, or their agencies, have set up formal panels to review the approach to safety in their advertising. These panels include advertiser and agency personnel who are in some way particularly familiar with actual consumer experiences with the products involved — for example, parents of young children. The National Advertising Review Board, an industry self-regulatory organization, has devel-

19 Gordon F. Bloom, "Government Regulation: The Hidden Tax on Food," (address at the Fifteenth Annual Underwood-Prescott Memorial Symposium, Cambridge, Mass., September 27, 1977), pp. 5-6.

20 H. Keith Hunt, "Advertising Regulation," *Exchange*, Fall–Winter 1976, p. 11.

21 U.S., National Business Council for Consumer Affairs, *Safety in the Marketplace* (Washington, D.C.: U.S. Government Printing Office, 1973), pp. 1-11.

oped the following checklist for reviewing company advertising to minimize the likelihood of violating federal product safety requirements:

> Is anything shown, described, or claimed in the advertisement that raises questions of consumer safety?
> Is everything known that should be known about the product's performance under both normal and misuse circumstances?
> Is there anything in the advertisement that might prove harmful to children who cannot comprehend the most familiar hazards in consumer products and tend to imitate what they see?
> Is allowance made in advertising situations for the susceptibility to suggestion of the elderly or the consumer predisposed toward risk-taking?[22]

The Review Board is associated with the National Advertising Division (NAD) of the Council of Better Business Bureaus. NAD serves as a national advertising complaint bureau. From mid-1971 through 1977 NAD processed 1,244 complaints, in 395 instances resulting in the advertising claims being modified or discontinued.[23]

Professor Jules Backman and John Czepiel have described today's marketing strategists as "broken field" runners, because they must traverse the field between what their organizations can do, what the consumer wants, and what society collectively allows.[24]

INTERNATIONAL OPERATIONS

The major impacts of government regulation on corporate international operations are mainly indirect. The added costs of meeting domestic regulatory requirements may at times place American-produced products at a competitive disadvantage in world markets. The result would depend, of course, on the relative regulatory costs imposed by other nations on the products produced abroad. Many other statutes affect the business operations of both foreign and domestic enterprises.

Specific government regulations may benefit domestic companies at the expense of overseas business, including the foreign sub-

---

[22] *Product Advertising and Consumer Safety* (New York: National Advertising Review Board, 1974), p. 5.

[23] William Sklar, "Consumer Advertising Issues: 1978 Perspective," *Business and Society Review*, Fall 1978.

[24] Jules Backman and John Czepiel, "Marketing Strategy: Some Basic Considerations" in *Changing Marketing Strategies in a New Economy*, eds. Jules Backman and John Czepiel, (Indianapolis: Bobbs-Merrill, 1977), p. 19.

sidiaries of American corporations. The most conspicuous example of such controls is the Buy American policy of federal procurement agencies. Passed in 1933 as an antirecessionary measure, the Buy American Act requires federal agencies purchasing commodities for use within the United States to pay up to a 6 percent differential for domestically produced goods. As much as a 50 percent differential is paid for military goods produced at home. The desire to reduce the defense burden on the United States balance of payments is the general justification for the special treatment to domestic producers.

American flag vessels must be used to transport at least 50 percent of the gross tonnage of all commodities financed with United States foreign aid funds. Most of the goods financed by the program are procured in the United States.[25] As shown in table 13-5, many state governments have comparable practices. The preferences granted to domestic suppliers range from the North Carolina practice of favoring domestic bids when the terms of foreign and domestic proposals are essentially the same to Idaho's policy of purchasing only domestic materials. Some of these restrictions have been challenged in the courts, and others are so vague as not to be generally enforceable. Indirectly, American exporters may suffer from these policies, at least to the extent that they encourage other nations to adopt similar restrictions. The Internal Revenue Code authorizes companies to set up so-called Domestic International Sales Corporations (DISC) to handle their export sales from the United States. So long as the income remains in the DISC subsidiary, only one-half of export profits is subject to the federal corporate income tax.

There also are laws that prohibit or limit foreign investments in certain sectors of the American economy for reasons of national security or to protect what are considered "essential" national interests. These sectors include atomic energy, domestic airlines, shipping, federally owned land, communications and media, and fishing. Many laws provide the government with authority to control foreign economic activities in specific areas, such as defense. The Department of Defense may deny security clearances required to do classified (secret) work for the government to any firm under "foreign ownership, control, or influence." Foreign ownership of producers of defense materials is not expressly prohibited, but it is effectively deterred by the prospect that such acquisition would likely cause the firm to lose its classified government business. Exports of arms are closely controlled.

[25] Norman S. Fieleke, "The Buy-American Policy of the United States Government," *New England Economic Review*, July-August 1969, pp. 2-6.

Table 13-5 State buy-American practices

State	Practice
Alabama	Requires use of U.S. materials "if available at reasonable prices" in cases of public works financed entirely by state funds.
California	Requires use of materials of U.S. origin (subject to court challenges).
Georgia	Requires state agencies to buy American products if price and quality are equal.
Hawaii	Establishes a scale of preferences for domestic products.
Idaho	Requires state bids to carry a clause restricting use of foreign materials.
Indiana	Restricts use of foreign steel and aluminum.
Kentucky	Discourages state agencies from requesting foreign-made products.
Maine	Reserves the right to reject bids involving foreign products when in direct competition with American products.
Massachusetts	Grants preference "other considerations being equal" to in-state products first and then to other American products.
New Jersey	Requires U.S. domestic materials to be used unless their cost is "unreasonable."
New York	Restricts use of foreign products through general specifications for bids.
North Carolina	Follows a policy of purchasing domestic products "wherever we deem we are not penalizing ourselves as to competition, availability, service and ultimate cost."
North Dakota	Requires certain bids to carry the phrase "bid domestically produced material only."
Oklahoma	Requires purchases of domestic goods and equipment unless a foreign product is of "equal quality" and also "substantially cheaper" or is of "substantially superior quality" and is sold at a "comparable price" to domestic products.
Pennsylvania	Prevents use in state projects of foreign steel and aluminum products made in countries that "discriminate" against American products.
South Dakota	Writes state specifications for American-made products; if foreign-made is bid, award is made on condition of acceptance by the state agency.
Wyoming	Generally discourages use of foreign goods.

Source: Norman S. Fieleke, "The Buy-American Policy of the United States Government," *New England Economic Review,* July–August 1969

In the wake of public concern over foreign purchases of farmland, Congress passed the Agricultural Foreign Investment Disclosure Act of 1978. Foreigners who own or purchase any interest in more than one acre of U.S. agricultural land or earn more than $1,000 from such land must report to the Secretary of Agriculture.

Under the Export Administration Act of 1969, the Department of Commerce controls the exports of goods and technology which would make a "significant contribution" to the military potential of any other nation which would prove "detrimental" to the national security of the United States. The Treasury Department also administers controls with respect to exports to Communist countries by foreign overseas firms controlled by Americans.

A more direct impact on the international operations of American business firms occurred following disclosures of widespread practices concerning legal and illegal payments involving government personnel of foreign nations (often called "mordita" or "baksheesh"). The payments have ranged from minor bribes to customs agents (at the equivalent of $5 to $10) to millions of dollars, via middlemen to senior officials of other governments. The practice of funneling cash into the hands of government officials or their representatives is long-standing and is defended by many business executives as the only way they can compete effectively abroad.

One businessman in Africa said in an interview, "You have to pay small bribes, called 'dash,' to get anything done. It's part of the price of visas, getting customs clearance on materials — even getting your suitcase."

The president of Bendix offers the hypothetical case of a foreign harbormaster holding up a shipment of perishable goods. He is demanding $5,000, or the shipment — which is worth twenty times as much — will be totally lost. In this example, the harbormaster is the prime minister's brother-in-law, so there is little point in complaining to the police.[26]

Nevertheless, such practices violate the mores and established modes of conduct in the United States, and since 1977 they have constituted a violation of American law. The Foreign Corrupt Practices Act of 1977 makes it a criminal offense for an employee of an American business to offer a bribe to a foreign government official (excluding those performing routine or clerical duties). The act also establishes standards governing a company's books and records and its system of internal accounting controls. The first court action brought by the Securities and Exchange Commission under the act related, not to the antibribery provision, but to alleged false entries in the company's books of account.[27] The maximum fine under the act — $1 million — is in striking contrast to the top fine of $10,000 that a court can assess for defrauding American investors under the securities law.

[26] William M. Agee, "The Moral and Ethical Climate in Today's Business World," *MSU Business Topics*, Winter 1978, p. 19; see also Michael C. Jensen, "U.S. Company Payoffs Way of Life Overseas," *The New York Times*, May 5, 1975, pp. 1, 52.

[27] *An Analysis of the Foreign Corrupt Practices Act of 1977* (Chicago: Arthur Andersen and Co., 1978), pp. 1-2.

Many other nations, of course, are also expanding their regulation of domestic and foreign business practices. The European Economic Community (EEC) especially has been attempting to develop uniform approaches for the Common Market countries, ranging from labeling and packaging of consumer products to curtailing misleading and unfair advertising.[28] American-based and other multinational corporations are finding their operations increasingly subject to the rules set by such international bodies.

The Organization for Economic Cooperation and Development, which is comprised of the major developed nations, has developed a code of conduct covering disclosure of information, competition, financing, taxation, employment policies, and investment in technology. When an American firm closed down its Belgian affiliate and found that the European subsidiary did not have sufficient assets to pay the required severance allowances, the parent company was forced to make the payments.[29]

APPENDIX: THE MARLIN TOY CASE*

In 1972 the U.S. Food and Drug Administration (FDA) banned two toys produced by the Marlin Toy Company of Horicon, Wisconsin, as hazardous substances and included them in published banned-products lists. This action led to the company's changing the products so as to eliminate the unsafe features and thus to qualify for removal from the ban list. After taking over administration of the Federal Hazardous Substances Act, the U.S. Consumer Product Safety Commission (CPSC) continued FDA's practice of periodically publishing such lists. In a list published on October 1, 1973, the commission inaccurately listed the toys as still hazardous. Marlin claimed to have lost many thousands of dollars in sales because of the commission's action. The commission acknowledged its mistake to Marlin in October 1973 and stated that it would include a retraction on its next published list. But it did not publish another banned-products list containing a retraction until June 1, 1974, eight months after the error.

[28] Carol Denning, "Consumer Reports, EC Style," *Europe*, March–April 1979, p. 43.

[29] "Neo-Mercantilism in the '80s," *Business Week*, July 9, 1979, p. 54.

*The material in this case is taken primarily from U.S., Comptroller General, *Banning of Two Toys and Certain Aerosol Spray Adhesives*, MWD-75-65, (Washington, D.C.: U.S. General Accounting Office, 1975), pp. 4-12.

Banning of Marlin Toys

As part of a toy safety survey in October 1972 FDA representatives in St. Louis identified Marlin's "flutter ball" toy as a possible mechanical hazard under the Hazardous Substances Act and acquired a sample for testing. Flutter ball was a transparent plastic ball with toy butterflies mounted on a rod and small plastic pellets. Both the rod and the pellets moved freely inside the ball.

FDA's Bureau of Product Safety tested the flutter ball on October 30, 1972, and found that the toy presented an unreasonable risk of injury or illness to children because it could be easily broken or shattered, creating the danger of inhaling, swallowing, or choking on the pellets. On November 1, 1972, FDA banned the toy as a mechanical hazardous substance.

The Hazardous Substances Act states that an article may be determined to present a mechanical hazard

> if, in normal use or when subjected to reasonably foreseeable damage or abuses, its design or manufacture presents an unreasonable risk of personal injury or illness (1) from fracture, fragmentation, or disassembly of the article, (2) from propulsion of the article (or any part or accessory thereof), (3) from points or other protrusions, surfaces, edges, openings, or closures, . . . (7) because the article (or any part or accessory thereof) may be aspirated or ingested, (8) because of instability, or (9) because of any other aspect of the article's design or manufacture.

The act prohibits banned hazardous substances from being delivered in interstate commerce and authorizes several methods, including seizure, fines, and imprisonment, for removing them from the marketplace. Through formal rule-making procedures (including such due process provisions as public hearings and public notice), FDA issued regulations for manufacturers, distributors, and retailers to follow in complying with the act (21 C.F.R. 191). Because such regulations had been issued, the toys were banned immediately after FDA determined that they did not conform to those regulations. Such immediate actions are authorized under the act.

On November 1, 1972, FDA notified Marlin that its flutter ball and any similar toys with like hazards were banned from interstate commerce and that any banned toys remaining in the market were subject to regulatory action, including seizure. In a subsequent meeting at Marlin's plant, FDA representatives learned that a similar Marlin toy — "birdie ball" — could also be hazardous. Birdie ball was basically the same as flutter ball, except it contained plastic birds instead of butterflies.

Late in November 1972 FDA obtained three samples of each ball to test before possibly seizing the balls as banned toys. Both types failed FDA's tests. On December 5, 1972, FDA notified Marlin that birdie ball had failed the test and that both balls were banned under the Federal Hazardous Substances Act.

After expressing displeasure and resistance to FDA's decision, Marlin agreed to modify the balls in stock and production but hesitated to recall those already distributed. Marlin stated that it would be an extreme financial hardship to recall those balls already distributed because it reportedly manufactured an estimated five million flutter and birdie balls during the previous 12 years. After Marlin's continued resistance to recalling the toys, FDA initiated seizure action and seized 88 balls from the marketplace.

Early in January 1973, shortly after the seizure, Marlin informed FDA that the two toys had failed the FDA tests because a supplier substituted an inferior grade of transparent plastic than Marlin had used to make the balls. Marlin subsequently informed FDA that it was recalling defective balls it had distributed and was excluding plastic pellets from future balls produced. Marlin said that flutter and birdie balls made with the higher-grade transparent plastic and without pellets would pass FDA tests.

Since Marlin planned to continue marketing balls similar to, but not the same as, the ones banned, Marlin and FDA agreed that the banned toys would be listed as those *with* plastic pellets to distinguish them from those that were not banned (those *without* plastic pellets). The record does not show whether FDA tested the balls with the higher-grade transparent plastic.

Inaccurate Listing of Marlin Toys

To inform manufacturers, distributors, retailers, and consumers of banned products, FDA periodically published lists of products that it had banned. These lists include the products' names, the manufacturers' names and addresses, the reasons for banning, and the dates banned. FDA intended to publish monthly lists of all products banned the previous month and semiannual lists of all products banned during the preceding six months. Although this plan was not followed precisely, FDA published six banned-products lists before the transfer of its functions under the Hazardous Substances Act to the CPSC in May 1973.

The Marlin balls appeared on FDA monthly lists issued in November 1972 (flutter ball) and January 1973 (birdie ball) — those issued after the banning of each ball. These lists properly labeled the toys as flutter ball and birdie ball, without any reference to plastic pellets. Both lists were issued before Marlin and FDA had agreed that future lists would specify that the ban pertained only to those balls with plastic pellets.

FDA added a note to the banned-products list of February 1, 1973, stating that the only versions of flutter and birdie balls classified as banned hazardous substances were "those containing pellets." Future lists including flutter and birdie ball entries were to list the two banned balls as those with plastic pellets.

On October 1, 1973, the CPSC published a cumulative list of products banned since FDA began its toy safety program in December 1970, including Marlin's flutter and birdie balls. Both balls were inaccurately described. Flutter ball was listed without any notation concerning plastic pellets, and birdie ball was listed as "'Birdie Ball' (without plastic pellets)," the opposite of what was intended.

On October 17, 1973, Marlin representatives informed the commission of the errors in the October 1 list. It was Marlin's understanding that after six months a banned toy would no longer appear on the list. Further, Marlin claimed to have lost many thousands of dollars in business because of the commission's actions and believed it was entitled to some form of compensation.

The commission acknowledged its inaccurate listing of birdie ball, agreeing that the toys should have been described as those with plastic pellets. It did not specifically acknowledge the inaccurate listing of flutter ball until the retraction was published. The commission said it would include a retraction in the next list. However, it did not have an anticipated publication date. The next list, published on June 1, 1974, included a retraction stating that the only versions of birdie and flutter balls that had been banned were those with plastic pellets.

The commission informed Marlin that the inaccurate listing was "an editorial error." The commission staff explained that the inaccurate listing resulted from several factors. The manually prepared note in FDA's banned-products list (February 1, 1973) was not picked up in the commission's computer-prepared list on October 1, 1973. There was a major change in personnel responsible for preparing the list. Moreover, commission staff did not discover the error when proofreading the October list before printing.

The commission told Marlin that the cumulative banned-products list (October 1, 1973) was issued because some previously banned toys were still on the market. The commission pointed out that, although banned products are removed from production, they still might be in retail stores. Also, the originally designed version of a banned product is banned permanently, but a redesigned product would not be banned unless found to be hazardous through further testing.

The commission informed Marlin that confusion might have arisen about a product appearing on the list for only six months. To help clarify the matter, the commission told Marlin that FDA had planned to publish banned-products lists each month and a cumulative list semiannually. Thereafter, items would remain banned but would not appear on new published lists. Marlin representatives may have interpreted this as meaning that the banned products would be listed for only six months.

The commission gave Marlin no explanation for its delay in publishing a banned-products list containing a retraction or for not publishing a separate retraction. Subsequently commission staff told investigators of the General Accounting Office that the major reason for the delay was that, knowing of other errors, the commission wanted to scrutinize and purify the list to improve its accuracy and usefulness. Banned products were to be more clearly identified, and reasons for their banning more fully explained.

The commission wrote Marlin two letters — one in November 1973 and another in March 1974 — acknowledging its error and explaining its intention to publish a retraction in the next banned-products list. Publishing a separate retraction was not considered economical because of the wide distribution of the banned-products list of October 1, 1973 — about 240,000 copies — and the commission's belief that a retraction in the next issue would be sufficient. Commission representatives also told the government investigators that Marlin could have used the commission's letters to Marlin to inform its customers of the commission's error and intention to publish a retraction. Although it did not tell that to Marlin, the commission believed that Marlin was responsible for informing its customers of the error and the planned retraction. The commission rejected Marlin's request for reimbursement because it did not have the authority to make such compensation payments. Marlin's recourse was to file a claim in the United States Court of Claims.

In a letter to the commission dated May 6, 1974, Marlin said that it was forced out of the toy business because the two balls were inaccurately listed. According to Marlin, 40 percent of its business was from sales of flutter and birdie balls, and the commission's November 1973 letter acknowledging the error and planning a retraction was "too little and too late." Marlin requested that the commission permit it to sue and let the courts determine whether and to what extent the commission was liable.

Lack of Procedures for Retracting Inaccurate Information

Since that episode the commission's Bureau of Compliance has installed procedures to upgrade the banned-products list through controls and other verification practices. Commission officials believe these prepublication controls should eliminate inaccurate lists. The commission, however, has not established any policy, regulations, or procedures for insuring prompt retractions. In practice, it discontinued the lists shortly after the Marlin episode.

Recognizing that the commission may err in attempting promptly to advise the public of its activities to protect consumers from hazardous products, section 6(b) of the Consumer Product Safety Act requires it to retract erroneously published data. Section 6(b) states:

> If the Commission finds that, in the administration of this Act, it has made public disclosure of inaccurate or misleading information which reflects adversely upon the safety of any consumer product, or the practices of any manufacturer, private labeler, distributor, or retailer of consumer products, it shall, in a manner similar to that in which such disclosure was made, publish a retraction of such inaccurate or misleading information.

The Hazardous Substances Act does not contain a similar provision. Therefore, although the banned-products list of June 1, 1974, included a retraction, the commission was not legally bound to issue retractions of information published in this case because the two balls were banned under the older law. However, in practice the commission does attempt to follow the spirit and intent of section 6(b) in retracting any inaccurate or misleading information published under any of the acts that it administers.

Commission officials say that publishing separate retractions in most cases would not be economically justified, and that publishing a retraction in the next issue of the list would be sufficient. Unsatisfied manufacturers could go to the courts for relief.

The CPSC, subsequent to this case, has indicated that it would be willing to send any manufacturer or other concerned party a retraction letter explaining an inaccurate listing and expressing the commission's intent to publish a retraction in the next list. The manufacturer could use such a letter to inform its customers of the error and planned retraction. Commission representatives believe it would be the manufacturer's, and not the commission's, responsibility to disseminate the letter to the customers — and presumably to request such a letter in the first place.

Although a letter written to a manufacturer would be beneficial, this retraction method is, of course, weaker than section 6(b) of the Consumer Product Safety Act. That law provides that the retraction be issued in "the same manner" as the original inaccurate statement.

Pending Litigation

In June 1974 two bills (S. 3666 and H.R. 15403) were introduced in the Ninety-third Congress that would provide for the payment of an unstated amount to Marlin in settlement of its claim for the erroneous description of its toys in the banned-products list. Senate and House resolutions (S. Res. 344 and H. Res. 1181) referred the two bills to the chief commissioner of the United States Court of Claims to determine the facts in this matter. Marlin filed a petition for its claim in the Court of Claims on October 11, 1974.

The CPSC was given an opportunity to comment on the bills and resolutions. On July 19, 1974, in letters to the House and Senate Committees on the Judiciary, it said that the two balls were inaccurately listed in the October 1, 1973, list. The commission urged that Marlin be given an opportunity to prove its reported financial losses in the Court of Claims.

CPSC and Marlin agreed in a cross-stipulation that $40,000 represents a just and fair claim, but that Marlin's exit from the toy industry was not caused by the appearance of its products on CPSC's list. Subsequently, the Court of Claims recommended that the federal government compensate Marlin to the extent of $40,000 to cover losses of new sales due to the errors in the banned-products list. The proposal was sent to Congress in November 1978, where it awaited action.

Conclusions

It would appear that the Federal Hazardous Substances Act was appropriately applied in banning Marlin's flutter and birdie balls as hazardous substances because FDA's interpretation of its test results showed that the two Marlin balls met the requirements for banning unsafe products. Due process was served with the publication and application of formal regulations before the banning.

The CPSC's subsequent description of the two balls in the October 1, 1973, list was an error that took eight months to retract. The commission acknowledged to Marlin its mistake and expressed its intentions to publish a retraction in the next list. However, it did not publish a retraction until June 1, 1974. Alternative retraction methods were discounted as being uneconomical, even though Marlin informed the commission that the inaccurate listing resulted in substantial financial loss.

No case similar to the Marlin incident has been reported since and, as noted, the ban list no longer is issued. However, the commission had not established a formal policy to guide it in making timely and appropriate retractions of inaccurate or misleading information. In practice, it would seem that the substantial adverse public and congressional reaction to the Marlin case did have a positive impact on the operating procedures of a relatively new regulatory agency.

Final Note

A few questions in this case still puzzle some observers. Would a larger business, knowing its way around Washington, have gotten the head of the commission to correct the problem promptly? Was the CPSC error the "last straw" that drove Marlin out of the toy business? Would the company just rather have had the $40,000 than maintain its intellectual position?

14

impacts on company staffs

Company staffs bear much of the responsibility for business response to government regulation. This added function is especially evident in such areas as personnel, finance, and facilities. Effects of regulation can range from who a firm can hire or fire to what a company must tell its stockholders, including how often and in what form the information must be communicated. Increasing controls over land use and requirements for comprehensive, complex environmental impact statements limit the physical alternatives for expansion and add new environmental parameters to the decision to relocate or enlarge existing facilities.

A portion of the material in this chapter raises issues discussed in previous chapters in order to show more directly their impacts on company staffs.

PERSONNEL FUNCTIONS

At times it seems that the primary thrust of many personnel departments is shifting from serving the staffing needs of the company to meeting the requirements of and pressures from government agencies.[1] On the positive side, the massive intervention by government has forced many companies to review their total employment process.

Regulatory agencies increasingly are affecting most of the important aspects of company personnel policies and practices: hiring, promoting, and training activities; employee testing; compensation, including fringe benefits; the composition and funding of pension plans; the physical working environment; and basic work relationships, such as discipline, job termination, union negotiation, and communicating with employees.

In some cases, a government agency has authority to approve or disapprove company actions (for example, qualification of company pension contributions as a tax deduction). In numerous other situations involving requirements that range from equal employment opportunity to the health and safety aspects of the job, federal agencies can file legal charges against companies and seem disposed to do so with growing frequency (see table 14-1).

Meeting the government's personnel requirements may not be easy. In June 1979 Merck and Company agreed to spend $3.2 million over the next three and a half years on new and expanded affirmative action efforts for its female and minority employees. Because it supplies pharmaceuticals to the Veterans Administration, the company comes under the affirmative action requirements for government contractors. Merck will spend the bulk of the money on job training and development programs and for "EEO awareness training" for supervisors. In another case, however, the Santa Fe Trail Transportation Company was found guilty by the Supreme Court of firing a white employee while retaining a black employee after both had committed the same offense.[2] On the other hand, at least two federal judges have ordered ex-employees to pay legal costs for what the judges said were "frivolous" discrimination suits against their former employers. One of the judges criticized litigants who file frivolous lawsuits because they have "nothing to lose" when they are provided with free court-appointed lawyers.[3]

To some extent, the importance of government policies is reflected in the internal evaluation of company personnel. For ex-

---

[1] See "Personnel Widens Its Franchise," *Business Week*, February 26, 1979, pp. 116-21.
[2] Rogene A. Buchholz, "Equal Opportunity: Why Not a Market Solution?" *Business and Public Affairs*, Spring 1979, p. 23.
[3] "Court Levies Charge for 'Frivolous' Suit," *Washington Post*, April 12, 1979, p. A-4; "Worker Loses Discrimination Suit, Told to Pay $5,000 in Legal Fees," *St. Louis Post-Dispatch*, March 23, 1979, p. 1D.

Table 14-1 Federal influence on company personnel activities

Federal Agency	Employment	Training and Promotion	Compensation and Fringe Benefits	Working Relationships	Physical Environment
National Labor Relations Board	□	□	□	□	□
Equal Employment Opportunity Commission	□○	□○	□○	□	□
Federal Contract Compliance Office	□	□	□	□	□
Wage and Hour Division			□○		
Internal Revenue Service			X○		
Occupational Safety and Health Administration		□		□	□○

□ = Federal agency can file charges
X = Federal agency can approve or disapprove
O = Federal agency receives reports

ample, some corporations now rate supervisors for their performance in meeting federal equal employment policies.

The General Electric Company, through a reporting system begun in 1968 which accompanies the annual review of a manager's performance and through a penalty-reward policy linked to executive compensation, has increased minority employment at all levels by 57 percent. GE thus requires its managers to give priority to a thoughtful examination of the numbers of women and minorities supervised, whether that number is representative of local population or labor supply, plans for training these individuals for promotions, and the like. The results of GE's efforts can be seen in table 14-2. In 1974 GE stated its policy evidencing the importance it accords equal employment considerations: "Goals should be definitely established and a measurement and audit process for the achievement of these goals be put in place with an appropriate reward and penalty system for each foreman, supervisor, or manager who has the responsibility for hiring and terminating employees."[4]

Training and Recruitment

The widening array of government regulatory legislation is requiring corporate personnel departments to expand their existing orientation programs and to establish new training programs. Supervisors, for example, need to be highly trained in many aspects of safety and health. Skills that are taught vary from the ability to administer first aid to the leadership capability necessary to convince employees to use personal protective equipment continually (as we have discussed, the company may be liable if its employees do not use required safety devices).[5]

Greater numbers of specialized personnel are being hired — safety directors and engineers, industrial hygienists, in-house medical staffs, and material buyers with special knowledge of protective clothing and nonhazardous equipment. Moreover, because required reports and applications, such as environmental impact statements, necessitate inputs from many disciplines, companies are finding that they must either increase the array of experts on their own staffs or receive more expert opinions via consulting arrangements. These specialists are involved in such fields as ecology, economics, sociology, geology, climate, engineering, mining, forestry, and aquatic

[4] Theodore V. Purcell, "How GE Measures Managers in Fair Employment," *Harvard Business Review*, November–December 1974, p. 104.
[5] "Safety Pros: They Save Lives for a Living," *Journal of American Insurance*, Spring 1978, pp. 16-19.

Table 14-2 Employment of women and minorities, General Electric Company, 1968 and 1973

Job Categories	All Employees			Women			Minorities		
	December 1968	December 1973	Percent Increase	December 1968	December 1973	Percent Increase	December 1968	December 1973	Percent Increase
Officials and managers	23,024	26,486	15.0	119	473	297.5	195	678	247.7
Professionals	53,624	44,905	-16.3	1,289	2,020	56.7	1,068	1,902	78.1
Technicians	19,846	15,377	-22.5	1,742	1,473	-15.5	726	964	32.8
Sales workers	4,599	7,622	65.7	336	595	77.1	79	362	358.2
Office and clerical	40,807	36,301	-11.1	28,898	27,068	- 6.3	1,844	3,558	93.0
Craftsmen	53,802	57,215	6.3	801	1,367	70.7	2,340	3,791	62.0
Operatives	88,910	101,099	13.7	41,869	46,856	11.9	11,182	18,703	67.3
Laborers	23,745	19,193	-19.2	8,663	8,869	2.4	3,489	3,385	-3.0
Service workers	3,689	3,011	-18.4	424	657	55.0	660	572	-13.3
Total	312,046	311,209	- 0.3	84,141	89,378	6.2	21,583	33,915	57.1

Source: Theodore V. Purcell, "How GE Measures Managers in Fair Employment," *Harvard Business Review*, November–December 1974.

life, as well as in public communications. Businesses also use specialized consulting services, both to provide advice on meeting Consumer Product Safety Commission (CPSC) and Occupational Safety
and Health Administration (OSHA) standards, and to provide more
health services to employees (for example, periodic examinations and
return-to-work checkups).[6]

One issue of *The New York Times* (June 17, 1979) contained a
variety of "help wanted" advertisements for positions that seem
either to have been established or expanded as a result of requirements imposed by government regulatory agencies. A sampling
follows:

> *Benefits Planning Analyst* . . . Full knowledge of all aspects of ERISA. . . .
>
> *Regulatory Affairs* . . . a Regulatory Affairs professional . . . 3–5 years
> experience in dealing with federal regulations as they apply to the manu-
> facturing and marketing of cosmetics, foods, and medical device products.
>
> *Project Manager, Environmental Assessment* . . . in charge of activities for
> the firm's Environmental Planning Division . . . Knowledge and familiarity
> with sludge, refuse and wastewater environmental engineering projects.
>
> *Packaging Equipment Engineer* . . . Knowledge of regulatory requirements
> (FDA, CGMP, OSHA) as they relate to packaging equipment.
>
> *Manager of Employment* . . . familiarity with AAP/EEO.
>
> *Pharmaceutical Project Engineer* . . . familiarity with GMP and OSHA
> requirements. . . .
>
> *Patent Attorney* . . . Some familiarity with trademark, copyright, fair
> packaging and labeling, food and drug, toxic substances, energy, and envi-
> ronmental matters is also required.
>
> *Corporate Beneftis Administrator* . . . be responsible for ERISA reports
> and other applicable state and federal filings.
>
> *Regulatory and Policy Analysis Consulting* . . . the assessment of the
> public and private impacts of existing and proposed government regula-
> tions in transportation and related fields. . . . The identification and esti-
> mation of the costs and benefits of regulations . . . analysis and evaluation
> of policies, including their technical and legal aspects. . . . Quantitative
> and qualitative regulatory impact analysis. . . . Cost-benefit and cost-
> effectiveness analysis of regulations. . . . Risk and probability analysis of
> regulations. . . .
>
> *Director of Public Relations* . . . articulate our growing role in the nation's
> economic and cultural life. . . . material to support company efforts in
> marketing and community relations.
>
> *Energy Consultants* . . . dealing with quantitative and qualitative energy
> issues in either the private or the public sectors. . . . Policy analysis and
> strategic planning. . . . Economic and financial analysis. . . . Technology
> assessment.

---

[6] See *Introduction to OSHA: A Complete Training Program* (Hicksville,
N.Y.: Research Media, Inc., 1974).

Government Marketing Representatives . . . experience in selling telecommunications or computer-related products and systems to the military. . . .

Attorney . . . relating to . . . SEC matters, stock transfers, and U.S. and foreign subsidiary activities.

Public Affairs Coordinator . . . coordinate contacts with local, state, and national governments.

Trade Association Assistant Manager . . . service 13 committees in arranging meetings, developing subject matter, preparing financial reports. . . .

Government Sales Engineer . . . experience dealing with military and/or government agencies and strong familiarity with government operations. . . .

Environmental Engineers . . . industrial waste water and sewer treatment technologies. Excellent writing skills required for the analysis and preparation of reports and documentation.

Compliance Assistant Director . . . in-house compliance experience to assist in the supervision and coordination of the firm's compliance activities. . . . Prior experience with NASD, SEC, or NYSE. . . .

Energy Conservation Manager . . . evaluate, plan, monitor and implement both current and new energy management systems.

Subcontracts Administrator . . . an in-depth knowledge of government procurement regulations is necessary.

Perhaps the most dramatic examples of government's impact on personnel decisions can be seen in some of the new breed of CEOs chosen by major corporations. The current chief executive of DuPont, for example, is neither a chemist nor a member of the DuPont family; Irving Shapiro is a lawyer by profession who spent part of his earlier career in government and much of his prior service with the company in dealing with government matters. Likewise, Bethlehem Steel Corporation recently chose for its president, not a traditional steel manager, but the vice-president for public relations; Richard F. Schubert earlier had served in Washington as an Undersecretary of Labor. Both men devote a major share of their time to representing their industries in dealing with government.[7]

Equal Opportunity

Personnel departments, as well as supervision at all levels, are placing more emphasis on meeting federal equal employment opportunity and affirmative action requirements (see fig. 14-1). The importance of equal employment opportunity considerations, and their turbulent effects at times, is vividly displayed by statements of the general counsel of one very large organization after watching

[7] Roger Smith, "Bethlehem President Is More Concerned with Regulators Than Mills," *Los Angeles Times*, June 26, 1979, p. 1 ff.

Could you be practicing illegal job discrimination— and not even know it?

Answer: True. Due to outdated policies or failure to understand the law, many employers do discriminate in the way they hire, fire, promote or pay.

Take this 30-second test and see where you stand.

An employer . . .   **True**   **False**

1. can refuse to hire women who have small children at home.   ___ ___

2. can generally obtain and use an applicant's arrest record as the basis for non-employment.   ___ ___

3. can prohibit employees from conversing in their native language on the job.   ___ ___

4. whose employees are mostly white or male, can rely solely upon word-of-mouth to recruit new employees.   ___ ___

5. can refuse to hire women to work at night, because it wishes to protect them.   ___ ___

6. may require all pregnant employees to take leave of absence at a specified time before delivery date.   ___ ___

7. may establish different benefits—pension, retirement, insurance and health plans—for male employees than for female employees.   ___ ___

8. may hire only males for a job if state law forbids employment of women for that capacity.   ___ ___

9. need not attempt to adjust work schedules to permit an employee time off for a religious observance.   ___ ___

10. only disobeys the Equal Employment Opportunity laws when it is acting intentionally or with ill motive.   ___ ___

Answers: The answers to 1 to 10 above are false. The Equal Employment Opportunity Act makes it against the law for an employer to discriminate on the basis of race, religion, color, sex or national origin. It's a tough law, with teeth, but most Americans think it is a very fair law. Yet unfair practices continue— in big business and in small. So, if you are in private industry, state or local government, or educational institutions, it is your business to know your rights and obligations. Contact your local EEOC office, listed in the phone book under U.S. Government or write to us in Washington, D.C.

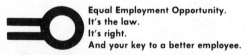

Equal Employment Opportunity.
It's the law.
It's right.
And your key to a better employee.

The Equal Employment Opportunity Commission Washington, D.C. 20506

Figure 14–1   TYPICAL PERSONNEL POSTER PREPARED FOR INDUSTRY BY GOVERNMENT

the bored reactions of a group of middle managers to a discussion of nondiscrimination laws.[8]

> Gentlemen, including back pay awards, this company has already spent hundreds of thousands of dollars on preparing, defending, and *losing* nondiscrimination cases in the federal courts. We do not intend to continue to do so.
>
> This meeting was called to tell you what the laws require. The attorneys on the other side are likely to be very able. And we now know that the courts intend to enforce these laws fully.
>
> If *you* do not expect to comply with all the nondiscrimination laws, consider this to be fair warning. You will be fired.

A "catch-up phase" is resulting in the need to train minority group candidates to enhance their opportunities for promotion to higher job levels. Equal employment regulations are being expanded to cover women, handicapped workers, and veterans. In a series of decisions, the courts levied substantial fines on companies that were held to discriminate against women and older workers in hiring, training, promotion, and firing practices. Meeting charges of discrimination against older workers during a general layoff can prove difficult, especially where supervisors have been preparing uniformly favorable or innocuous annual evaluations of their employees.

Companies holding federal contracts valued at $500,000 or more are now required to report on their treatment of handicapped applicants. The courts have clearly defined the only acceptable reason for discrimination as "business necessity." But this is a narrowly and rigidly defined "out." As stated in a United States Court of Appeals decision:

> Thus, the business purpose must be sufficiently compelling to override any racial impact; the challenged practice must effectively carry out the business purpose it is alleged to serve; and there must be available no acceptable alternative policies or practices which would better accomplish the business purpose advanced, or accomplish it equally well with a lesser differential racial impact.[9]

Hiring and promotion decision-making processes are increasingly scrutinized by government agencies. In New York State, for example, preemployment physical examinations must abide by the

---

[8] Ruth G. Shaeffer, *Nondiscrimination in Employment: Changing Perspectives, 1963-1972* (New York: The Conference Board, 1973), p. 3.

[9] *Robinson* v. *Lorillard Corporation*, U.S. Court of Appeals, 4th Cir. (Richmond), 444 F.2d 791 (1971).

requirements of the Human Rights Law. It must be demonstrated that any minimum physical standards adopted by a company are reasonably necessary for the work to be performed. The standards also must be uniformly applied to all applicants for the particular job category. General questions, such as "Do you have a disability?" are considered unlawful. Questions must be limited to those specific disabilities that relate to a particular job to be performed.[10] Formal testing has been reduced or abandoned in many instances because of the time and expense of demonstrating the validity and bias-free nature of the tests. The informal oral interview, of course, may present other, less measurable opportunities for bias.

Commenting on the personnel requirements that EEO has imposed on the Bell System, the affirmative action officer of another telephone system stated that Bell no longer has EEO goals. "They have quotas that have been mandated by the government. If they don't meet specific quotas—numbers of women and minority members hired and promoted—within a specific time period, the pressure and the fines will be laid on even more heavily." The officer went on to describe the adverse effects that can result:

> Any time a company gets itself in that kind of situation—one of dealing with numbers instead of people—bad things begin to happen. Suddenly, the time that's necessary to develop and train a minority group person for higher level positions isn't available any more. That's when the old cliché about EEO being a program that puts people into jobs they're not qualified for becomes true.[11]

Many of the people concerned with affirmative action programs may need to be reminded of the ultimate goal of such efforts, as so ably stated by Rafer Johnson, a black officer of the Continental Telephone Company, whose responsibilities include the equal employment opportunity program:

> We—and I'm talking about the country as well as the company—must get to the point where both the person being considered for a job and the person doing the considering are making decisions based strictly on the skills and potential that person can bring to his employer. EEO will be a complete success only when the color or race or creed or sex of a potential employee becomes no more than an afterthought.[12]

---

[10] "Discrimination for Disability," *Industrial Relations* (New York State Chamber of Commerce and Industry Bulletin), July 9, 1975, p. 1.
[11] "The Meaning behind the Words," *Continental System Communicator*, June 1975, p. 10.
[12] Ibid., p. 11.

The Rehabilitation Act of 1973 does strongly imply that the employer must make "reasonable" accommodations to the mental and physical limitations of the handicapped. The law does not seem to require a company to utilize a significantly less effective job design so that a disabled worker can be hired. But, according to Professor Richard Deane of Georgia Tech, in some cases an employer may be expected to restructure jobs slightly to accommodate a handicapped worker. This shows a good-faith effort to use the skills of the handicapped. The failure to offer any accommodations at all for the handicapped worker may subject the company to charges of discrimination.[13]

Innovative job designs may include using special fixtures to aid the arm movements of paralysis victims, replacement of foot controls with hand controls (or vice versa), and use of alternate sensory devices for blind workers.

Pension Plans and Retirement

The federal income tax system continues to be a means through which the federal government requires company pension plans to meet ever more stringent national standards. Moreover, the 1974 pension reform law requires that up to 30 percent of a company's net assets be available to meet its pension program liabilities. In addition, the pension law inundates employers with additional reporting requirements (see table 14-3). One impact of these increased costs and liabilities will be that some employers, especially those in smaller and/or new companies, are discouraged from setting up retirement programs.[14]

Unfunded pension liabilities (the difference between the amount the corporation has set aside for pension benefits and the amount of its obligation if the pension plan were liquidated today) pose still another problem for many corporations. A study of 1,200 corporations showed their total unfunded pension liabilities exceeding $38 billion. General Motors had the largest such liability, $6.1 billion, with other automobile and steel manufacturers also having unfunded pension liabilities in the billions of dollars.[15] The pension law requires employers to fund fully the yearly cost of their retirement

---

[13] Richard H. Deane, "The IE's Role in Accommodating the Handicapped," *Industrial Engineering*, July 1975, p. 17.

[14] "Private Pensions and the Public Interest," *Industrial and Labor Relations Report*, Fall 1974, pp. 12-25.

[15] "Unfunded Pension Liability in Billions for Some Firms," *Money Manager*, July 14, 1975, p. 17.

Table 14-3   Reporting requirements of the Employee Retirement Income Security Act (ERISA)

Reports to be filed with U.S. Department of Labor:

- Plan description, 120 days after the plan is subject to the reporting and disclosure provisions.
- Summary plan description, 120 days after the plan is subject to the reporting and disclosure provisions.
- Any change in plan description or material modification to plan, 60 days after its adoption.
- Updated plan description at such times as the Secretary of Labor may require but no more frequently than once every 5 years.
- Annual report, 210 days after the end of the plan year.
- Certain terminal reports for plans winding up their affairs.
- Plan documents and other information, if requested by the Secretary of Labor.

Reports to be filed with the Pension Benefit Guaranty Corporation:

- Annual report, within 6 months after the end of plan year.
- Intent to terminate, no later than 10 days before termination date.
- Certain events that indicate financial adversity ahead, within 30 days after plan administrator knows or had reason to know of their occurrence.
- Notification as soon as possible if any insufficiency develops after plan administrator has begun termination.
- Such other reports as the corporation may require from a plan administrator who has initiated termination proceedings.
- Notice of withdrawal of a substantial employer from a multiemployer plan, within 60 days.

Reports to be filed with the Internal Revenue Service:

- Annual Registration Statement, listing employees separated from service of plan, for plans subject to vesting standards due as prescribed by regulation.
- Notification of change of status, for plans subject to vesting standards, due as prescribed by regulation.
- Annual return for certain pension and deferred compensation plans.
- Actuarial statement of valuation for certain pension and deferred compensation plans, not less than 30 days before merger, consolidation, or transfer of assets or liabilities.
- Actuarial report for defined benefit plans for the first year that new funding requirements apply and every third year thereafter, or within time prescribed by regulation.

Source: U.S. Department of Labor, Labor Management Service Administration

program, and additional amounts must be contributed to amortize existing liabilities over a specified time period.

The pension reform law is also altering the investment philosophy being followed. In many cases there is now more emphasis on a strategy that will minimize the legal liability on the manager of the portfolio. This is in contrast to the traditional approach of attempting to maximize the return on the pension contributions.

The fear of legal consequences has also increased the documentation costs that the pension fund manager has to bear.[16]

With reference to retirement practices, the new mandatory retirement age will have differential effects on various types of businesses. According to Richard Cyert of Carnegie-Mellon University, those producing services rather than physical products may be most adversely affected. The jobs in service companies tend to be less physically demanding and therefore more attractive to keep for those approaching seventy than jobs on the assembly line. Given the difficulty in developing performance measures for many positions in the services, it may be difficult to remove older people on grounds of inadequate performance. Cyert points out that firing a worker over 65 will increasingly result in a court case for age discrimination. Thus, it will become harder for companies to eliminate errors in personnel selection, with resultant negative impacts on economic efficiency.[17]

Wage Controls

Another aspect of federal regulation involving personnel departments is so-called incomes policy — intermittent and varying forms of federal restraint on wage increases. These actions generally occur in conjunction with federal price actions, discussed previously in the section "Marketing." As in the case of prices, federal involvement in wage decisions likely will be greater during the coming decade than it has been during the past ten years. Wage (and price) controls do more than increase a company's paperwork burden. They complicate decision making, turning personnel officers' attention to learning the intricacies of government bureaucracy. Emphasis shifts to identifying legal subterfuges, such as substituting promotions for pay raises in order to stay within the "guidelines" issued by the government.[18]

Record Keeping

As a result of the government controls described above, there are increasing requirements for record keeping and reporting on

---

[16]Shoya Zichy, "How Small Funds Are Coping with the New Pension Law," *Institutional Investor*, September 1975, pp. 19-20.

[17]Richard M. Cyert, "Extending the Retirement Age" (Beta Gamma Sigma Invited Essay, March 1979), pp. 3-4.

[18]"How the Guideline Promotes Job-Hopping," *Business Week*, February 19, 1979, pp. 24-25.

OSHA NO. 100

Form Approved
OMB NUMBER 44R 1453

LOG OF OCCUPATIONAL INJURIES AND ILLNESSES

Case or file no.	Date of injury or initial diagnosis of illness. If diagnosis of illness was made after first day of absence enter first day of absence. (mo./day/yr.)	Employee's Name (First name, middle initial, last name)	Occupation of injured employee at time of injury or illness	Department to which employee was assigned at time of injury or illness	DESCRIPTION OF INJURY OR ILLNESS		EXTENT OF AND OUTCOME OF INJURY OR ILLNESS					
					Nature of injury or illness and part(s) of body affected (Typical entries for this column might be: Amputation of 1st joint right forefinger Strain of lower back Contact dermatitis on both hands Electrocution-body)	Injury or illness code See codes at bottom of page.	Fatalities	Lost Workday Cases		Nonfatal Cases Without Lost Workdays		
							Enter date of death (mo./day/yr.)	Enter workdays lost due to injury or illness (see instructions on back.)	If, after lost workdays, the employee was permanently transferred to another job or was terminated, enter a check in the column below	If no entry was made in columns 8 or 9, but the injury or illness did result in: Transfer to another job or termination, or; medical treatment, other than first aid, or; diagnosis of occupational illness, or; loss of consciousness, or; restriction of work or motion; Enter a check in the column below	If a check in column 11 represented a transfer or termination, enter another check in column 12
1	2	3	4	5	6		7	8	9	10	11	12

Company Name
Establishment Name
Establishment Location

Art 14

Injury Code
10 All occupational injuries

Illness Codes
21 Occupational skin diseases or disorders
22 Dust diseases of the lung (pneumoconioses)
23 Respiratory conditions due to toxic agents
24 Poisoning (Systemic effects of toxic materials)
25 Disorders due to physical agents (other than toxic materials)
26 Disorders due to repeated trauma
29 All other occupational illnesses

Figure 14-2 LOG OF OCCUPATIONAL INJURIES AND ILLNESSES

various aspects of employee characteristics and actions — including prehiring procedures and results of periodic physicals. Figure 14-2 shows an extract from the log of injuries and illnesses that OSHA requires employers to maintain. Many companies, particularly those with large work forces, find it useful to automate their personnel records. Personnel department staffs are expanding to meet the added federal requirements.[19]

The paperwork burden imposed by the equal employment program on government contractors is becoming particularly heavy. All prime contractors or subcontractors having 50 or more employees and a contract of $50,000 are required to provide reports analyzing each job category to determine whether women and minority groups are being "underutilized." If this is found to be the case, the contractors must provide cogent explanations. The analyses are to cover such factors as pay, lines of job progression, and usual promotional sequences.

In addition to the new record keeping requirements for personnel departments, other corporate divisions are bearing added paperwork burdens. Already noted are those connected with product recalls and health and pension plans. The requirements for more extensive information can be especially onerous for corporate finance departments. More staff, solely for record keeping, is often needed in divisions such as R&D or legal.

FINANCE FUNCTIONS

A fundamental impact of the federal government on company financial practices is that a rising share of the economy's investment funds are being funneled to business firms and other borrowers through government credit agencies. Thus, United States corporations are more frequently competing for money in credit markets dominated by federal financial institutions. During periods of extreme credit stringency, the federal government may resort to more direct methods of rationing capital. It may establish a temporary "capital issues" committee to assure that available funds are channeled into uses that the government considers of highest priority.

Another impact resulting from the government's increasing regulation of business financial activity and demands for more infor-

[19] U.S., Occupational Safety and Health Administration, *Recordkeeping Requirements* (Washington, D.C.: U.S. Government Printing Office, 1973); U.S., Department of Labor, *What Every Employer Needs to Know About OSHA Recordkeeping* (Washington, D.C.: U.S. Government Printing Office, 1973).

mation on company operations is an increase in the size and budgets of financial departments. Corporate finance departments increasingly are reacting to external demands for information, rather than merely meeting the corporation's own data requirement. This is a good indicator of the shifting locus of business decision making from entirely within the firm to an environment in which a variety of other organizations and considerations figure actively.

Reporting

Government regulatory agencies are specifying in increasing detail the financial information that companies must provide to their shareholders and to the public.[20] Headquarters and divisional finance departments bear the brunt of demands for statistical information from regulatory agencies. Many such requests result from continued public distrust of private business. The greater amount of information, in turn, may make possible even more detailed regulation of business.

After initial opposition by business, the FTC is now obtaining line-of-business sales and profits information from the nation's largest businesses. In addition to classifying sales and profits by product line, companies subject to SEC jurisdiction are required to show separately federal, state, local, and foreign taxes. Partially in response to public concern over companies that report relatively low payments of United States corporate taxes, the SEC is ordering corporations that pay federal income taxes at a rate other than the standard 48 percent of profits to explain the difference. This requirement may be particularly burdensome to petroleum and other natural-resource-based companies granted depletion allowances and special tax incentives and to multinational corporations receiving credit for the income taxes they pay to other countries.

The SEC also requires companies to disclose more information about leasing, a measure especially affecting capital-intensive industries that lease such items as airplanes, railroad cars, nuclear fuel, and buildings. The balance sheets for such companies do not look as attractive as they did without notation of such large contingent financial liabilities.

Every publicly held company has to divulge details about how its board of directors operates, including the function and membership of the audit, compensation, and nominating committees; the

---

[20] Frank T. Weston, "Prepare for the Financial Accounting Revolution," *Harvard Business Review*, September–October 1974, pp. 6–8 ff.

identity of any director who fails to attend 75-percent of all board and committee meetings and those directors with whom the company does 1 percent or more of its business. The company also has to give financial details on the varieties of executive compensation and the "perks" it offers, including commissions, bonuses, pension plans, options, and stock appreciation rights. The compensation of the top five officers must be disclosed, if they make $50,000 or more a year, in three categories: cash; the cash value of insurance, medical coverage, perquisites, and deferred compensation; and contingency remuneration. Perks that serve a business as well as personal purpose do not have to be shown, nor those totaling less than $10,000 per individual, or which are very costly to compute.[21]

New Securities and Exchange Commission regulations have brought about substantial changes in the information provided in corporate annual reports. The SEC now requires that annual reports include:

Certified financial statements for two fiscal years.

A five-year summary of operations. The presentation must include sales, cost of goods sold, interest expense, taxes, earnings, dividends, and the effect of discontinued operations, extraordinary items, and accounting changes.

Management analysis, in plain English, of the financial information and the company's competitive position in its field.

Operating information listed by line of business or classes of product.

Identification of corporate officers and directors, including their outside business affiliations.

Statement regarding the exchange or market where the stock is traded, market price ranges, and the dividends paid for at least the most recent two years.

In addition, the annual report must state that the 10-K report, the extensive financial statement required by the SEC, is available to any shareholder on request and without charge.

In June 1979 the SEC adopted a rule to encourage companies to disclose economic and related projections. This so-called "safe harbor" rule provides that companies will not be held liable if their projections prove inaccurate as long as they are made with a reasonable basis and in good faith. The projections include various financial items, management plans and objectives, future economic performance, and analysis of earnings.

If companies publish forecasts of their financial results, certain

[21] John Perham, "The Tough New Disclosure Rules," *Dun's Review,* January 1979, pp. 59-60.

technical capabilities will have to be obtained or expanded. Executives will need to become more knowledgeable and informed about sophisticated forecasting techniques. Information systems will have to be developed so that publishable forecasts can be prepared quickly and with minimum effort. Shareholders must be educated concerning proper interpretation of company forecasts and the accuracy and limitations of such information.[22]

At times, the SEC has shown concern over the problem of "information overload." In April 1979 a federal district court ruled that the commission acted properly when it decided against requiring companies to disclose detailed information about environmental and job discrimination matters. The SEC had decided not to adopt proposals by several "public-interest" groups that would have required disclosures on pollution and cleanup and on the hiring of minorities and women. The court pointed out that shareholders were generally not interested in such information.

Accounting

A rider attached to the 1977 law prohibiting American corporations from bribing officials of foreign governments also gave the SEC power over the adequacy of the accounting systems of all publicly owned corporations — whether the companies have any overseas activities or not. Under the 1977 act companies must keep financial records which, "in reasonable detail," accurately and fairly reflect transactions and asset dispositions; they also must maintain a system of accounting controls sufficient to provide reasonable assurance that transactions are properly authorized and recorded and that assets are safeguarded. The first lawsuit filed by the SEC under the new statute accused a domestic coal company, Aminex Resources Corporation, of failing to keep accurate books or to maintain adequate accounting controls. The former officers of the company agreed to pay back $1.2 million allegedly misappropriated. The firm subsequently went into bankruptcy.

The enlarged role of audit committees of corporate boards of directors often adds to the workload of both the internal audit staff and the corporation's outside auditors. Because of the requirement that the audit committees be composed entirely of "outside" directors, the accounting staff often finds that it has a special pipeline for transmitting its information, in addition to the normal chain of corporate command.

---

[22] James D. Edwards and Carl S. Warren, "Management Forecasts: The SEC and Financial Executives," *MSU Business Topics*, Winter 1974, pp. 51-55.

FACILITIES FUNCTIONS

According to the chief environmental engineer of Parsons, Brinckerhoff, Quade & Douglas (a leading architectural and engineering contractor), environmental factors have become a crucial consideration of management in planning the expansion of existing facilities, the introduction of new production processes or products, and the building or relocation of factories.[23]

Although Congress has not enacted general land-use control legislation, some specific federal land-use statutes already are on the books. For example, section 208 of the Federal Water Pollution Control Act provides for the regulation of "the location, modification, and construction of any facilities that may have discharges. . . ." The Flood Disaster Protection Act of 1973 required that (by July 1975) all communities in areas officially designated as "flood-prone" enact new zoning and building codes. As discussed in an earlier chapter, the regulations issued under the Clean Air Act Amendments of 1977 constitute, in effect, a powerful federal policy on the use of private land and facilities.

Environmental impact analysis involves more than preparing detailed analyses for government review (see table 14-4). The process also provides for greater community participation in determining whether the project should be built at a given location — particularly if considerable social and aesthetic consequences may result.[24]

In addition to examining the direct physical and economic impacts, environmental analyses increasingly deal with the indirect ("second-order") effects, including the implications of the planned facility for regional development patterns; the effects on demand for housing and public utilities; and the possibility of further technological development that might have subsequent impacts. Emphasis also is being placed on how the benefits of the facility are to be distributed in the community, and especially how they will affect different economic, social, and ethnic groups. Thus, due to the comprehensive nature of these environmental impact statements, they have been both costly and time-consuming to prepare. Based on the experience of utility companies providing environmental impact statements for proposed facilities, the cost of the study for each facility would range from $300,000 to several million dollars.[25]

[23] Stephen S. Rosen, "Environmental Considerations in Building Construction," *Management Review*, August 1978, p. 31.
[24] Michael J. Walker, "The Impact of Environmental Impact Statements," *Management Review*, January 1974, pp. 25-29.
[25] Statement of Richard D. Godown on behalf of the National Association of Manufacturers before the Securities and Exchange Commission, 1975.

Table 14-4 Range of required environmental impact analyses for a typical residential construction project

Condition to be Examined	Existing Physical Environment — Natural and Man-made	
	Required to Analyze	Example of an Analysis
Land and climate	Soil (general characteristics, load-bearing capacity, existing and potential erosion, permeability) Topography (general characteristics, slope grade of site) Subsurface conditions (geologic characteristics, geologic faults) Special conditions: flood plain or other unique landscape features; potential for mudslide, subsidence, or earthquake; aerial or underground transmission lines and right-of-way Unusual climatic conditions: subject to very high rainfall, flashfloods, hurricanes or tornadoes, strong winds, extremes of temperature, and so forth	No special climatic, subsurface, or unusual conditions. Soil — permeable, clayey. Topography — average, 3% slope.
Vegetation, wildlife, and natural areas	Extent and type of vegetation and wildlife; existence of on-site or proximity to unique natural systems (stream systems, wildlife breeding area, parks)	Site 50% covered with beech, oak, sassafras, and dogwood trees. Adjacent to 20-acre urban park.
Surrounding land uses and physical character of area	Type of development (family or high-rise residential, industrial, commercial, open space, mixed); land-use configuration; densities; building height and design; lot sizes	Mixed: single family, high-rise, and open space area. Density — about 60 dwelling units per acre in immediate site area.
Infrastructure	Water supply, sanitary sewage and solid waste disposal, storm sewers and drainage, energy, and transportation facilities (roads, public transit, parking) servicing site	Site controlled by city water system and sanitary and sewer system. There is ample capacity. Site on bus line and arterial street. Parking garage on same block. All electric project.

Air pollution levels	Extent of pollution (smog, dust, odors, smoke, hazardous emissions) in relation to local/state standards, and standards of health and safety (frequency of inversions, air pollution alert, or emergency) and in relation to the rest of the metropolitan area (conditions peculiar to the site and immediate area)	No obvious dust, odors, or smoke in site area. Community does have smog alerts periodically throughout summer months.
Noise levels	Source (nearby airport, railway, highway); noise levels in relation to HUD standards; vibrations	Project is not located in vicinity of airport or railroad. Project is on major arterial road, but noise exposure is minimal.
Water pollution levels	Ground and surface water relevant to site and area (drainage basin, source of water supply, water bodies with implications for health and recreation uses, and so forth)	No streams are on project site; there are no bodies of water nearby.
Community facilities and services	Description: general description; location; responsible organizations; relation of capacity to existing demand of schools, parks, recreational and cultural facilities; police and fire and health facilities servicing the site and area	Complete community facilities within walking distances of site, i.e., 200-bed hospital, library, museum, police, and fire station.
Employment centers and commercial facilities	Employment centers and commercial facilities servicing site	Shopping center ¼ mile from site. Site is located 1½ miles from downtown central business district.
Character of community	Socioeconomic and racial characteristics	Immediate community is mainly white, 30% black, 4% Spanish-speaking, and 10% elderly. Community employees are about 50% professional (lawyers, bankers, and so forth) and 50% blue collar and clerical.
Existing aesthetic community	General aesthetic characteristics; special features (natural or man-made; existence on site or proximity to significant historic, archaeological, or architectural sites or property, including those listed on, or being considered for nomination to, the National Register of Historic Places); scenic areas and view	The Historic Society is across the street from the site.

Source: U.S. Department of Housing and Urban Development

One underappreciated limitation on the construction of new manufacturing facilities is the diminished availability of sites for disposing of the hazardous wastes that may be produced. According to an EPA-sponsored study of 12 major waste-generating industries, their current volume of 46 million metric tons of hazardous waste exceeds the environmentally sound treatment, storage, and disposal capacity available. The key limit on the availability of these sites is neither economic nor technological; it is the political pressures which have to be faced. The Minnesota experience is indicative. In 1975 EPA granted the state Pollution Control Agency $3.7 million to establish a chemical landfill. All 12 of the locations initially proposed by the agency were rejected because of public opposition. An additional four locations were dropped after vocal objections. In August 1978 the state returned the grant money to EPA.[26]

LEGAL AND CONSULTING STAFFS

The proliferation of regulatory agencies is enlarging the role of many corporate legal staffs and their outside law firms. Although many companies continue to rely heavily on private law firms, the role of house counsel is expanding as a result of the growing body of government laws and regulations affecting day-to-day business operations. An official of Dow Chemical Company states, "Any company will tell you its fastest growing department is its legal department, and its legal department is dealing mainly in regulatory matters."

The internal counsel can be particularly valuable in advising the various operating departments on how to conduct their affairs in accordance with ever-changing federal legal requirements. For example, increasing consumer product regulation is expanding the number of legal actions necessary to minimize company liability for products ruled to be unsafe or defective. Product liability insurance is being more widely used as the size and frequency of product safety suits rise. On the other hand, warning labels can reduce legal exposure. Since 1964, when the Surgeon General's warning was put on every pack of cigarettes, no tobacco company has lost a suit involving cigarette-related cancer.

The expansion in government control of business is also creating a growing market for consulting firms that can advise businesses on

---

[26] U.S., Comptroller General, *How to Dispose of Hazardous Waste*, CED-79-13 (Washington, D.C.: U.S. General Accounting Office, 1978), pp. 5, 6, 13.

how to operate in the new regulatory environment, notably in pollution control and job safety. In response to suggestions by the Consumer Product Safety Commission, *ad hoc* associations are being established in industries where no trade organizations have existed so that industry standards may be developed that are acceptable to the commission. But the Federal Trade Commission is developing rules restricting the ability of private associations to develop standards for their members. Should the government in effect adopt standards to guide the private sector in the development of its standards, the role of legal counsel probably would increase further.

15

government
relations functions

As government becomes more involved in day-to-day business activities, companies are expanding resources devoted to government relations. Virtually every company must develop the capability to know what present and future developments in the federal government relate to its activities. Firms of substantial size generally maintain Washington offices, while smaller companies rely primarily on their trade associations as well as on Washington-based attorneys and consultants. The full-time Washington representative is no longer limited to the major government contractors (for example, aerospace and electronics) or the closely regulated industries (such as transportation and drug manufacture).[1]

THE WASHINGTON REPRESENTATIVE

Most large corporations maintain one or more full-time representatives in the nation's capital. Their offices vary from one person

[1] Paul Cherington and Ralph Gillen, *The Business Representative in Washington* (Washington, D.C.: Brookings Institution, 1962).

Table 15-1   Factors affecting size of D.C. offices

Size of firm (e.g., automobile manufacturers)

- Most larger firms have some direct representation
- Economies of scale and variety of interests
- Greater public exposure

Importance of government markets (e.g., aerospace companies)

- Day-to-day contract administration function
- Market intelligence and forecasting
- Support base for sales efforts

Extent of regulation (e.g., ethical drug houses)

- Day-to-day dealings with regulatory agencies
- Desire to influence regulatory climate – through Congress and the media

Concern of management (e.g., petroleum corporations)

- Subjective factors, such as attitude toward social responsibility
- Level of civic awareness or concern with national policy

Degree of public exposure (e.g., conglomerates)

- Defensive – to counteract adverse media and congressional attention
- Offensive – to obtain greater public exposure for government marketing purposes and as institutional advertising

plus a secretary to large operations with annual budgets of $250,000 or more. Large government contractors traditionally have maintained representation in Washington, and many commercially oriented firms, including medium-size ones, are establishing a permanent presence in the capital. The expansion of government controls over business has led to "protective reaction" on the part of many companies that historically have had little knowledge of or direct relationship with the federal government. About 500 companies had on-the-scene Washington representation in 1979, compared with only some 50 a decade previously. The typical corporate office in Washington employs six to seven persons and is headed by an officer of vice-presidential level.[2]

Activities of Washington offices vary substantially according to the industry and markets served, the size of the firm, and tradition (see Table 15-1). One major company compares its Washington office to an embassy in that it follows and interprets actions of the federal government that have significant impact on it, helps to formulate positions on those actions, and serves as the principal channel

[2] Ann M. Reilly, "Washington Information Boom," *Dun's Review*, March 1979, p. 60; Leila K. Lesko, *Business Representation in Washington* (Washington, D.C.: Washington Researchers, 1977), p. 1.

for communicating the company's views to the government. Five primary functions are often performed by Washington offices:

1. Supplying information to the home office.
2. Rendering services to visiting home office personnel.
3. Providing marketing assistance.
4. Providing legislative representation.
5. Supplying analyses of government programs and policies.

Supplying Information

Virtually all corporate offices established in the national capital provide a "listening post" for the home office. A constant flow of information is supplied to corporate officials on current government policies and on future plans and actions that might affect company operations. Although trade associations and industry publications are useful, at times a company's unique concerns best can be met by company personnel on the Washington scene. Some companies refer to this intelligence function as an "early warning" system; it is the most time-consuming function of the typical corporate office in Washington.

Various communication channels are used. Representatives of some large companies prepare daily newsletters that are sent to senior executives in headquarters and operating divisions. Often information is passed along entirely by telephone, either because of urgency or because it is preferable not to maintain a written record on sensitive matters. The Washington office also may have day-to-day dealings with members of the government bureaucracy in order to follow up questions or complaints by company personnel on specific regulatory actions.

A substantial amount of company information and views also may be provided to federal agencies. Such a "two-way street" relationship can help to provide a more cordial welcome to company personnel making inquiries at a federal agency; it can also enhance the weight given to the company's expressed concerns. In September 1978, for example, EPA announced its streamlining of the complicated system for issuing pollution control permits. The agency pointed out that Caterpillar Tractor Company had originally brought the problem to EPA's attention.[3]

The more successful Washington representatives also have some effect on company policies and operations. In contrast to the traditional company attitude on public affiars ("if they only saw our side

---

[3] "EPA Trims Red Tape," *Chemical Week*, September 27, 1978, p. 27.

of the story, they would understand"), the Washington office may help to adapt corporate actions to changing national policies. In this regard, much depends on the status and effectiveness of the head of the Washington office. It is often desirable for the personnel stationed in Washington to make periodic visits to headquarters and other company locations to acquire and maintain a "feel" for the problems and outlook of company executives.

The need for such professional advice on communicating with government decision makers is underscored by a survey of members of Congress by *Industry Week* magazine. The following—in large part, negative—congressional responses were received to the question, "Which of the following do you most often find true of industry communication with your office?":[4]

Reflex reactions to "government"	28%
Usually against and seldom favoring	24
Suggesting problems rather than solutions	24
Polished but impersonal	20
More constructive than most	20
Based more on concern than on facts	20
Narrowly self-serving	16
Naive concerning economic realities	16
Timely and to the point	16
Representing management rather than employees	16
Often relates to "principles" and not issues	8

Several congressmen responding to the survey provided specific suggestions for business executives, as well as comments on business effectiveness in communicating its views:

How could business be worse? Labor is so much more effective in Washington than business. Business is defensive, timid, and scared of the government. (Rep. James M. Collins, Texas.)

As a general principle, it seems to be always the same few companies who are well-informed on the issues and whose opinions are therefore most taken into account. Most companies provide too little, too late. (Sen. Charles H. Percy, Illinois.)

A personal letter from top management is more helpful than a form letter. Send to your member of Congress company magazines, newsletters, and reports on a continuing basis. It allows the congressman and his staff to become familiar with your company and its problems. (Rep. G. William Whitehurst, Virginia.)

[4] "How Well Does Industry Communicate with Congress?" *Industry Week,* May 14, 1973, pp. 42-43.

We need factual information on how proposals affect you in specific terms. We get too many generalities reflecting association literature. (Rep. Glenn R. Davis, Wisconsin.)

I believe industry can improve the quality and timeliness of its communications with my office by doing a better job of studying legislation while it is pending rather than after it is passed. (Rep. Harold R. Collier, Illinois.)

Do not assume the legislator is familiar with your industry or its problems; explain as clearly as possible from a layman's point of view the problem or request. (Rep. John H. Dent, Pennsylvania.)

Thank those who support your position so they know they are supported. (Rep. Philip M. Crane, Illinois.)

Service to the Home Office

To some extent the Washington office serves as a "coffee and donuts brigade," assisting officials of the home office or operating divisions who are not fully familiar with government procedures. The assistance may vary from obtaining public documents and specialized studies to arranging appointments with federal officials and embassy personnel to meeting the board chairman's airplane. For senior officers, the aid may include getting theater tickets and renting a limousine for dinner at the White House. But the emphasis is shifting toward more important services, such as arranging and participating in high-level contacts and meetings, and briefing corporate officials before congressional and agency hearings or other important public appearances.

The Marketing Function

For many Washington offices, marketing is the basic "bread-and-butter" justification of their existence and may account for the presence of the majority of the personnel assigned to the office. A variety of market research, selling, and contract administration activities may be involved. It is often considered the responsibility of the Washington office to keep the company abreast of emerging new government product requirements, so that engineering and advance design departments can be prepared for formal "requests for proposal."

On-the-scene representation may result in the company participating, officially or informally, in the development of government specifications for the products that it wants to sell to federal agencies. The basic objective usually is to assure that the products of the company meet government requirements. Representation and work on specifications being developed by government procurement agencies also provide advance information on future sales possibilities, as well as the opportunity to qualify company products. In the process, the company may learn of and bid on exploratory research and development contracts that the government will be awarding prior to the actual production phase of a major project.

Although much actual selling may be performed by company marketing and engineering personnel assigned to the home office, the Washington-based staff may be in a better position to maintain day-to-day liaison with federal research and development and procurement offices, and to "open doors" for company specialists. In addition, by virtue of its location, the Washington office can expedite the often numerous and complicated steps involved in government contracting: obtaining the detailed bidding specifications; ensuring attention to company contract proposals; securing the necessary signatures; assuring company compliance with federal procedural requirements; and expediting payments for work performed. Some Washington offices also take advantage of their location in developing contacts with the embassies of foreign governments that may provide market potential.

Representation

The effective Washington office is the focal point of a company's relations with the federal government, serving especially as the principal channel for communicating the company's views on matters of major importance to legislators and executive branch officials. In good measure, the office is a coordinator, drawing on specialized talents in the corporate office, such as the legal, engineering, and public affairs staffs. One senior government official has stated, "The influencing of Washington's largest industry, government, has become the city's second-largest industry."[5] An experienced lobbyist, however, described his function as "a damage control operation."

Although many company representatives try to avoid using the term, "lobbying" may be a primary part of their total function. One experienced Washington office director, who previously had served as legislative assistant to a leading senator, defines lobbying in very straightforward terms: "Lobbying is a communication with public officials to influence their decisions in a manner harmonious with the interests of the individual or group communicating. ... A lobbyist's

---

[5] Lee Richardson, "A Voice for Consumers," *Fortune*, July 17, 1978, p. 140.

purpose is selfish in the sense that he seeks to persuade others that his position is meritorious."[6]

The total lobbying activity includes direct relations with legislative and executive branch officials and, in addition, dealings with the media and the private policy analysis groups that abound in the nation's capital. Thus, the Washington office of a large national corporation may provide access to key reporters and influential columnists that cannot be obtained by senior management located in a more remote area.

Lobbying has changed dramatically from the flamboyant, power-play-oriented stereotypes. As *The New York Times* describes him (or her), "Today's lobbyist, whether working for a large corporation, a trade association or a labor union, tends to be a dun-colored organization man who fades easily into the background — and likes it that way."[7] As one highly regarded lobbyist stated the matter, "Visibility is the last thing I need."[8]

Increasing emphasis is being placed on subtle forms of lobbying. Because so many lobbyists crowd the stage, greater attention is given to innovative, offbeat techniques incorporating public relations, political action, and subtle influence. For example, Amoco Oil Company sponsors a weekly FM radio program in Washington, D.C., area, featuring a guest conductor who selects the music for that particular program. Each week the guest conductor is a different member of Congress. Interspersed in the program are commercial messages by the sponsor on such subjects as why oil prices should not be regulated and why higher petroleum taxes will only lead to higher gasoline prices. Also in the program is a complimentary profile of the "guest conductor." One major retail chain sends each member of Congress a birthday cake, and a large trade association presents each lawmaker with a blank photograph album suitably engraved.[9]

The liaison with the legislative branch may serve both an "offensive" and a "defensive" function. The former is designed to get the company's views on pending legislation of special interest across to senators, representatives, their aides, and committee staff members. Increasingly, these efforts are geared to opposing or at least amending the rising flow of federal legislation that results in

---

[6] Richard W. Murphy, "Lobbies as Information Sources for Congress," *Bulletin of the American Society for Information Science,* April 1975, p. 22.

[7] James Deakin, "Lobbying Is Fine Art in Washington," *The New York Times,* November 17, 1974, p. 1.

[8] "How the Weapons Lobby Works in Washington," *Business Week,* February 12, 1979, p. 128.

[9] Tom Littlewood, "Lobbyists Resort to Subtlety," *St. Louis Post-Dispatch,* April 21, 1975, p. B-1.

greater government control over business decision making. The "defensive" function — less widely known — is geared to avoiding embarrassing investigations of and attacks on the company. This may be accomplished by providing additional information, and the "other side of the story," at an early stage of a committee's operations. Moreover, continuing liaison, although perhaps involving nothing more than an occasional luncheon or cocktail party, may help to soften or even avoid unpleasant encounters by introducing into the situation the natural reluctance to confront one's friends.

When Congress is actively considering a piece of legislation deemed vital to the company, the Washington office may arrange for a corporate officer to be invited to testify, then draft the actual testimony and prepare the officer for cross-examination and public interviews. Much influence on congressional deliberations, however, may come from informal telephone or face-to-face contact in a senator's or representative's office, rather than at a formal committee hearing. Formal "lobbying" activities are subject to statutory control.

The basic legal authorization for lobbying is found in the Constitution: "Congress shall make no law respecting . . . the right of the people . . . to petition the Government for a redress of grievances." A minimum of restrictive legislation has been enacted since. Under the Regulation of Lobbying Act of 1946, lobbyists are defined as those individuals whose "principal" purpose is to influence legislation by direct contact with members of Congress. These legally defined lobbyists must register with Congress and give quarterly reports on their spending for lobbying activities.

Because enforcement of current legislation has been very limited and because of the many individuals active in government liaison work who have not judged their primary activity to be lobbying, new legislation in this area has been under active consideration in Congress for some years. In the summer of 1979 a subcommittee of the Judiciary Committee of the House of Representatives approved a compromise bill which provided that an organization must register as a lobbyist if it pays $5,000 or more to a firm within a three-month period to do lobbying or if it has paid employees to lobby at least thirteen days each three months. This would be far stronger than the current requirement that only organizations or individuals whose "principal purpose" is lobbying must register, which exempts almost all business firms.

Registered organizations would have to list total lobbying expenditures, gifts to federal employees exceeding $35, the names of individual lobbyists, and all major issues actively supported or opposed. The lobbying organization would have to list all other organizations, including corporations, giving $3,000 or more each year. However, contributions by individuals would not have to be reported. As the late Justice Robert H. Jackson stated in a noted dissenting opinion (*U.S.* v. *Harris*, 347 U.S. 612, 1954), ". . . to reach the real evils of lobbying without cutting into the constitutional right of petition is a difficult and delicate task."

Washington office personnel also participate in various business organizations and trade associations. This activity may be part of the function of maintaining the information flow, as well as a method of obtaining access to government decision makers. Senior officers from headquarters are, however, more likely to serve on the policy boards of these associations. Another area of representation is with the press and other media that have increasingly built up their Washington staffs.

Analysis

A few companies, such as General Electric, have developed in-house "think tanks" in conjunction with their Washington offices. These units often concentrate on forecasting and evaluating future markets in the public sector and in tracking new developments in public policy toward business. Their staff members interact with government and private planning groups and with the growing array of public policy analysis organizations that have been established in Washington and which range over a broad spectrum of political and social values. These groups include the American Enterprise Institute for Public Policy Research, the Brookings Institution, the Center for Strategic and International Studies, the Committee for Economic Development, the Heritage Foundation, and the Institute for Policy Studies.

As may be surmised, the four functions of a corporate Washington office are closely interrelated. Much of the intelligence furnished by the office leads to advice recommending company positions on major issues. As the focal point for communicating the company's views in Washington, the office can help to devise, for any given issue, a strategy of advocacy that takes into account the political and other realities of the Washington scene.

Staffing the Washington Office

Although many Washington representatives or their key assistants have served previously in other capacities in the company, these positions are frequently filled by men and women who have worked in and around the federal government for a number of years. The senior corporate representatives include former White House officials, cabinet and subcabinet officers, and members of Congress. Others are former congressional staff members or personnel from middle-level positions in executive agencies and departments of the government.

As the array of government powers over business expands, Washington offices are shifting more of their emphasis from marketing to representation before Congress and the regulatory agencies in the executive branch. Thus, the personnel staffing these offices increasingly consists of lawyers, economists, and others versed in regulatory matters, in addition to the traditional complement of engineers and sales representatives.

The head of a company's Washington office has often reported to a vice-president in the marketing' area or has been a relatively junior vice-president. The current trend is to confer vice-presidential status on the firm's top official in the Washington office and have that individual communicate directly with the corporation's top management.

Washington representatives are being given greater authority to contact and direct personnel throughout the company. In addition, the discretion given to them in making statements in behalf of the company grows as the "reaction time" for government decision making is reduced and as the issues become more complex and specialized. Their knowledge of the organization and its industry, as well as of the federal government, can be major determinants of their effectiveness.

There are obvious limits to the role of a company's Washington office. It is typically not the sole medium for communicating with the federal government. Lacking the array of expertise, it cannot substitute for the ongoing contacts by company engineers, lawyers, economists, and such, with their technical counterparts in the government. It can monitor and coordinate those relationships. At the most senior level the Washington representative cannot displace the visit by the chief executive officer or members of the senior management with key legislators and other high officials in the government on matters of concern to the company. The office, however, can identify the proper contacts, arrange appointments, and furnish the necessary background for these visits, as well as take care of any follow-up activities. Here is what the head of the Washington office of one billion-dollar corporation stated one year after opening the office: "In retrospect, I wonder how we did without it."

Companies are more frequently drawing upon trade associations to assist them in participating in the process of government decision making. In addition, more companies find it advantageous to provide personnel to serve on federal advisory committees. Service on these groups permits company officials to obtain access to government decision makers.

Representing the corporation to the executive branch of government may involve both attempts to influence future policy and efforts to learn of current developments and how the company might successfully adjust to them. Serving on government advisory committees can be a desirable form of unpaid public service in that the government becomes aware of a broad array of views prior to taking action. In addition, it may have the effect of marshaling public support for such action.

Virtually all federal agencies have set up one or more public advisory committees. These range from the Department of Defense's prestigious Industry Advisory Council (IAC) to the Business Research Advisory Council (BRAC) of the Bureau of Labor Statistics. The IAC, composed of senior management members of some of the major defense contractors, advises on Pentagon procurement policy, while the BRAC consists of economists, statisticians, and other company specialists who comment on price indices and such technical matters.

Table 15-2 illustrates the different patterns of representation on federal advisory committees for the utility, defense, automobile, and petroleum companies.[10] Traditionally regulated companies, such as AT&T, are far more active on federal advisory committees than are other firms, such as Monsanto. Similarly, major defense contractors, for example, Lockheed, have more advisory memberships than do more commercially oriented corporations, such as Procter and Gamble. The variety of these business-government relations can be extensive; they range beyond the obvious agencies such as Commerce, Defense, and Transportation to include Agriculture; Health, Education and Welfare; Interior; and State.

Advisory committees vary from those dealing with major matters of policy to bodies charged with providing advice on statistics and other technical matters. Some of these groups are designed to provide professional and technical expertise that the federal government may not possess. For example, the advisory panels of the

[10] M. L. Weidenbaum, "Private Advisors and Government Policy-making," *Policy Analysis*, January 1975, pp. 101-114.

Table 15-2 Number of representatives of selected companies on federal advisory committees, 1972

Department or Agency	AT&T	Exxon	General Motors	IT&T	Litton	Lockheed	Monsanto	Procter and Gamble	U.S. Steel
Agriculture	2	—	—	—	—	—	—	—	—
Commerce	9	4	9	3	3	1	11	5	3
Defense	18	1	3	5	6	9	—	—	2
Health, Education and Welfare	7	1	1	—	2	—	—	—	1
Interior	3	12	—	—	—	—	1	—	—
Labor	8	2	4	19	—	2	1	—	11
State	37	2	2	—	4	7	—	—	—
Transportation	4	4	7	—	1	—	—	—	—
Treasury	—	—	—	—	1	—	—	—	—
Atomic Energy Commission	2	—	—	—	—	—	1	—	2
EPA	—	1	—	—	—	—	3	1	—
FCC	57	9	2	64	9	17	—	—	4
Federal Power Commission	—	12	—	—	—	—	—	—	—
Interstate Commerce Comm.	—	3	—	—	—	—	—	—	—
NASA	4	1	1	1	—	4	1	—	—
National Science Fnd.	9	—	2	—	—	—	1	—	—
Office of Economic Oppty.	—	—	—	—	1	—	—	—	—
Office of Mgt. & Budget	—	—	—	—	—	—	—	—	1
OTP	—	—	—	1	—	—	—	—	—
SEC	—	—	—	1	—	—	—	—	—
Other	4	1	2	—	—	—	—	—	—
	164	53	33	94	26	42	19	6	24

Source: Compiled from data supplied by U.S. Senate, Committee on Government Operations

National Science Foundation have one major and clearly defined task — to review and make recommendations on proposals for research grants that have been submitted to the foundation in their area of expertise (economics, mathematics, physics, and so on). This essentially is a "peer group" review process, whereby academicians and other professionals evaluate research to be undertaken by their colleagues in their profession.

On the other hand, the advisory committees to the Bureau of the Census — there is one each appointed by the American Economic Association, the American Marketing Association, and the American Statistical Association — have a much broader scope. They review the various internal research and reporting programs of the entire bureau. The role of these advisory groups is substantially less precise and perhaps more difficult. To a very considerable extent, they listen to presentations on, and are asked to comment on, tasks that have been authorized and are already under way. The outside advisors may thus provide both technical expertise and an aura of scholarship to the government's own research undertakings.

Other advisory committees deal with aspects of government decision making of a more operational character. For example, the Department of the Treasury meets four times a year with two committees who advise it on the quarterly financings of the public debt: the Government Borrowing Committee of the American Bankers Association and the Government Fiscal Policy Committee of the Securities Industry Association. This process has been subject to some criticism, because the advisors are also heavily involved in the subsequent purchases of government securities. Yet the advisors provide an extremely knowledgeable input to the government without the Treasury revealing any special information to them. The government's decisions on terms, size, and timing of the financings are made quite independently of the two committees. Moreover, the recommendations of the two groups frequently differ.

Another function of advisory committees is to provide a sounding board or at least a mechanism for the exchange of views by various private-interest groups. An interesting variation is used by the Department of Labor. The Bureau of Labor Statistics has for many years organized two parallel but completely separate groups of advisors — the Business Research Advisory Council, consisting of economists, statisticians, and other executives of business firms, and a Labor Research Advisory Council, consisting of economists, statisticians, and other labor union officials.

The two groups always have been kept separate, never meeting jointly. Thus, the Labor Department would seem able to enjoy the role of the mediator or, at least, to occupy the high central ground in any dispute. In practice, both groups deal with technical questions related to the composition of price indices, the measurement of the labor force, and so forth.

Much may depend on the level of representation. In contrast to the staff officials who serve on the BLS committees, the Department of Defense has appointed senior management members of some of the major defense contractors and other large industrial corporations to its Industry Advisory Council. That council at times has provided a major vehicle for the defense industry to present its views to the key officials in the Pentagon, on such vital questions as changes in the regulations and procedures that the department establishes in its dealings with the firms doing business with it. Contrary to the general impression, professors from colleges and universities rather than business executives constitute the bulk of the memberships on government advisory committees.

REVISED ORGANIZATIONAL STRUCTURES

To deal with the increasing array of government involvement, many companies find it necessary or at least desirable to revamp their organizational structures. Initially, these changes may be modest, such as the previously discussed expansion of the Washington office or establishment of company interdepartmental committees on job safety, consumer affairs, or energy conservation. The growth of public-interest groups (often with an antibusiness orientation) is another factor encouraging business firms to expand their government relations staffs.

In some cases more substantial changes are made. For example, a major headquarters office on government relations may be established, with direct ties to each of the operating departments. Such offices may be given clearance authority on company actions ranging from introducing new products to price changes to personnel practices. On occasion, the head of such a government relations office may become a member of the corporation's top management and a major advisor to the board of directors. Several large enterprises have designated a new vice-chairman of the board of directors to be concerned primarily with government and public relations in a very broad and comprehensive sense.

Chrysler has set up an office of public responsibility, directed by a vice-chairman of the board of directors. The office has been assigned the task of monitoring and coordinating the company's efforts in safety, environmental affairs, consumer relations, and improving job opportunities for minority groups. Mobil Oil has created a position of vice-chairman of the board responsible for explaining company policy and actions to congressional, consumer, and environmental critics. The Bank of America has designated an executive vice-president to be in charge of social policy. This post, which is viewed as a functional responsibility, oversees operations in the areas of consumerism, minority affairs, and environmental problems.

At Connecticut General Insurance Company, the Corporate Government and Industry Relations Department (CGIR) has overall responsibility for "issue management" activities. This staff of eight professionals approaches issue management under the broad banner of "external affairs," encompassing social, economic, and political trends; public opinion research; government legislation; and regulation. The CGIR staff prepares a quarterly *Corporate Issues Inventory* for the company's CEO and division heads. For each issue, specific officers are designated with lead responsibility, together with inter-divisional task forces, as needed.[11]

Some companies take a more accommodating view toward the rising role of government in business decision making. They merely add compliance responsibilities to the functional jobs of general or line managers. Others take a composite position, whereby the senior management assumes a more active role in public policy and the operating management concentrates on meeting government-imposed requirements. For example, Union Carbide's Chemical and Plastics Division has set up a Department of Safety, Health, and Affairs Related to the Environment (SHARE), headed by a vice-president. SHARE is charged with the corporate responsibility of communicating and protecting the environment and in-plant working conditions of the company's employees.

One of the main responsibilities of the department is to put into operation waste-water treatment facilities in company plants. It is charged with assuring that the water and air burdens from the manufacturing processes are reduced to permissible levels to meet applicable standards. The department works with research and development personnel to design systems to ensure permissible levels of operation. SHARE meets regularly with the legal staff, toxicology experts, corporate environment staff, marketing personnel, and

---

[11] *The Fundamentals of Issue Management* (Washington, D.C.: Public Affairs Council, 1978), pp. 5–8.

```
FUNCTIONS OF A GOVERNMENT RELATIONS DEPARTMENT

 • Federal legislative monitoring and analysis
 • Regulatory agency liaison and response
 • State and local legislative monitoring and analysis
 • Domestic and international market development assistance
 • Trade association liaison
 • Federal appointment assistance
 • Political analysis and response
 • Federal and state information services
```

Figure 15-1

others. It also has authority to review and approve all new capital projects for environmental, safety, and health features.

Often, a major adverse experience with government regulators will trigger an organizational response by a company. Such was the case with the pharmaceutical producer, G. D. Searle and Company, which reacted in the fall of 1975 to a hostile congressional hearing on questions relating to its submission of test data to the Food and Drug Administration. Searle responded to the adverse public reaction by establishing a corporate committee of social scientists to study economic and political trends and determine how they are likely to affect the company. It also retained a Washington-based lobbying firm to gain more insight into congressional deliberations and to present its views more effectively.

The company also started to educate its employees on major public issues, ranging from drug pricing to the operations of the private enterprise system. It urged them to take more active roles in local civic affairs. It set up a council of management officials to review community relations and public attitudes toward business and to propose methods of dealing with those issues. The company also moved the regulatory compliance function from the divisional level to the corporate office.

Air Products and Chemicals, Inc. (a corporation with annual sales of approximately $1 billion) set up a separate government relations department in 1976 (see fig. 15-1 for the array of functions assigned to the new office). A 1979 survey by the Conference Board revealed that approximately two-thirds of the companies reported that they had government relations units which were at least three years old.[12]

---

[12] Phyllis S. McGrath, *Redefining Corporate-Federal Relations* (New York: Conference Board, 1979), p. 59.

Business is increasingly turning to the public to exert pressure on government for reforms it believes desirable. Numerous existing channels of communication are available to companies for communicating their views on public policy. They range from employee newspapers to customer magazines to annual reports to shareholders. In the past, such house organs have tended to be dominated by routine announcements, pictures of employees receiving ten-year pins, and bowling league scores. Many companies are now including more substantial editorial content in these publications.

A company may make most types of "noncoercive" statements to its employees, including solicitations of political contributions, expressions of political support and corporate philosophy, and exhortations to political or legislative activity. The legal restraints on employer-employee communications are limited to form, reportability, and tax deductibility. Employee communications involving legislative matters are subject to the Federal Regulation of Lobbying Act.

Section 142 (e)(2) of the Internal Revenue Code denies deductibility of expenditures for participating in any political campaign or in attempting to influence a segment of the "general public" on legislative matters (so-called "grass roots lobbying").[13] Regulations of the Internal Revenue Service permit deductions for advertising that presents views on economic, financial, social, or other questions of a general nature. But the distinction between tax-deductible "informational" messages and nondeductible "persuasional" communication is at best arbitrary.[14]

A series of rulings by the Internal Revenue Service in 1978 appeared to set some strict limits on tax-deductible grass roots lobbying and related activities. Internal Revenue Ruling 78–111, for example, stated that the cost of printing and distributing the text of the remarks of a company president on a pending state environmental bill was nondeductible, even though the shareholders were not actually requested to contact their representatives. That activity, according to the IRS, was an attempt to influence shareholders to oppose the legislation. In Revenue Ruling 78–112, IRS held that the costs of advertisements stating the company's objection to certain proposed land-use legislation and suggesting an alternative program

[13] John Lucas, "Legal Guidelines for Communications with Corporate Employees," *Enterprise*, March 1979, p. 13.
[14] S. Prakash Sethi, "Tax Deductibility and Business Ads," *The New York Times*, July 18, 1978, p. D-2.

also violated the prohibition on "grass roots lobbying," regardless of the absence of a specific request that the reader contact a representative in the legislature. (See table 15-3 for an analysis of the tax-deductibility of different types of corporate communications.)

On the other hand, an important U.S. Supreme Court decision in April 1978 (*First National Bank of Boston* v. *Bellotti*) held that corporations have a constitutional right of free speech to propagate their political and social views. The Bellotti case did not, however, deal with tax deductibility; rather, it struck down a Massachusetts law that prohibited corporations from making expenditures for the purpose of "influencing or affecting the vote on any question submitted to the voters, other than one materially affecting any of the property, business or assets of the corporation." The First National Bank of Boston had opposed a proposed state graduated individual income tax. The decision held that corporations have a right of free speech.

There can be important feedback effects of corporate communications efforts. A strong statement of company position on a controversial issue of public policy may engender strikingly negative responses from one or more elements of the community. However, such reactions can be valuable to the extent that they induce a more informed company response to the issues involved. Such interchanges of opinion with a variety of interest groups can broaden the horizons of company managements and enable them to function more effectively in the more open environment which is facing the modern business firm.

For the first time in 14 years, General Motors in 1975 solicited the support of its stockholders to secure a five-year postponement of tougher emissions and safety standards. In a mailing to its 1.3 million stockholders, 13,000 dealers, and 19,000 suppliers, GM helped to communicate this sentiment to lawmakers by enclosing names and addresses of the senators and representatives from the appropriate state.[15]

Company managements are looking to their shareholders as an important but neglected constituency. William S. Mitchell, president of Safeway Stores, Inc., called for the development of a business activist movement. He suggested that the more than 60,000 Safeway shareholders be the nucleus for such a movement or at least active participants, ". . . 31 million communications from 31 million stockholders would cause a ground swell that could not be ignored."[16]

---

[15] "GM's Political Pitch to Its Stockholders," *Business Week*, February 17, 1975, p. 27.

[16] William S. Mitchell, "Why Government Neglects the Stockholder," *Nation's Business*, August 1975, p. 51.

Table 15-3 Corporate communications with shareholders

	Political		Grass Roots		Institutional Advertising
	Partisan	Nonpartisan	Legislative	Regulatory	
Permitted	Yes	Yes	Yes	Yes	Yes
Tax consequences	Nondeductible	Deductible	Nondeductible	Deductible	Deductibility depending on audience

Source: Thomas J. Houser, "Legal Guidelines," *Enterprise*, April 1979

Not all public relations need necessarily be negative or defensive. For example, in April 1973, the Minnesota Isaak Walton League presented an award to United States Steel for its conservation efforts in developing and operating its Minnesota ore operations. It should be noted that this was not a matter of public relations after the fact. United States Steel asked the group for its advice in planning the facility in view of the vast quantity of water used in processing taconite. Ninety-five percent of the water is reused via an extensive closed-circuit system of separators and tailings basins.[17]

INTERACTION WITH STATE GOVERNMENT

The rising share of federal expenditures which takes the form of grants-in-aid to states and localities indicates that a greater proportion of public-sector responsibilities is being assumed by state and local governments. This, in turn, is leading more business firms to set up formal liaison activities with the state legislatures and agencies that affect their operations. In some cases similar offices are being established to work with the larger county and municipal governments.[18]

The revitalization of state governments is often making a company representative in Sacramento or Albany almost as important as the one in Washington. State legislatures are moving in a variety of areas of concern to business (see table 15-4). In addition to the traditional areas of taxes and labor, they are now deeply involved in job safety, environmental controls, land use, product packaging, and transportation systems. The Environment Information Center, a clearinghouse for environment and energy information, reported that in 1977 a total of 316 major environmentally related laws or regulations were enacted by the 50 states, bringing the total of state environmental statutes to more than 2,000[19] (see table 15-5). Between May and September 1978, in just one area of concern, nine states signed sixteen bills into law and introduced five others regulating the manufacture, use and management, packaging, storage, licensing, and disposal of chemicals and toxic substances.[20]

---

[17]"Conservationists Salute Minntac," *U.S. Steel News*, July–August 1973, p. 10.

[18]John S. McClenahen, "Is Business Ready for New State Power?" *Industry Week*, November 12, 1973, pp. 56–60; Martin R. Haley and James M. Kiss, "Larger Stakes in Statehouse Lobbying," *Harvard Business Review*, January–February 1974, pp. 127–32.

[19]*Land Use Digest* (Urban Institute), June 1978.

[20]*State Legisletter* (Chemical Specialties Manufacturers Association), December 2, 1978, pp. 1–6.

Table 15-4   Major business issues at the state level

Lobbying laws
Land-use planning
Environment
Consumer affairs
Taxation
Labor law
Product safety
Job safety and health
Legislature modernization

Source: Public Affairs Council

Table 15-5   State environmental statutes, 1976–77

Statute Subject	Existing at Year-End, 1976	Added during 1977*
Air	582	66
Water	431	79
Land use	168	75
Radiation	111	18
Pesticide	168	23
Noise	26	2
Solid waste	253	25
Hazardous substances	23	7
General environment	104	31
Total	1,866	326

*Some 1977 laws repeated or replaced earlier statutes.
Source: Environment Information Center

As a result, some companies are either expanding their state government relations efforts or establishing whole new programs. As in the case of the Washington representative, a state director of public affairs can be a "watchdog" maintaining an early warning system to alert the company on coming government action that may affect its plans or operations. Thus, he or she can identify at an early stage those bills that will have significant impact on the company, and corporate views can be presented before legislative positions become hardened. The state relations representative also may be a repository of knowledge about the mechanics of state government. Many company managers — particularly technical specialists in engineering, manufacturing, or finance — lack sufficient understanding of committee structures and the mechanics of legislative processes.

Conferring on legislation at the state level may often be easier than at the federal level. Individual state legislators may be more approachable by business representatives. Typically, they possess less staff and official information sources and may come to rely on business representatives for factual information on various issues. As one soft-drink manufacturer recommended in a newsletter to the company's bottlers: "State legislators say that a visit from a soft drink bottler, where he explains the basis of his concern for support or change of a proposed measure, is much more persuasive than any requests for action received by mail. . . . It is time again for 7UP developers to take positive action and carry proposals to their state government."[21]

The older forms of special access and personal relations are giving way in the new lobbying framework. Lunches, banquets, small favors, and year-round remembrances are still welcome as tokens of civility. But as techniques of influence they are being overtaken by specialized knowledge, integrative analysis, and planning. Sound research and professional expertise frequently can be critical ingredients in influencing government policy formulation. State legislators often lack well-staffed committees or good research services. For them the lobbyist can be a helpful resource.

With most of the nation's governors possessing an item veto on appropriations bills, the executive branch should not be overlooked either. The well-prepared company representative, with established access to the executive offices, is able to offer advice on appointments to advisory commissions, to influence approval or veto of legislation, and to contribute to a more favorable political climate for business.

Although state laws on lobbying differ very substantially, there are several common threads that pervade many of them. Almost every state government requires lobbyists to register (although the precise definition of "lobbying" varies among the states). Seventeen states also require lobbyist employers to register. In the case of several states — including California, Massachusetts, Texas, and Washington — lobbyists before executive branch agencies of state government must register for that purpose, in addition to registering for lobbying members of the legislature. Thirty-three states require the lobbyist and/or his or her employer to file financial reports.[22]

Washington State has set up a special regulatory agency to monitor the activities of lobbyists. Persons coming within the lobby-

---

[21] *Environmental Information* (Seven-Up Company), January 31, 1975, p. 1.

[22] William Hoffer, "Associations Face Tough State Lobbying Laws," *Association Management*, August 1975, p. 46.

ing statute must register and file detailed financial reports weekly, monthly, and quarterly. The law also provides a "bounty hunter provision," whereby an individual citizen can sue a lobbyist and the employer for violating the act and receive as much as 50 percent of any resulting fine.

California has established a Fair Political Practices Commission, with an annual budget in excess of $1 million. One of the key duties of the commission is to audit annually the books of every registered lobbyist. Lobbyists are prevented from spending more than ten dollars a month on any one item of legislation. Monthly reports are required and lobbying funds must be kept in a separate, designated bank account. California has adopted a bounty hunter provision similar to the state of Washington law.

Some enlightened business association executives have urged their members to take the lead in promoting the passage of strict but reasonable lobbying laws and to clean up any abuses that may exist in their organizations. In the words of one senior association official, "That's not the plaintive cry of a frazzle-haired liberal. That's the calm statement of a concerned association executive. Drag your members kicking and screaming into the 20th century."[23]

[23] Ibid., p. 47.

Part Three

SHAPING
THE
BUSINESS-
GOVERNMENT
ENVIRONMENT

16 ||

trade
associations
and government

Business firms have been utilizing trade associations ever since
the Rhode Island candlemakers banded together in 1762. In more
recent years, business corporations have been using their trade
associations more frequently to assist them in dealings with the
government. These associations traditionally have performed services
in data collection, education, and other standard and relatively low
profile areas. Now, they are taking a more positive role in public
affairs, particularly in five areas of government regulation of business:
health and safety, consumer affairs, the environment, wage and price
standards and controls, and energy (see table 16-1).

Most business firms, large or small, belong to one or more trade
associations (a great many of which are now located in Washington,
D.C.). These groups perform a variety of functions. They keep their
members informed of new government regulations and pending
legislation. On important issues affecting their industry, the associations develop positions and express them to the government, Congress,
and the public. In addition, the trade groups sponsor conferences and
other meetings, initiate litigation when necessary, undertake studies

Table 16-1   Key activities of associations

Activity	Percent of Associations Performing Activity
Inform members of congressional developments	92
Help members express views to senators and congressmen	87
Inform members of federal administrative actions	87
Inform members of state and local legislative developments	81
Testify before Congress or state legislatures	76
Make recommendations on legislation	71
Provide data to state governments	66
Include speakers on legislation in convention programs	57
Draft legislation	55
Lobby and inform Congress of industry views	54
Provide data to federal government	49
Report federal court decisions	46
Train members to become active in politics	29
Collect and distribute political funds to candidates	27
Arrange plant tours to help government expose foreign visitors to U.S. industry	23
Sponsor courses on political participation	15
Assist members with customs, tariffs, and trade agreements	12
Represent industry in tariff negotiations	9
Assist government in foreign trade fair participation	8

Source: American Society of Association Executives

and analyses, issue a variety of reports and publications, and provide many educational programs for the public and industry.

The wider range of products and services a company provides, the more associations it is likely to belong to. The Air Products and Chemicals Company, for example, holds memberships in the American Iron and Steel Institute, the American Petroleum Institute, the Chamber of Commerce of the United States, Chemical Manufacturers Association, Environmental Industry Council, Fertilizer Institute, Machinery and Allied Products Institute, Manufacturers of Emission Controls Association, National Association of Manufacturers, National Constructors Association, National Paints and Coatings Association, National Petroleum Refiners Association, and Society of the Plastics Industry.

A single organization may serve such a narrow membership that it cannot always cover all of the varied interests of a diversified national corporation. Also, the position of a specific association on a given issue may be at variance with the company's. Thus, membership in a variety of trade groups can provide a company management with considerable flexibility on public policy issues.

Modern trade associations have been characterized as "organizations in the middle," standing between government and business.[1] Thus, they increasingly interpret government actions and attitudes toward business, and vice versa. Some of the ways in which this mission is accomplished is through testifying at congressional hearings on matters affecting the industry, appearing in proceedings before government agencies and regulatory bodies on issues of concern to the industry, and contributing to precedent-making cases before the courts.

Similarly, trade associations often interpret government to business by informing member companies of the attitudes and problems of various government bodies and by making available information that the government is anxious to get into the hands of business executives. Trade association personnel often cooperate with government by serving voluntarily without pay on various advisory committees. As collectors of statistics for their industries, many trade groups may provide government agencies with information that may not be otherwise available.

The use of the statistical information developed by trade associations often extends far beyond the members of the industry. Such regular annual publications as *Aerospace Facts and Figures* (Aerospace Industries Association), *Statistical Yearbook of the Electric Utility Industry* (Edison Electric Institute), *Annual Statistical Report* (American Iron and Steel Institute), and *National Fact Book* (National Association of Mutual Savings Banks) have become basic research sources used by government officials and private scholars. In addition, numerous specific statistical releases are issued by these organizations, such as the Edison Electric Institute's quarterly surveys of rate case decisions and its year-end summary of the electric power situation.

The critical relationship between the federal government and most trade associations has not been in the area of lobbying for or against new legislation. Rather, in most cases, it has been dealing with the rules and regulations that government agencies issue with increasing frequency.

Soon after the Arab oil embargo in October 1973 the Pharmaceutical Manufacturers Association (PMA) assembled an energy task

---

[1] Reuel W. Elton, *How Trade Associations Help Small Business*, Management Aids no. 32 (Washington, D.C.: U.S. Small Business Administration, 1961), p. 1.

force of 11 key executives from major drug companies to deal with the then new Federal Energy Administration. The task force first conducted a comprehensive survey of the member firms to determine the likely effects of a reduction in the energy supply. While the industry's needs for petrochemicals and fuels were found to be relatively small in comparison with that of other industries, the impact of a shortage of fuel or petrochemicals was considered likely to constitute a serious health hazard. On the basis of this analysis, the FEA granted the pharmaceutical industry priority in the allocation of certain distillates and residual fuel oils.

As federal agencies establish newer forms of controls over business, member companies more commonly look to their associations to explain the new rules to them, as well as to take public stands that they may not want to take individually. Federal agencies often foster this relationship by encouraging many companies in a given industry to present their views through a single association representing them rather than meeting with the companies individually. For example, the Secretary of the Treasury meets four times a year with two industry association committees that advise the department on the quarterly financing of the public debt.

In contrast to this very high level, nationally focused activity, the Timber Operators Council (TOC) consists of hundreds of small plywood, lumber, and logging firms in the Pacific Northwest that have banded together to develop a better understanding of the OSHA standards that apply to them. The TOC provides safety consultation services, hygiene counseling, and engineering advice on improved machine guarding and sound enclosures. It buys workmen's compensation as a group, thus obtaining more favorable rates for the member firms. TOC staff also perform "dummy" walk-through inspections complete with sound-level surveys.[2]

Because relatively few companies can afford professional safety and health experts, the establishment of OSHA has given a new or expanded role to many trade associations. The National Roofing Contractors Association has published *Roofing Contractors Guide*, listing the most serious hazards in the roofing industry. The National Association of Sheet Metal and Air-Conditioning Contractors set up a committee to develop safety standards.

The meat products industry created an industrial safety committee and has published an analysis of meat plant injuries; the lumber and wood products industry established a committee to

2 "Big Help for the Little Man," *Job Safety and Health*, February 1974, p. 19.

develop guidelines for compliance with the OSHA act. A ten-hour course on occupational safety and health, offered by the New York City Building Trades Employers Association, has been completed by 1,000 construction supervisors and employees.[3]

The Grocery Manufacturers of America has prepared a 100-page study, *Guidelines for Product Recall*, to help members of that industry to cope with an increasingly frequent by-product of government regulation. The voluntary guidelines set forth in the report, which had been discussed previously with the Food and Drug Administration, cover organizational arrangements, distribution systems, and communications aspects.

The Milk Industry Foundation provides a recurrent publication, *Milk Order Roundup*, to keep its members informed on the great variety of regulations issued by federal and state agencies. Similarly, the foundation's releases, *Information about Energy* and *Ecogram: Ecology and Environment*, are continuing efforts to keep milk processors abreast of two relatively new and rapidly changing areas of government regulation.

In a different area, the Comics' Magazine Association was established in 1954 as a result of the Kefauver Senate Subcommittee's investigation of the relationship between comic books and television programs and juvenile delinquency. The association's code governing the presentation of crime, sex, violence, and advertising in comic books has been successful in removing the public's major objections to the magazines. The extreme crime and horror comics to a large extent have been withdrawn from the market.[4]

Voluntary standards promulgated by other trade associations for product safety have likewise had favorable results. The Cosmetic, Toiletry and Fragrance Association (CTFA) began in 1971 a voluntary program to provide assurance of cosmetic safety to the Food and Drug Administration. CTFA provides information (most of which is not required by law) on where cosmetics are manufactured, what they are made of, and safety-related complaints. The association also developed, with cooperation from the FDA, the *CFTA Cosmetic Ingredient Dictionary* to develop uniform names for cosmetic ingredients. This industry's most important effort, however, has been the formation of a Cosmetic Ingredient Review to bring

[3] *The President's Report on Occupational Safety and Health* (Washington, D.C.: U.S. Government Printing Office, 1973), pp. 20–21; "High on Safety," *Occupational Safety and Health*, July 1974, p. 11.
[4] David J. Pittman and M. Dow Lambert, *Alcohol, Alcoholism and Advertising: A Preliminary Investigation of Asserted Associations* (St. Louis: privately published booklet, 1978), pp. 6–7.

together worldwide data on the safety of cosmetic ingredients for review by a panel of scientific experts.[5]

Another voluntary program has been that of the Chain Saw Manufacturers Association to develop, with the help of the Consumer Product Safety Commission, performance rules to reduce the "kickback" hazards of gas and electric chain saws. (A "kickback" is the sudden and unexpected movement of the chain saw blade toward the user's body.) The CPSC stated that the voluntary program by industry would cost $330,000 and take two years to develop, whereas mandatory standards would cost about $1.75 million and take four years to develop.[6]

In a related area, however, voluntary standards for power mowers proposed by an association met with rejection. The Outdoor Power Equipment Institute petitioned the CPSC in 1973 to adopt its already existing voluntary standards for mowers, which had been approved by the American National Standards Institute, an international standard-setting organization. These standards were adhered to by 90 percent of all mower manufacturers. Instead, the CPSC commissioned the Consumers Union to develop mandatory standards, which, if adopted, would have cost consumers $371 million in their first year of application.[7] As of mid-1979, no mower standards had been adopted by the commission.

Location of Associations

Many associations with headquarters in cities closer to their constituents' industrial environment have opened subsidiary offices in Washington, but many more have moved their central offices to the nation's capital. A radius of ten blocks of the White House now contains many of these offices. According to James P. Low, executive vice-president of the American Society of Association Executives (naturally, there is an association for associations), "Every time HUD hiccups, 20 construction industry associations hold a meeting."

As recently as 1974 New York City was still home for the largest single share of the nation's associations, especially because of the proximity of advertising, marketing, and publishing companies

---

[5] *Introducing the Cosmetic, Toiletry and Fragrance Industry Today* (Washington, D.C.: The Cosmetic, Toiletry and Fragrance Association, n.d.).

[6] Consumer Product Safety Commission news release, March 30, 1978; Larry Kramer, "Manufacturers to Write Chain Saw Safety Rules," *Washington Post*, April 3, 1978, p. D-12.

[7] "The Long Road to Standards Development," *Association Management*, March 1979, pp. 39-40.

that provide important services to them. Nevertheless, a rising proportion of business associations has been locating in Washington. In 1978 Washington had 1,800 trade association headquarters, which employed over 40,000 persons.[8] Industries that cater heavily to the government market — including the Aerospace Industries Association, the Electronics Industries Association, and the National Security Industrial Association — traditionally have located their trade associations in the capital. Others now located there are the American Advertising Federation, the American Bankers Association, the American Gas Association, the American Petroleum Institute, the American Newspaper Publishers Association, the Atomic Industrial Forum, the Bicycle Manufacturers Association, the Chemical Specialties Manufacturers Association, the Mortgage Bankers Association, the National Association of Furniture Manufacturers, the National Association of Manufacturers, and the National Shrimp Congress.

The continued expansion of federal control over private industry will further the tendency of trade associations to locate all or at least a major part of their operations in Washington, D.C. They also will be devoting a rising share of their resources to government relations. A recent survey by the American Society of Association Executives reported that 22 percent of member trade associations devoted one-fifth or more of their budgets to government relations activities.

Some business groups have moved to the national capital area because other associations with which they can cooperate are already there, and valuable information about legislation and government actions can be shared. Many associations cite the concentration of reporters in Washington as another important reason for moving to the capital. As one association head remarked, "You don't see many datelines from Boston."[9]

The American Petroleum Institute is a good example of a large Washington-based trade association working for an industry that is strongly affected by government actions. Its 1979 budget of $35 million supported 500 employees, 12 of whom were formally registered as lobbyists. A major producer of statistics on the petroleum industry, the institute has established a policy analysis division to examine proposed legislation and to provide information to Congress. It is strengthening its ties to state and regional oil associations and providing more speakers to local radio and television talk shows, all

---

[8] Steven V. Roberts, "Trade Associations Flocking to Capital As U.S. Role Rises," *The New York Times*, March 4, 1978, p. 23.
[9] Ibid., p. 44.

in an effort to increase "grass roots" support for the industry's positions on petroleum-related legislation.

THE RISE OF "UMBRELLA" ORGANIZATIONS

To counter the increasing impact of other interest groups, there is a new tendency for business associations to combine forces, at least for some overriding issues. A recent innovation in this regard is the occasional joining of forces by the two largest general associations of business interests, the Chamber of Commerce of the United States and the National Association of Manufacturers (NAM). The move of the NAM to Washington has made such cooperation feasible; the Chamber of Commerce historically has been located in the capital.

In October 1973 the Chamber of Commerce and the NAM issued their first joint letter in 70 years — an appeal to the President to remove all wage and price controls. In December 1973 the two organizations sent the President another letter on the subject. (The wage and price control legislation was allowed to lapse in April 1974). The two associations have jointly testified before Congress on foreign trade legislation. They also have formed an Energy Users' Conference, designed to represent the nation's major industrial and commercial consumers of energy; the conference has become a major business link with the DOE. The heads of the two associations lunch together regularly and are frequently joined by the Secretary of Commerce.

The Chamber of Commerce also has been instrumental in organizing the Association Advisory Group on Product Safety, representing 30 different trade and professional associations who have joined forces for a common front. The group has dealt with the Consumer Product Safety Commission on industrywide problems, such as the publicity given the raw data obtained through the hospital network, known as the National Electronic Injury Surveillance System.[10]

The chamber itself is perhaps the largest and most broadly representative business association in Washington. It is comprised of over 80,000 members who represent virtually every kind of business. The chamber has formed 2,300 Congressional Action Committees, each made up of about thirty business executives around the country, at the "grass roots" level, who personally know their senators and congressional representatives and who keep in touch

---

[10] "Chamber Dialogue Underway with CPSC," *Washington Report*, December 30, 1974, p. 2.

with them on legislative activity. The chamber attempts to influence the legislative process through congressional testimony, the work of its lobbyists along with the Washington representatives of its member companies, other trade association lobbyists, and through the "grass roots" contacts in the Congressional Action System. A sophisticated computer operation allows the chamber to contact large segments of its membership when a bill is about to be acted upon in Congress.

Although utilizing a somewhat similar structure as the chamber, the National Association of Manufacturers covers, of course, a somewhat more specialized grouping of American businesses. Yet its membership of over 13,000 firms and its annual budget of over $8 million makes it one of the major voices of private enterprise in the United States.[11]

Of all of the broad-based organizations, the newest and perhaps most influential is the Business Roundtable. Comprised of 190 chief executive officers of the nation's largest and most prestigious companies, the Roundtable has its own staff and activities, although it does work with the older and larger groups. It is a specific vehicle for getting members of top management personally involved in presenting business views to Congress and to senior officials in the departments and agencies. The staff of the Roundtable is kept at a minimum, with the organization relying mainly on the efforts of executives in the employ of its member companies. Committees are active in such areas as construction, labor-management, public information, and antitrust legislation.

The Roundtable operates with an annual budget of about $2.5 million. Much of its expenses are born directly by the member companies whose executives serve on its committees or talk directly to members of Congress and executive-branch policy officials. Annual dues range from $2,500 to $35,000, depending on the size of the company. The membership includes the three largest automobile manufacturers, the three largest banks, seven of the biggest oil companies, major retail organizations, several utilities, and a variety of other industrial firms.[12]

The trend toward the formation of more business "umbrella" organizations in Washington is likely to continue as federal regulations extend to nationwide activities, rather than being limited to a single regulated industry.[13]

[11] Ann M. Reilly, "Washington Information Boom," *Dun's Review*, March 1979, pp. 60–71.

[12] Eileen Shanahan, "Antitrust Bill Stopped by a Business Lobby," *The New York Times*, November 16, 1975, p. 1.

[13] "Harmonizing Business' Voices," *Industry Week*, June 24, 1974, pp. 50–52; Andrew J. Glass, "NAM's New Look Is toward Goal of Business Unity," *National Journal Reports*, January 5, 1974, pp. 15–23.

Some trade association executives are sensitive about being termed "lobbyist," preferring such terms as "government liaison" or "government representative." Many see themselves as conduits between business and government, acting mainly as message carriers. The effectiveness of the message being delivered may depend in good measure on the association's ability to get member companies to agree on strong common stands on controversial issues. For example, manufacturers of a product with a large foreign sales operation may well prefer a different stand on tariff issues than other companies in the same industry that are faced with severe import competition. For this reason, many large companies are active members of a variety of trade associations and also maintain large offices in Washington. This dual form of representation provides flexibility, allowing a company to band together with other firms in the industry on some issues, while taking an independent stance on other matters.

Most associations still conduct traditional activities, such as setting standards, gathering statistics, publishing information about the industry, maintaining public relations, and performing educational functions. However, government relations has become the dominant function for many of them. One result has been that association staffs have been growing in both quantity and quality. Relatively few associations still call their top staff people "executive secretary." The title "president" is more in vogue, with salaries often matching the added stature; on occasion, they may exceed $100,000 a year. Associations are attracting former government officials for top staff jobs.

The trade association field has taken on added professional stature as a result of an intensive educational program begun by the American Society of Association Executives, in which hundreds of association staff members have qualified for a certified association executive designation by passing a written examination. At least one educational institution, Florida Atlantic University, now offers a master's degree in association management. The ASAE sponsors many courses for association executives covering finance, management, publications, working with governments, and leadership. Table 16-2 indicates the contents of the first-year course in association management sponsored by the U.S. Chamber of Commerce at six major universities.

A special three-day Communications Workshop prepares members for appearances on television, presentation of testimony, and press conferences. In the Workshop, television cameras, videotape

Table 16-2   Program of a first course in association management

Organization structure, policy, and programming

Types of associations. Elements of the organization structure. Role of the manager, staff, and members. Techniques for developing a policy. Techniques for developing a program. Techniques for communicating the policies and program.

Finance and budgeting

How to develop financial policies for an association. Setting up the financial structure. Fundamentals of cash and accrual accounting methods. The use of a budget as a planning and control tool. How to develop a budget. Procedures for assuring internal control.

Government relations

The importance of government relations. Steps in developing a government relations program. Importance of policy in government relations. Developing membership support. Techniques for legislative representation. The "do's and don'ts" of political involvement.

Law

Basic knowledge of federal statutes that affect associations. Legal organization of an association. Activities that are clearly legal and clearly illegal. The executive's responsibility in association law. Techniques and procedures to help assure legality of activities.

Communication

Functions of communication. The communication process. The relationship between language and communication.

Power relationships of people and groups

Ways of looking at power relationships. Emergence of power relationships — formal and informal. Connection of power and organization.

Group action

Components of group action (motivation). Concepts of group dynamics and the social structure of groups. The necessity for developing and implementing a philosophy of group action.

Task force management

Use of committees — their role in the organization. Types of committees. Selection of committee chairmen and members. Working with committees.

Developing external manpower

How to determine volunteer leadership needs. Techniques for identifying potential volunteer leaders. Recruiting and developing volunteer leaders and potential leaders. How to evaluate performance. The role of the manager and staff in developing volunteer leadership.

Source: Chamber of Commerce of the United States

recordings, and playback equipment are used for demonstrations and personalizing the educational experience.[14]

Educational activities of associations also extend to their member companies, especially smaller companies without their own management development staffs. The operational management sessions of the National Soft Drink Association, for example, draws 1,800 participants on such subjects as security, energy conservation, and employee communications. The Edison Electric Institute conducts a four-week Graduate Management Course for upper-level executives of the industry, covering management skills, oral communications, and current electric utility industry problems.

The American Association of Executives has set up a program for the voluntary accreditation of trade groups. The formal evaluation is a three-stepped affair:

1. The applicant association submits a self-evaluation report using the ASAE's Association Evaluation Guidelines.
2. A site visit is made by an evaluation team of three persons made up of two ASAE member executives and a staff member.
3. The evaluation team submits a written report to the ASAE's chief staff executive officers.[15]

To be sure, not all of the activities of trade associations have generated uniformly favorable public reactions. Labor unions and other interest groups from time to time have attacked what they have considered to be improper or excessive influence that business associations have exerted on government policy makers. Many of the criticisms seem to boil down to the fact that members of certain industries, notably petroleum, are heavily represented on government advisory committees.[16] Some of the specific concerns, however, have a stronger base than that, as was the case of the U.S. Geological Survey.

Until April 1974 the Geological Survey consulted a committee of oil industry representatives before establishing regulations for offshore drilling on the continental shelf of the United States. The agency's practice was to circulate its proposed regulatory orders to the Offshore Operators Committee, composed entirely of industry representatives, before making the information public via publication in the *Federal Register*.

[14] "New Opportunities for Executive Development," *Association Management* (July 1975), p. 75.

[15] "Accreditation Program Approved by ASAE Board at Annual Meeting," *Association Management*, October 1975, p. 99.

[16] Norman Medvin, "How Big Oil Influences Government,"*American Federationist*, December 1974, pp. 16-19.

The change in procedure came about after Representatives Henry S. Reuss and Guy Vander Jagt, chairman and ranking minority member of the House of Representatives Subcommittee on Conservation and Natural Resources, complained to the Secretary of the Interior that the procedure deprived the public of knowing what the federal agency proposed initially. The revised practice is to make the proposed regulations public before soliciting the industry's comments.[17]

THE FLOW OF INFORMATION

One of the problems facing business associations, and resulting in the upgrading of their personnel, is how to develop more sophisticated ways of dealing with the rapidly growing flow of information from government agencies and related research institutions. The traditional newsletter to the top management of member companies frequently is not considered sufficient. Conferences, television, a variety of printed publications, and other media are used to present and tailor information on government actitivies for the growing variety of users in member companies.

The work of Washington trade associations has become much more information oriented than it has been in the past. Trade associations seek information, but so do the legislators who must act on congressional bills and who also keep their constituents informed about Washington developments and their implications. The associations are, therefore, useful to members of Congress in more than a "self-serving" way. A staffer for the Senate Energy Committee, for instance, has remarked that the American Petroleum Institute analyzes legislation "in excruciating detail" and that it often provides "good material, useful for technical insight."[18]

Trade associations produce a wide range of publications. Several associations publish very professional magazines, which deal with issues of public policy and also inform the industry of the impact of current and prospective government activities. Examples include the Mortgage Bankers Association's monthly *Mortgage Banker* and the Edison Electric Institute's bimonthly *EEI Bulletin*.

The Milk Industry Foundation, in conjunction with the International Association of Ice Cream Manufacturers, regularly provides

[17]Murray L. Weidenbaum, "Private Advisors and Government Policymaking," *Policy Analysis*, January 1975, pp. 110-11.

[18]"America's Oil Lobby — The Way It Works," *U.S. News and World Report*, May 7, 1979, pp. 59-60.

its membership with two series of reports on various aspects of government relations: *Thrust*, a relatively technical publication, describes and evaluates the effect of state and federal standards, labeling regulations, and enforcement activities. *Alert*, a more popularly written release, covers critical issues affecting the industry, such as proposals for requiring regulatory agencies to consider the costs that they impose on business.

The NAM recently has computerized many of its activities. Member firms have been categorized according to congressional districts as well as the standard industrial classification (SIC) used by federal statistical agencies. A computerized profile of each member of Congress also has been prepared. As legislative issues arise, the NAM staff in Washington hopes to be better equipped to pinpoint the companies most directly affected by proposed legislative changes or executive action. The data will also help to determine where the association's government representation efforts should be focused.

In addition to assisting the information function of the individual corporate offices in Washington, trade associations also can be useful in obtaining "access" to government decision makers in both the legislative and executive branches. While such officials may be reluctant to meet privately with the representatives of a single company, they frequently accept invitations to attend meetings sponsored by an association representing an entire industry. Employees of a company thus can make initial informal contacts with key government people at association luncheons, dinners, cocktail parties, conferences, and other meetings.

On occasion, companies in a given industry have cooperated in setting up organizations to develop new information and research findings, often in response to government regulatory activities. One example was the formation in 1975 of the Chemical Industry Institute of Technology, jointly funded by 32 chemical companies. The institute aims at generating, assessing, and disseminating health and safety data on industrial chemicals. The testing and other factual outputs of the institute are expected to help the chemical industry meet an increasing array of federal regulation, including that from EPA, FDA, CPSC, and OSHA.

In recent years, moreover, trade associations have made many efforts to educate and to communicate directly with the public via a variety of publications. This mode of "consumerism" is designed to foster a better understanding of their products, their business operations, and their services.

For example, the National Paint and Coatings Association took action after it learned that a large number of people did not understand how to use paints properly. It published a 100-page *Household*

Paint Selector that tells consumers how to save money by picking the right paint for the right surface. The association also took action on the issue of faulty nozzles on aerosol spray paint cans by devising label standards in clear language that passed federal scrutiny. Likewise, the Chemical Specialties Manufacturers Association distributes two special pamphlets aimed at combating teen-age abuse of aerosol spray products.

The Pharmaceutical Manufacturers Association disseminates information in several forms on the purchase of drugs and on drug addiction symptoms, especially among youths. And one of the National Consumer Finance Association's booklets tells consumers how to set up a family budget.

An effective system for dealing with consumer complaints has been the Major Appliance Consumer Action Panel, a joint effort of the Association of Home Appliance Manufacturers, the Gas Appliance Manufacturers Association, and the Retail Merchants Association. This panel, composed of private citizens not associated with industry, hears complaints that have not been settled by a retailer or manufacturer and makes recommendations that generally result in action (in one year, it resolved over 3,100 out of 3,800 complaints presented to it). Moreover, the first of the associations engaged in this cooperative effort has its own extensive consumer education and complaint-handling program. The AHAM actively cooperates with government, educators, utility companies, home economist groups, and consumer specialists in the media to handle and promote consumer affairs. It has warned of the dangers of children being trapped in refrigerators and freezers, and it has worked with the CPSC in an education program that includes a series of public service announcements.[19]

Through these programs associations can at times spot consumer problems early and deal with them through "self-policing" efforts before becoming the target of further regulation.

FUTURE PROSPECTS

Trade associations may be one of the most underutilized mechanisms for improving public policy. With some adaptation these groups of companies could become the moral conscience of the

[19] Nathan J. Margolin, "Trends in Consumerism: A Look at What Associations Are Doing," *Association Management*, May 1979, pp. 81–89; Michael S. Hunt, "Trade Associations and Self-Regulation: Major Home Appliances," in *Regulating the Product*, eds. Richard E. Caves and Marc, J. Roberts (Cambridge, Mass.: Ballinger, 1975), pp. 39–51.

business community, at least to a larger extent than at present. In the middle 1970s, for example, during the investigations of illegal corporate contributions, individual companies were often reluctant to take a stand with regard to the public criticisms directed against the wrongdoers. Such inaction was not due to approval of the wrong-doing, but fear that subsequent investigation might reveal that their own skirts were not completely clean. Here the trade associations were in a better position to enunciate the acceptable standards of private behavior, although generally they did not take advantage of the opportunity.

17

business
participation
in politics

The rising impact of government regulatory activities on business decision making is resulting in renewed interest by business executives in participating directly in the political process. The substantial political role of other interest groups, such as labor and agriculture, and the antibusiness orientation of many political activists working under the banner of the public interest, continue to encourage business people to enter the political arena more actively.

Although numerous industry leaders attempt to use the political process as a way of slowing government intervention in the private sector, they are often circumspect in their efforts. Legislation has been enacted to deal with the illegal political contributions by business which were exposed to glaring national publicity in the early 1970s. Since then many corporate executives have become far more knowledgeable of the legal limits to political participation.

Corporations can participate legally in a wide variety of political activities. Federal law governs only political activities involving candidates for President, Vice-President, and Congress. Involvement in state and local campaigns is governed by varying state statutes and local ordinances.

A corporation may encourage its employees and stockholders to register and vote, but it may not recommend to employees *how* they should vote. Candidates may tour a company plant or office to meet employees or may stand at an entrance to greet them, but the company must grant *all* candidates that right. However, it need not specifically invite *every* candidate.

The management of a company has a right to state its position on public issues affecting the company's well-being, including legislative proposals before Congress. It also may communicate to its employees and stockholders information on members of Congress and candidates for office, such as voting records. Company-sponsored programs explaining how to be effective in politics are another permissible form of political activity.

A corporation can provide political education programs for employees, and it can actively promote, on a nonpartisan basis, its employee's voluntary involvement in direct political action on their own time. An employee also may be granted a leave of absence without pay to work on a political campaign.

A survey by the Conference Board of the 1,000 largest industrial firms revealed that 28 percent had formal policies covering employee participation in political activities; 17 percent had informal policies. Most of the remainder handle each request on an individual basis; 9 percent stated that the question of a leave for political reasons has never been raised in their companies. Of the formal company policies on political participation, most encourage employees to be active in political work and offer leaves of absence without pay to employees elected or appointed to public office. Leaves are usually restricted to one term, after which an employee is considered to have chosen a career in politics.[1]

Under the 1974 election reform law, business partnerships may contribute to federal candidates, although corporations and labor unions may not. The Federal Election Commission has ruled that any candidate receiving a donation from a partnership must, to comply

---

[1] Grace J. Finley, *Policies on Leaves for Political and Social Action* (New York: Conference Board, 1972), pp. 1-4.

with the limitation on individual donations, divide the amount received among the individual partners "in relation to each partner's interest in the partnership's profits." The campaign organization must get that information within 30 days or return the contribution.[2]

METHODS OF SUPPORTING POLITICAL CANDIDATES

For many years it was illegal for corporations or unions to solicit political funds from employees or members. At first, unions circumvented the law by forming "educational" groups such as the AFL-CIO's Committee on Political Education (COPE) as a funnel for political contributions. But until comparatively recently, businesses and trade groups had no such outlet and were restricted to individual voluntary contributions by executives. Prior to the reforms in campaign financing laws enacted in the 1970s, these personal contributions could be made in virtually unlimited amounts.

Although corporations and associations are still prohibited by law from making political contributions and making expenditures for federal elections, they in practice now can use company funds to set up Political Action Committees (PACs) comparable to labor's COPE. Specific statutory provisions contained in the 1971 Federal Election Campaign Act and spelled out in greater detail in amendments in 1974 and 1976 allow business- and union-sponsored PACs to support candidates actively. As separate legal entities organized to solicit and accept contributions from shareholders and "executive or administrative personnel" and their families, PACs in turn can make political contributions to candidates for federal office (twice a year they can solicit other company employees). Despite the complex rules governing their operation, the number of business PACs has increased rapidly, from fewer than 100 in 1974 to more than 1,200 in 1978 (PACs disbursed $37 million that year). Table 17-1 lists the sixty firms with largest PAC expenditures.

Individual contributors to PACs are limited to $1,000 per calendar year. Each PAC is allowed to contribute only $5,000 per election to each candidate. But there is no limit on total contributions by a PAC.[3]

Besides making cash payments directly to candidates, political action groups can provide support "in kind." For example, a PAC

[2] Walter Pincus, "Making Campaign Rules Complex," *Washington Post*, September 15, 1975, p. A-22.
[3] Edwin M. Epstein, "The Business PAC Phenomenon: An Irony of Electoral Reform," *Regulation*, May–June 1979, p. 35.

Table 17-1   Sixty largest corporate political action committees, fiscal year 1977–78

Sponsoring Company	Expenditures in 1977–78	Sponsoring Company	Expenditures in 1977–78
Standard Oil of Indiana	$266,308	Pacific Lighting	84,099
American Family	260,140	Burlington Northern	80,517
International Paper	240,336	Republic Steel	77,575
LTV	208,804	Monsanto	76,755
General Motors	198,842	Atlantic-Richfield	76,142
General Electric	176,076	Weyerhaeuser	75,541
Chicago and North Western	169,067	Lockheed	74,135
Grumman	156,435	Southern Railway	70,624
General Dynamics	155,956	McDonnell-Douglas	70,206
Boeing	135,377	Southern Pacific	69,509
United Technologies	130,725	Occidental Petroleum	69,500
Dart Industries	128,914	Steak and Ale Restaurants	68,557
U.S. Steel	124,230	Sun Company	66,925
Winn-Dixie Stores	123,611	L. M. Berry and Company	62,174
Union Camp	117,900	Union Pacific	61,269
Pfizer	115,842	Ashland Oil	60,977
General Telephone of California	112,047	Consolidated Edison	60,928
Greyhound	110,400	Olin	60,740
Coca Cola	106,812	Standard Oil of California	60,042
Westinghouse	103,075	Texaco	58,930
Eaton	101,600	Bank of Everett	58,008
Brown and Root	100,385	Beneficial Management	58,008
Union Oil of California	100,245	Getty Oil	57,350
Hughes Aircraft	98,357	Dresser Industries	56,863
FMC	92,437	Abbott Laboratories	56,340
Wheelabrator-Frye	89,700	Coors Industries	56,140
Florida Power and Light	88,515	Colt Industries	55,860
Flowers Industries	86,016	Alcoa	54,700
Georgia Pacific	85,768	Columbia Gas System	54,376
Ford Motor	85,525	Minnesota Mining and Manufacturing	53,843

Source: Business-Industry Political Action Committee, *A Directory of Corporate and Trade Association Political Action Committees Registered With the Federal Election Commission* (Washington, D.C.: National Association of Manufacturers, 1979).

may pay the salary and expenses of a consultant who goes into a congressional district to counsel a candidate or otherwise work on his or her behalf. It may conduct a target mailing to employees, shareholders, or others in a given congressional district, urging the election or defeat of a candidate. Such in-kind assistance can provide

Table 17-2   Political action committees of *Fortune* ranked firms, September 1978

Size Category	Number of PACs
First 50	35
Second 50	34
Third 50	30
Fourth 50	25
Fifth 50	17
Subtotal, first 250	(141)
Second 250	52
Third 250	24
Fourth 250	7
Total	224

Source: Edwin M. Epstein, "The Business PAC Phenomenon" *Regulation,* May–June 1979, p. 39.

an opportunity for greater interaction with a candidate and staff than do ordinary cash contributions. Also, in-kind contributions can give the PAC greater control over how its help is used.[4]

Professor Edwin Epstein of the University of California at Berkeley, a leading authority on business political activity, concludes that "what is astonishing is how few corporate PACs there are, given how many there might be."[5] He notes that, of the top 1,000 industrial corporations listed by *Fortune* magazine, in 1977, only 224 had a PAC as of September 1978 (see table 17-2).

Moreover, on the basis of Federal Election Commission data for 1976, it is apparent that business usually follows a predictable, low-risk pattern in its contributions. The bulk of the money goes to incumbents rather than challengers (in a ratio of 4 to 1), a practice which tends to favor Democrats over Republicans. Business prefers to contribute to general elections rather than primaries or runoffs and rarely helps in open-seat elections. Business groups very frequently give contributions to chairmen of congressional committees who have jurisdiction over legislation of concern to the industry or company, regardless of the candidate's political philosophy or need for funds.[6] Thus, much of business's political donations have the effect of maintaining "access" to current policymakers rather than of

[4] "The Growing Influence of Political Action Committees," *NSDA Quarterly,* Fall 1978, pp. 8–9 ff.
[5] Epstein, "The Business PAC Phenomenon," p. 39.
[6] Edwin M. Epstein, "The Emergence of Political Action Committees," in *Political Finance,* ed. Herbert E. Alexander (Beverly Hills, Calif.: Sage Publications, Inc., 1979), pp. 159–97.

attempting to change the actual composition of government decision makers.

Business efforts in political fund raising may also be industry-wide and patterned after similar efforts by labor unions. The National Association of Manufacturers sponsors a Business-Industry Political Action Committee. Bankers have established a Banking Profession Political Action Committee (BANKPAC), and the American Bakers Association have a Bread Political Action Committee (BREADPAC). Doctors, with help from drug firms, have set up an American Medical Political Action Committee (AMPAC). Other industry groups that raise funds for political candidates include the Construction Equipment Political Action Committee (CEPAC), the Life Underwriters Education Fund and Political Action Committee, and the Milk Industry Foundation. These committees generally contribute to the campaigns of legislators who are favorable to business or to their specific industry.

Some bona fide sales of goods and services to campaign organizations at times turn out to be involuntary contributions if full payment is not made. Because of widespread abuses of this nature during 1968, especially by losing candidates, Congress passed some restrictive legislation. Pursuant to the Federal Election Campaign Act of 1971, the CAB, the FTC, and the ICC have issued regulations limiting the extension of unsecured credit for transportation and communication services to political candidates.

Businesses may legally make indirect contributions to political parties. Corporate officers and directors may take positions in political parties, often in connection with fund raising. While these officials function in an individual capacity, their corporate affiliations usually are known, and their activities can result in political goodwill for the firm, at least in the case of winning candidates. Moreover, corporations are rarely monolithic in the political sympathies of their individual executives, and frequently some members of management will actively support one candidate while others back the opponent. This is an important point to remember when business is accused of "undue" influence in the political sphere.

Corporations may advertise directly in convention and anniversary publications issued by political parties. Under current legislation, a company may deduct the cost of advertisements printed in national presidential convention programs if that cost is deemed reasonable in light of the business that the advertiser expects to gain. However, the Federal Election Commission in 1975 prohibited political parties from accepting services, such as free automobiles or buses, which business firms had customarily donated for use at national political conventions.

Members of Congress and state and local legislators, as well as candidates, may be invited to speak before trade associations, company management clubs, chamber of commerce groups, and similar business-oriented organizations. Their remuneration may range from merely having a convenient platform to present their views to generous honoraria. The 1974 election reform law set a limit of $1,000 (plus travel expense) for a speech, appearance, or article by a federal official, and an annual ceiling of $15,000 for each such individual. Once a government official becomes a candidate, the Federal Election Commission treats the honoraria as political contributions if the speech is made "before a substantial number of people within his (or her) electorate."

Any newspaper reader in recent years can readily recall numerous instances of flagrant abuse involving business and political campaigns — and attention to the less savory aspects of the subject is surely warranted. Nevertheless, it is useful to note the findings of Professor Epstein that even in politically active years, only about one out of five officers and directors of the very largest industrial firms, including government contractors, contribute to political parties. Since large manufacturing firms, particularly those strongly influenced by government decisions, have generally had higher rates of political contributions by their officials than other businesses, the 20-percent figure is probably a generous indicator of the financial participation of business as a whole.[7]

Epstein views aggregate corporate political participation as a continuum along which individual companies can be placed with regard to both the scope and the magnitude of their operations. Businesses in practice vary in their political efforts from, at one pole, no conscious participation by company executives, to an occasional letter or phone call to a member of Congress or a hundred-dollar campaign contribution to, finally, continuous and comprehensive government and electoral activity by political specialists on the company payroll.

Although most corporations engage in some form of participation in the political process, this activity varies substantially with a number of factors. These influences include the size of the firm, the degree of regulation of the enterprise by the government, and the

[7] Edwin M. Epstein, "Corporations and the Political Imperative," *Business and Society Review*, Summer 1972, pp. 54–67.

extent to which company business and well-being depend upon governmental decisions. As would be expected, the larger the firm and the greater the importance of government decisions to its operations, the greater is likely to be the scope and magnitude of its involvement in political activity.

OTHER POLITICAL CONTRIBUTIONS

The substantial contributions by other interest groups should not be ignored in any balanced treatment of the subject of political activity. In the fall of 1974 labor unions were reported to have contributed $333,300 to 141 members of Congress who supported a bill to require that eventually 30 percent of all oil imports be shipped in American vessels, staffed by union crews. The largest donation, $20,000, went to the senator who served as floor manager of the bill. President Ford subsequently vetoed the bill on the grounds that it would result in higher fuel bills and larger government subsidies to shipping.[8]

Much of labor's election effort does not show up in official reports, and hence is not subject to legal limitations. Examples include the virtual full-time assignment of union organizers and clerks to get-out-the-vote duty. In the 1976 national election campaign, more than 10 million calls were placed from COPE's telephone banks and 120,000 "volunteers" were involved in its car pools and doorbell ringing. Here is how Al Barkan, the director of COPE, evaluates the operation of this union-sponsored organization:

> On election day, we provide transportation to the polls for members needing it, babysitters, pollwatchers — probably more and better trained than in either political party. . . . As important as funding is in politics, however, COPE's strength is people . . . the thousands of volunteers who make the COPE program go and who provide the nuts-and-bolts support services that are so crucial to winning elections.[9]

In contrast, it is difficult to find companies or trade associations which assign their executives to full-time campaigning as part of

[8] "Unions Back Shipping Bill with $333,000," *St. Louis Post-Dispatch*, September 16, 1974, p. 2A. For other examples see Bryan E. Calame, "Unions and Politics," *Wall Street Journal*, January 29, 1974, p. 1 ff.
[9] H. H. Raskin, "The Labor Scene: COPE's Impact on Election Outcome," *The New York Times*, December 28, 1976, p. D1.; Al Barkan, "The Action Started Early: U.S. Workers Have a Long Political History," *Viewpoint*, First Quarter 1976, pp. 9–11.

their paid work or which devote their reports to shareholders and executives to the campaigning in which union publications openly engage.[10] Surely, there is nothing illegal in these union activities per se. But their widespread existence provides further encouragement for business to support the use of PACs as a counterweight.

Business executives need to understand, however, that, at least in the current environment, labor's political contributions do not receive the public attention that comparable business efforts do. A cogent contrast was provided by the case of Senator Harrison A. Williams of New Jersey, who was simultaneously chairman of the Committee on Labor and Public Welfare and chairman of the subcommittee of the Banking Committee that handles securities industry legislation. The $34,600 that members of the securities industry donated to the senator's reelection campaign in 1975 became the source of considerable public controversy in view of his key role with reference to a major bill regulating the securities industry. These relationships between the industry's contributions and Senator Williams were the subject of a 28-inch article in *The New York Times*. It is interesting to note that buried in the same article was a short reference to the fact that the senator's reelection campaign had also received $23,100 from labor groups. In the words of the reporter, "It is the securities industry donations, however, that have aroused controversy."[11]

The typical relationships of businesses to politics have been at times obscured by the series of reports of highly improper and often blatantly illegal business activities in the political sphere, especially in connection with the 1972 presidential campaign. The Minnesota Mining and Manufacturing Company, for example, admitted in early 1975 that it maintained an illegal political fund totalling $634,000. Five of its officers agreed to pay $475,000 to the firm to settle a shareholder suit involving illegal donations to the 1972 campaign of former President Nixon.[12]

In late 1974 the Northrop Corporation settled a class-action suit that had been filed after the disclosure that it had made $150,000 of illegal corporate contributions to the Nixon campaign. The chief executive officer of the company was required to relinquish the post of president and to repay the company for $50,000 of the improper

---

[10] "Few Corporations Have Exercised Their Right to Convey Political Opinions to Shareholders, Executives," *The New York Times*, November 1, 1976, p. C-33.

[11] Martin Tolchin, "Securities Industry Gave Senator Williams 25% of Election Fund," *The New York Times*, June 22, 1975, p. 42.

[12] 3M Firm Admits Keeping Slush Fund," *St. Louis Post-Dispatch*, January 2, 1975, p. 12D.

political gifts. This was in addition to a previous reimbursement of
$122,000 to cover legal fees and other expenses to the company.[13]

Several other companies were fined for their illegal contributions to the 1972 presidential campaign, including American Airlines,
Ashland Oil, Braniff, Goodyear, Greyhound, and Phillips Petroleum.
The Gulf Oil Corporation has admitted that it had made secret
political contributions of more than $10 million in the United States
and abroad during the period 1966–73, some of the expenditures
being demonstrably illegal. In many of the cases, senior management
has left the company or resigned from the boards of directors of
other corporations.

Business, quite properly, took it on the chin as these numerous
revelations of so-called political slush funds were uncovered. It is
altogether fitting that such lawbreaking be exposed and punished. As
pointed out earlier, corporate contributions to federal election campaigns are clearly illegal. In addition, setting up the illegal funds
often involved violating securities and income tax laws.

Yet there is another, usually ignored apsect of these illegal
business contributions to political causes. When we turn to more
traditional types of crime, we find that the progressive thinking is
not limited to punishing crime, but it extends to uncovering the
causes of crime. By identifying the conditions that breed crime, it
is hoped that public policy can be modified so as to reduce or eliminate those conditions — a preventative approach to lawbreaking.

The illegal contributions were usually a response, sometimes
reluctant, to the demands from the representatives of a powerful
government administration in the position to do great harm to the
company. Whether the government would abuse its vast power in
the absence of an adequate payment was a risk that many managements decided not to take. But is is not surprising that so many of
the executives who were implicated held positions in corporations
that are dependent upon government in important ways — firms that
hold large defense contracts, airlines that have government-approved
route structures, and companies that otherwise are either recipients
of special subsidies or subject to stringent federal regulation.

Those corporate executives — and indeed there were many —
who turned down the outrageous demands of the Nixon campaign
representatives were at the time exhibiting a special form of courage.
In retrospect, of course, their reaction turned out to be the course of

---

[13] "Northrop Tentatively Settles Class Action over Illegal Gifts to '72
Nixon Campaign," *Wall Street Journal,* November 21, 1974, p. 14. Subsequently,
investigation uncovered a pattern of Northrop contributions to foreign government officials in connection with the company's overseas sales.

wisdom as well as honor. On the other hand, however, it may not be too wide of the mark to consider at least some of those illegal corporate payments as a form of "protection" money given to prevent action harmful to the company. Viewed in this light, the precipitating reason for the lawbreaking can be seen as the tremendous and often arbitrary power that the society has given the federal government over the private sector.

Thus, the eradication of this particular form of white collar crime can be seen to involve more than the necessary tighter auditing standards and improved laws on political financing. It would also require abstaining from the further expansion of government power over the private sector, and instead embarking on efforts to reduce the arbitrary decision-making authority that many federal agencies now possess in their dealings with business firms.

Some of the attacks on business participation in the financing of election campaigns, although fully justified, may be too narrow from the viewpoint of developing appropriate public policy. For example, the practice of voluntary political contributions by individual executives to a company or industry fund was based on an earlier innovation in the political campaign financing process introduced by labor unions. Their membership often agree to "voluntary" checkoffs of contributions to political funds controlled by union officers.

The basic point should not be misunderstood. Lawbreaking, whether by business executives or others, should not be condoned. It should be ferreted out and punished according to law. Simultaneously, it is naive — and it may be ineffective as well — to ignore the basic forces that give rise to the lawbreaking. In the area of business contributions to the political process, much of the basic thrust seems to come from the awesome power that — through the political process — government has been given over business, power that ranges from awarding contracts and subsidies to withholding approval of new products and facilities.

In response to the public concern over improper corporate political activities, some companies have been adopting more open and at times rather severe policies on the subject of campaign contributions. DuPont, the nation's largest chemical firm, adopted in July 1975 a policy of publicly disclosing all United States political contributions by its top executives. In addition, all solicitations for more than $1,000 and responses to those requests are made public for inspection by reporters, shareholders, and employees. The largest oil company, Exxon, announced in 1976 that it was prohibiting all corporate contributions to political candidates or to political parties.

This policy extended to state and local and foreign elections where such political support by business is often entirely legal.

THE OUTLOOK

Despite the continued interest in full federal funding of national election campaigns, it is unlikely that Congress will eliminate all private contributions to political parties or to individual candidates for public office. The federal government, however, clearly is becoming a more important factor in election campaigns, and the Treasury is now a significant fund raiser for presidential candidates of the major parties.

Since 1972 each taxpayer has had the opportunity to check off on his or her individual income tax return a $1 contribution from the U.S. Treasury to the forthcoming presidential election campaign ($2 for married taxpayers filing jointly). Another effort to increase the role of small contributors to election campaigns — and thus to lessen the impact of major interest groups — is the tax treatment of private campaign contributions. Since 1972 each taxpayer has been permitted to deduct up to $50 of political contributions from his or her taxable income ($100 in the case of married taxpayers filing a joint return); or the taxpayer may credit half of such contributions against his or her tax liability, up to a maximum of $12.50 ($25 in the case of joint returns by married taxpayers). As these provisions become widely used and are augmented by direct appropriations from the U.S. Treasury, the dependence of political parties on large contributors will be reduced substantially.

Business executives, as well as the public, might well bear in mind Peter Drucker's thoughts on this subject: "If I were to have a

Table 17-3   Seminar on political campaign management

Program Outline	Program Outline
Research and surveys	Computers and automated devices
Planning strategy	Profile of a successful campaign
Fund raising, advertising, and publicity	Reaching special classifications:
Direct mail	Absentee ballots
Campaign organization	Campus votes
Volunteer activities	Rural votes
Graphics and photography	Votes in high-rise apartments
Campaign law	Print and electronic advertising

Source: Chamber of Commerce of the United States

criticism of the American businessman, it is that he has made no attempt to understand the political process. He attempts to influence it without understanding it."[14]

Some business organizations are attempting to meet Drucker's challenge. The U.S. Chamber of Commerce has been sponsoring a series of political campaign management seminars. Designed to be nonpartisan in nature, the seminars are aimed at business executives who may become involved in campaigns for public office at various levels — federal, state, and local. The sessions are aimed at potential candidates, campaign managers, finance chairmen, as well as rank-and-file volunteers. Staffed by professional campaign consultants, the seminars show the various steps in developing a campaign, including administrative and financial aspects. Table 17–3 reproduces the program outline of the chamber's political campaign management seminar. The sponsors stress that the sessions are devoted to techniques of political campaigning and avoid advocating positions on specific issues or supporting any candidates or political parties.

In 1976 the Chamber of Commerce sponsored the creation of Citizen's Choice, a national membership organization based roughly on Common Cause, the citizen's group established by John Gardner. Although it has not received the public recognition of Common Cause, Citizen's Choice has become increasingly active in informing its membership of over 36,000 of the details of current legislative issues facing American business. It operates in much the same way — with a monthly bulletin, a "hot line" toll-free telephone message, and "action alerts" to members.

In viewing the entire subject of participation in politics, a word of caution may be in order. One public affairs consultant maintains that the unwary management can get into "deep trouble" by a naive participation in funding election campaigns. For example, contributions to political action groups are required to be voluntary, without pressure on employees in solicitation. L. L. L. Golden fears that heavy-handed solicitation on the part of some firms could cause a backlash, both within the company and in the public arena. In any event there may be little to argue with in his point that politicians are not going to support a cause if they think voters are opposed to it.[15]

---

[14] "Inside Peter Drucker," *Nation's Business*, March 1974, p. 63.
[15] L. L. L. Golden, "A Dangerous Rush to Political Action," *Business Week*, September 25, 1978, p. 14.

18 ‖

reforming
government
regulation

A key area of public policy in which business can and does participate actively is the effort to reform government regulation. The advent of a professional literature on the costs and other measurable impacts of regulation of business has contributed to a growing concern in improving the effectiveness and reducing the burden of the vast network of rules, prohibitions, and requirements imposed on the private sector. Simultaneously, useful work is under way to subject regulatory action to formal analytical review—which provides further opportunity for improvement, or at least change.

THE COSTS OF COMPLIANCE

Table 18-1 contains the results of an initial effort to estimate the many costs arising from the regulations issued by federal government agencies. The figures include the expenditures incurred by the government and the larger costs by business in responding to regula-

Table 18-1   Annual cost of federal regulation, 1976 (millions of dollars)

Area	Administrative Cost	Compliance Cost	Total
Consumer safety and health	1,516	5,094	6,610
Job safety and working conditions	483	4,015	4,498
Energy and the environment	612	7,760	8,372
Financial regulation	104	1,118	1,222
Industry specific	484	19,919	20,403
Paperwork	—*	25,000	25,000
Total	3,199	62,906	66,105

*Included in other categories.
Source: Washington University, Center for the Study of American Business

tion. In the first category outlays include such government administrative costs as salaries of inspectors, office supplies, and the government's own paperwork flow—all of which is included in the federal budget. These are the expenses of writing, managing, publishing and policing regulations.

Compliance costs, the second category, are incurred mainly by the private sector (and also by some government agencies) in the process of meeting the mandates contained in government regulation. Unlike the administrative costs incurred by government, which are financed by taxes, compliance costs are paid largely through higher prices to consumers who purchase the goods and services affected by regulation. The basic approach followed in table 18-1 was to cull from the available literature the more reliable estimates of the costs of specific regulatory programs, put those estimates on a consistent basis, and aggregate the results for 1976.[1] Industry-specific regulations (such as those of the ICC, CAB, etc.) figure so prominently in part because of the wealth of data available on their activities. For many of the newer regulatory programs (notably consumer safety and energy) adequate information is not available for all categories and hence the numbers reported tend to be underestimates. As shown in earlier chapters, it is the newer, social regulation which has been growing most rapidly in recent years.

The total annual cost of federal regulation in 1976 was estimated at approximately $66 billion, consisting of $3 billion of taxpayer costs to operate the regulatory agencies and $63 billion (or

[1] Murray L. Weidenbaum and Robert DeFina, *The Cost of Federal Government Regulation of Economic Activity* (Washington, D.C.: American Enterprise Institute, 1978).

Table 18-2   Estimated cost of federal regulation of business (Fiscal years. In billions of dollars)

	1977	1978	1979	1980
Administrative costs	$ 4.1	$ 4.9	$ 5.8	$ 6.0
Compliance costs	82.0	98.0	116.0	120.0
Total	$86.1	$102.9	$121.8	$126.0

Source: Washington University, Center for the Study of American Business

twenty times as much) for business to comply with the regulations. Thus, on the average, each dollar that Congress appropriates for regulation tends to result in an additional $20 of costs imposed on the private sector of the economy.

If we apply the same multiplier of twenty (between the amounts budgeted for regulatory activities and the private cost of compliance) to the budget figures which are available for more recent years, we can come up with more current approximations of the private sector's cost of compliance (see table 18-2). On that basis, the costs arising from federal regulation of business in the United States (both the expenses of the regulatory agencies themselves as well as the costs they induce in the private sector) come to a total of $126 billion in 1980, or about $570 per capita.[2]

EFFORTS TO REFORM

The growing awareness of the high and rising costs of regulation has provided the impetus to the executive branch of the government to undertake some changes on its own. In November 1974 President Ford instituted a requirement whereby federal agencies prepare "inflation impact" statements prior to issuing new regulations.[3] With modifications, this requirement continues.[4] In January 1978 President Carter created a Regulatory Analysis Review Group (RARG), headed by the chairman of the Council of Economic Advisers, to review the economic impact of 10 to 20 of the major regulations which are forthcoming each year. The very knowledge

[2] Murray L. Weidenbaum, *The Cost of Government Regulation of Business*, Joint Economic Committee Print (Washington, D.C.: U.S. Government Printing Office, 1978); Kenneth Chilton, *A Decade of Rapid Growth in Federal Regulation* (St. Louis: Washington University, Center for the Study of American Business, 1979), pp. 1–3.

[3] Executive Order 11821, November 27, 1974.

[4] Executive Order 12044, March 24, 1978.

that a proposed regulation would be reviewed by RARG has increased the awareness of costs and other economic impacts on the part of the regulatory agencies. But the extent to which the review procedure actually has resulted in less costly regulation is difficult to judge.[5]

In October 1978 President Carter set up another body, a Regulatory Council, composed of the major regulatory agencies. This new group is charged with "coordinating" common regulatory approaches among agencies that have overlapping responsibilities. Its major output so far, however, has only been a calendar listing important proposed regulations, with varying amounts of factual material concerning them.

With great fanfare the Occupational Safety and Health Administration in 1978 dropped 928 minor safety rules (so-called "Mickey Mouse" regulations) governing, among other things, the size of toilet seats. Almost simultaneously, however, it promulgated a General Carcinogenic Proposal with far-reaching costs and consequences. In addition, the Environmental Protection Agency has made some moves to relax standards on urban smog; yet at the same time it has been gearing up to enforce the Clean Air Act Amendments of 1977 which, as described earlier, may constitute a major barrier to industrial expansion.

The forementioned reforms notwithstanding, the overall pace of regulation of business is continuing on an upward trajectory. As shown in Chapter 2, the number of agencies, regulatory programs, and authorizing statutes — and the budgets to carry them out — are all continuing to grow rapidly. Moreover, a very substantial further expansion of regulation is in the government pipeline. Many of the laws passed in recent years are in the early growth stages of development. Thus the data in Tables 18-1 and 18-2 do not reflect in any significant way the costs that will be incurred to meet the regulations which are being prepared under the Resource Conservation and Recovery Act of 1976, the Toxic Substances Control Act of 1976, and the 1977 amendments to the Water Pollution Control Act and the Clean Air Act.

Moreover, the ability of the executive branch to change the basic regulatory system is limited. Each regulation is issued in accordance with a law passed by the legislature and each regulatory agency is financed by appropriations and other authorizations also enacted by the legislature. Reform measures, therefore, cannot simply be "proclaimed," generally they must be legislated. John Quarles,

---

[5] Susan J. Tolchin, "Presidential Power and the Politics of RARG," *Regulation*, July-August 1979, pp. 44-49.

former deputy administrator of EPA, describes an effort by the head
of his agency to weed out unnecessary regulations:

> He found his hands were tied. Of approximately 125 regulations under
> development, all but a few were specifically required by a statute or by a
> court order interpreting a statute. Shortly after assuming office . . . EPA's
> current administrator, Douglas Costle, conducted a similar review — with
> the same results.[6]

Thus it is not surprising that the concern about the cost of regulation
has resulted in the introduction of over 150 bills on the subject in
Congress. These proposed laws cover a wide variety of approaches,
ranging from requiring economic impact statements for proposed
regulations to giving Congress a veto over individual agency rulings.
Several key alternatives, not necessarily mutually exclusive, have
received the bulk of the attention in legislative hearings to date:[7]

Economic Impact Statements

The Ford administration's institution of economic impact
statements for new regulations was an important and useful innovation which, with modifications, has been continued by the Carter
administration. But that approach has basic limitations. The so-called
"independent" regulatory commissions, such as the ICC (in contrast
to the cabinet departments and operating agencies), contend that
they are not subject to presidential review on regulatory matters.
Moreover, many regulatory agencies of both types (FDA and OSHA)
state that their legislative charters prohibit or limit the weight that
they can give to economic factors in their decision making. A general
law passed by Congress requiring each government agency to consider the economic impacts of its regulations prior to issuing them
might overcome such objections, and several variations have been
introduced.

Under a measure introduced in December 1977 by Representative Elliott Levitas (H.R. 10257), the government official responsible
for issuing a proposed rule also would be charged with preparing a
statement analyzing many of its impacts, including: (1) cost to con-

---

[6] John Quarles, "Runaway Regulation? Blame Congress," *Washington Post*,
May 20, 1979, p. B-8.
[7] See *Regulation and Regulatory Reform: A Survey of Proposals of the
95th Congress* (Washington, D.C.: American Enterprise Institute, 1978).

sumers and business; (2) effects on employment, productivity, competition, and supplies of important products; and (3) alternatives, including an explanation of why they were rejected. Such requirements for merely analyzing the impacts of regulation constitute the mildest reform approach. Benefit-cost tests represent a logical follow-through.

Benefit-Cost Analysis

Specifying the weight given to economic factors in agency decision making presents another opportunity for reform. After all, a reluctant agency can merely go through the motions of studying the effects of its actions on the economy and proceed as it originally intended. To deal with this concern, proposals have been introduced to require a formal benefit-cost analysis prior to the issuance of any new regulation. The general notion that a regulation should not be promulgated until it can be shown that it will generate more good (benefits) than harm (costs) is attractive.

Thus, regulation would be carried to the point where the added costs equal the added benefits, and no further. Overregulation (regulation for which the costs exceed the benefits) would be avoided. But the actual implementation involves difficult conceptual and measurement questions (see the following section of this chapter).

An agency not directly involved in regulation, such as the General Accounting Office or the Office of Management and Budget, probably should be chosen to set governmentwide standards for performing the analyses of proposed regulations. The standards for the analyses could cover such aspects as concepts and methods of performing economic evaluations of regulations, estimation of benefits and costs, and determination of the interest rates to be used in discounting future costs and benefits. In the absence of such standards, there is a natural tendency for a government agency (or any other organization) to be generous in estimating the good that it does and depreciating the magnitude of the resources required to achieve those results.

At the beginning of the Ninety-fifth Congress, Representative Samuel Devine introduced H.R. 351, which would have required the regulatory agencies to perform a comprehensive assessment of "reasonably foreseeable" costs and benefits, estimating the net public benefit and also examining "reasonable alternatives." The cost-benefit assessment required by this bill would have had to be comprehensive, considering effects that would be short-run or long-run, direct or indirect, and quantifiable or nonquantifiable.

A Regulatory Budget

The appropriations for the regulatory agencies are relatively small portions of the government's budgets — the totals for the 56 regulatory agencies in fiscal 1980 came to about 1 percent of the entire federal budget. As a result, limited attention is given to regulatory expenses during the budget preparation and review process. In fact, as shown in chapter 2, the budgets for regulation have, in the aggregate, been growing faster than the rest of the federal budget. One reform approach is to give each regulatory agency a "budget" of private costs that it can cause to be incurred by its regulations. Not only would an agency be given x million for operating costs, but also a ceiling of y billion of social costs that it can impose upon the nation during the same year. Thus, under the regulatory budget concept, Congress would be focusing on the *total* costs involved in the process of government regulation. Table 18-1, in effect, was a rudimentary effort in that direction.

In October 1978, Senator Lloyd Bentsen introduced S. 3550, a bill to establish a regulatory budget (a companion bill, H.R. 14370, was introduced by Representative Clarence Brown). Under the terms of this proposal, a budget for maximum allowable regulatory compliance costs in a given year would be prepared and submitted to Congress along with the regular budget. As part of the regulatory budget preparation process, each agency would submit to the President a report containing: (1) a proposed regulatory budget with justifications; (2) a breakdown of the previous year's compliance costs; and (3) an explanation for any costs which exceeded the previous year's budget.

A Legislative Veto ✓ *Supreme Ct. says it is unconst.*

One of the popular reactions at congressional hearings at which regulatory shortcomings are exposed is to urge Congress to give itself veto power over individual regulations. This mechanism, it is claimed, would curb the "excess zeal" of government regulators. The constitutionality of this approach has been questioned, insofar as it may violate the separation of powers. Nevertheless, the veto concept has been applied to at least 176 types of regulation.

A practical shortcoming may well prove fatal to the chances of enactment of the legislative veto as a general tool — the sheer inability of Congress and its committees to review the vast tide of regulations which are issued each year without ignoring its existing legislative duties. In a given year approximately 27,000 pages of new or revised regulations may be published in the *Federal Register*. Internal congressional decision making may be crucial, notably the selection of the committees having "oversight" jurisdiction over a given regulatory area. An excessively protective attitude may shield an agency from thorough review.[8]

A number of virtually identical bills carrying the title Administrative Rule Making Reform Act were introduced in the Ninety-fifth Congress to impose a legislative veto on agency rule making. The bills would have established the following procedure: After a new regulation was promulgated, it would become effective unless, within 90 days of continuous session of Congress, either the Senate or the House of Representatives passed a resolution of disapproval or reconsideration. The agencies would have 180 days to revise regulations after a reconsideration resolution was passed; otherwise the rules would lapse. A special category of emergency regulations addressed to "problems" of immediate importance" would be exempt from the veto but would expire after 210 days.

Sunset Laws

Many government programs tend to prolong their existence far beyond their initial need and justification. Under a "sunset" approach, each regulatory agency would be reviewed by Congress periodically to determine whether it is worthwhile to continue it in light of present circumstances. This procedure would provide Congress with a formal opportunity to revise the underlying regulatory statutes or to determine that a given agency is no longer needed and that the "sun" should be allowed to "set" on it. In the case of the older, one-industry regulatory agencies, such as the Interstate Commerce Commission, the sunset mechanisms might be an effective way of pursuing a deregulation approach.

The "sunset" approach is viewed by its proponents as an action-forcing mechanism, because the prospect of termination of an agency's charter (in the absence of congressional action) would force needed reviews of existing regulatory programs. However, as some skeptics note, the impact of this reform may be less than intended. The reviews may be perfunctory and the extension of popular regulatory legislation might even be the occasion for adding irrelevant or undesirable "riders" to the renewal statute.

The Ninety-fifth Congress held extensive hearings on S. 600, a

---

[8] Barry Weingast, *Congress and Regulation* (St. Louis: Washington University, Center for the Study of American Business, 1979).

sunset bill for regulatory agencies introduced by Senators Charles Percy, Robert Byrd, and Abraham Ribicoff. In 1978 part of S. 600 was added as an amendment to a general sunset bill introduced by Senator Edward Muskie (S. 2), which passed the Senate without any counterpart action in the House of Representatives.

Reducing Regulation

To date, none of the procedural reforms described in the foregoing discussion have been enacted by Congress. Perhaps the most significant single legislative action in the regulatory reform area in recent years was the law which cut back a single regulatory program, that administered by the Civil Aeronautics Board. The Airline Deregulation Act of 1978 (signed on October 24, 1978) phases out the regulation of the airline industry. By January 1, 1982, the Civil Aeronautics Board will lose its authority to make domestic airline route assignments and to certify airlines. On Januray 1, 1983, the CAB will no longer have authority over domestic air fares, mergers, acquisitions, and charters. Unless Congress changes its mind, the agency will go out of business on January 1, 1985. The initial reaction to airline deregulation has been a reduction in fares and increases in both passenger demand and airline profits.

The CAB experience has generated increased attention to the general notion of using alternatives to regulation for achieving public objectives. In the case of other traditional one-industry types of regulation of business (such as railroads, interstate trucking, and natural gas), a greater role might also be given to competition and to market forces. Professor Stephen Breyer of the Harvard Law School reminds us that "unregulated" markets are subject to the antitrust laws, a form of government intervention designed to maintain a workably competitive marketplace. Antitrust enforcement is a form of government regulation but unlike other regulation, it seeks to achieve the conditions of a competitive market, rather than attempt to correct its defects.[9]

In the area of consumer safety, as we have seen in Chapter 4, a greater provision of information on potential hazards may often be more effective than banning specific products or setting standards requiring expensive alterations in existing products. The information approach takes account of the great variety of consumer desires and capabilities. More widespread dissemination of data on product-

[9] Stephen Breyer, "Analyzing Regulatory Failure," *Harvard Law Review,* January 1979, p. 578.

associated accidents, for example, might encourage business firms to devote more attention to safety in the design of the goods that they sell.

Although mandatory disclosure is a form of regulation, it may be viewed at least in part as a preferable alternative mechanism because it neither interferes with the production process nor restricts individual choice. Moreover, the greater flow of information may be seen as an effort to achieve a more competitive economy. However, as noted in earlier chapters, when the government sets the standards for information rather than relying on competitive forces, many inefficiencies can result, such as overloading the consumer with unusable details.

Through its taxing authority, government can send strong signals to the market. Pollution control taxation may indeed provide a more effective and less costly mechanism than the existing standards approach in achieving desired ecological objectives. As noted in chapter 6, such taxes, by increasing the prices of highly polluting means of production and consumption, could encourage shifts to ecologically sound production and consumption patterns. The basic approach, hence, would be to reduce the incentive to pollute — on the assumption that people and companies alike pollute when it is easier or cheaper to do so. (Initial experiments along these lines are being conducted by the Los Angeles Air Pollution Control District.) Price incentives tend to force the environmental agencies to consider explicitly the cost of cleaning up pollution, while direct controls make it very easy to adopt extremely expensive if not unrealistic goals (such as zero pollution).

Thus, fees for discharging effluents into bodies of water would encourage the most extensive efforts to improve pollution abatement by those who can do so at relatively low cost and who would thereby avoid paying the fees. Less antipollution efforts would be made by those for whom the costs of reducing pollution would be greater than the required fees. Standards, in contrast, do not make such distinctions. By virtue of their "uniformity," standards result in higher costs in attaining the same total environmental cleanup. So perhaps the greatest virtue of pollution taxation, in lieu of rigid standards, is the ability to provide incentives for behaving in a socially desirable fashion without freezing technology or eliminating individual choice. Incentives using the price system always reward additional reductions in pollution. The less the firm discharges, the lower its tax bill. This continuing incentive to find more effective ways to reduce pollution is absent once a company meets the detailed standards in the conventional approach.

Yet another alternative to detailed regulation is to rely on the courts more heavily for handling individual claims. In such cases as product hazards, job accidents, and environmental pollution (where risks may not be well known), scholars have suggested changes in tort law that would encourage the production of safer products or the greater use of pollution-free processes. The notion behind these proposals is to increase the risk of liability, and thus the cost, for those firms which can most readily reduce the risk of accidents or the level of pollution.[10] However, the costs of using the courts can be high and the deterrent effect may not be sufficiently great in the case of some hazards to obviate the need for standards or other regulatory approaches.

Clearly, there are many ways of responding to the concerns which give rise to government regulation of business. Given the great variety of areas subject to regulation and the multiplicity of regulatory devices that are used, it is unlikely that any single set of reforms will eliminate the shortcomings that are present in the status quo. There does, surely, seem to be a useful role for more formal analysis of regulatory impacts to provide at least an ancillary guide to policymakers in this area. The following section presents an introduction to such economic analyses.

BENEFIT-COST ANALYSIS

The motive for incorporating benefit-cost analysis into public decision making is to lead to a more efficient allocation of government resources by subjecting the public sector to the same type of quantitative constraints as those in the private sector. In making an investment decision, for example, business executives compare the total costs to be incurred with the total revenues expected to accrue. If the expected costs exceed the revenues, the investment is usually not considered worthwhile. To be sure, capital constraints require a further sorting to determine the most financial attractive investments.

The government agency decision maker, however, usually does not face such constraints. If the costs to society of an action by an agency exceed the benefits, that situation has no immediate adverse impact on the agency, as would be the case if the private business executive makes a decision error. In fact, such analytical information rarely exists in the public sector so that, more often than not, the government decision maker is not aware that he or she is approving a

---

[10] Ibid., p. 583.

regulation that is economically inefficient. In requiring agencies to perform benefit-cost analysis, the aim is to make the government's decision-making process more effective, presumably eliminating those regulatory actions whose net benefits are negative. This result is not ensured by benefit-cost analysis, since political and other important but nonquantifiable considerations may dominate and result in actions which are not economically efficient, but which are desired on grounds of equity or income distribution. Yet benefit-cost analysis can provide valuable information for government decision makers.[11] (See appendix to this chapter for a case study.)

The Economic Rationale

It may be useful to consider briefly the economic rationale for making benefit-cost analyses of government actions. Economists have long been interested in identifying policies that promote economic welfare, specifically by improving the efficiency with which a society uses its resources. This assumes, of course, that an increase in economic welfare will raise total welfare, and ignores some theoretical problems such as making interpersonal utility comparisons.

Benefits are measured in terms of the increased production of goods and services. Costs are computed in terms of the foregone benefits that would have been obtained by using those resources in some other activity. The underlying aim of benefit-cost analysis, therefore, is to maximize the real value of the social income (GNP). For many years, benefit-cost analysis has been applied by certain federal agencies (such as the Corps of Engineers and the Bureau of Reclamation) to the evaluation of prospective projects. Despite important operational difficulties, including that of choosing an appropriate discount rate which would correspond to a realistic estimate of the social cost of capital, these analyses have helped to improve the allocation of government resources. They have served as a partial screening device to eliminate obviously uneconomical projects — those for which prospective gains are less than estimated costs. The analyses also has provided some basis for ranking and comparing projects and choosing among alternatives. Perhaps the over-riding value has been in demonstrating the importance of making relatively objective economic evaluations of essentially political

[11] See Peter G. Sassone and William A. Schaffer, *Cost-Benefit Analysis: A Handbook* (New York: Academic Press, 1978); E. J. Mishan, *Cost-Benefit Analysis* (New York: Praeger Publishers, 1976).

actions and perhaps narrowing the area in which political forces dominate.[12] Thus, if economically inefficient programs are adopted, at least government decision makers know the price that is being paid for those actions.

Benefit-Cost Analysis Regulation

Figure 18-1 shows the basic relationship of costs and benefits that tends to hold over most varieties of regulatory programs. Typically, the initial regulatory effort — such as cleaning up the worst of the pollution in a river — may well generate an excess of benefits over costs. But the resources required to achieve additional cleanup become disproportionately high, and at some point the added benefits may be substantially less than the added costs. For example, a study of the impact of environmental controls on the fruit and vegetable processing industry revealed that it costs less to eliminate the first 85 percent of the pollution created than the next 10 percent.[13] Similarly, in beet sugar plants, it costs less than $1 a pound to reduce BOD — a measure of the oxygen required to decompose organic wastes — up to 30 percent. But it costs an additional $20 for a one-pound reduction at the 65-percent control level and an added $60 for a one-pound reduction when over 95-percent control is achieved.[14]

A more aggregate comparison is equally telling. The pulp and paper industry spent $3 billion between 1970 and 1978 complying with federal clean water standards, and achieved a 95-percent reduction in pollution. But to reach the new reduction goal proposed by EPA — 98 percent by 1984 — would cost a further $4.8 billion, a 160-percent increase in costs to achieve a 3-percent improvement in water quality. Thus, it is important to look beyond the mere relationship of the total costs and the total benefits of a proposed government undertaking to the additional (marginal) benefits and costs that would result from each extension or addition to the government activities in a given field.

---

[12] Murray L. Weidenbaum, "Program Budgeting — Applying Economic Analysis to Government Expenditure Decisions," in *Planning, Programming, Budgeting*, ed. Fremont J. Lyden and Ernest G. Miller (Chicago: Markham Publishing, 1967), pp. 165–80.

[13] U.S., Congress, Joint Economic Committee, *The Economic Impact of Environmental Regulations* (Washington, D.C.: U.S. Government Printing Office, 1974), p. 203.

[14] *Environmental Quality, Second Annual Report of the Council on Environmental Quality* (Washington, D.C.: U.S. Government Printing Office, 1971), p. 118.

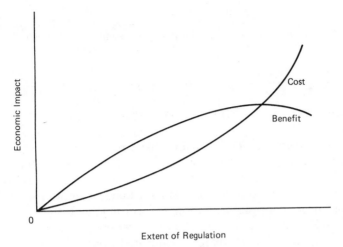

Figure 18-1   BENEFIT-COST ANALYSIS REGULATION

Ultimately, if the regulatory power goes unchecked, the result could tend to be an excess of total costs over total benefits. Thus, performing benefit-cost analyses may be helpful in identifying the optimum amount of regulation, rather than merely being a tool for debating the general pros and cons of regulation.

When there is more than one alternative for attaining a regulatory goal, benefit-cost analysis also can be used to compare the various methods and help to choose the most attractive. Consider the following hypothetical example: Suppose a government agency wishes to control the amount of pollutants a factory is spilling into a river. Assume present technology allows for two possible means of reducing the pollution, System A and System B, of which System B is costlier but more effective (see table 18-3).

System B, in this simple example, has greater benefits per dollar spent than System A. Despite the fact that System B has a larger total annual cost than System A, we see that System B will yield the larger annual net benefit to society. In the creation of government policy, such simple cases are not frequently encountered. Indeed, the process becomes considerably more complicated.

If a business decision in the private sector places an external burden, such as pollution, on its neighbors, the individual firm does not include such a cost in its accounting, since it does not bear the burden. Public sector decision makers, however, must or at least ought to consider the effects of a decision on the entire society. Unlike their private sector counterparts, regulators should attempt to

Table 18-3   Applying benefit-cost analysis

System	Total Annual Cost	Total Annual Benefit	Benefit-Cost Ratio
A	$ 14,000	$ 17,500	1.25
B	26,000	34,000	1.31

include all costs and benefits, including those external to the government itself.

The agencies should do so because any regulatory action will have indirect effects on the economy. Requiring safety belts in automobiles has direct impacts on the cost of automobiles and on the safety belt industry. But it will also influence the number of accidents and have a ripple effect on the suppliers of the safety belt industry and their suppliers, and so on. At some point in the benefit-cost analysis, good judgment must be relied upon in deciding which indirect effects are important and which are not.

Quantification

In general terms, the benefits and costs attributable to regulation are measured by the difference between the benefits and costs that occur in the presence of regulation and those that would prevail in its absence. Although the basic idea may seem to be quite straightforward, its application can be complex. Determining what would occur in the absence of regulation — which establishes a benchmark or reference point for the calculations — may involve a considerable amount of judgment.

Table 18-4 shows how the incremental costs (the expenses that would not have been made in the absence of regulation) were computed in one study of water pollution control.[15] It is interesting to note that the bulk of the costs apparently would have been undertaken voluntarily.

Sometimes the indirect effects of regulation may be as important as the direct. Consider, for example, the question of mandatory standards to ensure the production of less hazardous consumer products. Suggestions have been made from time to time to require more protection in helmets and other recreational equipment used in playing football. Those using the safer helmets would be expected to receive the benefits of fewer or less severe injuries. However, such a safety standard could impose substantial costs on lower-income

[15] Michael E. Simon, "The Business Roundtable Study; What We Did," *Regulation*, July–August 1979, p. 21.

Table 18-4 Calculation of incremental cost of regulation

Steps	Example
Company identifies an action taken to comply with a specific regulation.	Installation of waste-water pretreatment system to remove 99% of pollutants in compliance with Title 40 *CFR*, Chapter 1, Part 128.
Would action have been taken otherwise?	Pretreatment system without Title 40 would have been designed to remove 95% of pollutants.
What was the cost of the action?	$1,200,000 (from fixed-asset ledger data).
How much would the action that would have been taken in the absence of regulation have cost?	$800,000 (the cost of installing a 95% system).
What was the incremental cost?	$1,200,000 - $800,000 = $400,000.

Source: Arthur Andersen & Company

youngsters. Perhaps of greater concern, the standards might even contribute to more injuries if the price increases result in more youngsters playing football without any protective equipment at all. This example illustrates another basic thrust of benefit-cost analysis — to view the proposed government action not from the viewpoint of the initial impact on the business firm but from the vantage point of the ultimate effects on the consumer.

A large but difficult to measure type of regulatory costs is a grouping that economists refer to as "deadweight losses." As shown in earlier chapters, regulation often limits the range of permissible prices, practices, or processes; those legal restrictions inhibit the most productive use of resources. The loss of the higher output, output that would have resulted in the absence of the regulatory activity — those "deadweight losses" — arises from producing an inefficient combination of output as well as producing goods and services with an inefficient mix of inputs. For example, if regulated shipping rates result in freight moving by railroad that could have been hauled at lower real cost by truck, the total efficiency of the economy is reduced.[16]

When it is not appropriate or practical to put a dollar sign on the benefits, the analyst can utilize a cost-effectiveness approach. This methodology, which was originally developed for military programs, estimates the dollar cost of a variety of alternative ways of accomplishing a given objective. Cost-effectiveness analyses permit policymakers to identify least-cost solutions. In this more limited

[16] Marvin H. Kosters, "Counting the Costs," *Regulation*, July–August 1979, p. 24.

approach, the analyst takes the objective as something worth accomplishing in the first place. In the regulatory field this approach may be most useful in dealing with programs to reduce personal hazards. Rather than dealing with such imponderables as the cost or value of a human life, the emphasis shifts to identifying those regulatory approaches that will maximize the lives saved or pain avoided from a given use of resources. Rather than a green eyeshade approach, such attempts at objective analysis, it is contended, show true compassion for our fellow human beings by making the most effective use of the limited resources that are available to society.[17]

Discounting

A regulatory action today has an impact not only in the present but also in the future. It is necessary, therefore, to value future costs and benefits less than costs and benefits immediately available — the basic notion being that a dollar today is worth more than a dollar tomorrow. For this reason, we discount the value of future benefits and costs; that is, we modify their monetary value so that they have less weight in our current decision than presently received benefits and costs.

This practice is important in evaluating regulatory actions. If the total costs and benefits of two actions appear equal, yet for one of the actions most of the benefits occur at the end of five years, as opposed to immediate benefits for the other action (with the equal costs occurring currently), then the preferred alternative is the one whose benefits occur immediately. We value this action more because the value of a benefit occurring in five years is less than the value of the same benefit today. Discounting of the future thus implies that the timing of any action's costs and benefits is crucial in its evaluation.

Assuming we are able to quantify all the costs and benefits in a given instance, it is then necessary to correctly discount the net benefits accruing in future periods. The correct discount rate (r) can be crucial, as is clear in the highly simplified, two-period example shown in Table 18–5.

If all costs accrue in Period 1 and the discount rate is 10 percent, then clearly Plan A is superior to Plan B. However, if the correct discount rate is 5 percent not 10 percent, then Plan B is preferable. The appropriate discount rate is obviously very important in benefit-cost analysis. Such analyses can be biased, however, if congress or an agency designates an unrealistically low interest rate.

[17]James C. Miller III and Bruce Yandle, *Benefit-Cost Analyses of Social Regulation* (Washington, D.C.: American Enterprise Institute, 1979), p. 4.

Table 18-5   The role of interest rates

Plan	Benefit Period 1	Benefit Period 2	Cost Period 1	Discounted Benefit in Period 1 $r = 10\%$	$r = 5\%$
A	$200	0	$100	$200	$200
B	0	$215	$100	$195	$205

Uses and Limitations of Benefit-Cost Analysis

Reliable measures of costs and benefits are not easily achieved. Quantification is not always possible. Should the loss of a forest area be quantified by the value of the timber eliminated? What of the beauty destroyed? What of the area's value as a wildlife habitat? Given such questions, it is unlikely that agency decision makers will be faced with simple choices.

The quantification problem is further complicated by a lack of information. The adverse impact of some products on health is often uncertain. Asbestos, for instance, has only recently been found to be a cancer-causing agent, and the extent of the damage caused by use of this material is at this time not discernible. It is often the case that both total costs and total benefits will contain some nonquantifiable variables, leaving much opportunity for political value judgments and determinations.

It should be noted, however, that the difficulties involved in estimating the benefits or the costs of regulatory actions need not necessarily serve as a deterrent to pursuing the analysis. Merely identifying some of the important and often overlooked impacts may be useful. Examples on the cost side include the beneficial drugs that are not available because of regulatory obstacles, the freight not carried because empty trucks are not permitted to carry backhauls, and the television stations that are not broadcasting because they could not be licensed. On the benefit side, examples range from the more productive work force that results from a lower rate of accidents on the job to savings in medical care as a result of the safer products and healthier environment achieved from compliance with the regulatory efforts.[18]

At times the imperfections of benefit-cost analysis may seem substantial. Nevertheless, this type of analysis can add some objectivity to the government's decision-making process. While benefit-cost analysis is capable only of representing efficiency considerations, the subsequent decisions of elected officials and their appointees

[18] See A. Myrick Freeman III, *The Benefits of Environmental Improvement* (Baltimore: Johns Hopkins University Press, 1979).

Table 18-6   Attributes of regulations with high incremental cost

Type of Regulation	Characteristics
1. Continuous monitoring	Requires evidence of compliance by means of round-the-clock monitoring devices or continuous maintenance of comprehensive records of actions taken and results achieved.
2. Forcing new technology	Requirements to meet a level of compliance not achievable with available technology, often effected through legislation specifying a stringent deadline.
3. Capital intensity	Requires the purchase of new equipment or modification of existing equipment.
4. Recurring costs	Requires actions which lead to continuing costs of operation or maintenance.
5. Retrofitting	Requires modification of existing facilities, not just application to new facilities.
6. Specified compliance action	Requires a specified method of compliance without flexibility to recognize differing circumstances for application of alternate techniques to achieve the desired objective.
7. Inadequate risk assessment	Requires compliance with a stringent standard even though the risks have not been adequately assessed.
8. Engineering solutions	Requires the elimination of a hazardous substance or condition by engineering methods rather than specific mechanical protection of endangered workers or others.
9. Changing requirements	Requires adaptation to rules which are frequently changed or are subject to delay in being defined; capital spending plans are made without knowledge of requirements to be met.

Source: Arthur Andersen & Company

might be envisioned as representing society's evaluations of the equity effects of regulatory actions. Economists can provide these decision makers with information via benefit-cost analysis and analysis of the distributional impact of regulations, leaving the final decision to society's representatives. These individuals are better able to make objective decisions with such information on the impacts of the actions they contemplate. Despite its shortcomings, benefit-cost analysis is a neutral concept, giving equal weight to a dollar of benefits as to a dollar of costs.

A useful by-product of such analyses may be the identification of less costly ways of achieving society's regulatory objectives. For example, detailed estimates of industrial compliance with federal regulation, produced by Arthur Andersen & Company for the Business Roundtable, revealed the types of regulation that tend to generate especially high costs (see table 18-6). Such information may help government policymakers to select less costly approaches.

In the final analysis, however, the political factors in regulatory decision making cannot be ignored. As pointed out by Robert Crandall of the Brookings Institution, most social regulation involves a transfer of economic resources from a large number of people to a small group of beneficiaries. OSHA's coke oven standard, for example, protects fewer than 30,000 workers but is paid for by everyone who buys a product containing steel. Crandall warns that so long as regulators avoid concentrating the costs on a small group that could organize political counterpressures, excessively costly regulations can easily be promulgated.[19]

APPENDIX: BENEFIT-COST ANALYSIS OF TRAFFIC SAFETY STANDARDS*

Congressional concern over the increasing number of motor vehicle deaths led to the enactment of the National Traffic and Motor Vehicle Safety Act of 1966, whose purpose was to reduce motor vehicle accidents and the deaths and injuries resulting from them.

As one means of reducing these deaths and injuries, the act directed the Department of Transportation to establish motor vehicle safety standards. The National Highway Traffic Safety Administration does such work for the Transportation Department. The act required that the standards be reasonable, practicable, and appropriate for the particular type of motor vehicle or item of equipment to which they applied.

In reporting on the proposed legislation that became law, both the Senate Commerce Committee and the House Committee on Interstate and Foreign Commerce stated that safety was to be the overriding consideration in issuing a standard. Both committees

[19] Robert W. Crandall, "Curbing the Costs of Social Regulation," *The Brookings Bulletin*, Winter 1979, p. 2.

*The material in this section is based on U.S., Comptroller General, *Need to Improve Benefit-Cost Analyses in Setting Motor Vehicle Safety Standards*, B-164497(3) (Washington, D.C.: U.S. General Accounting Office, 1974), nn. 1-14.

pointed out, however, that the motoring public's cost to purchase and maintain safety equipment required by a standard also should be considered. In this regard, the Senate Committee said that, in addition to the technical feasibility of the standard and adequate lead time for the industry to develop and produce safety equipment, reasonableness of equipment cost should be considered. The House Committee said that all relevant, including economic, factors should be considered in determining practicality of a standard.

Benefit-Cost Analyses

The National Highway Traffic Safety Administration uses benefit-cost analyses primarily to establish an internal order of priorities among all safety standards. The analyses are considered in evaluating the merits of a proposed safety standard, along with technical feasibility; legislative mandates; congressional, public, and industry views; and legal considerations.

A benefit-cost analysis of a safety standard involves estimating, in dollars, the benefits from establishing the standard and the consumer costs to comply with the standard. Comparing these totals, usually by dividing dollar benefits by dollar costs, gives a benefit-cost ratio. A ratio greater than 1 indicates that the estimated dollar benefits from establishing a safety standard exceed the estimated cost to comply with the standard. The Safety Administration measures benefits by estimating how much accidents, fatalities, injuries, and property damage cost society and by evaluating a standard's effectiveness in reducing such costs. Costs to comply with the standard include the consumer's cost for the safety equipment.

Comparisons of Estimated Costs of Motor Vehicle Accidents

The U.S. Safety Administration and the private National Safety Council estimated the annual costs of motor vehicle accidents. The Safety Administration's estimates were for use in benefit-cost analyses, and the Council's estimates were for use by state highway officials in requesting appropriations and by research workers and others in the field of safety. The estimates shown in the following table vary widely because of differences in base years, data sources, statistical bases, assumptions, and calculations of future costs.

The Safety Administration and the Safety Council estimates are given in present-value terms. Under this method, the current value of future costs is calculated by using a discount rate. Discount-

Estimated costs of motor vehicle accidents in 1971 (in millions)

Type of Cost	Safety Administration	Safety Council
Costs estimated by both:		
Future earnings lost	$18,100	$ 3,700
Medical costs	1,950	1,100
Property damage	7,100	5,000
Insurance administration	6,600	6,000
Total	33,750	15,800
Costs estimated only by Safety Administration:		
Home and family	4,500	—
Pain and suffering	3,800	—
Legal and court costs	1,050	—
Service to community	900	—
Time and money losses to others	800	—
Miscellaneous losses	800	—
Asset losses	300	—
Employer losses	50	—
Funeral costs	50	—
Total	12,250	—
Total costs	$46,000	$15,800

	Safety Administration		Safety Council
		(In billions)	
Fatalities	$ 7.3		$ 2.4
Injuries	10.8		1.3
Total	$18.1		$ 3.7

ing future costs makes them comparable to present costs, that is, the present value of costs. The higher the discount rate used, the lower the value that is placed on future costs. The Safety Administration used a 7-percent discount rate and the Safety Council used a 3.5-percent discount rate.

The Safety Administration measured all costs that directly or indirectly caused a reduction in society's total welfare. It pointed out that each vehicle accident diminished individual and societal welfare. The Safety Administration contended that society's welfare was considerably greater than its economic well-being and that money could be used only as a proxy measure for estimating changes in welfare. It further contended that, although the severe shortcomings of measuring welfare in terms of money were obvious, there was no better standard of value useful for public policy decision. Accordingly, the agency attempted to measure and translate identifiable inconvenience and hardship associated with motor vehicle accidents, such as pain and suffering, inability to perform home and family duties, loss of service to community, and similar types of costs, into dollar-and-cent equivalents.

The Safety Council, in contrast, tried to measure economic costs in what it considered to be the real dollars lost as a result of motor vehicle accidents. Inconvenience and hardship costs were not included in its estimates because it believed that such costs, although very important to the individual who suffered as a result of an accident, did not represent a cost to the rest of society.

Costs Estimated by Both Groups

Costs estimated by all future earnings lost. The main reasons for the different estimates of earnings lost were the differences in statistical bases, assumptions, and computations used in estimating average annual earnings lost and the number of injuries.

The Safety Administration estimated that $132,000 in average lifetime earnings would be lost for each of 55,000 traffic fatalities. The estimate was based on assuming that, in the absence of an accident a person would be productively employed between the ages of 20 and 65 and would earn $9,196 annually at the time of death.

The computation assumed that a child who died in an accident otherwise would have entered the work force at age 20 and remained productively employed for 45 years and that an adult who died in an accident otherwise would have remained productive for an average 20 more years. The Safety Administration separately determined the earnings lost for children and for adults and computed a weighted average wage loss, using the ratio of child to adult fatalities. It based its estimate on gross earnings, adjusted for annual income growth, because it contended that, if a potential accident victim was prevented from dying as a result of some safety investment, society's benefit was equal to the full amount of the person's earnings. In comparison, the Council used net earnings — earnings less the cost of self-maintenance — on the assumption that loss to the family of the deceased more properly measured the economic loss resulting from a traffic fatality.

It estimated that average lifetime earnings of $44,000 would be lost for each of 54,700 traffic fatalities. The Council grouped people by sex, race, and age, and for each group determined motor vehicle fatality rates and net earnings lost, considering annual income growth, unemployment, and mortality rates.

A major cause of variation in the estimate of earnings lost was the difference in estimates of the numbers of injuries and average earnings lost. The Safety Administration estimated that about 3.8 million people suffering injuries of varying severity would lose earnings of about $10.8 billion. It based its estimate of total injuries on a 1969 National Health Survey adjusted to 1971. Its estimates of the severity of injuries — 8,000 persons permanently, totally disabled; 250,000 persons permanently partially disabled; and 3,545,000 persons temporarily disabled — were derived from an analysis of a 1970 Department of Transportation study on the automobile personal injury claims. Calculations of average income lost were made under the assumptions established for estimating income lost in fatality cases and were adjusted for the degree of severity of the injuries.

The Safety Council estimated that persons suffering injuries of varying severity would lose about $1.3 billion in earnings. It assumed one-half as many injuries as the Safety Administration used. This difference is attributable to the fact that the Safety Administration included all individuals who have had to restrict their activities or receive medical attention because of injury, whereas the Council did not include less seriously injured individuals in its estimates.

Medical costs. Major differences in the estimates of medical costs resulted primarily from differences in the Safety Administration's and the Safety Council's estimates of average medical costs for the several classifications of injury severity. The Safety Administration used the same number of fatalities and injuries for estimating medical costs that it had developed for estimating earnings lost. It based its estimates of average costs on a Department of Transportation study on automobile insurance and compensation and on a medical cost study prepared by the Social Security Administration. The average costs ranged from $315 for each of an estimated 3,545,000 persons experiencing temporary disability to $7,900 for each of 8,000 persons suffering permanent, total disability.

The Council's estimate of average medical cost was based on National Center for Health Statistics data and information from state accident reports, social security bulletins, and the *American Hospital Journal*. The average costs ranged from $8 for each person experiencing a nondisabling injury to a high of $1,090 for each person suffering a disabling injury requiring hospitalization.

Property damage. Differences in the estimates of property damage appear primarily attributable to differences in sources used by the two organizations. The Safety Administration's estimate was partly based on accident cost studies made for Illinois, Ohio, and Washington, D.C. The Council's estimate was based on the consumer price index for auto repairs and maintenance and on data made available by insurance companies.

The Safety Council defined insurance administration costs as the difference between premiums paid to insurance companies and claims paid by them. Insurance claims paid were included in the estimates of earnings lost, medical and hospital expenses, and property damage. Thus, on the assumption that in the absence of accidents there would be no need for automobile insurance, the inclusion of insurance administration costs has the effect of including all automobile insurance costs in the estimate of automobile accident loss. Insurance administration costs were estimated at $6 billion.

The Safety Administration also included insurance administration expenses as a cost of automobile accidents, although it recognized that there was a problem in trying to determine the extent to which the expenses could be reduced if the number of accidents decreased. It used the Council's data but made several errors in distributing the factor among the various levels of accident severity — fatality, permanent total disability, and so on. As a result, its estimate was $600 million greater. The Safety Administration is now using revised data.

Costs Estimated Only by the Safety Administration

Unlike the National Safety Council, the Safety Administration included in its estimate about $12.3 billion that is associated with the inconvenience and hardships of automobile accidents.

Home and family duties. The Safety Administration decided that certain nonemployment-related activities, such as housekeeping and home and yard maintenance, contribute to individual and societal welfare, although they are not represented in the gross national product. It assumed that the average person involved in an accident spent about one-fourth of his or her working hours, or ten hours a week, on home-related productive actitivies. The Safety Administration placed a value on inability to perform home and family duties equal to about a quarter of the amount computed for income lost. The average losses computed ranged from $50 for each of 3.5 million persons experiencing temporary disability to $35,000 for each of 8,000 persons suffering permanent, total disability. The overall loss was estimated at $4.5 billion.

Pain and suffering. The Safety Administration also decided that society's welfare decreased because of pain and suffering incurred by the victim of a traffic accident, regardless of whether the victim or his or her estate was compensated. On the basis of reviewing a number of court awards for pain and suffering, the Safety Administration computed average amounts for accident victims suffering injuries of varying degrees of severity. These amounts ranged from $100 for each of 3.5 million persons experiencing temporary disability to $50,000 for each of 8,000 persons suffering permanent, total disability. Overall, the Safety Administration estimated the loss associated with pain and suffering at $3.8 billion.

Other estimated costs. The Safety Administration placed dollar values on some additional categories of costs, such as legal and court costs, loss of service to the community, time and money losses to others, and miscellaneous losses, which in total amounted to about $4 billion. Legal and court costs were based on a study by the Travelers Research Corporation, which showed that police and court costs associated with accidents amounted to about $900 million, and was based on the Safety Administration's estimate that the average person spends about two hours a week for volunteer work in the community.

Time and money losses to others were estimated at about $800 million on the basis that the family and friends of accident victims suffered large noncompensated time and money losses. The estimate included travel costs to visit accident victims and attend funerals, costs of time spent visiting and attending funerals, and costs of time spent by members of the family attending accident victims.

Significance of Different Estimating Methods

Estimated costs of motor vehicle accidents form the basis for determining the benefit to be derived from a proposed safety standard. Therefore, reasonable cost estimates must be used to show fairly whether a proposed safety standard is cost effective. As we saw, the specific estimates of the Safety Administration and the Safety Council varied widely. The resulting differences for each motor vehicle accident, fatality, injury, or property damage are shown in the following table:

	Average Cost	
	Safety Administration	Safety Council
Typical accident	$ 2,800	$ 960
Typical fatality	200,700	52,000
Typical injury	7,300	3,100
Typical property damage	300	440

For most categories, the federal agency's cost estimates are substantially higher than those of the private organization. The effect of these differences can be seen from the benefit-cost ratios obtained when the Council's average costs for a fatality and injury are substituted for the costs used by the Safety Administration in its benefit-cost analyses for two standards. In the case of the windshield standard, the benefit-cost ratio is reduced substantially but still is extremely favorable. But in the case of the bus standard, substituting the Safety Council's numbers converts a favorable benefit-cost ratio to an unfavorable one.

	Benefit-Cost Ratio	
Standard	Safety Administration	Safety Council
Windshield zone intrusion	16.0	6.0
Bus passenger seating and crash protection	2.22	.88

Uncertainty in Estimating Effectiveness of Proposed Safety Standards

The potential effectiveness of a proposed motor vehicle standard is measured by the reduction in fatalities, injuries, and/or accidents that can be expected to result directly from its implementation. The estimate of effectiveness is an integral part of the benefit-cost analysis, because, multiplied by the Safety Administration's average estimated costs of fatalities, injuries, or accidents, it represents the anticipated benefit. For example, if a proposed standard were expected to reduce accidents by 400,000 annually, the estimated benefit would amount to about $1.1 billion (400,000 accidents times the estimated average accident cost of $2,800).

The effectiveness of a proposed standard can be estimated best by using analyses of accident data showing how the vehicle contributed to an accident, injury, or fatality. The Safety Administration spends about $6 million a year to collect accident data and make analyses to evaluate the effectiveness of proposed and existing safety standards. Although it has collected accident data ranging from basic information in police accident reports to in-depth analyses conducted by multidisciplinary accident investigation teams, this information is of limited value for projecting the effectiveness of proposed safety standards because of the lack of sufficient data on the causes of accidents and the problems associated with collecting data.

In the absence of fully usable accident data, the Safety Administration has to rely on judgment in estimating the effectiveness of a proposed standard. Attempting to issue standards in the absence of adequate accident data can be quite difficult. For example, in January 1971 the Safety Administration proposed a revision of Safety Standard 111, "Rearview Mirrors," because "Today's standard rearview mirrors offer the driver inadequate indirect fields of view to the sides of the vehicle and a limited one to the rear." To support this position the Safety Administration reported:

> Analysis of the statistics published in Accident Facts (1969 ed.) indicates that 22.5 percent of all motor vehicle crashes, or approximately six million crashes per year, occur in the indirect field of view area to the sides and rear. Systems providing broad and clear vision to the rear, in general use, have the potential of reducing this number of accidents by over a million per year.

The Automobile Manufacturers Association, Inc., criticized the Safety Administration's accident statistics, commenting that broad, clear rear vision does not have the potential of eliminating over one million accidents a year. It cited a research study which concluded that lack of rear vision causes less than 3 percent of all collisions, and this was not a significant contributor. Many motor vehicle manufacturers supported this position and added arguments of their own. One manufacturer said, "In our view, there is insufficient data available to support the proposed indirect visibility system." For this and other reasons, the Safety Administration, in March 1973, decided to do more research before issuing a safety standard. The agency did point out that 3 percent of all collisions can represent a significant absolute. In 1972, for example, 3 percent of all collisions accounted for some 510,000 accidents.

Collecting Accident Data

The Safety Administration has developed a national investigation system to collect accident data. Major data sources include summaries of basic police accident reports, investigations in which police data are supplemented by more detailed inquiry into specific topics, and multidisciplinary accident investigation teams, which conduct clinical in-depth studies of selected accidents. The Safety Administration also contracts for "trilevel studies" that use data from all of the three sources.

Police accident reports provide limited causal data on a large volume of accidents. Although the Safety Administration has obtained certain data from police reports on over 15 million accidents since 1968, the reports rarely pinpoint specific vehicle-related factors that contribute to accidents, injuries, and their severity. The reports, therefore, have limited usefulness for evaluating benefits from safety standards.

Accumulating accident data from detailed investigations is extremely slow and time consuming. Over 88,000 accidents have been investigated at this level. The administrative procedures for requisitioning the work to be done, briefing police or investigators, waiting for the specified type of accident or injury to occur, collecting and summarizing data, and analyzing the data can involve a period of two years or longer. If the investigation is made to evaluate the potential benefit of a proposed safety standard, implementation of the standard could be greatly delayed.

Multidisciplinary accident investigation data are a major source of detailed accident and injury information for a small number of accidents — about 5,500. Team members from various disciplines, including medicine, law, and engineering, are organized by universities, municipalities, and private corporations to make in-depth studies of selected accidents. The teams examine the precrash, crash, and postcrash phases of an accident to determine the involvement of the basic elements of the system — the occupant, the vehicle, and the environment. Findings range from obvious motor vehicle system and component failures to subtle causal factors that can only be detected by the more sophisticated methods used in this study. Careful sorting and analysis of the data can give the Safety Administration insight into specific problem areas. But, because of the limited number of investigations and the selective basis on which samples are chosen, the data gathered have limited usefulness for developing and evaluating standards.

The Safety Administration also obtains trilevel studies, which use the accident data-gathering techniques from all three of the fore-going levels of data collection, to focus on specific problems, such as

1. Determining the relationship between vehicle defects and crashes.
2. Examining the influence of interior vehicle component modifications on injuries.
3. Evaluating the probability of injury in relation to dissimilar vehicle weights.

Collecting data at all three levels is expensive, and the lead time to set up alerting systems, collect police reports, and assemble and process data usually is a year or two. Consequently, it takes two or three years before meaningful results can be obtained.

Some Continuing Questions

As seen in this case, the format of benefit-cost analysis is espe-cially effective in raising important questions about the desirability of proposed government actions, even though it may not always yield definitive answers. For example, was the U.S. National High-way Traffic Safety Administration correct in adding categories of accident costs which were not included by the National Safety Council? Does this procedure tend to bias the resulting benefit-cost analysis? What confidence can decision makers have in the data underlying these analyses? What is the remaining role for judgment and for highly subjective political and social forces?

19

the rising government presence in business decision making

A fundemental change is now taking place in business-government relations in the United States, a shift so pervasive that it is tantamount to a second "managerial revolution." The current wave of government regulation of business is altering the locus of decision making for a large portion of private-sector activities.[1]

The increased government presence in business management is far more fundamental than the more obvious cost and efficiency effects that arise from the multitude of regulations of business. These less visible effects can be stated in terms of the changing responsibility for the outcomes of private-sector activities.

[1] See Murray L. Weidenbaum, "The Future of Business-Government Relations in the United States" in Max Ways, ed. *The Future of Business* (Elmsford, N.Y.: Pergamon Press, 1978), pp. 48-76; Murray L. Weidenbaum, "Business and Government: The Changing Relationship," in Frank Bonello and Thomas R. Swartz, ed. *Alternative Directions in Economic Policy* (Notre Dame, Ind.: University of Notre Dame Press, 1978), pp. 78-124; Murray L. Weidenbaum, "The Second Managerial Revolution," in Walter Goldstein, ed. *Planning, Politics, and the Public Interest* (New York: Columbia University Press, 1978), pp. 45-69.

The first managerial revolution was noted by Berle and Means almost five decades ago and given the title by James Burnham four decades ago. They were referring to the divorce of the formal ownership of the modern corporation from the actual management.[2] The second managerial revolution now under way is a silent, bureaucratic development, in the course of which much — but certainly not all — of the decision making in the American corporation is shifting once again. This time the move is from the professional management selected by the corporation itself to the vast cadre of government regulators who are influencing and often controlling the key managerial decisions of the typical business firm.

This revolution is neither deliberate nor violent. But a revolution it truly is — in forcing a fundamental change in the structure of our society. The traditional concerns and debates in business-government relations ("Are we moving toward socialism?" Are we in the grips of a military-industrial complex?") should be recognized as dealing with an age that already has passed.

Extending the analysis of Berle, Means, and Burnham to the current situation, we see that it is not who owns the means of production but who makes the key decisions that is crucial in evaluating the relative distribution of public and private power. What lines of business to go into? Which investments to undertake? What products to make? Under what conditions to produce them? What prices to charge? As we have seen, government officials and their rule books loom increasingly large in the process through which these questions are answered.

There are few examples of outright nationalization of specific industries and firms in the United States. Rather, the current trend is, as has been noted in earlier chapters, for the government to take over or at least share many of the key aspects of decision making of all firms. We must also recognize that this is a silent revolution in many ways. For one thing, it is not led by a host of noisy trumpeters. In fact, in the main it is not even intentional or noticeable to the day-to-day observer. But that does not alter its deep impact.

Finally, the change that the national economy is undergoing

----

[2] "In the corporate system, the 'owner' of industrial wealth is left with a mere symbol of ownership, while the power, the responsibility, and the substance which have been an integral part of ownership in the past are being transferred to a separate group in whose hands lies control." A. A. Berle, Jr., and G. C. Means, *The Modern Corporation and Private Property* (New York: Macmillan, 1932), p. 68; see also James Burnham, *The Managerial Revolution* (Bloomington, Ind.: Indiana University Press, 1941).

must be understood as a bureaucratic revolution, but not as a conspiracy. Rather, what is involved is the lawful efforts of government civil servants going about their routine and assigned tasks — tasks which in concept are hard to speak ill of. Who is opposed to cleaning up the environment? Or enhancing job safety? Or improving consumer products? Or eliminating discrimination in employment?

If we step back and assess the long-term impacts on the private enterprise system of the rapidly growing host of government inspections, regulations, reviews, and subsidies, we find that the entire business-government relationship is being changed in the process. To be sure, the process is far from complete — and it proceeds unevenly in its various phases — but the results to date are clear enough: The government increasingly is participating in and often controlling the internal decisions of business enterprise, which are at the heart of the capitalist system.

It is important to understand that this silent bureaucratic revolution is not intended to undermine the capitalistic system. The men and women involved are patriotic citizens who are attempting to carry out high-priority national objectives, which are considered to be basic to the quality of life in America.

Yet, those who have assigned them these tasks — the legislatures and the executive branch leadership — often have failed to appreciate the significance of what they have been doing. If specific laws had been proposed or regulations promulgated for the government formally to take over private risk bearing and initiative, the problem would have been faced head on, and the proposals likely defeated. That, of course, is one of the most significant aspects. This silent revolution is unintentional; it is merely an unexpected by-product — but far more than a minor side effect — of the expanding role of government in our modern society. Former President Ford, who served in the House of Representatives for 24 years, has stated, "Most members of Congress don't realize the burdens that are placed upon business by the legislation they pass."[3]

The late Senator Hubert Humphrey offered a similar criticism:

> The government goes around willy-nilly making decisions of consequence. There was no estimate of the economic impact of the Occupational Safety Act, for example. I happen to be for the occupational safety program, but what were its economic implications? Did anyone think that through? No.[4]

[3] Juan Cameron, "Suppose There's a President Ford in Your Future," *Fortune*, March 1974, p. 206.
[4] Hubert H. Humphrey, "Planning Economic Policy," *Challenge*, March-April 1975, p. 22.

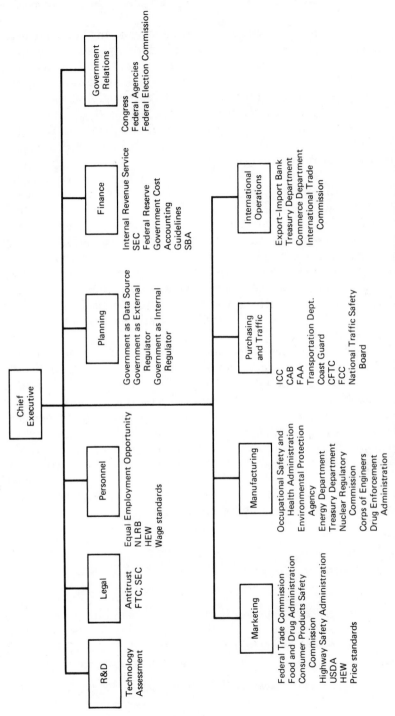

Figure 19-1 TYPICAL INDUSTRIAL CORPORATION AND FEDERAL GOVERNMENT
RELATIONS

Most proponents of greater government planning and regulation truly believe that these activities can be superimposed on the business system without damaging its central and desirable features, such as risk taking, efficiency and productivity, scientific progress, and enhanced employment opportunities. But Professor Thomas Ehrlich, former dean of the Stanford Law School, has used the term *legal pollution* to describe what he calls the growing feeling that it is almost impossible to move "without running into a law or a regulation or a legal problem."[5]

Certainly the great majority of public policy changes affecting business–government relations in the United States in recent years has been in the direction of greater government involvement — environmental controls, job safety inspections, equal employment opportunity enforcement, consumer product safety regulations, energy restrictions, and recording and reporting of items varying from domestic illnesses to foreign currency transactions. Indeed, when we attempt to look at the emerging business-government relationship from the business executive's viewpoint, a very considerable public presence is evident in what ostensibly, or at least historically, have been private affairs.

No business official today, neither the head of a large company nor the corner grocer, can operate without considering a multitude of governmental restrictions and regulations. His or her costs and profits can be affected as much by a bill passed in Washington as by a management decision in the front office or a customer's decision at the checkout counter. The organizational chart of a hypothetical industrial firm, in Figure 19-1, is an attempt to convey graphically the diverse nature of federal involvement in so many aspects of business. The precise nature of business-government relationships, of course, will vary by industry, size of firm, location, and types of products produced and markets served.

PRESSURES FOR INCREASING
THE GOVERNMENTAL PRESENCE

The rising government presence in internal business decision making is a phenomenon that is still in the process of development, rather than one that has attained a "steady state." The basic factors causing the change are diverse, ranging from the concern by some

[5] "Complaints about Lawyers," *U.S. News and World Report*, July 21, 1975, p. 46.

with the quality of life to the desire by others to increase the social responsiveness of business enterprise. Those pressures show little evidence of exhaustion in the short run. Numerous proposals for changes in public policy affecting business are virtually all variations on a single predictable theme: to increase the scope and degree of government involvement while shifting costs from the federal treasury to the products and services that consumers buy. One indication of future policy changes may be the bill introduced by several dozen members of Congress (H.R. 76, the proposed National Employment Priorities Act). That bill deals with what its proponents call the phenomenon of the "runaway plant." H.R. 76 would require that employees and affected communities be given two-year advance notifications of plant closings or relocations if the action would result in 15 percent or more of the employees (or 15 percent of the employees who are members of any labor union) losing their jobs. For "good cause," the Secretary of Labor may approve notification in a shorter period. The company's notification must include the following information:

1. The reasons for the proposed closing or transfer.
2. Alternatives to closing or transfer.
3. The unemployment loss that would result.
4. Plans to alleviate the effects of the job loss.
5. The "economic circumstances" of the plant, including profitability and future investment, employment, and production plans.
6. The "economic circumstances" of the overall company and the opportunity for transferring personnel elsewhere.

Should the Secretary of Labor rule that the proposed closing or transfer is not justified, the company would lose a variety of tax benefits for up to ten years, including the investment credit, the accelerated depreciation range, the foreign tax credit, and deductions for ordinary and necessary expenses related to the transfer. Even if the plant closing or transfer is determined to be justified, these penalties can be invoked if the Secretary of Labor determines that the company's move or closing could have been avoided had the company accepted the special federal assistance that would be established by the bill. The federal government would be given great discretion to provide grants, loans, and interest subsidies to companies qualifying for such aid.

Some labor unions are showing a strong interest in the "runaway plant" proposal. In the words of Douglas Frazer, president of the United Auto Workers Union, "moving a plant without regard to the people laid off or the communities affected is unacceptable social

conduct in a democracy and should be ended."[6] The supporters of
the proposed legislation contend that their purpose is not to deny
companies the freedom to move their operations but to make them
bear the "social cost" of their relocations. Inasmuch as these proposals ignore any "social benefits" that result from business investment, their enactment surely would limit the mobility of capital
and labor. The possibility thus looms that it literally may be difficult to go out of business, without at least some form of federal
review.

A more basic expansion in government influence on private-
sector decision making would leapfrog the entire current generation
of regulatory activity: that is, the establishment of a formal system
of national economic planning in the United States. In recent years,
the Federal Budget and the Annual Economic Report of the President
have been utilized as vehicles for presenting broad-gauged, long-term
projections of future economic conditions and of national priorities,
at least to the extent that the changing allocation of federal financial
resources indicates revisions in the relative importance of the major
program and policy areas. The initial suggestions for a more formal-
ized planning system are in terms of planning information, especially
forecasts of future needs, to guide decision makers in the private
sector.

Although the rhetoric favoring national planning is phrased in
terms of merely developing better information, even a cursory examination of the literature on business planning demonstrates that
planning encompasses far more than improved information accumu-
lation. A standard definition is this one: "A plan is a predetermined
course of action . . . to accomplish a specific set of objectives."[7] One
expert offers the most terse rendition: "Planning is to a large extent
the job of making things happen that would not otherwise occur."[8]

According to the Initiative Committee for National Economic
Planning, "The planning office would not set specific goals for
General Motors, General Electric, General Foods, or any other
individual firm." But the proposed new central planning office would
indicate the number of cars, the number of refrigerators and the
quantity of frozen foods that the American public is expected to
require in, say, five years, and it would try "to induce" the relevant
industries to act accordingly.

[6] Robert Howard, "Runaway Plants," *New Republic*, May 26, 1979, p. 17.
[7] Malcolm H. Sherwood, Jr., "The Definition of Planning," in *Readings in
Business Planning and Policy Formulation*, ed. Robert J. Mockler (New York:
Appleton, 1972), p. 103.
[8] David Ewing, *Long-Range Planning for Management* (New York: Harper,
1964), p. 3.

But suppose that General Motors or General Electric wishes to rely on its own market surveys rather than on the forecasts of the government planners? Strong hints of coercion are visible in the Initiative Committee's proposal. The inducements would be laws, as specific as necessary, on taxes, subsidies, and environmental problems. In the words of the committee, "The heart of planning is to go from information to action."[9]

To be sure, long-range planning techniques are in widespread use in the private sector. But there are many differences between business and government planning. Boiled down to its fundamentals, it is the difference between forecasting and reacting to the future and trying to control it. Corporate planning of necessity is based on the principle of trade — attempting to persuade the rest of society that it ought to purchase the goods and services produced by a given firm; the controls that may accompany the plan are internally oriented. If things go wrong, the onus falls on the officers, employees, and shareholders. In striking contrast, the government is sovereign and its planning can ultimately involve coercion, that is, the use of its sovereign powers to achieve the results that it desires. Its controls are thus externally oriented, extending their sway over the entire society. If things do not work out as well as expected in public planning, it is the taxpayer and the consumer who bear the main burden.

When we consider the period beyond the next few years, the possibility emerges that a fundamental restructuring may occur in the nature of the corporation. Large nationwide corporations — at least in some industries operating in the field of basic natural resources — may be required to obtain federal charters, the rationale being that the individual state governments cannot effectively regulate their total operations. Particularly those companies that receive large federal subsidies may find that the government will appoint one or more members of their boards of directors or require that they be designated by some other group. These "outside" officials may not be responsible to the shareholders, but rather to the public in general or to interests external to the firm, such as labor unions or consumers.

In the early nineteenth century Congress did grant federal charters to various private enterprises, including railroads, telegraph, canal, and bridge companies. States soon began chartering local businesses, usually those residing in the state of incorporation. With the development of the state role in this field, congressional involvement

---

[9] "For a National Economic Planning System," *Challenge* (March–April 1975), pp. 51–53.

was curtailed sharply.[10] In recent years Congress has in general limited itself to incorporating enterprises with special ties to the federal government, notably the Communication Satellite Corporation, Amtrak, and the Corporation for Public Broadcasting.

Of direct concern to American-based multinational corporations are the statutory requirements of several Western European countries that local companies appoint employee representatives to their governing boards. The West German government requires companies having more than two thousand employees — including German subsidiaries of United States firms — to give half the seats on their supervisory boards (equivalent to our boards of directors) to representatives of the employees; however, at least one of the "worker" directors represent management employees, and the chairman, in practice, is elected by the shareholder representatives. Nowhere else in Western Europe has codetermination or worker representation in the boardroom attained the level of importance it has in Germany. In France worker representatives are only observers at board meetings, with the right to obtain information and offer advice. European business executives acknowledge that employee participation at the board level has helped to ease labor-management tensions, but at the price of reduced flexibility and a slowdown in business decision making.[11]

Professor George C. Lodge of the Harvard Business School predicts, for the United States, that more use will be made of the corporate chartering power to harmonize corporations with the public interest. He sees the corporate charter increasingly as an instrument for defining the purposes and functions of large corporations.[12]

Government may also loom larger in basic business decisions on corporate size and structure. Efforts are already under way in the United States to amend the antitrust laws to prohibit mergers involving companies of a given size — regardless of their competitive practices and often of their market position. In 1979 the Senate Judiciary Committee held hearings on Senator Edward Kennedy's proposed Small and Independent Business Protection Act. The Kennedy bill includes the following prohibitions:

- No company with assets or annual sales of $2 billion or more would be allowed to acquire another company.
- No companies with assets or sales over $350 million would be allowed to merge unless they could show that the transaction would have the

---

[10] Willard F. Mueller, "Federal Chartering of Corporations," *American Federationist* (June 1973), p. 18.
[11] Theodore Geiger, "The Movement for Industrial Democracy in Western Europe," *Challenge* (May–June 1979), pp. 14–21.
[12] "Recovery and Beyond," *Saturday Review*, October 22, 1975, p. 24.

"preponderant effect of substantially enhancing competition" or "would result in substantial efficiencies."
- No company with over $350 million assets or sales would be allowed to merge with a company that has 20 percent or more of any market having at least $100 million in annual sales.

These prohibitions could be avoided only if the larger party to the merger divested itself of one or more "viable business units" equal in total size to the smaller party within one year before or after the merger. Such a new law would give the government clear authority to block so-called conglomerate mergers of companies in noncompeting lines of business. It would be based on the notion that "big is bad," a doctrine that the courts have not embraced. Under present law the Justice Department generally has to show that a merger would tend to create a monopoly or diminish competition.

The government's chief antitrust officer, Assistant Attorney General John H. Shenfield, supports the Kennedy approach on the ground that "one is reluctant to leave in the hands of private, unregulated firms" power so great that it could "have a major, shaping effect on society."[13]

Although such sweeping legislation may not be enacted in its present form, the possibility of some modified version being adopted should not be ruled out in any realistic appraisal of future prospects. Much will depend on the public's evaluation of the future performance of American business, an evaluation that increasingly is concerned with factors other than profitability. These additional factors range from the basic honesty and integrity of corporate management to its ability to help achieve a variety of social goals. As Professor Lee Preston of the University of Maryland has noted, the corporation is created out of a public policy process, not from a biological process. Its continued existence depends on public approval.[14] Although the scope of government influence in the operation of business firms in the years ahead is going to increase, it does seem likely that large corporate entities will remain the primary unit of economic activity in the United States for the foreseeable future. Lodge contends that there are no instruments of public management or government entrepreneurship that hold out any promise of better governing the large sector of the economy that historically has been left up to the interplay of market forces.[15]

[13] Edward Cowan, "Law for Size Limits on Mergers Sought," *The New York Times,* December 30, 1978, p. 25.

[14] See Lee F. Preston, "Socializing the Corporation," (lecture presented at Rochester Institute of Technology, March 14, 1974), p. 6.

[15] "Recovery and Beyond," p. 26.

PRESSURES FOR REDUCED CONTROLS

Not all the pressures for change in business-government relations in the United States are in the direction of expansions in government power. The rising citizen disenchantment with "big government" also has its counterpart here. Several dramatic examples of curtailment of government regulation have occurred in recent years. In 1974, as noted in Chapter 3, Congress eliminated the interlock system on the passenger automobile, in response to great citizen concern. In 1977 aroused diabetics and other users of artificial sweeteners convinced Congress to postpone the FDA's proposed ban on saccharin — and to extend the postponement in 1979. In 1978 the Supreme Court agreed with a protesting businessman and struck down OSHA's no-knock inspection power. During this entire period Congress refused to approve one of the major proposals of corporate activists — the formation of a consumer advocacy agency — on the grounds that it would be an unnecessary additional layer of bureaucracy.

Moreover, a number of active participants in public policy, such as Harold M. Williams, chairman of the SEC and former dean of the UCLA Graduate School of Management, have warned that, to the extent the regulatory presence becomes pervasive, it tends to undermine the foundation of the private sector, "the qualities of will and initiative and self-sufficiency which are essential to the growth and preservation of private enterprise."[16]

It is important to appreciate the direct connection between extensive regulation by government, in the first instance, and the pleas that result for more detailed government intervention in business. When government policies add to the cost of private production and thus to the prices charged to consumers, those policies can result in strong pressures for even greater government involvement in wage and price decisions. When excessive government regulation of business reduces the ability and incentive of business to engage in technological innovation and the development of new products and markets, the economy suffers a further reduction in its capability to achieve such important national objectives as greater job opportunities, rising standards of living, and an improved quality of life.

Moreover, when government policies sharply curtail the ability of the private sector to generate adequate savings to finance eco-

[16]Harold M. Williams, "SEC and Mutual Funds: Hands-off Regulation to Be Given College Try," *Money Manager*, August 14, 1978, p. 6.

nomic growth, not only is the government viewed as the banker of last resort, but the basic vitality of the business system is called into question. Public dissatisfaction with business performance increases greatly. This, in turn, sets the scene for another round of government involvement, ranging from proposals to nationalize specific industries to the subsidizing of others (always, of course, with the imposition of still more restrictions and regulations). Energy is a clear example of this phenomenon; and the automotive, pharmaceutical, and health care industries are providing more vivid illustrations.

Clearly, the proper division of power in a society between the government and the corporation is a difficult one to determine. It is not apparent how far government should intervene in attempting to protect public interests or private welfare. Surely the growing recognition that such intervention has great costs — notably inhibiting business innovation, efficiency, and growth — may provide some salutary restraint.

A NEW APPROACH
TO BUSINESS-GOVERNMENT RELATIONS

By and large, the relationships between business and government in the United States can be described as basically adversary in nature. Government probes, inspects, taxes, influences, regulates, and punishes. At least that appears to be the dominant view in many quarters, in both the public and private sectors. In many ways, this unfavorable view does seem to come uncomfortably close to approaching reality.

The contrast is striking between this situation (or at least this view of it) and what is often taken to be the dominant European and Japanese approach, a "partnership," or at least close cooperation, between business and government. This has lead to suggestions that we import the foreign model of business-government relations. It is often contended that such closer working relations would improve our competitive position abroad as well as enhance productivity at home. However, this approach, by expanding further government power over the private sector, could result in far more harm than good, especially by submerging public and consumer interests.

Yet, the status quo has many undesirable features. It does not seem sensible to expect American business to be successful in waging a two-front war, struggling against increasing government encroachment at home and competing against government-supported enterprises abroad.

Hence, a third approach is suggested here, which might be considered a variant of the attitude toward international relations often called "peaceful coexistence." That is, public policy might well explore the possibilities of a sensible division of labor between the public and private sectors in achieving basic national objectives. A short summary may turn out to be more caricature than description, but the following is offered as portraying the current method of decision making on national priorities, with particular reference to the impacts on business. Subsequently, a new model of national decision making will be presented.

In practice, decisions on government budgets, particularly on the spending side, are made in the small. Congress acts on a great many individual authorization bills and appropriation statutes. When the bits and pieces are added up, that is done usually on a functional basis—so much for defense, a bit less for welfare, much less for education, and so on. In this approach, business (if it is thought about at all) is regarded as an input, one of a variety of tools or mechanisms that can be drawn upon. In the case of defense spending, business firms are very heavily utilized, although not always in an effective manner. In the case of the rapidly expanding income-maintenance programs, in contrast, they are hardly involved at all.

Thus, a shift in emphasis in budget priorities from warfare to welfare, as indeed has been occurring in recent years, means— perhaps altogether unwittingly—a reduced emphasis on the direct utilization of business firms in carrying out national priorities. The earlier concern about moving toward a "contract state," in which key government responsibilities are delegated to private corporations, quite properly has faded away.

Another fiscal development, however, has been occurring, which raises a quite different concern. The desire to exercise a greater degree of control over the size and growth of the federal budget—be that due to the economic concern over inflationary effects of budget deficits or the more philosophical resistance to the growth of the public sector—had led to an effort to "economize" on direct government spending by using government controls whose costs are hidden in private-sector prices.

Consequently, we need a fundamental rethinking of the tendency for government increasingly to involve itself in what essentially is internal business decision making. One model that could be followed is one where the process of determining national priorities would be viewed as a two-step affair. The first step should continue, as at present, to focus on determining how much of our resources should be devoted to defense, welfare, education, and so forth, at least to the extent that these basic issues are now decided by design at all.

But this determination should be accompanied by a general and tentative allocation of responsibilities among the major sectors of the economy. This type of indicative planning would recognize that the constant and increasing nibbling away at business prerogatives and entrepreneurial characteristics has a very substantial cost — a reduced effectiveness in achieving some basic national objectives, notably (to use the language of the Employment Act of 1946) "maximum employment, production, and purchasing power." The proposed planning approach would also take account of the different mix of constituencies that the public and private sectors are primarily geared to serve.

In this day when benefit-cost analysis has become fashionable, we should not be oblivious of the very real if not generally measurable effects of converting ostensibly private organizations into involuntary agents of the federal establishment. Rather than pursuing the current course, the nation should determine which of its objectives can be achieved more effectively in the private sector and go about creating an overall environment that is more conducive to the attainment of those objectives.

Without prejudging the results of such an examination, it would appear reasonable to expect that primarily social objectives — such as improved police services — would be the primary province of government. And primarily economic objectives — notably training, motivating, and usefully employing the bulk of the nation's work force — would be viewed as mainly a responsibility of the private sector, and especially of business firms.

This attitude would recognize that the typical American corporation is becoming more responsive to the changing needs of the society of which it is a part. That voluntary response does not necessarily arise from any eleemosynary impulse but from the basic instinct to survive and prosper by meeting the needs and desires of the public. Business behavior increasingly responds to interest-group pressures and public opinion, whether those factors are welcomed or not and regardless of whether they are helpful or not. No company can afford to ignore public attitudes and expectations — simply because to do so will result, directly, in loss of sales and customer goodwill and, indirectly, in increased costs (when those pressures lead to further government involvement in business).

The new model of national decision making envisioned here hardly calls for an abdication of government concern with the substantive issues previously enumerated. Rather, it would require a redirection of the methods selected for achieving these essentially worthy ends. In the environmental area, for example, much of the current dependence on direct controls should be shifted to utilizing the more indirect but powerful incentives available through the price system. Specifically, imaginative use of "sumptuary" excise taxation, as we have grown accustomed to in the cases of tobacco products and alcoholic beverages, can be used to alter basic production and consumption patterns.

Other areas of the economy could benefit from using alternatives to government intervention in business operations. One such area, as we have seen, is the direction over the flow of saving and investment, a basic aspect of a capitalistic or other advanced economy. A result of the expanded use of governmentally sponsored credit agencies, such as the Federal Intermediate Credit Banks, the Export-Import Bank, and a host of others, is that a rising portion — as much as a third in recent years — of all the funds raised in ostensibly private capital markets in the United States now funnels through these federal financial intermediaries. In every period of credit tightness, there is a clamor for setting up additional intermediaries, such as an energy development corporation, to assure yet another category of borrowers ready access to capital markets.

Yet none of these federal instrumentalities do anything to add to the available pool of investment funds. In practice, their creation and expansion amounts to robbing Peter to pay or lend to Paul. These instrumentalities simultaneously reduce the tendency of the market to allocate capital resources to the more efficient undertakings and result in the "unprotected" and truly private borrowers bidding up interest rates to obtain the funds they require. A more positive and fruitful approach to national policy in this area would be to create an overall economic environment that provides more incentive to individuals and business firms to save, and thus to generate, more investment funds available to the society as a whole.

In the OSHA area the law has lost sight of the basic objective — to achieve a safer working environment. Instead, the current emphasis is on the establishment of bureaucratic procedures and the punishment of violators. An appraisal of the first four years of OSHA by one of its congressional sponsors focused, not on the results that it had achieved, but instead on the "inputs" — the number of officials that had been hired, the comprehensive standards that had been promulgated, and the large number of inspections that had been conducted.[17] As pointed out by Professor James Chelius of Purdue

[17]William Steiger, "OSHA: Four Years Later," *Labor Law Journal*, 25, no. 12 (1974), 723-28.

University, the danger for organizations such as OSHA is that its intermediate goals (for example, number of inspectors) become the ultimate goals of the organization. "That danger is, of course, more critical for a government organization because it lacks the ultimate discipline of the marketplace."[18]

In the more positive spirit of the approach suggested here, the basic emphasis of occupational safety and health legislation would be changed from prescribing specific practices to be followed in a company's operations to focusing on reducing the accident and health hazard rate in a given industry or plant. Government policymakers might also give greater weight to Lee Preston's observation that most companies and industries have evolved safety and health systems well above those that could be justified by any strict profit-cost calculation. He attributes that to a variety of factors, including union pressures, industrywide activities, and simple humanitarianism.[19] In this regard, moreover, the General Accounting Office (GAO) study cited in Chapter 13 urged OSHA to release to private industry the data the agency has obtained on the nature and causes of industrial accidents. GAO noted that business firms could use such information to adjust work procedures, change equipment, and to make workers more aware of job hazards.

It should be recognized that the results of such decentralized decision making may not necessarily coincide with those of a more centralized system. We would undoubtedly have a different mix of goods and services under the two approaches. That implicit reordering of priorities may be a real price we pay for the reduction of centralized control. Yet, the reordering of priorities may only happen in a relative sense. If our nation's resources are utilized more effectively as a result of reducing the costly burden of government controls, influence, and reporting, the increased national output could yield perhaps the same or even more of the new lower-priority items (in absolute terms). In any event, the total level of economic welfare should be enhanced — or, at the minimum, we will have a greater opportunity for enhancing it — as a result of the increased efficiency and productivity that is to be anticipated, and in a less inflationary environment.

The revised division of labor between public and private undertakings envisioned here should not be expected to remain invariant over time. Rather, it should change with underlying circumstances, foreign and domestic, and as experience is gained from following a

[18] James R. Chelius, *Expectations for OSHA's Performance: The Lessons of Theory and Empirical Evidence*, March 1975 (unpublished), pp. 6–7.
[19] Preston, "Socializing the Corporation" p. 13.

strategy of peaceful coexistence between business and government in the United States. Hopefully, that dividing line between public and private responsibilities will shift back and forth in the future, rather than move in a predictable single direction as has been the past experience.

It is pertinent that such a strong advocate of the free market as Professor F. A. Hayek has made a compelling case for some significant government role in the economy, pointing out that he did not mean "that government should never concern itself with any economic matters." Rather, he points out:

> A functioning market economy presupposes certain activities on the part of the state; there are some other such activities by which its functioning will be assisted; and it can tolerate many more, provided that they are of the kind which are compatible with a functioning market. . . . The range and variety of government action that is, at least in principle, reconcilable with a free system is thus considerable.[20]

OUTLOOK

Some students of the American corporation have come up with extremely negative evaluations of future prospects. One of the darkest appraisals is that of Michael Jensen and William H. Meckling of the University of Rochester Graduate School of Management. They see the large private corporation as a casualty of the continued encroachment of government on private initiative. "The corporate form of organization," warn Jensen and Meckling, "is likely to disappear completely." In any event, they contend, the larger corporations as we know them are "destined" to be destroyed.[21]

But, as we have seen, there are many forces at work in American society and few have ever achieved all of their objectives. Public-interest groups, labor unions, and corporations do not have monolithic views on all issues. Changing alliances among them make for great variation (albeit a lack of symmetry) in the development of public policy in this country.

Although the results by their nature can only be indicative rather than definitive, an extremely detailed "futurist" evaluation in 1979 of trends in government-business relationships provides a useful

---

[20] F. A. Hayek, *The Constitution of Liberty* (Chicago: University of Chicago Press, 1960), pp. 224-25.

[21] Michael C. Jensen and William H. Meckling, "Can the Corporation Be Saved?" *MBA*, March 1977, p. 16.

basis for speculation. A group of 39 "opinion makers" surveyed by the Center for Futures Research at the University of Southern California (ranging from corporate executives to public-interest group leaders) forecast no radical change in the freedom of American business to produce goods and services profitably and efficiently. Neither nationalization of industry nor widespread deregulation was viewed as a likely alternative.[22]

Part of the futurist study involved the preparation of a surprise-free "scenario," showing the future as viewed by 20 leading researchers in the field of business and society. The panel of scholars forecasted a much slower growth in government regulation of business, but no wide-scale dismantling of regulatory mechanisms. The most far-reaching change would occur in the late 1980s, when Congress is envisioned to enlarge the planning authority of its budget office, and set five- and ten-year national goals in the areas of manpower, natural resources, and economic performance. The legislation, however, would primarily affect federal fiscal policies and contain no authority to compel action in the private sector to meet the indicated goals.

By turning down proposals for federal chartering of corporations, Congress is seen as attempting only to influence indirectly the internal governance of large corporations. It passes a full-disclosure law and establishes a limit on the number of inside directors permitted to serve on boards of directors. Stringent safeguards are placed on corporate data banks containing information about employees and customers, and whistle blowers (employees who report legal violations) are protected.[23] This scenario corresponds to the notion of "regulated capitalism," recently advanced by R. Joseph Monsen.[24]

These futuristic views are supported, in large measure, by the general shape of the past. When we look back at the course of American economic history, we find that political and economic change in the United States usually has been a gradual, evolving process. Dramatic departures have been few and infrequent. It is reasonable to predict, therefore, that the future of business-government relationships in the United States will be a continuing reconciliation of conflicting forces rather than an inevitable movement to a polar alternative.

[22] James O'Toole, "What's Ahead for the Business-Government Relationship," *Harvard Business Review*, March-April 1979, pp. 94-105.
[23] Ibid., pp. 99-100.
[24] R. Joseph Monsen, "The Future of American Capitalism," *California Management Review*, Spring 1979, p. 14.

index